Doors of Santa Fe

Second Edition, 2024

John Lonergan

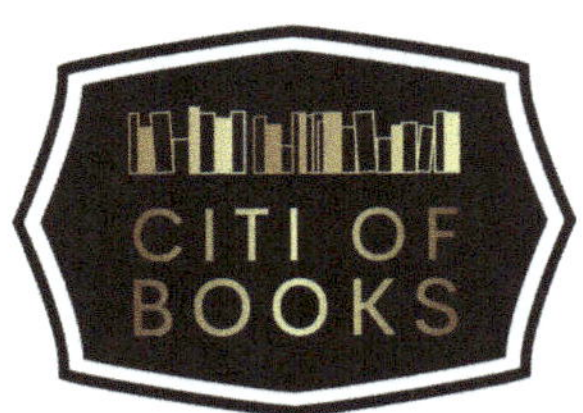

CITIOFBOOKS, INC.
3736 Eubank NE Suite A1
Albuquerque, NM 87111-3579
www.citiofbooks.com
Hotline: 1 (877) 389-2759
Fax: 1 (505) 930-7244

Ordering Information:
Quantity sales. Special discounts are available on quantity purchases by corporations, associations, and others. For details, contact the publisher at the address above.

Printed in the United States of America.

ISBN-13:   Softcover   979-889391-224-1

Library of Congress Control Number: 2024908962

This is dedicated to Mimi, whom I met and married in Santa Fe.
She opened the door to my heart

Doors reveal the spirit of those who live behind them. Sometimes, if one is lucky, doors reveal the character of a place with such specificity that one cannot mistake where they are located. Santa Fe, New Mexico, is such a place. Founded over 400 years ago, its inhabitants have forged a style from Spanish (not Mexican!), pueblo and Anglo styles that result in a look that is different from anywhere else.

The colors reflect and contrast with those of the high desert blue sky, the subdued blues of the distant mountains, the reds of the ferrous soils, and the greens of the juniper trees. They contrast with the various adobes (five official colors in Santa Fe) in ways that make them stand out from their surroundings.

This book is about more than doors. It's about entering a unique lifestyle, a way of looking at the world, and of reflecting the world in which one lives. Doors are the first thing one sees when coming to one's home, or the home of a friend. Doors represent. They both reflect and contrast with the landscape.

A key question we had while preparing Doors of Santa Fe. Open, or closed? An open door represents welcome. A closed door is conservative, secure, unwelcoming. The Spanish custom was to have small entrances leading on to big courtyards…and the doors were always closed. Santa Fe has kept this custom. One comes upon a door and opens it to be surprised by the welcome within.

And what about the elements around the door? Some entrances are messy—mailboxes, electrical wires, newspapers, dirt and wear. A book about new doors, pristine and proper, would not hold the same interest. Doors are about living and aging. One seldom sees a perfectly square, newly-painted door in Santa Fe. The clutter and weathering add character.

Enjoy!

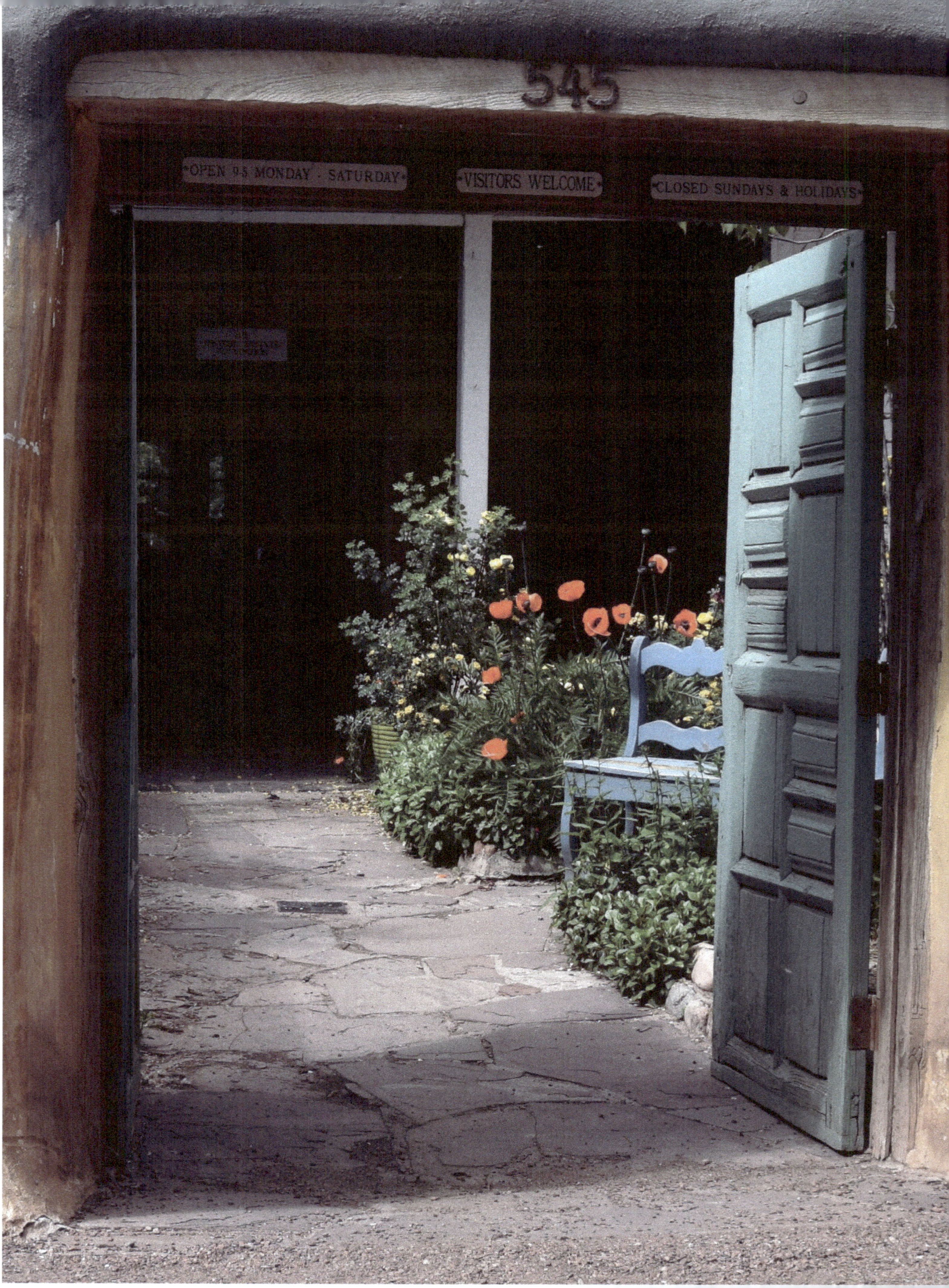

545
·OPEN 9-5 MONDAY · SATURDAY·
·VISITORS WELCOME·
·CLOSED SUNDAYS & HOLIDAYS·

Wabi-Sabi: the art of imperfection

...wabi-sabi is the art of finding beauty in imperfection and profundity in earthiness, of revering authenticity above all. In Japan, the concept is now so deeply ingrained that it's difficult to explain to Westerners; no direct translation exists.

Broadly, wabi-sabi is everything that today's sleek, mass-produced, technology-saturated culture isn't. It's flea markets, not shopping malls; aged wood, not swank floor coverings; one single morning glory, not a dozen red roses. Wabi-sabi understands the tender, raw beauty of a gray December landscape and the aching elegance of an abandoned building or shed. It celebrates cracks and crevices and rot and all the other marks that time and weather and use leave behind. To discover wabi-sabi is to see the singular beauty in something that may first look decrepit and ugly.

from: Wabi-Sabi, the Art of Imperfection, by Robyn Griggs Lawrence, Natural Home, September-October 2001

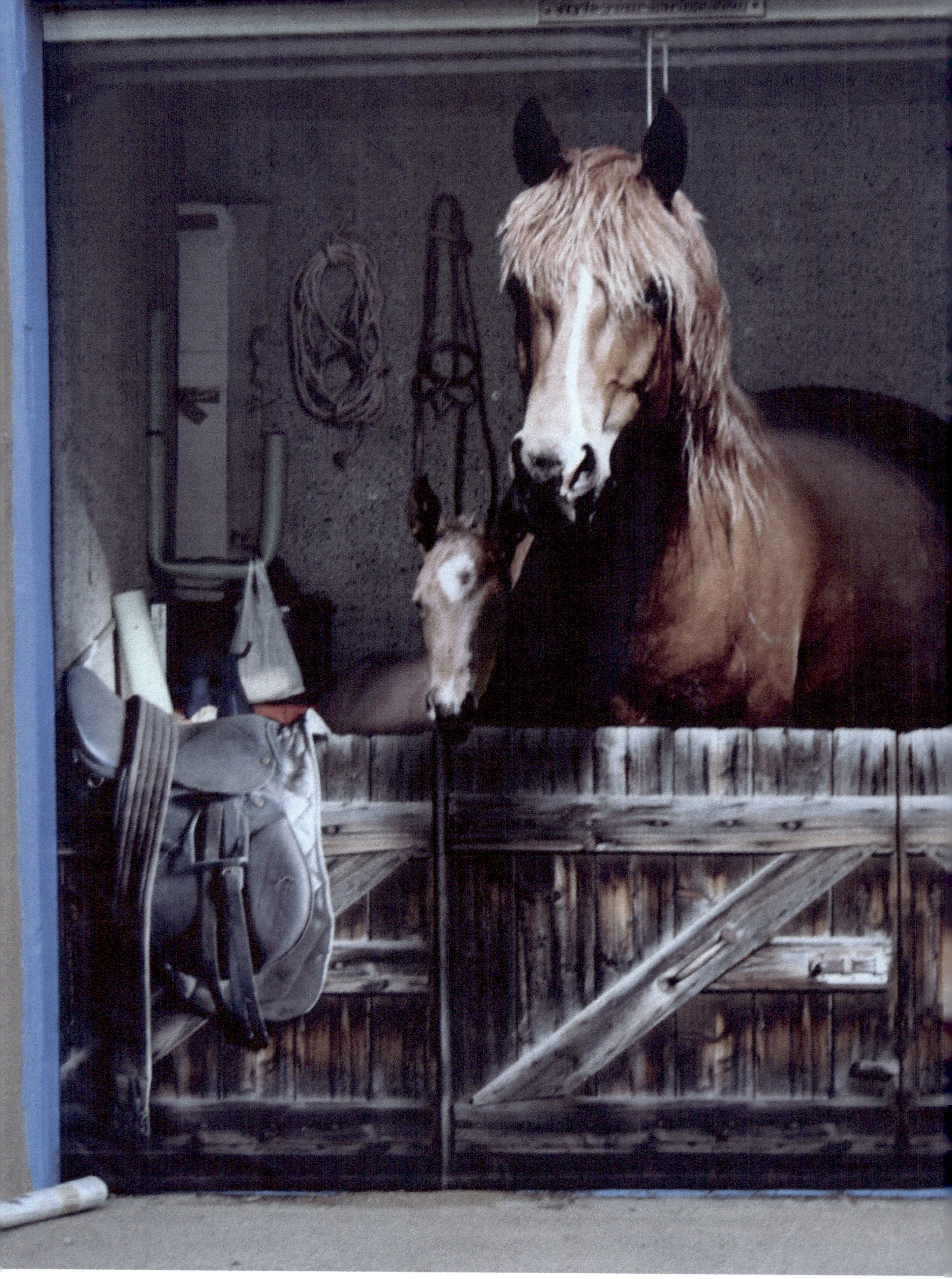

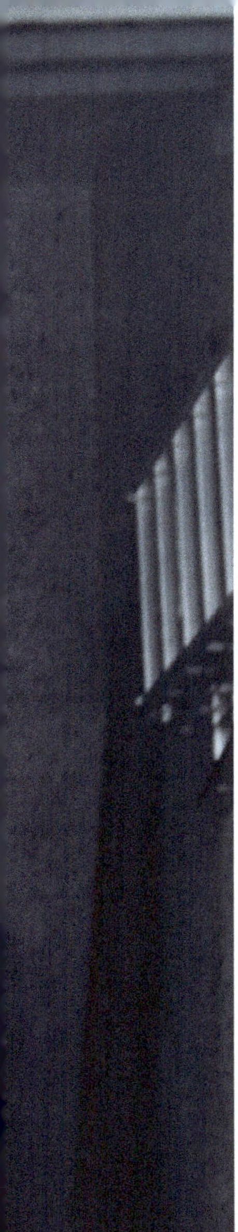

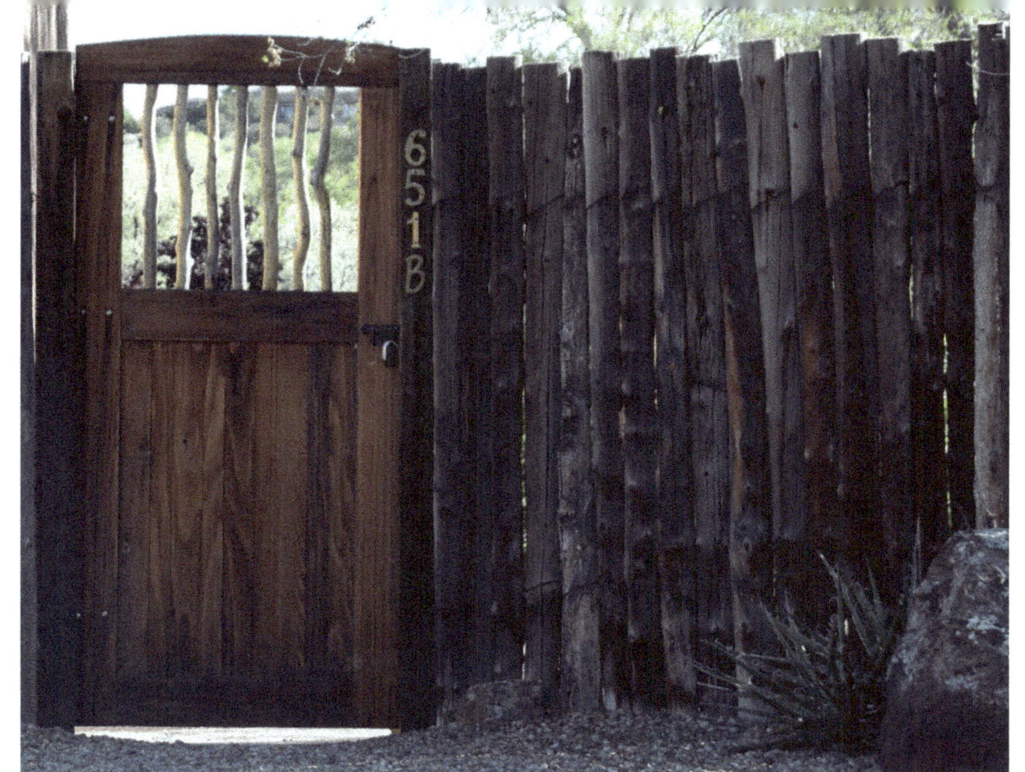

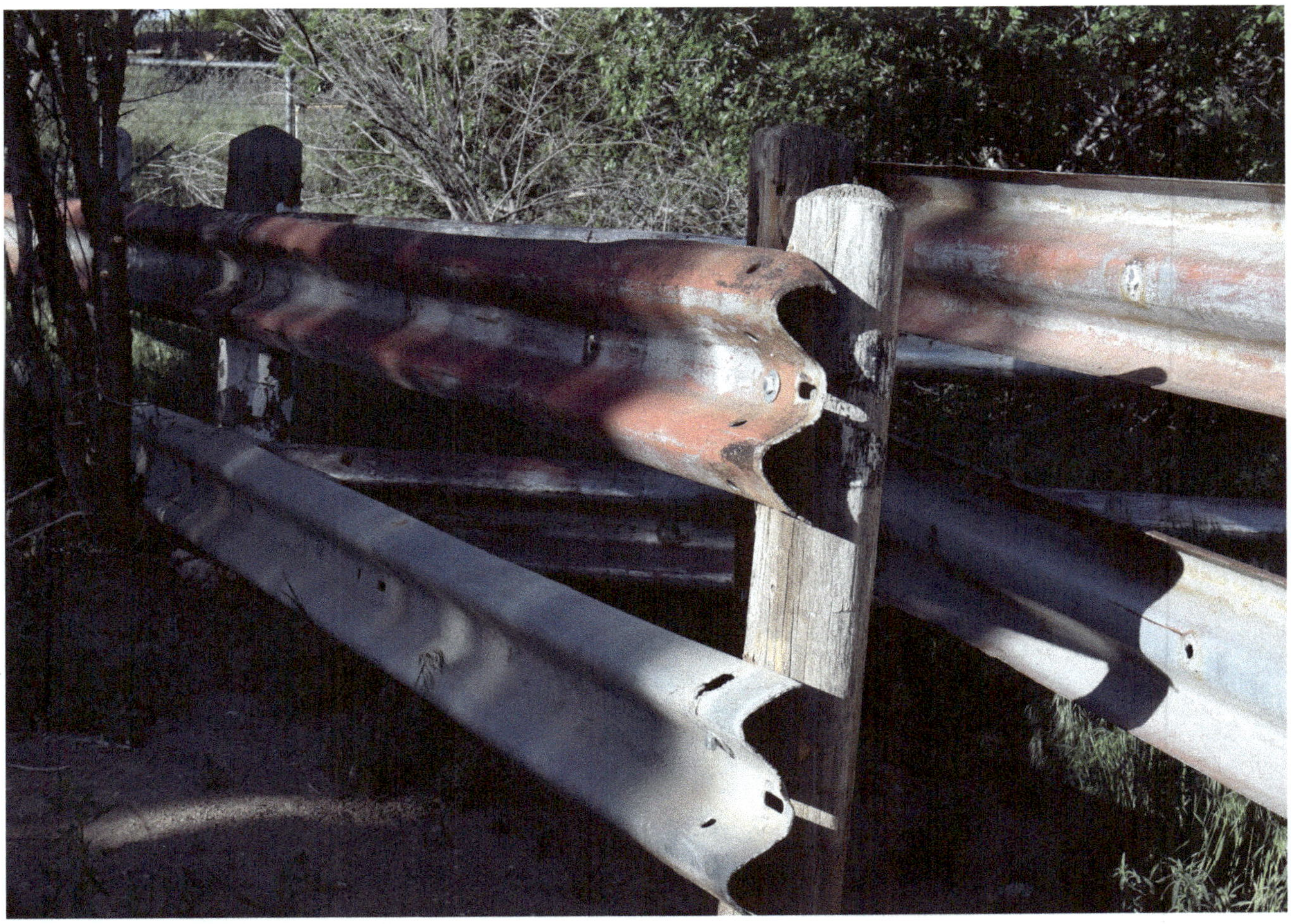

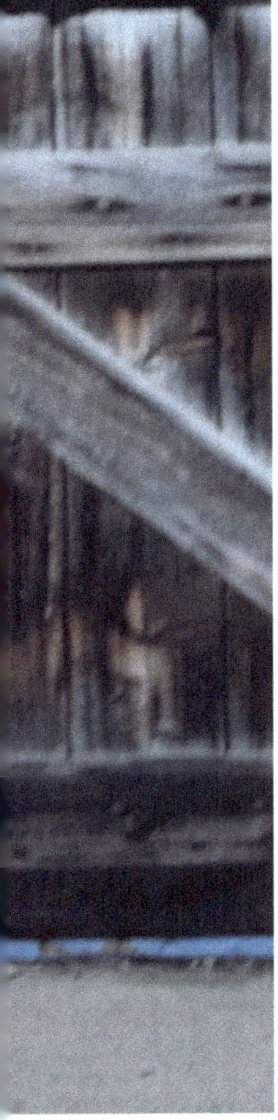

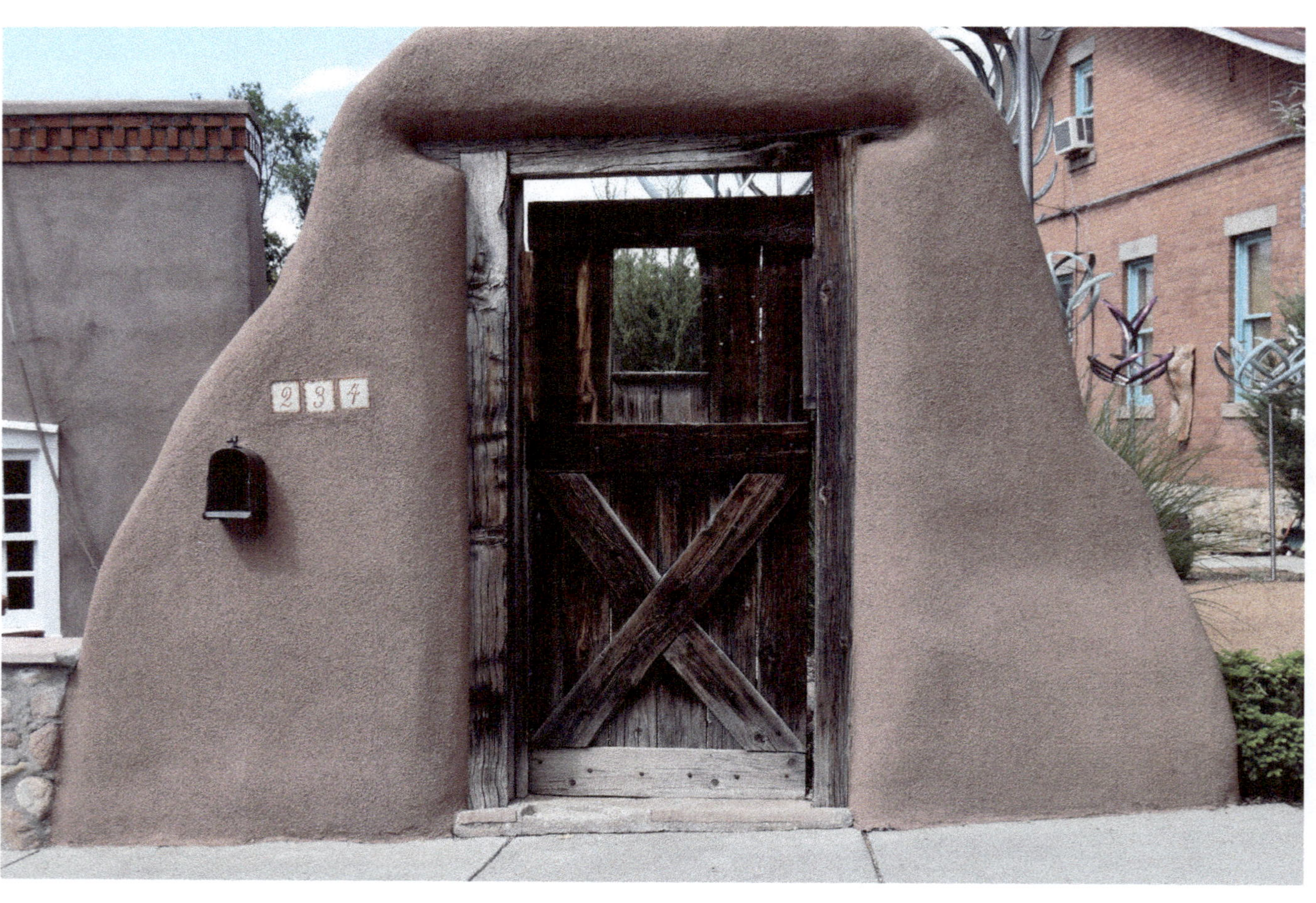

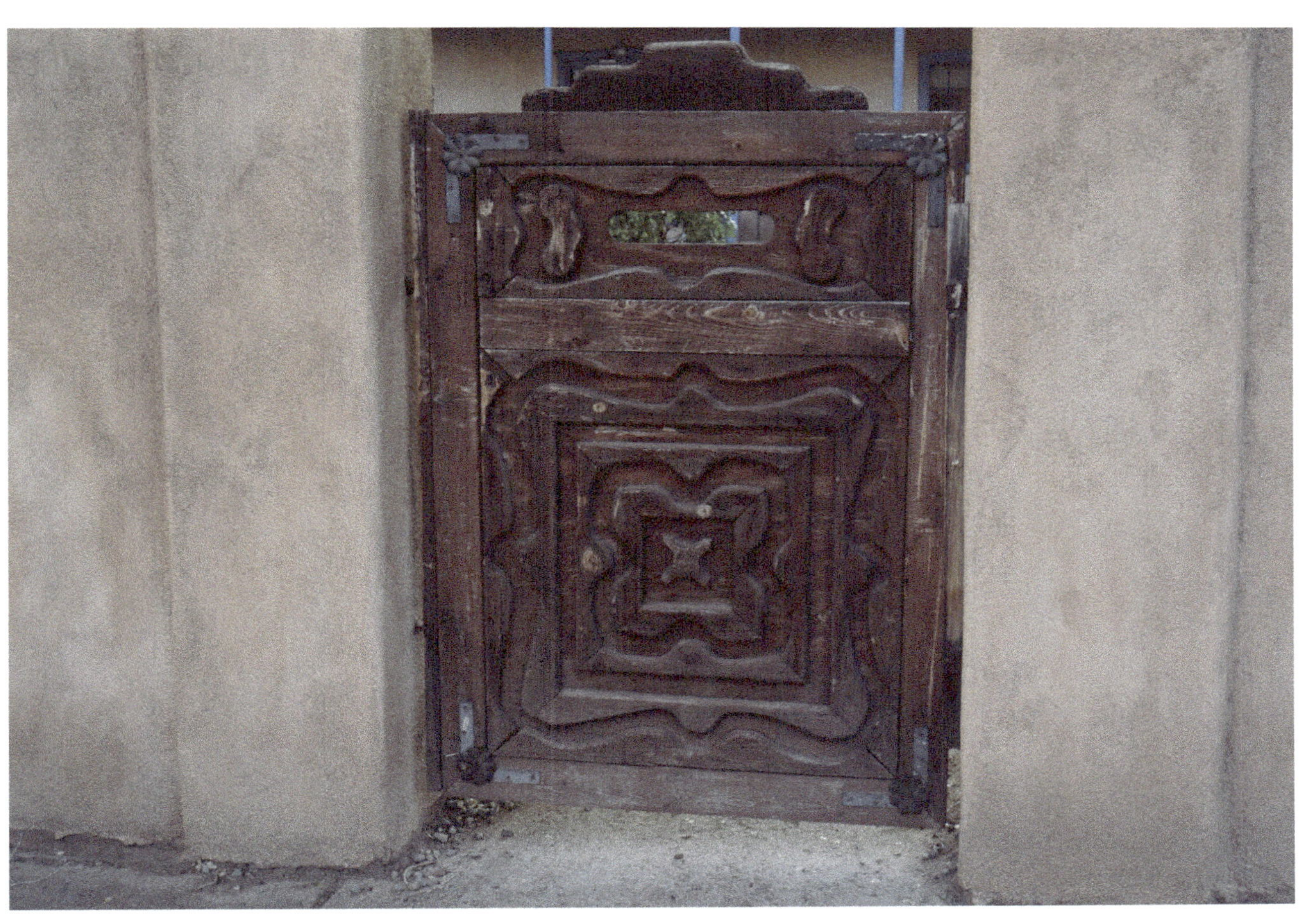

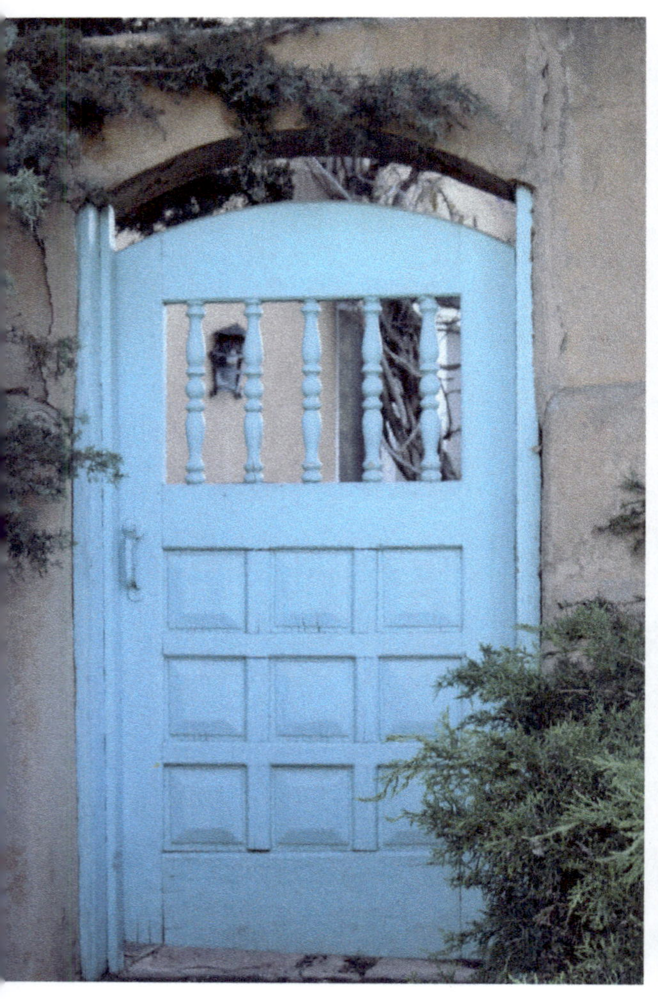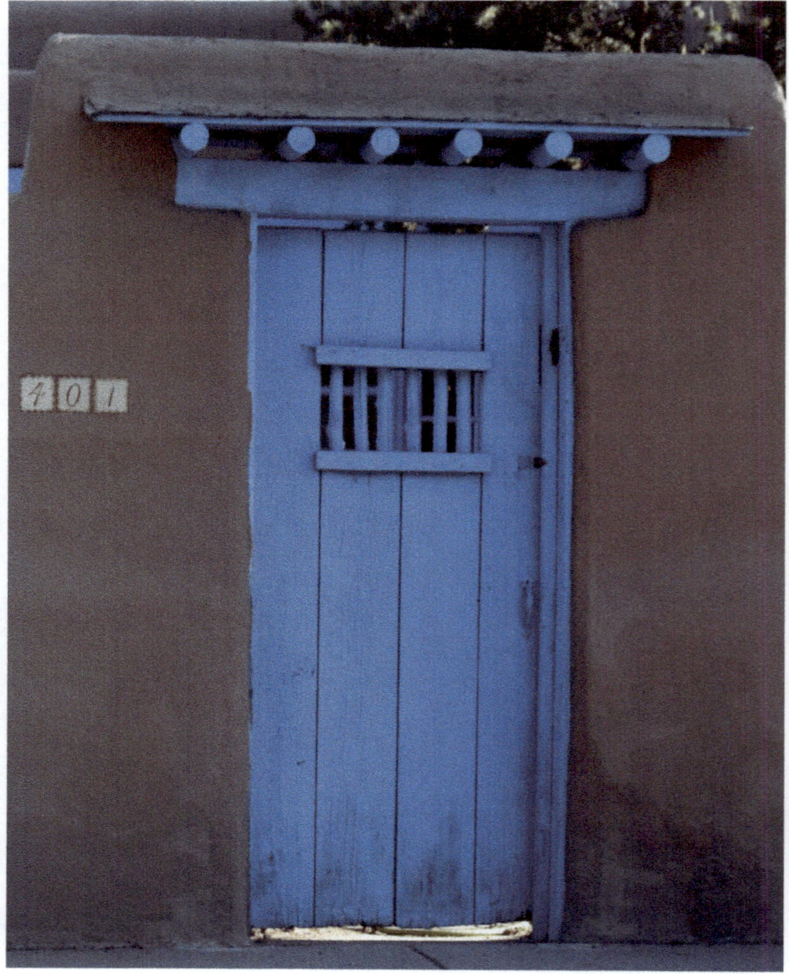

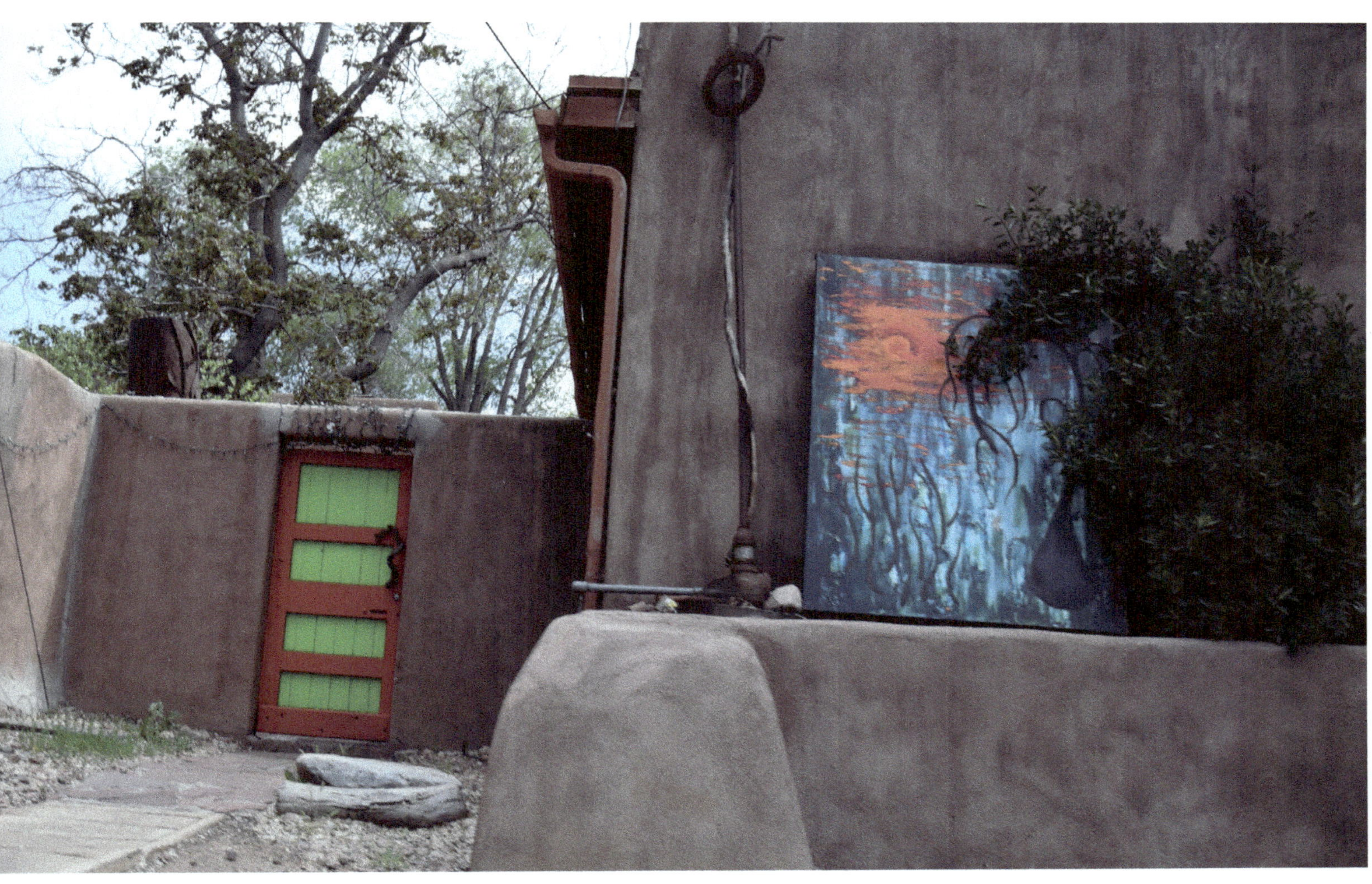

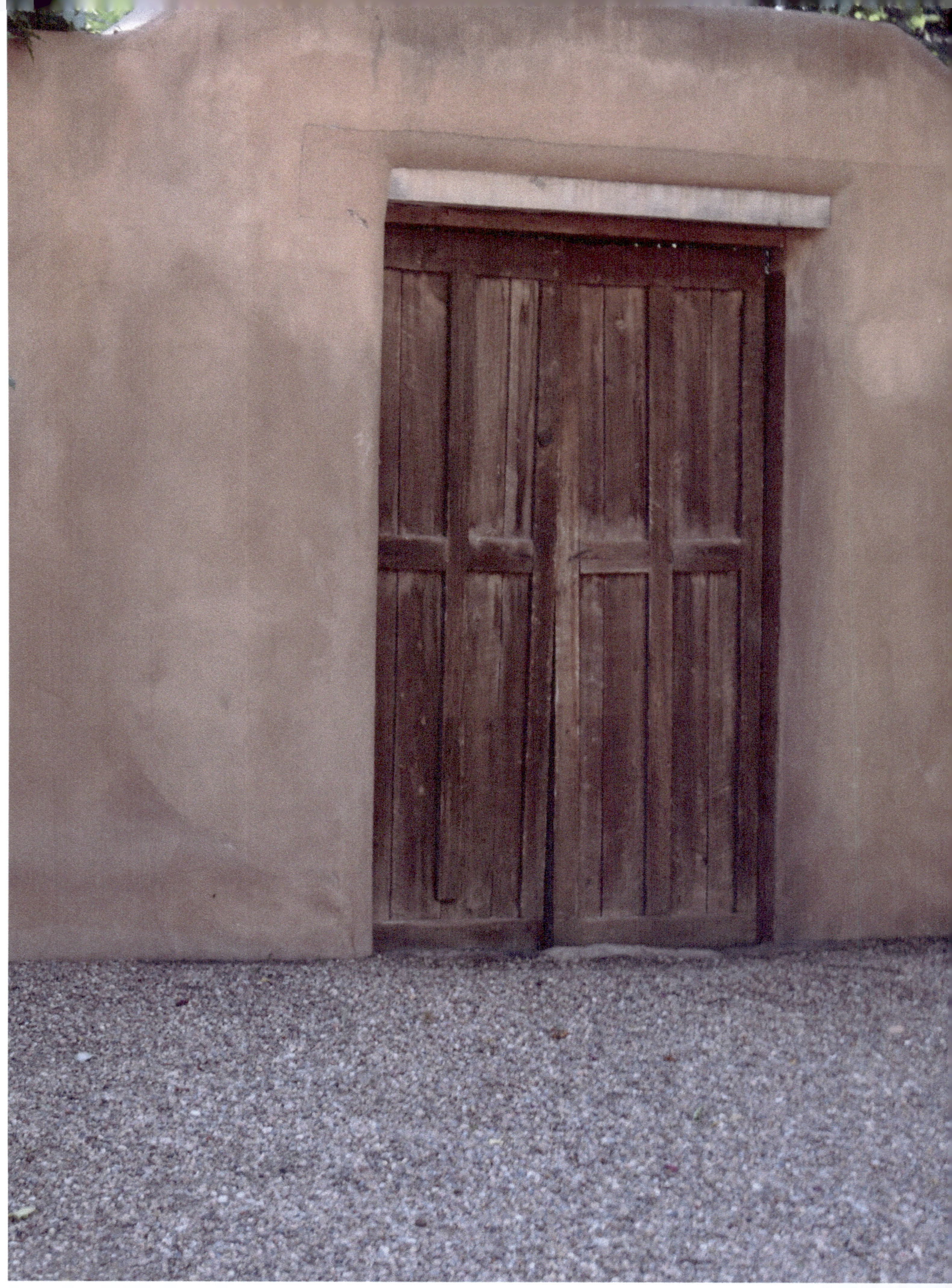

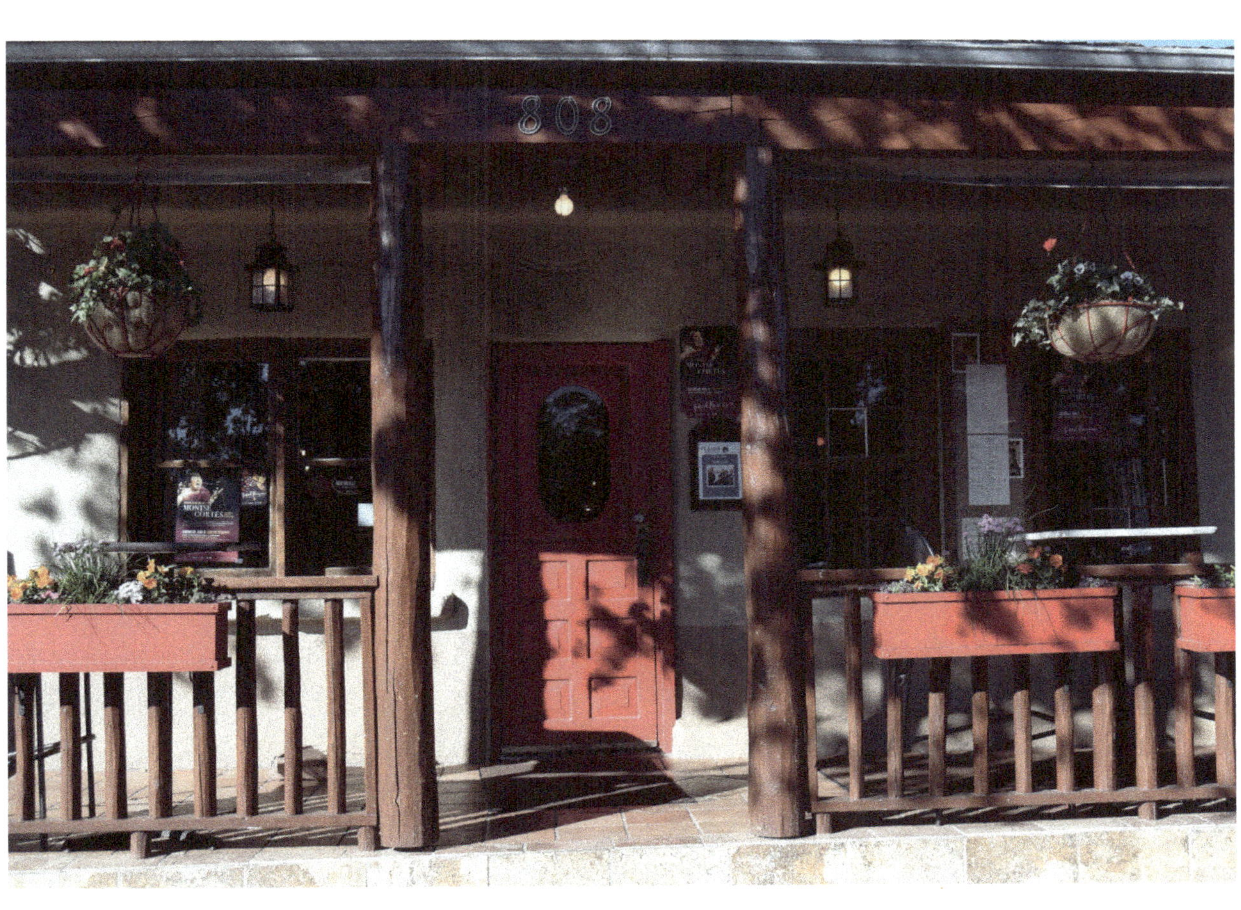
808

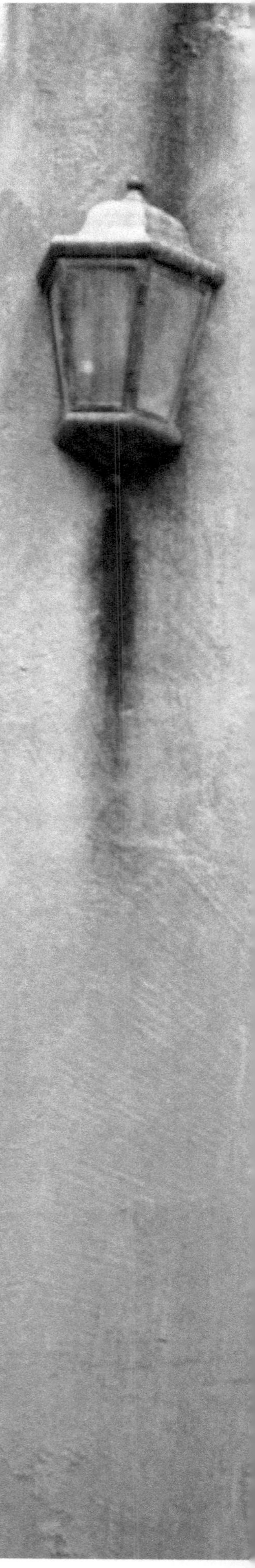

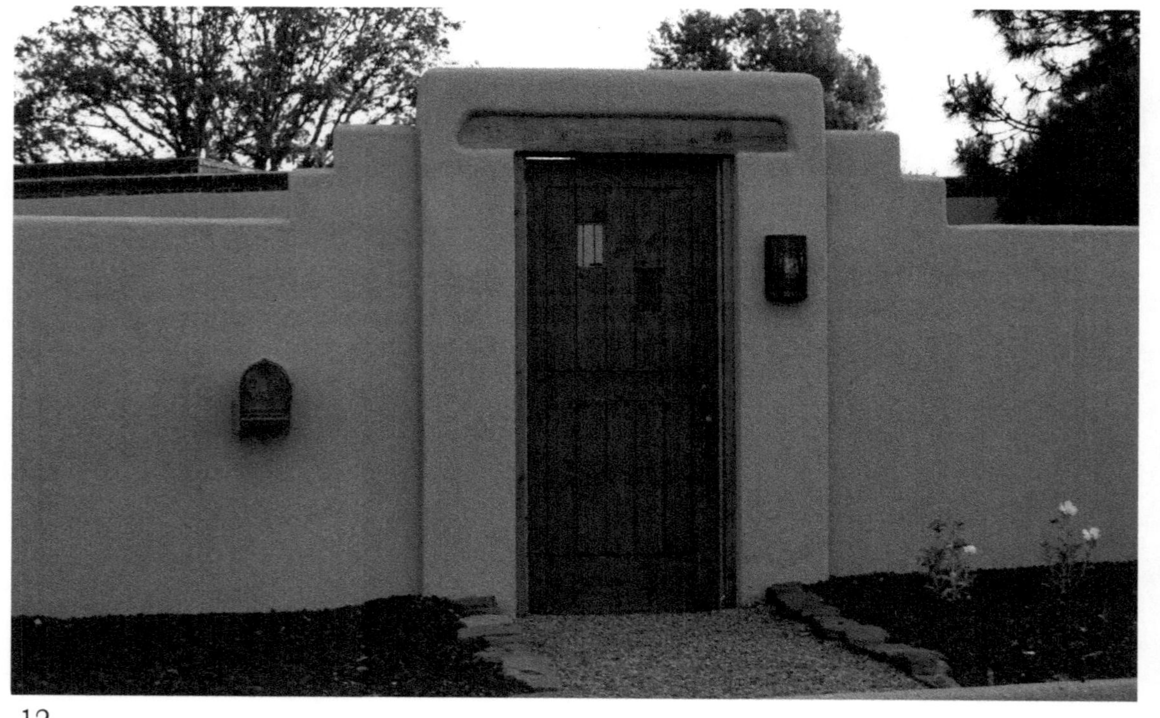

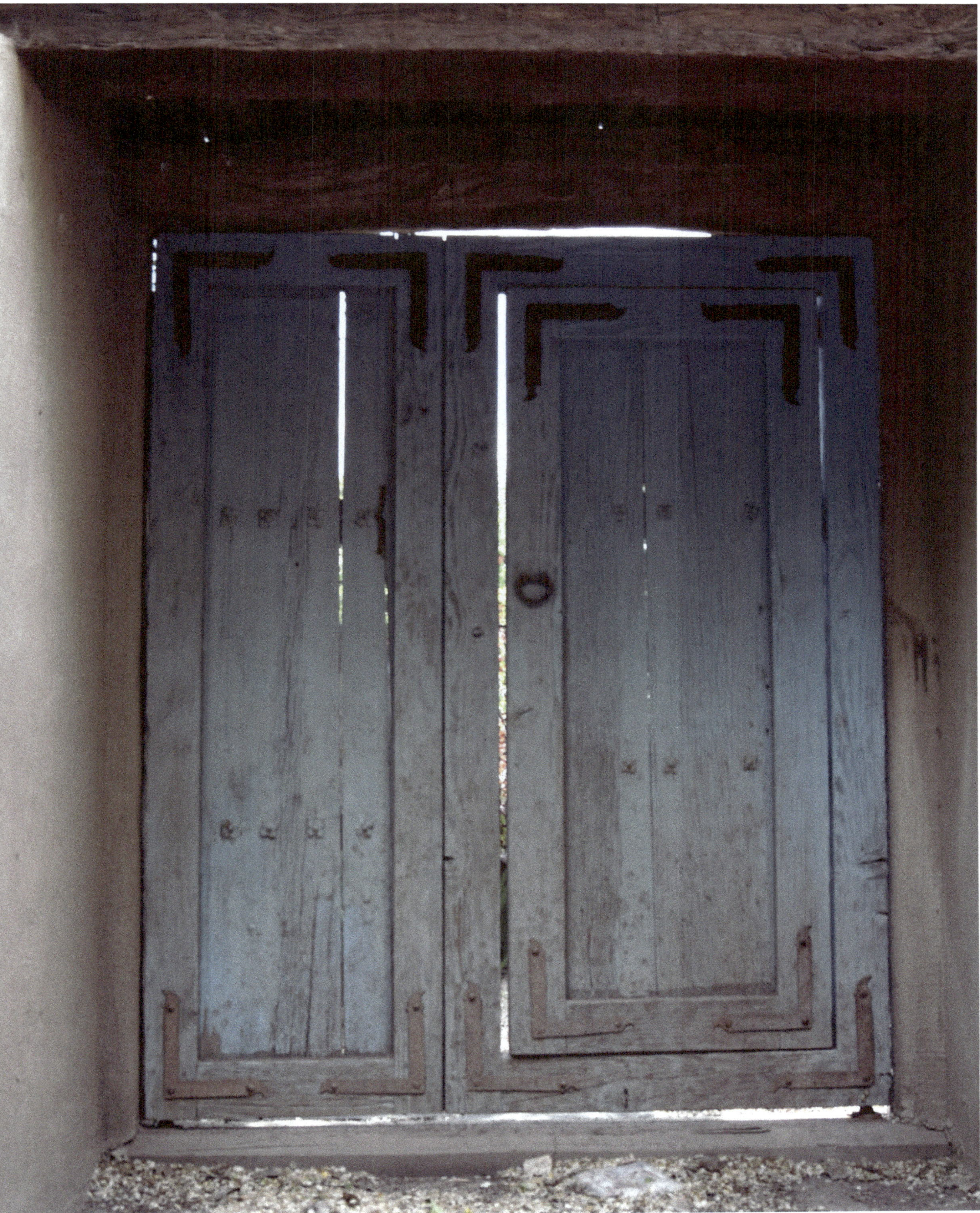

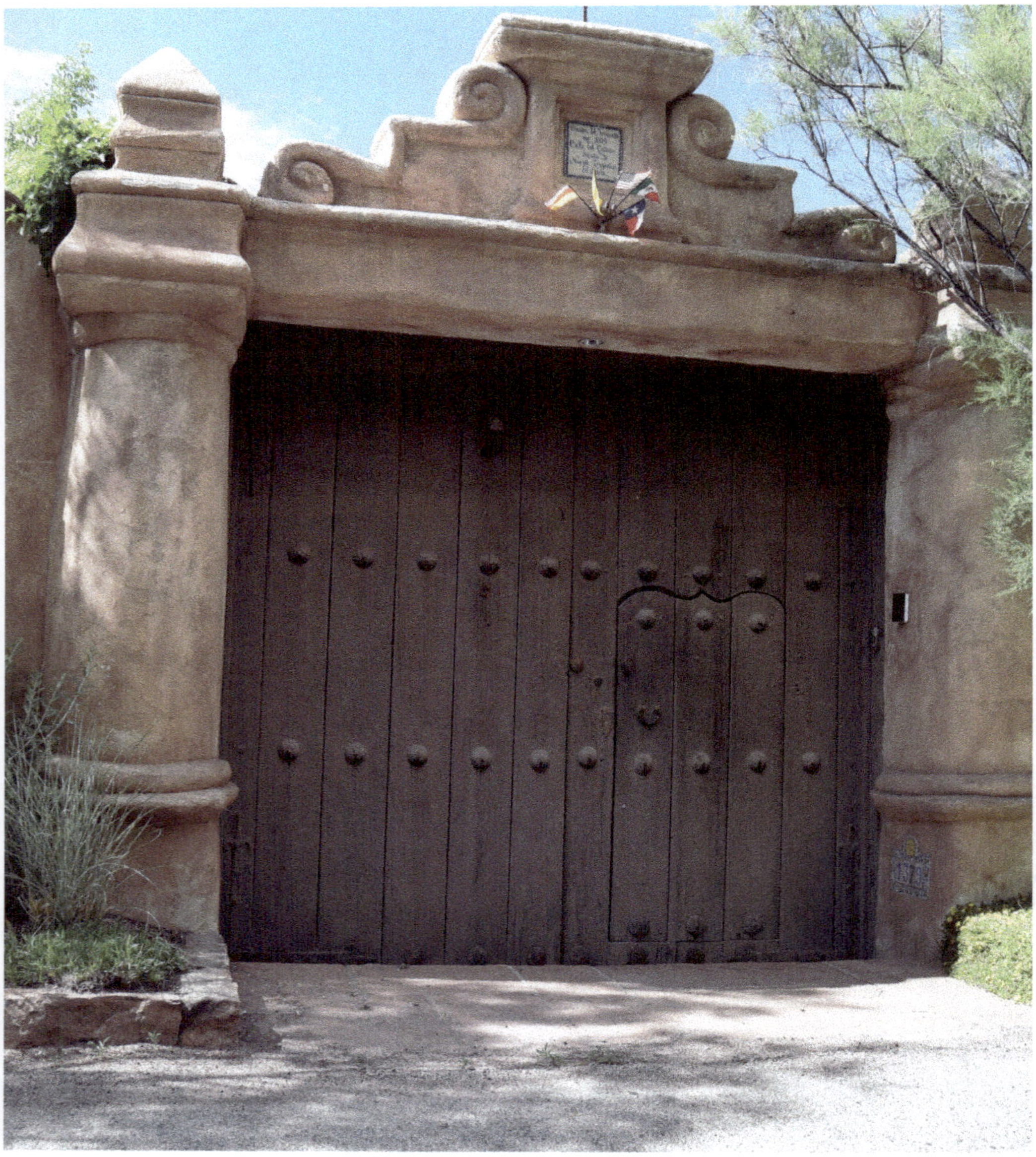

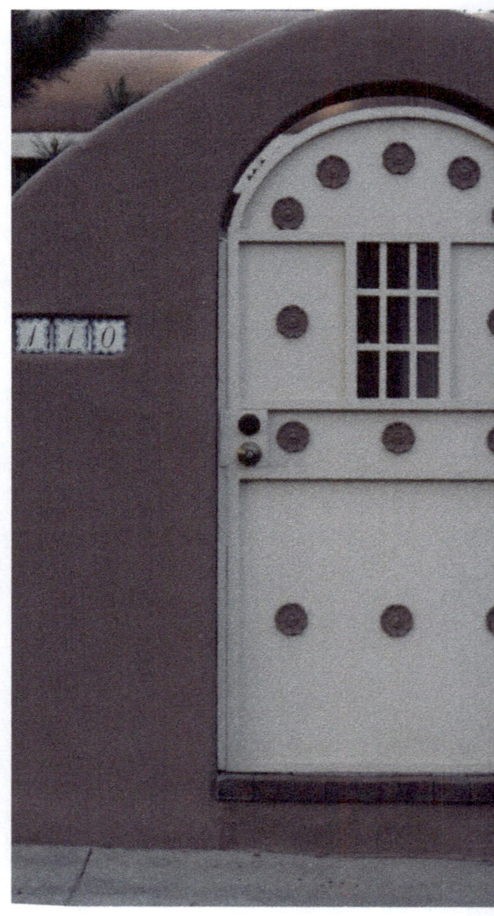

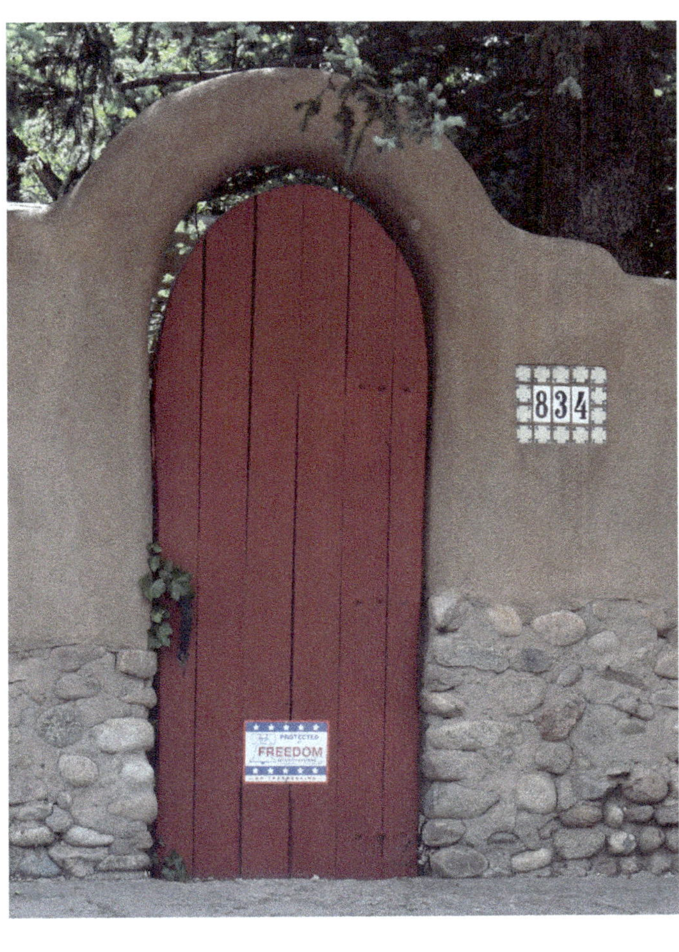

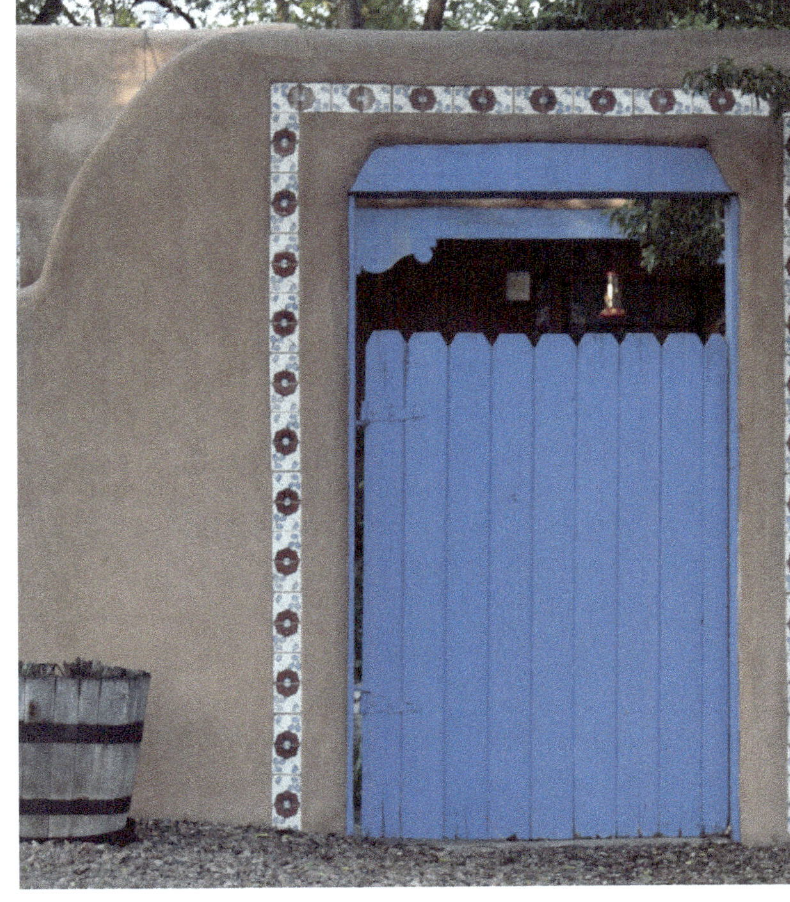

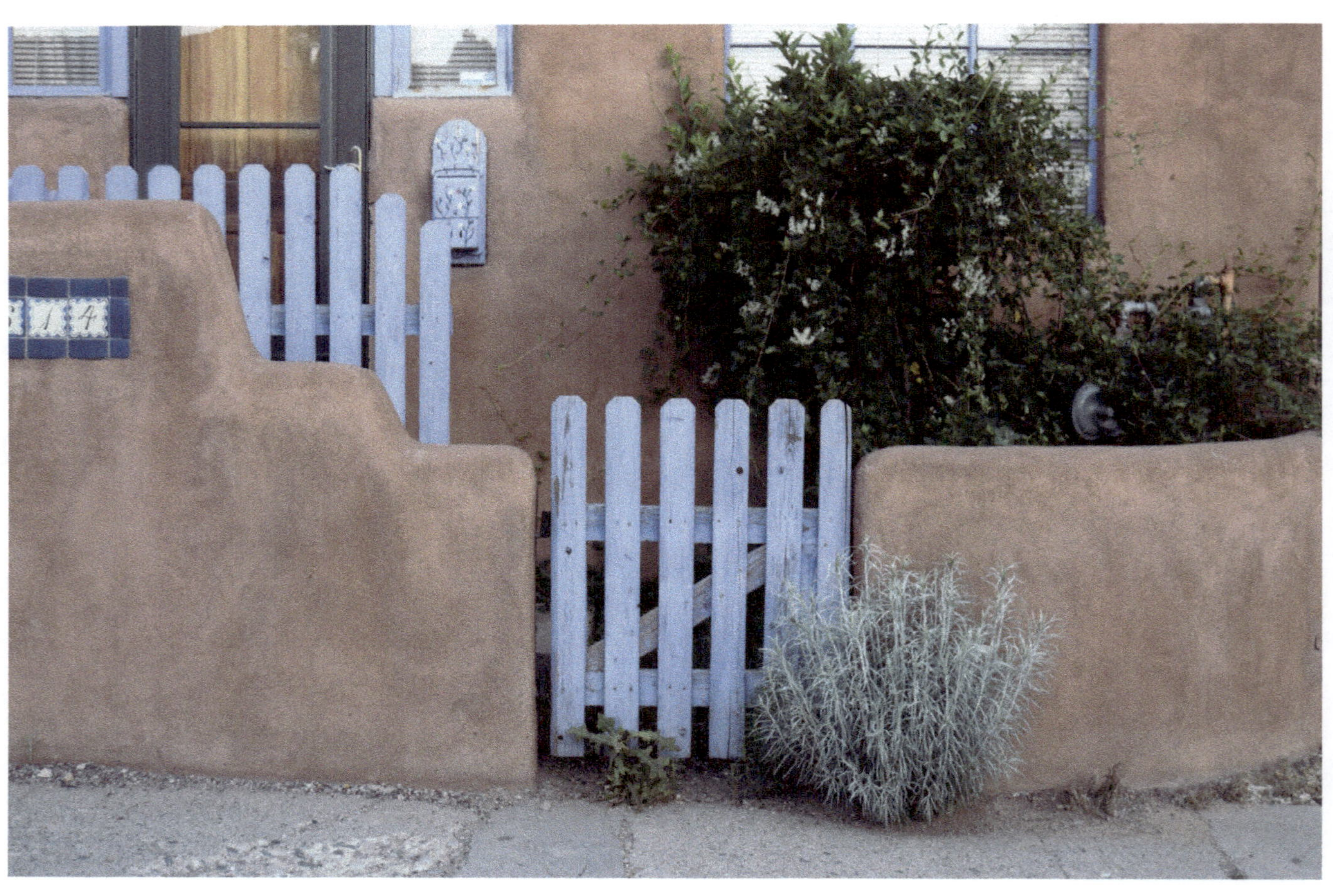

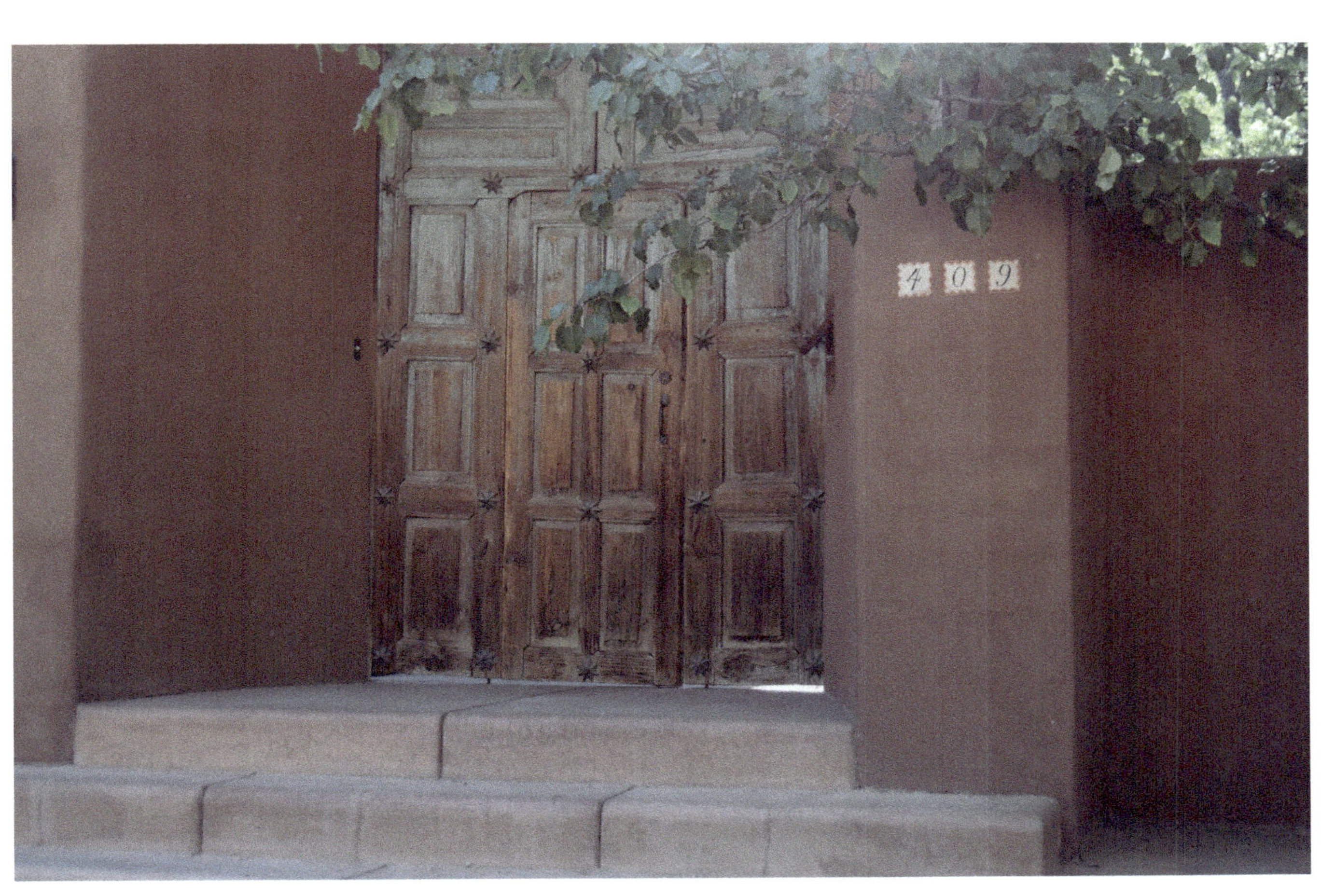

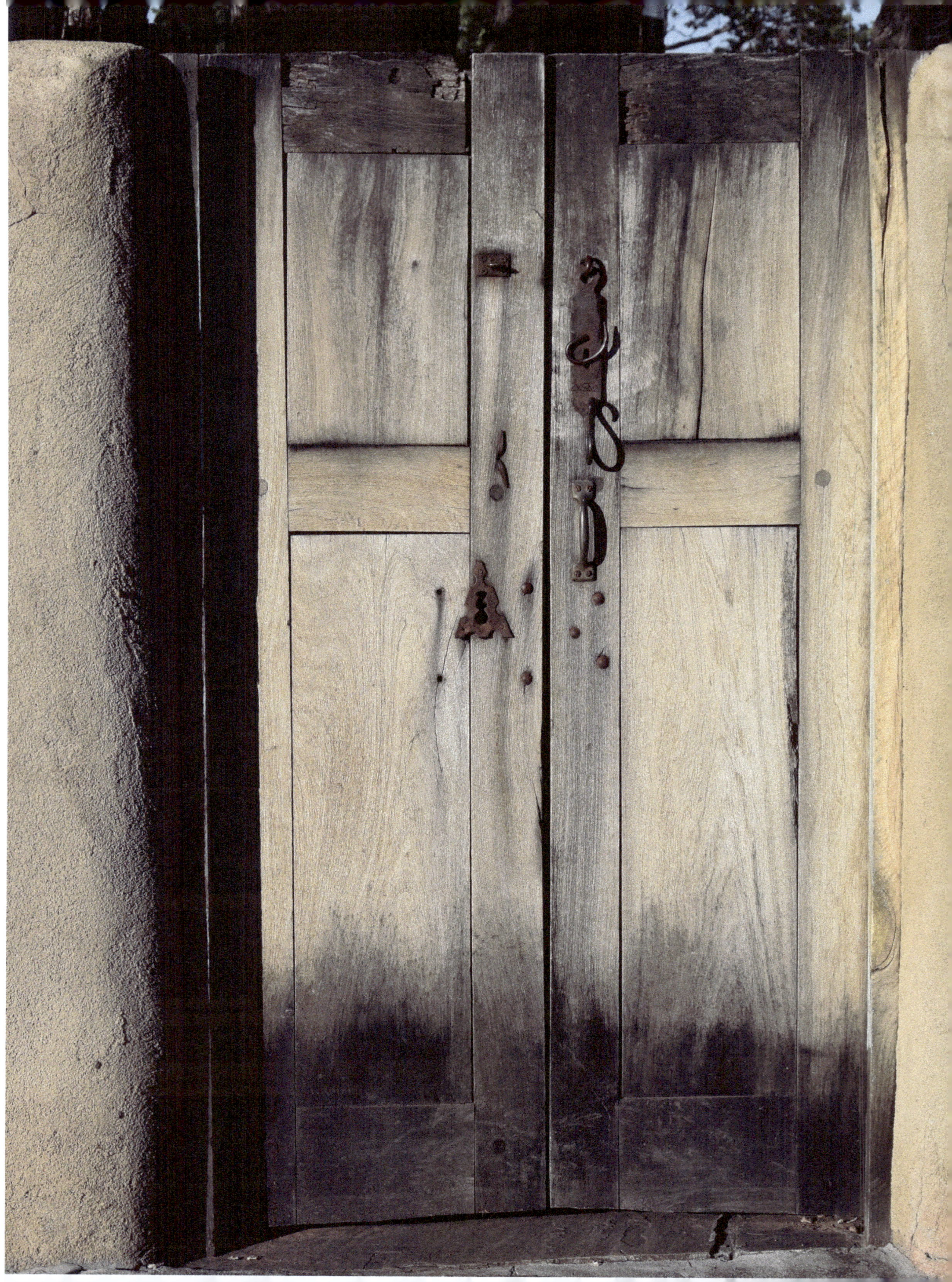

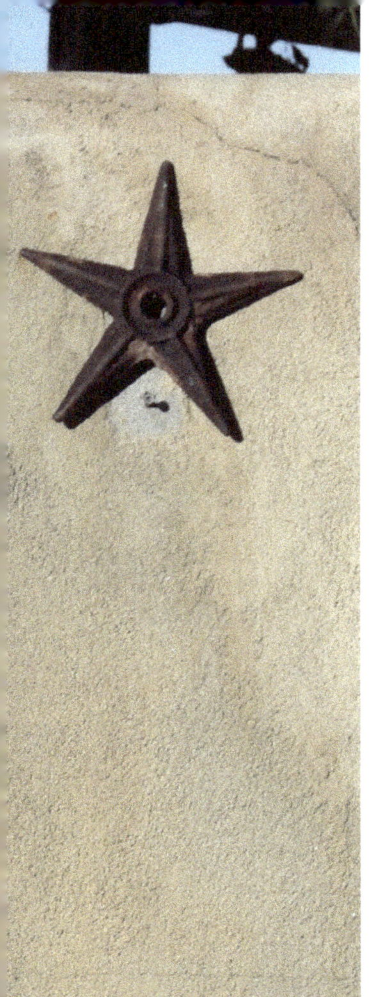

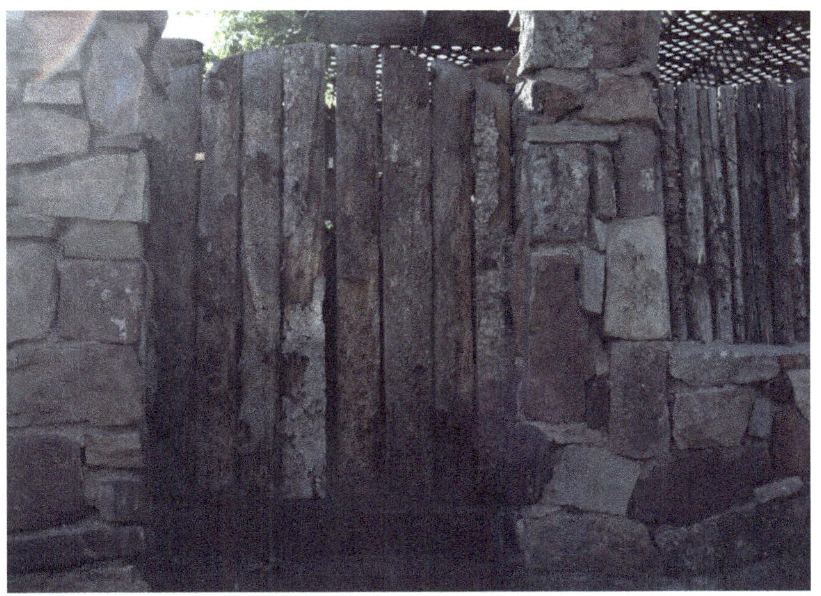

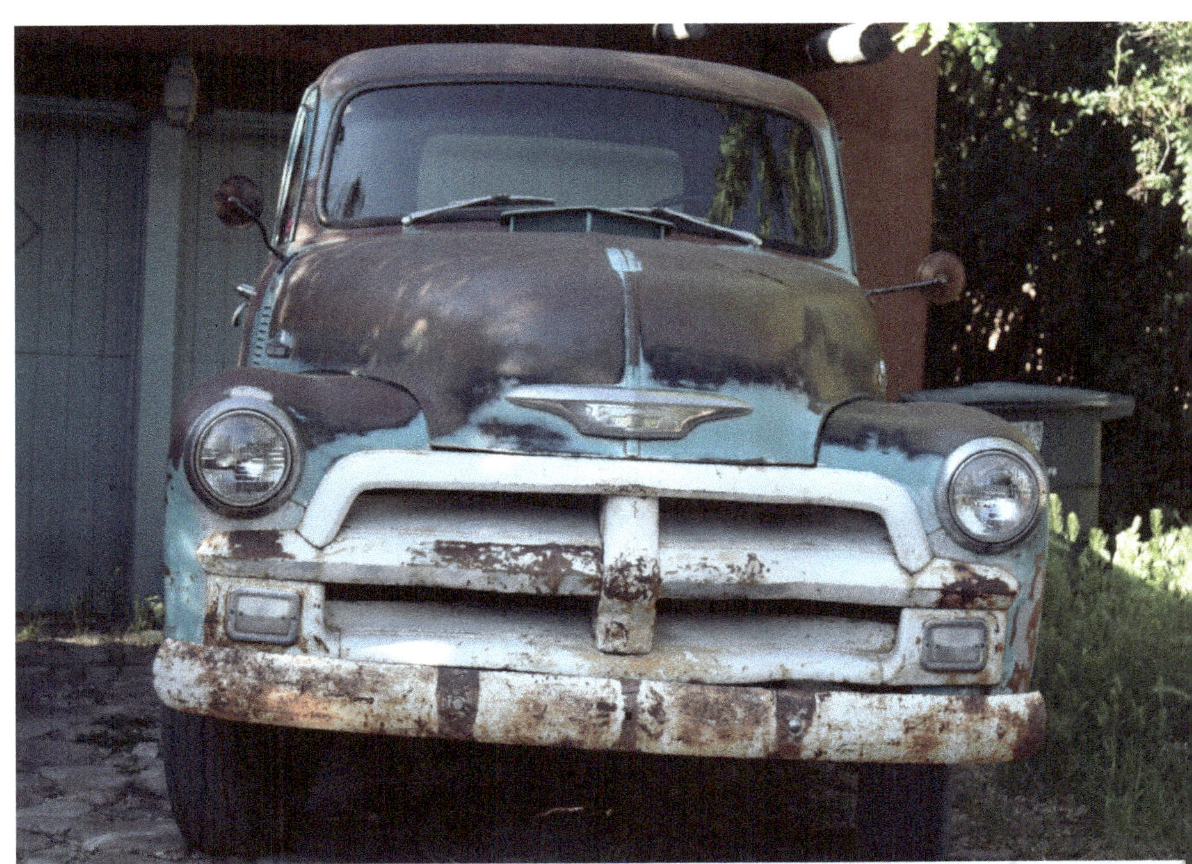

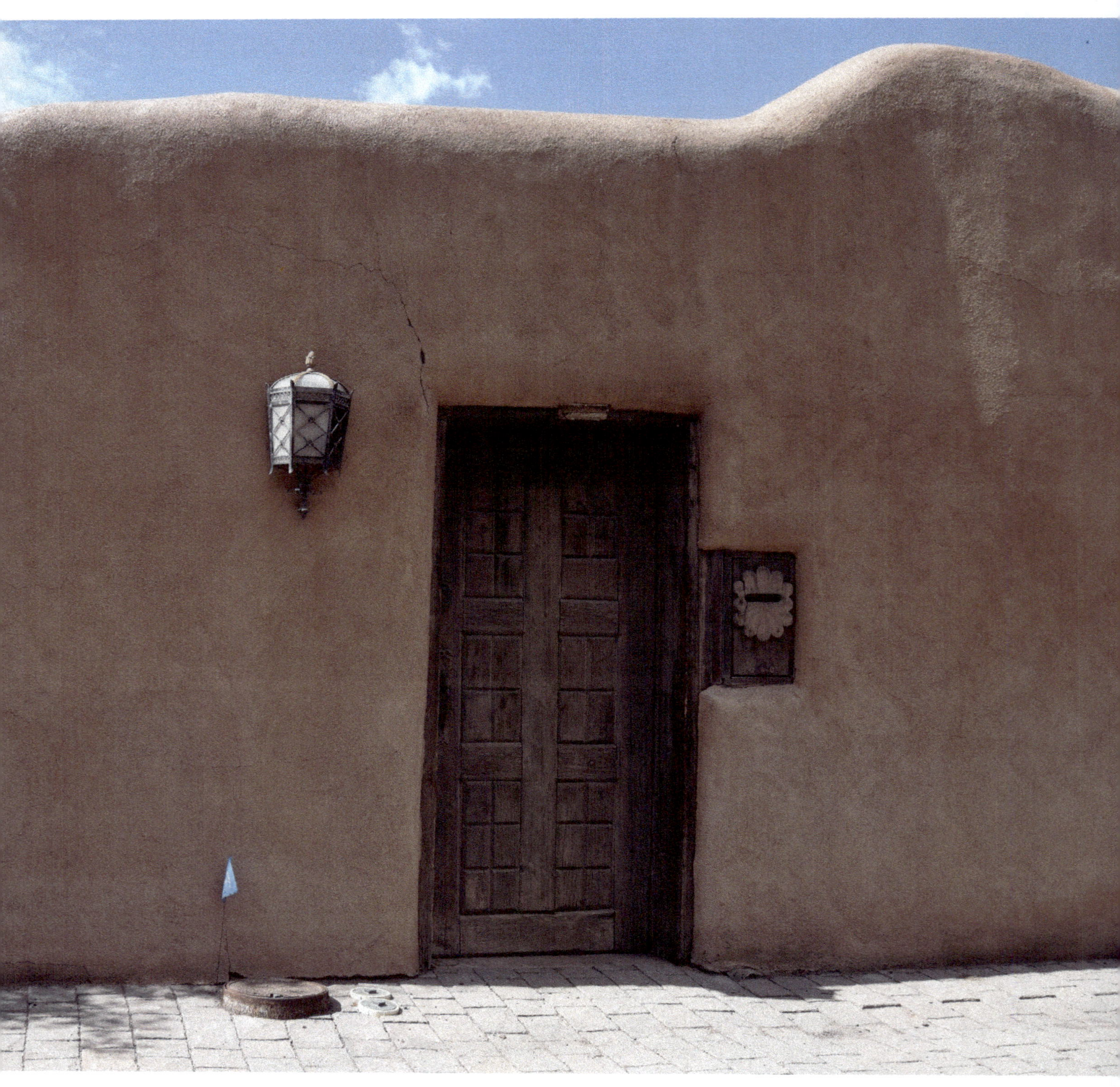

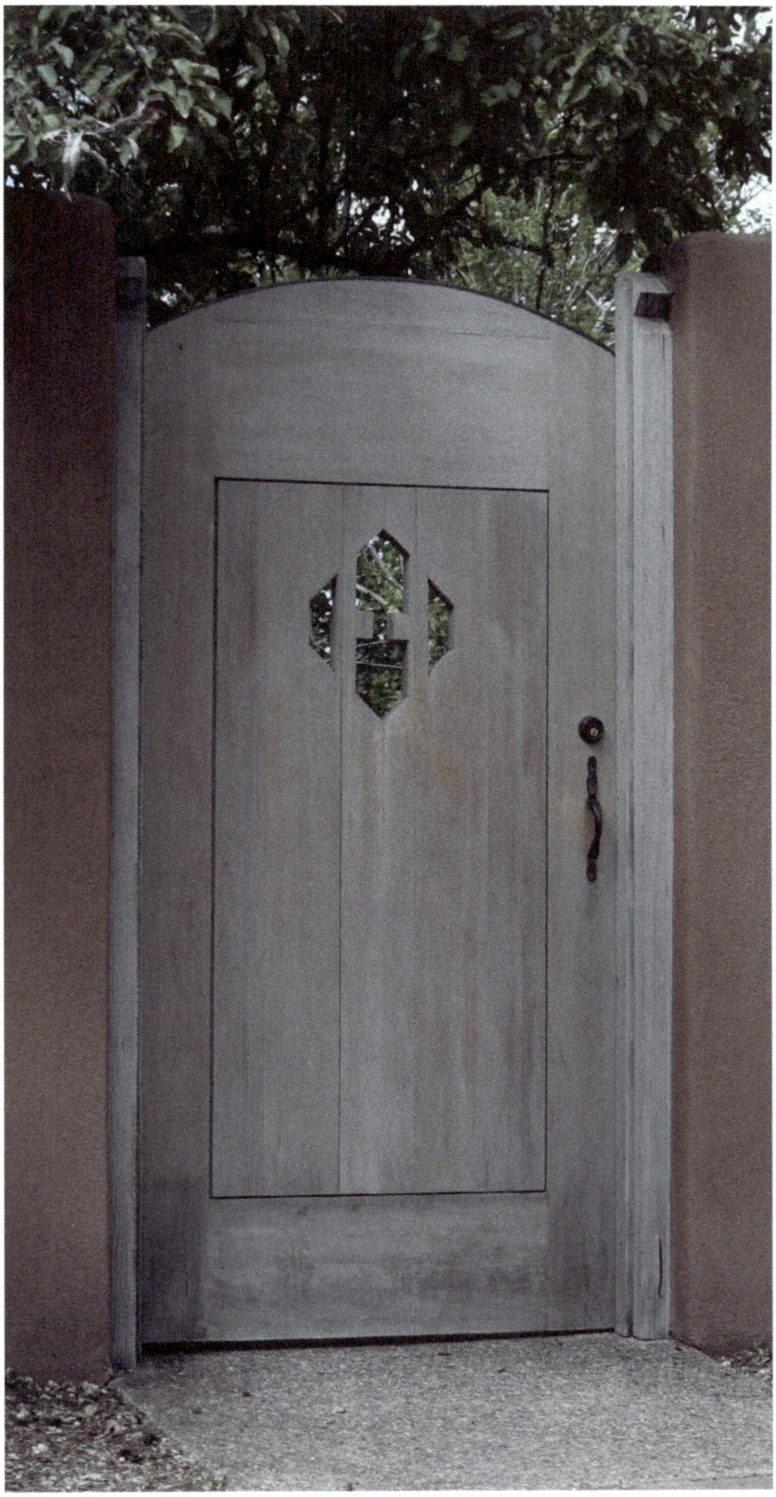

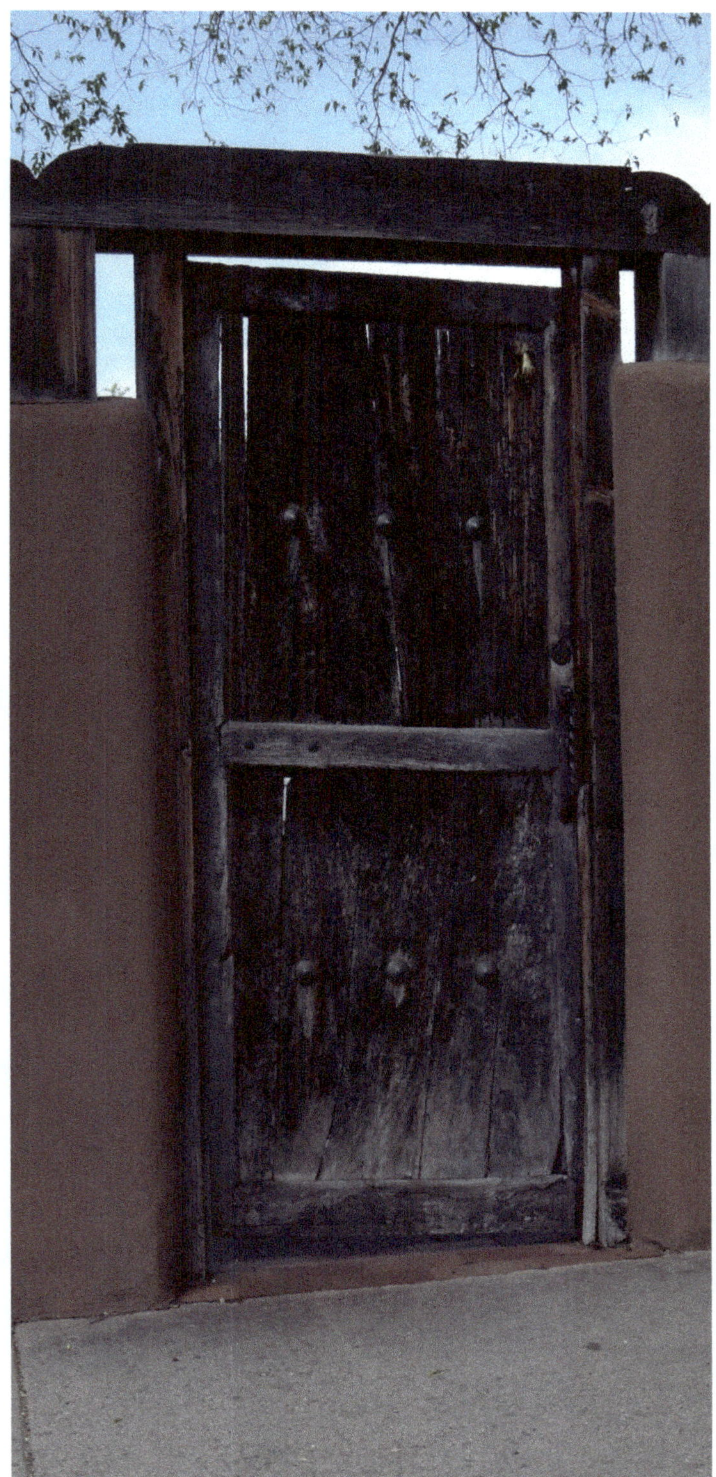

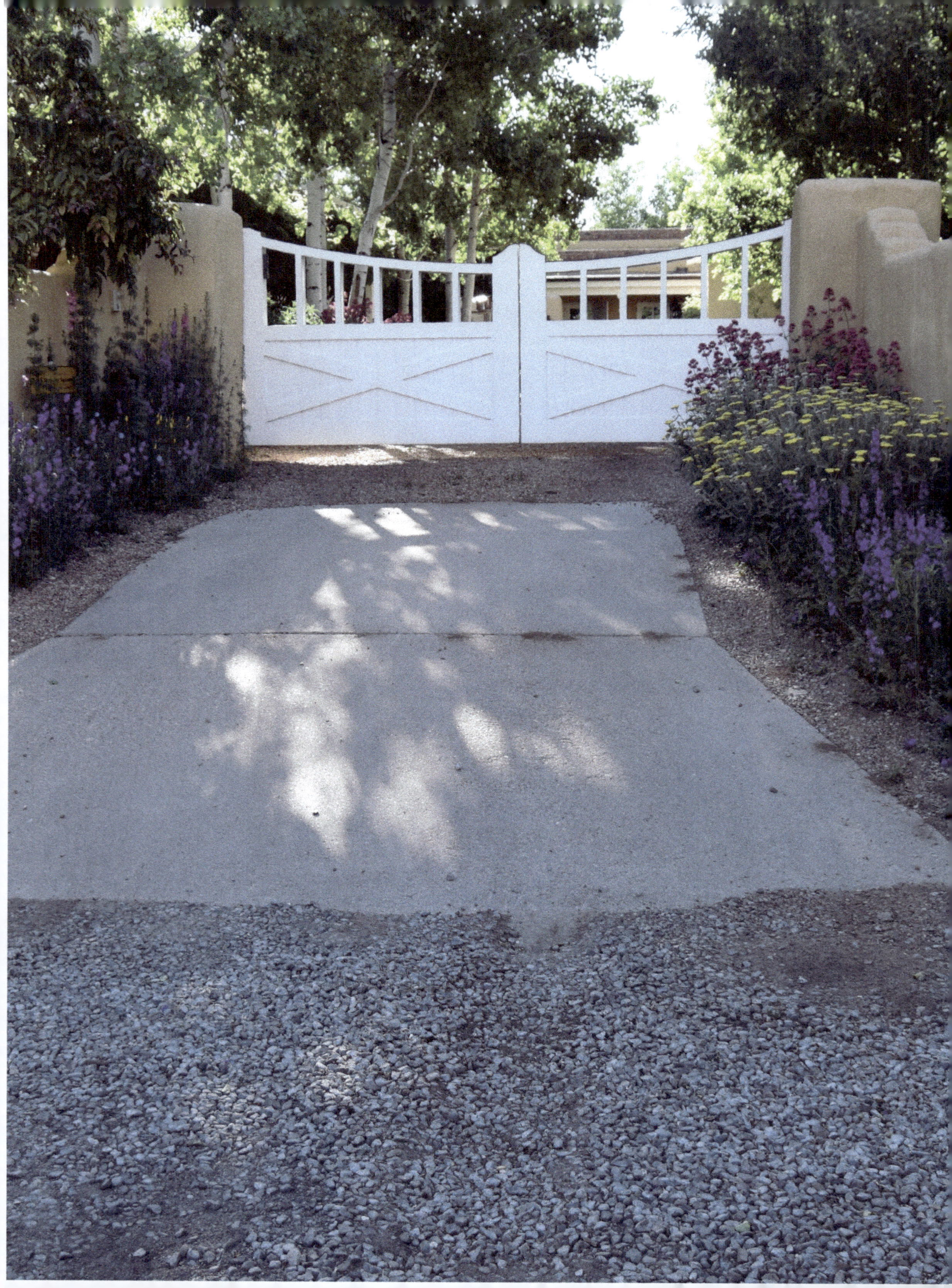

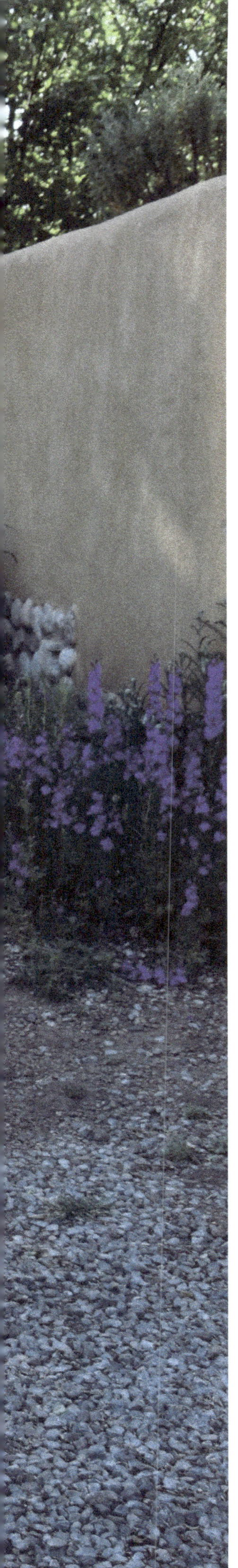

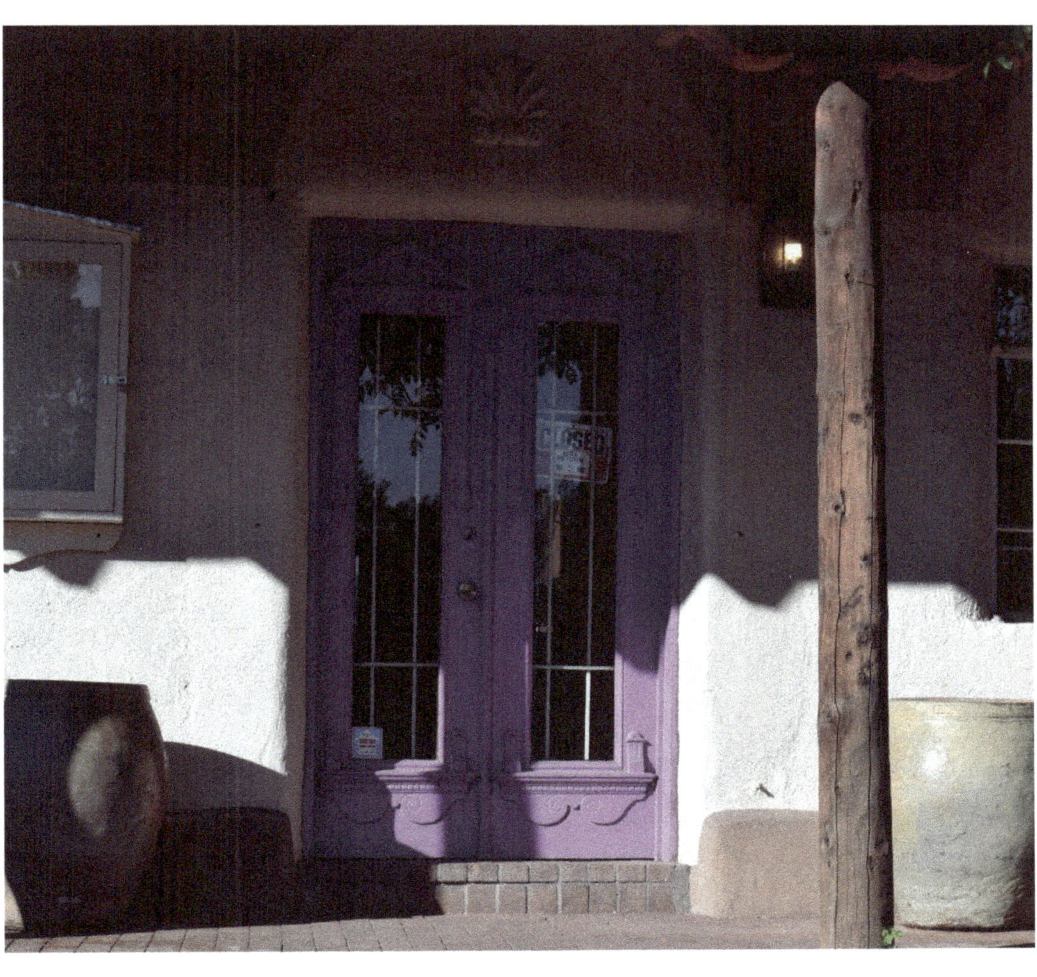

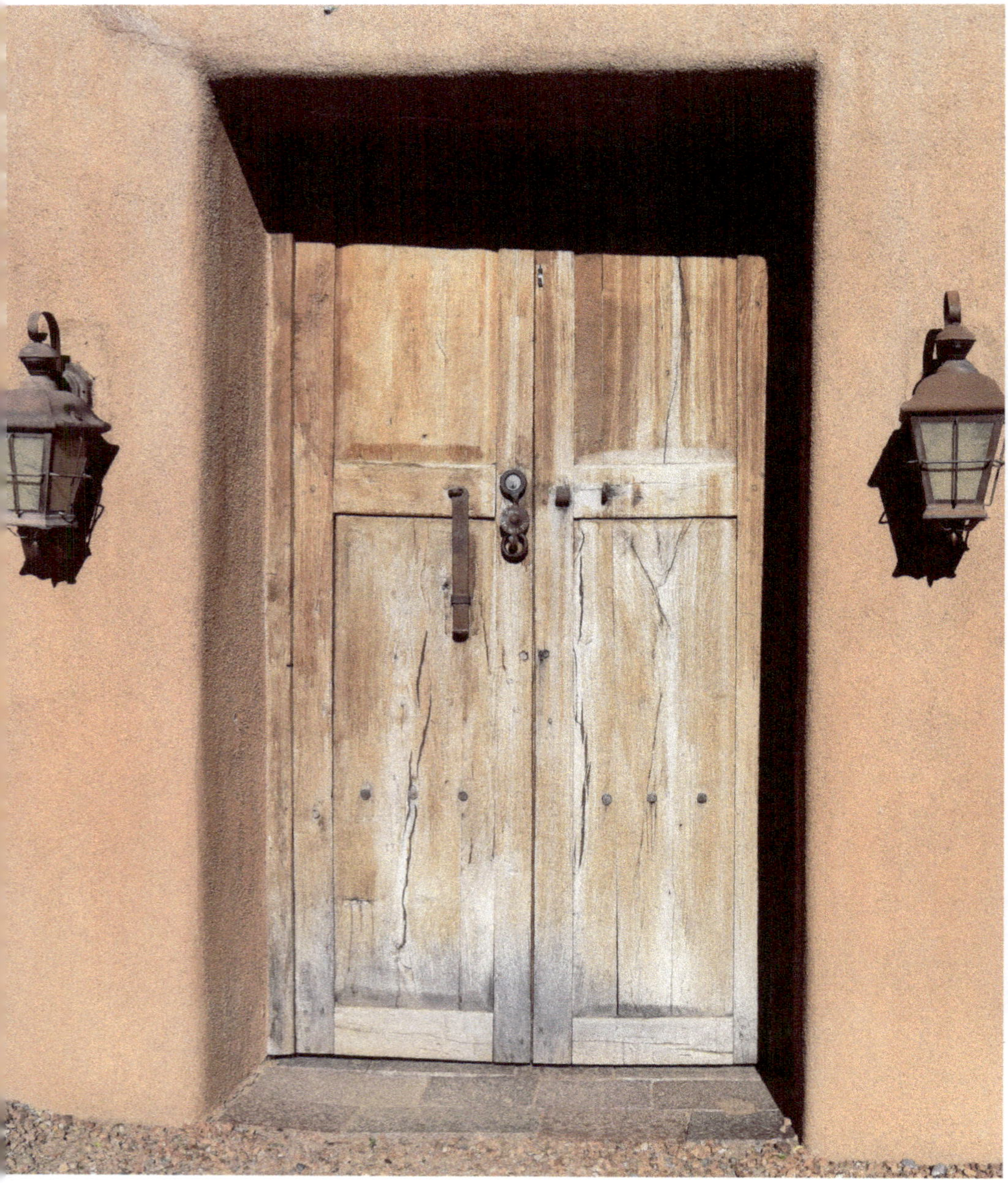

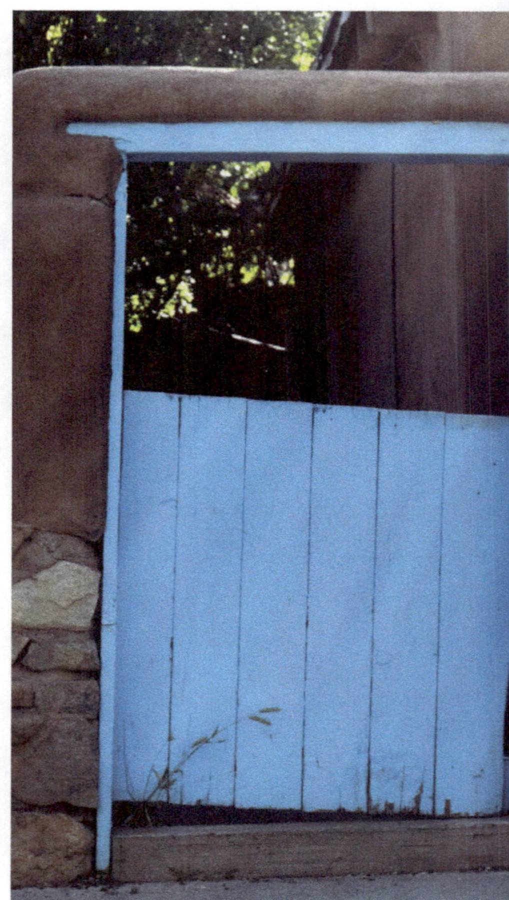

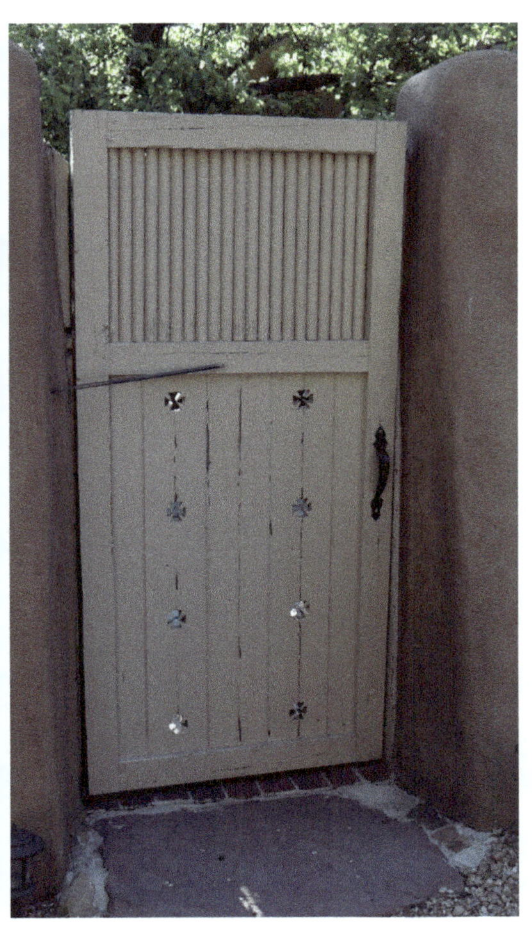

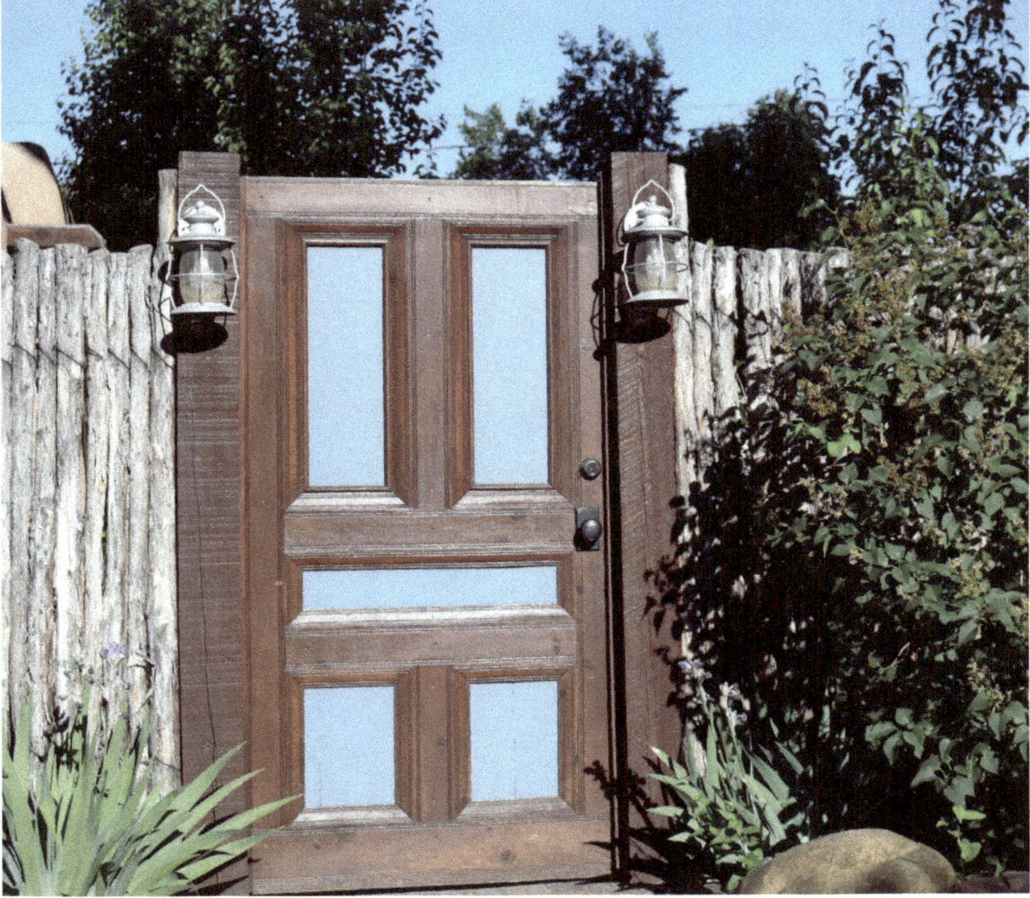

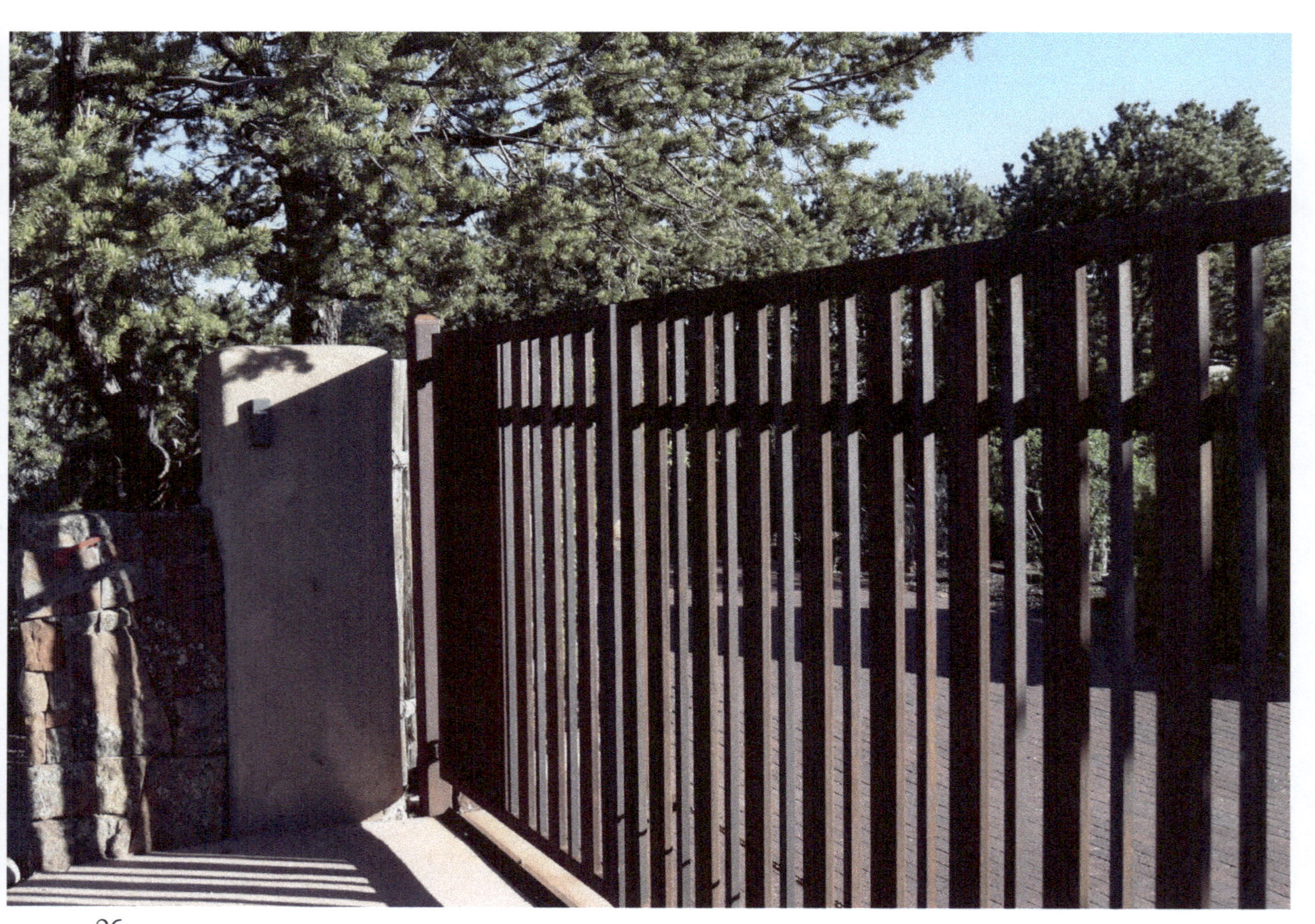

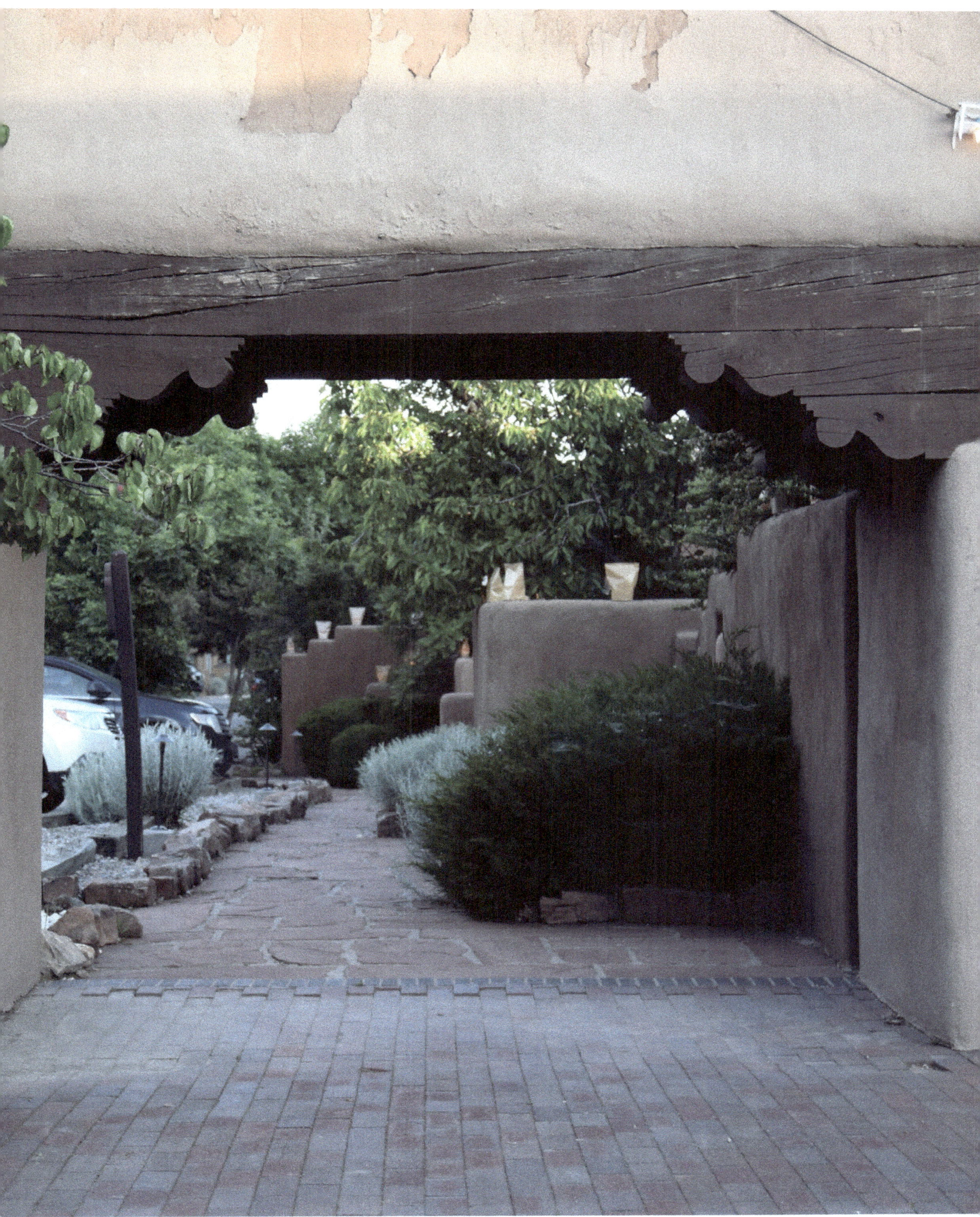

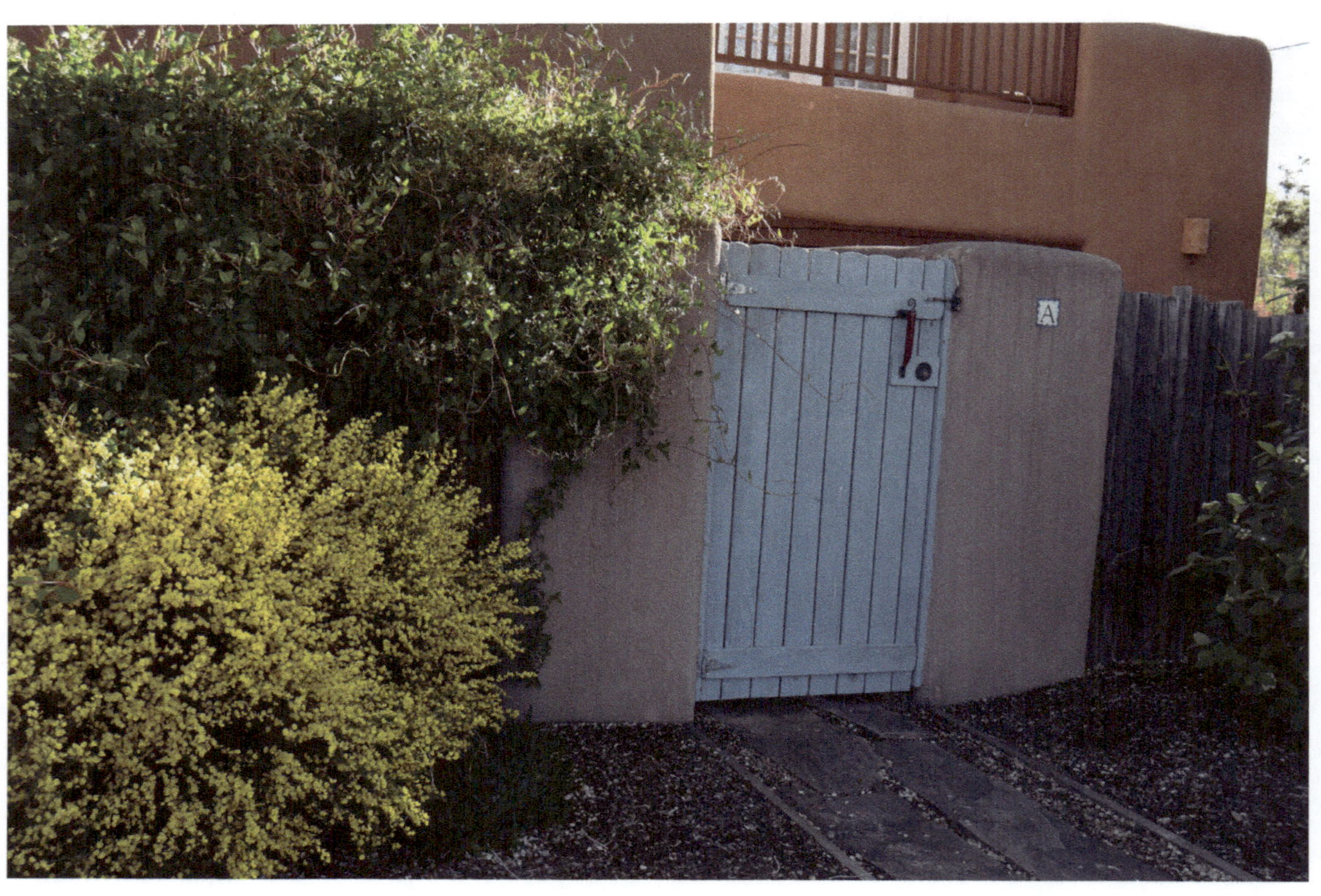

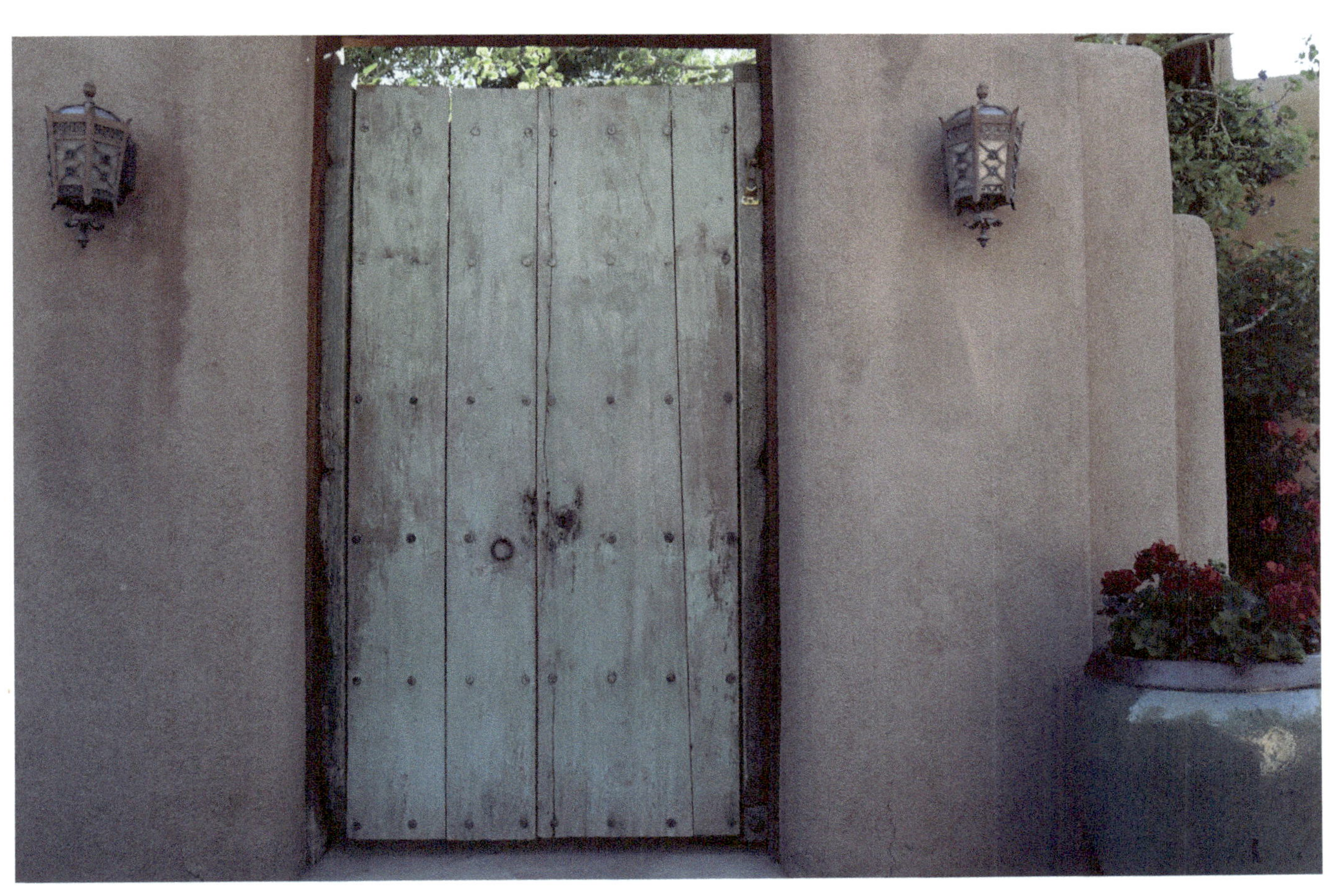

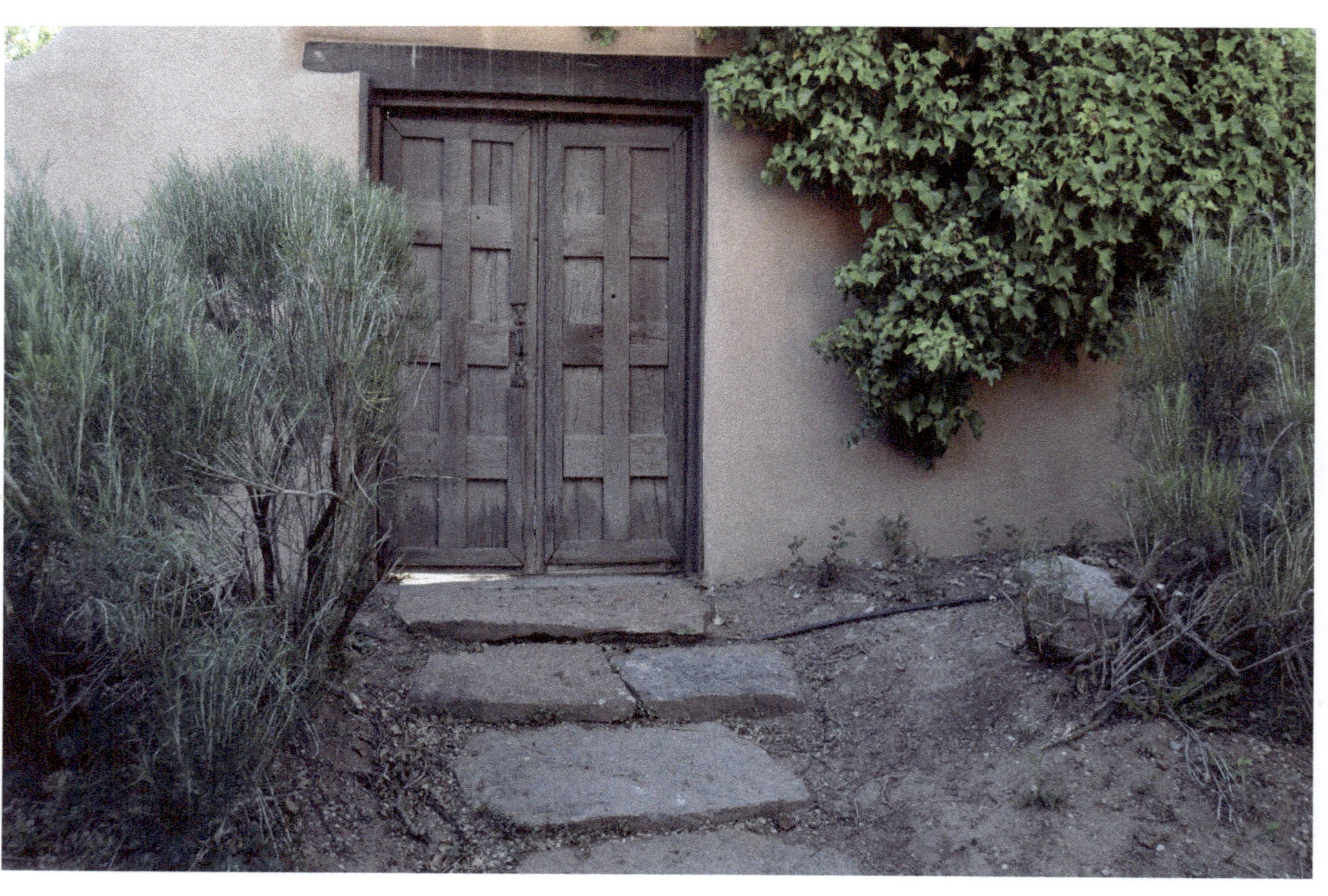

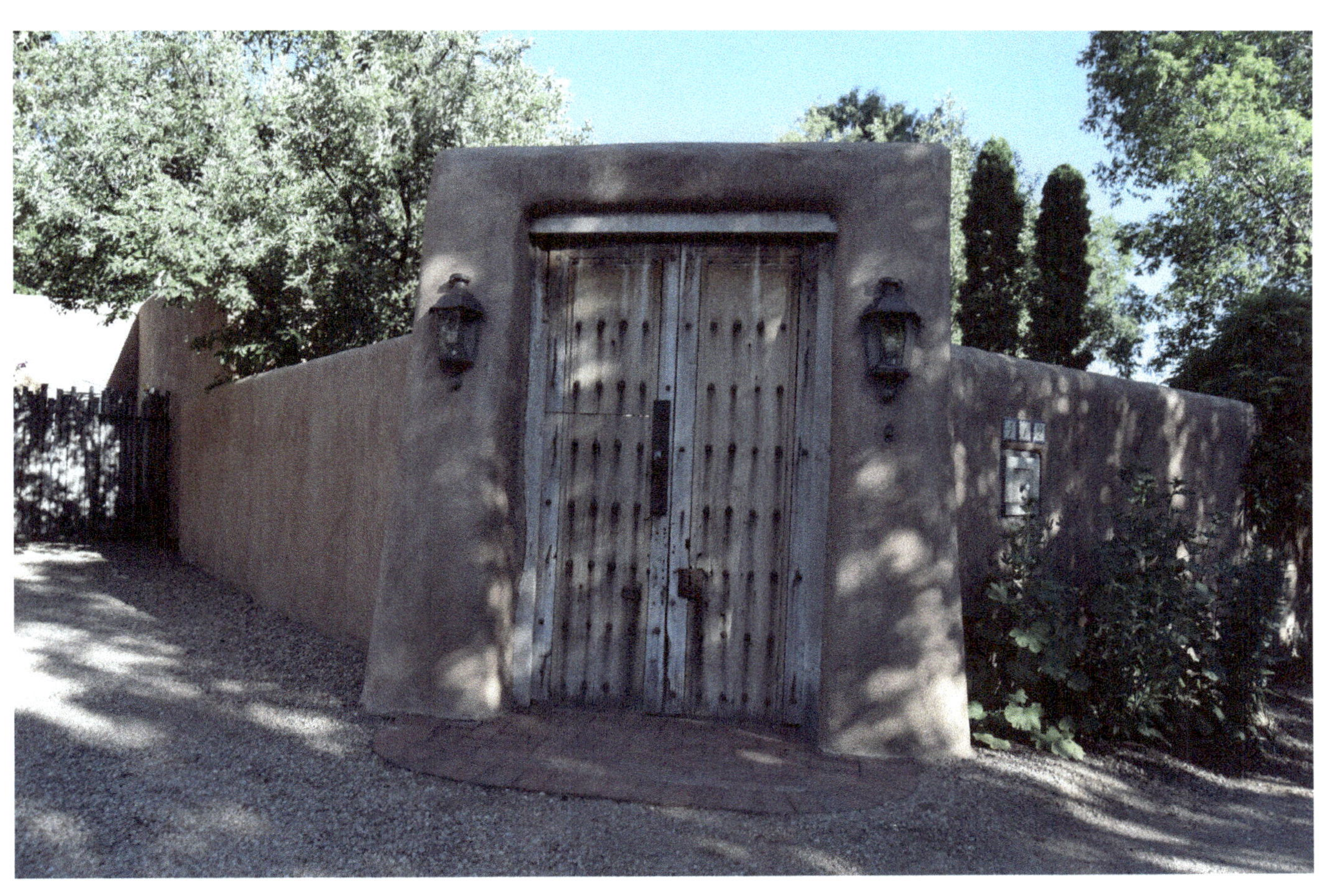

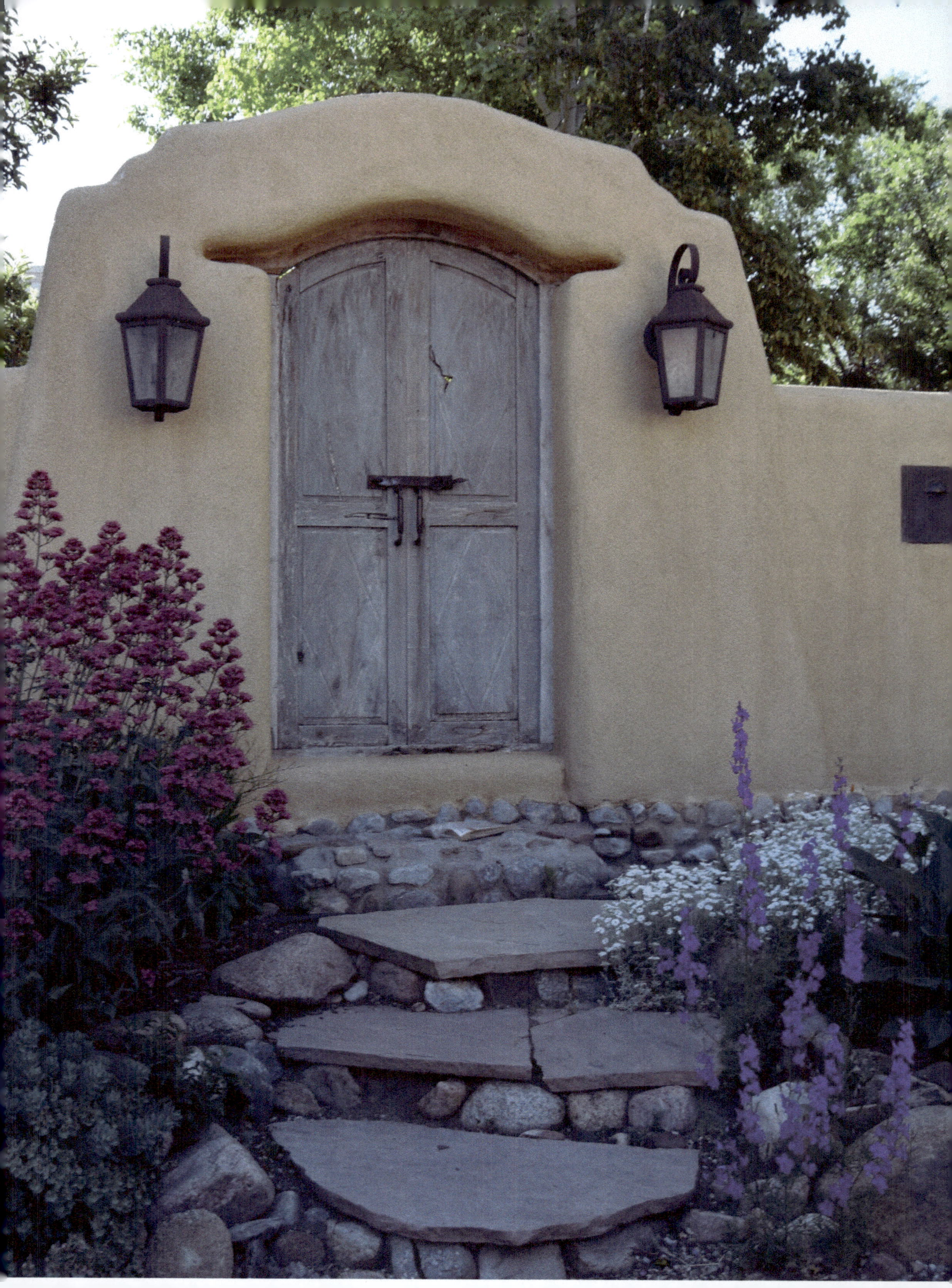

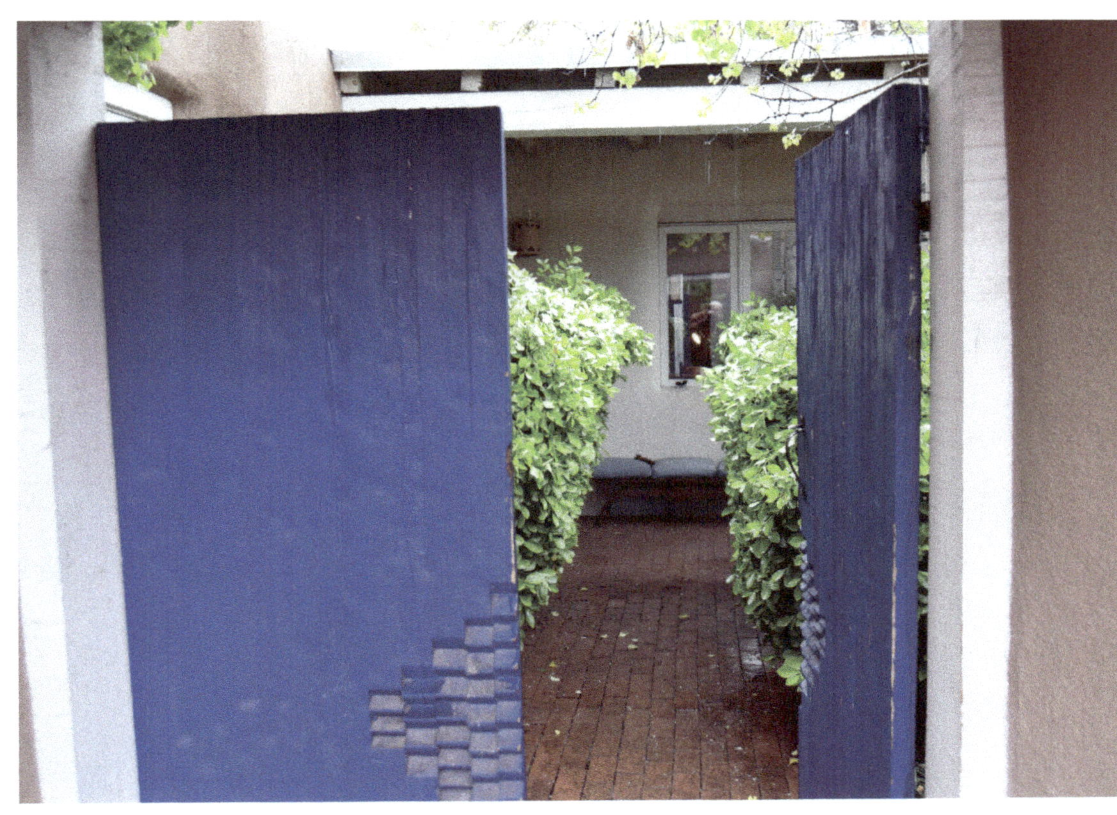

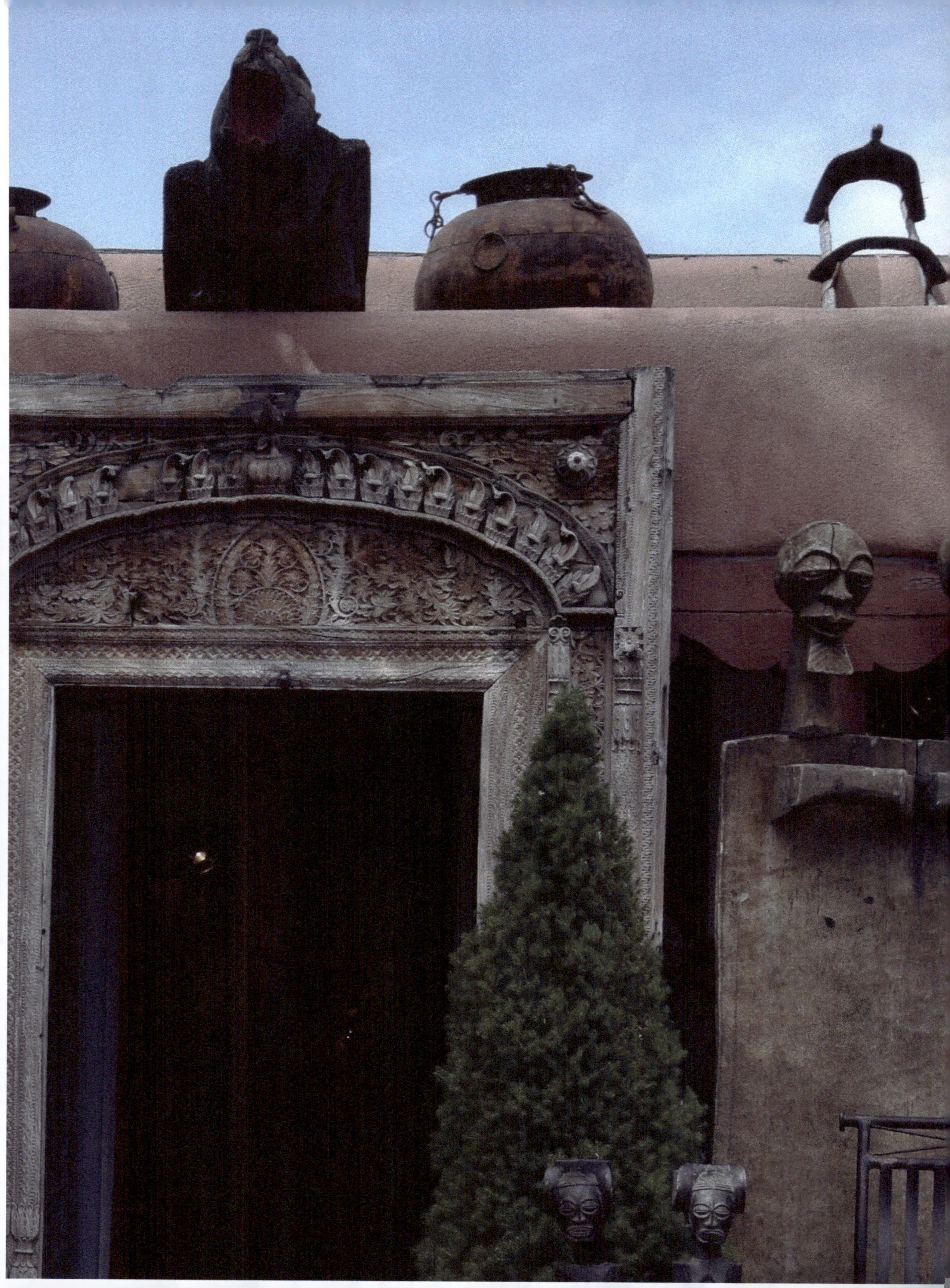

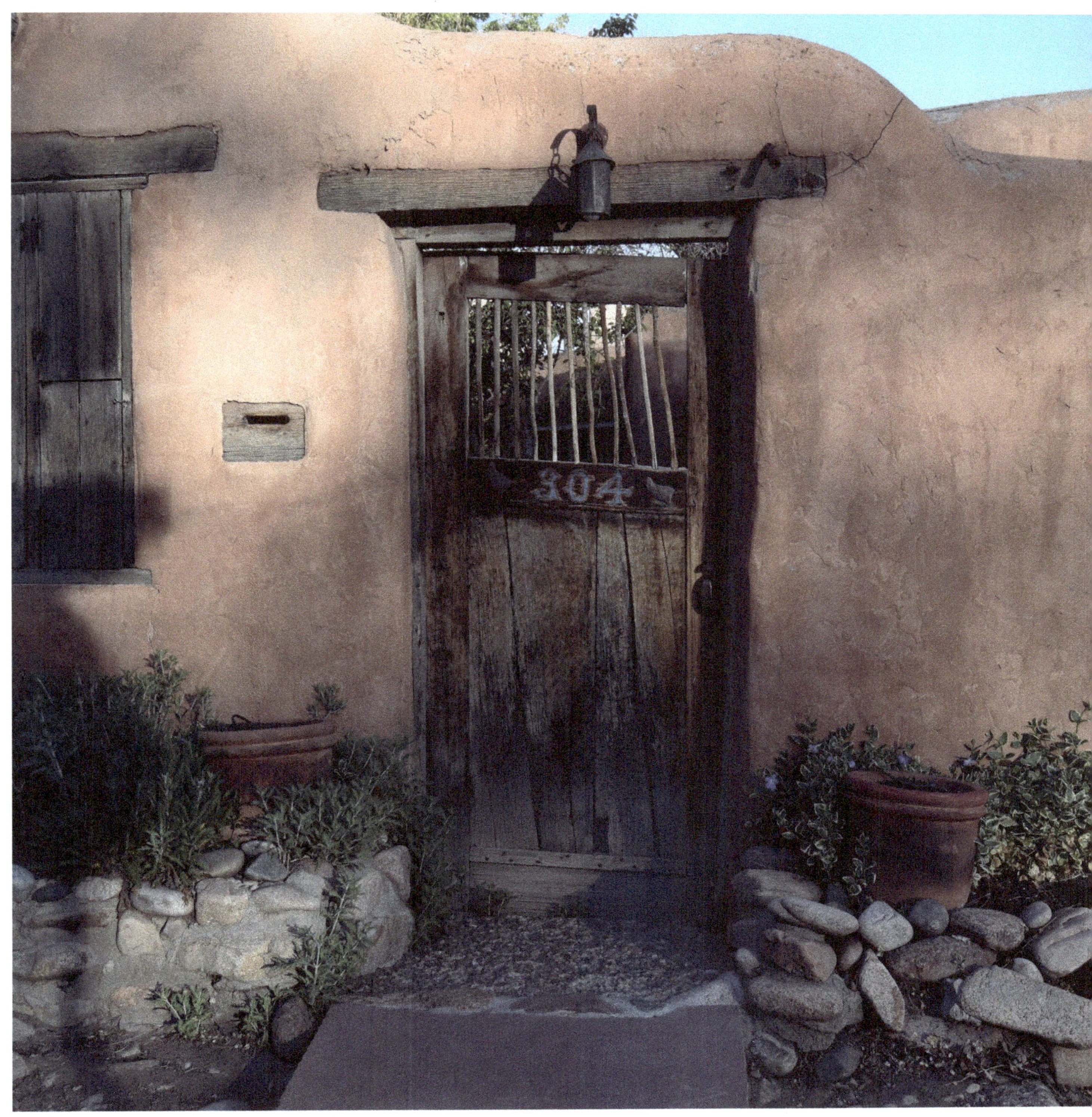

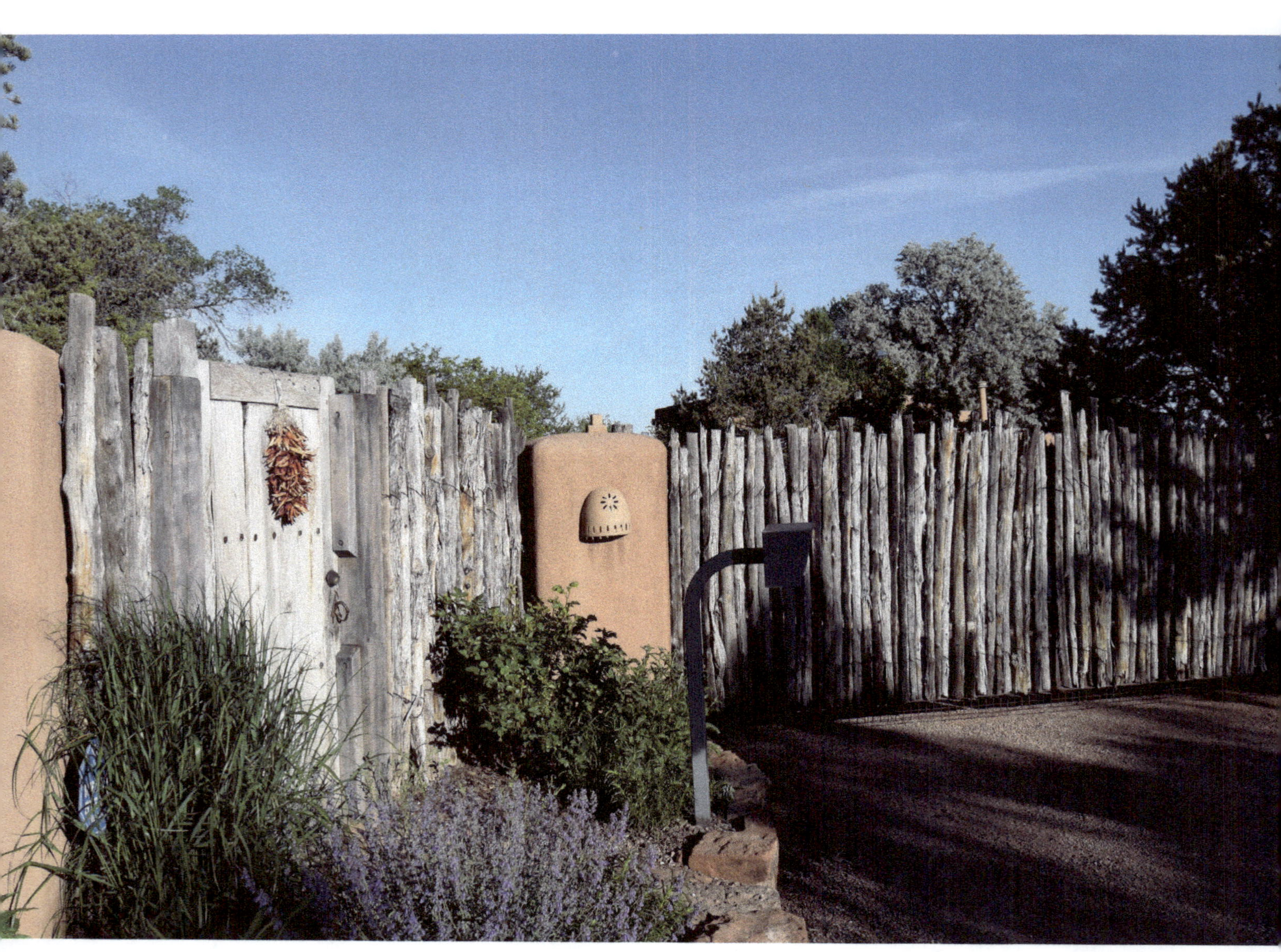

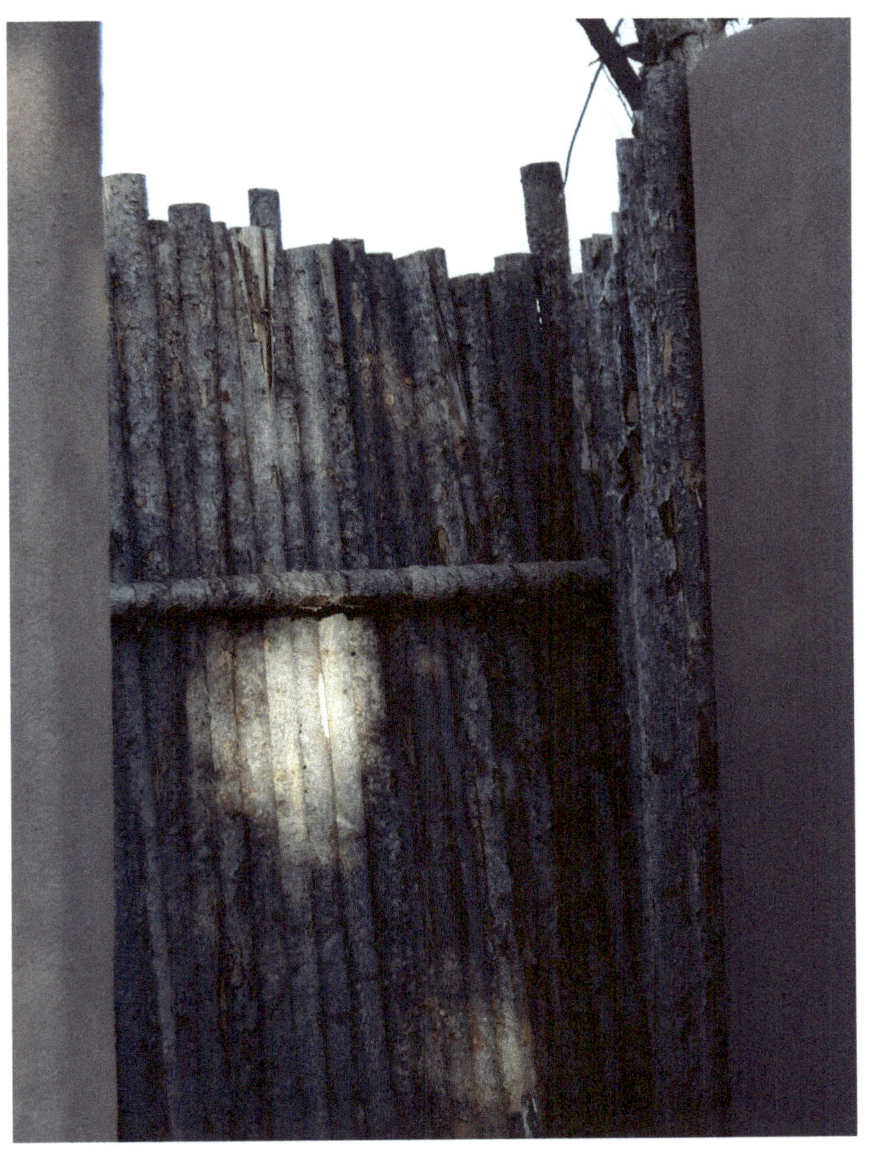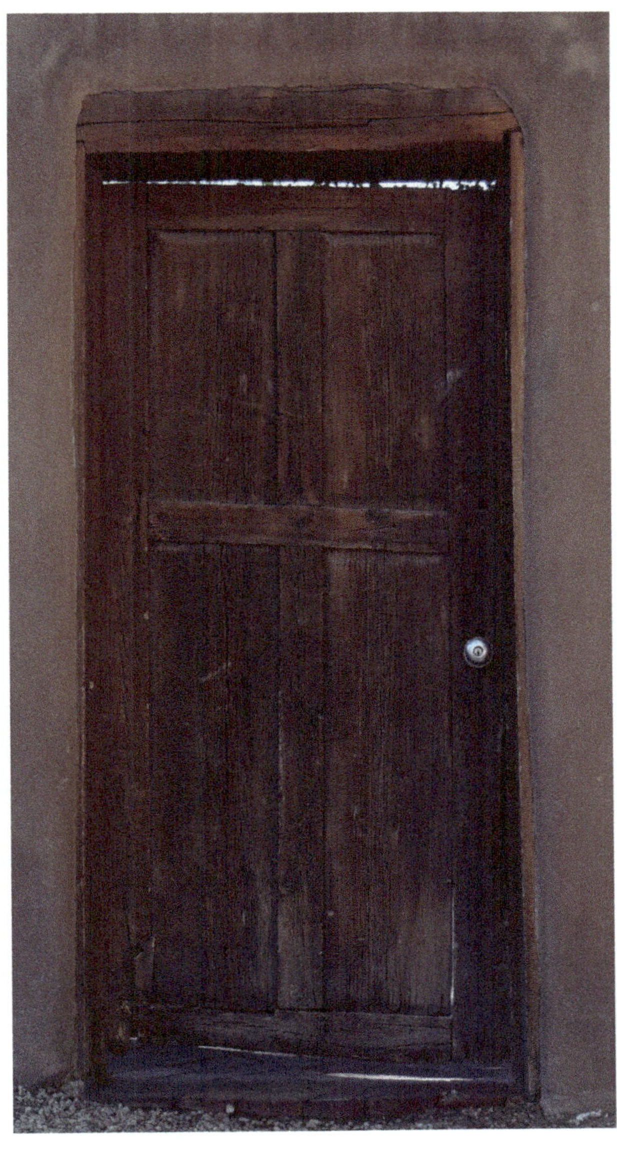

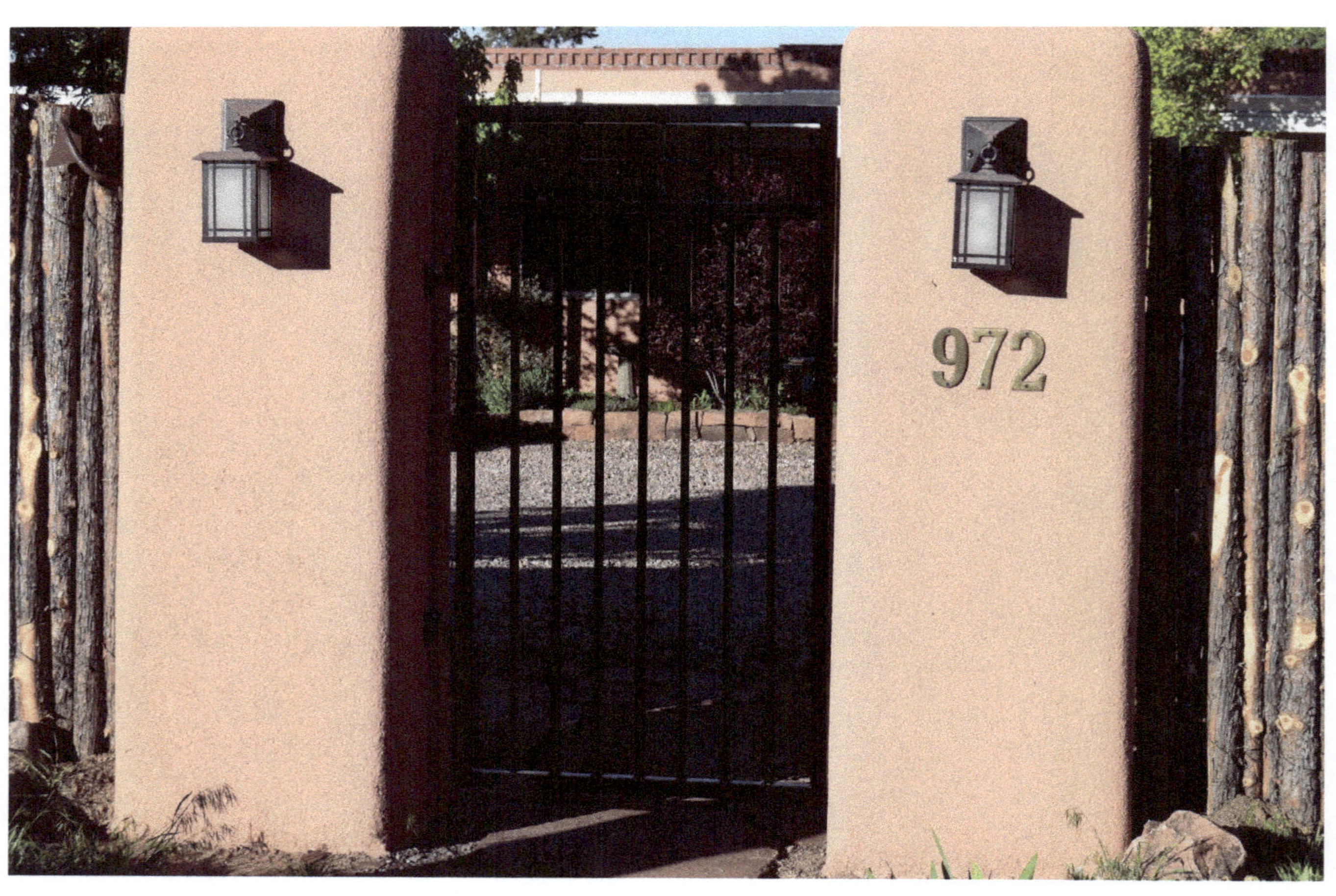
972

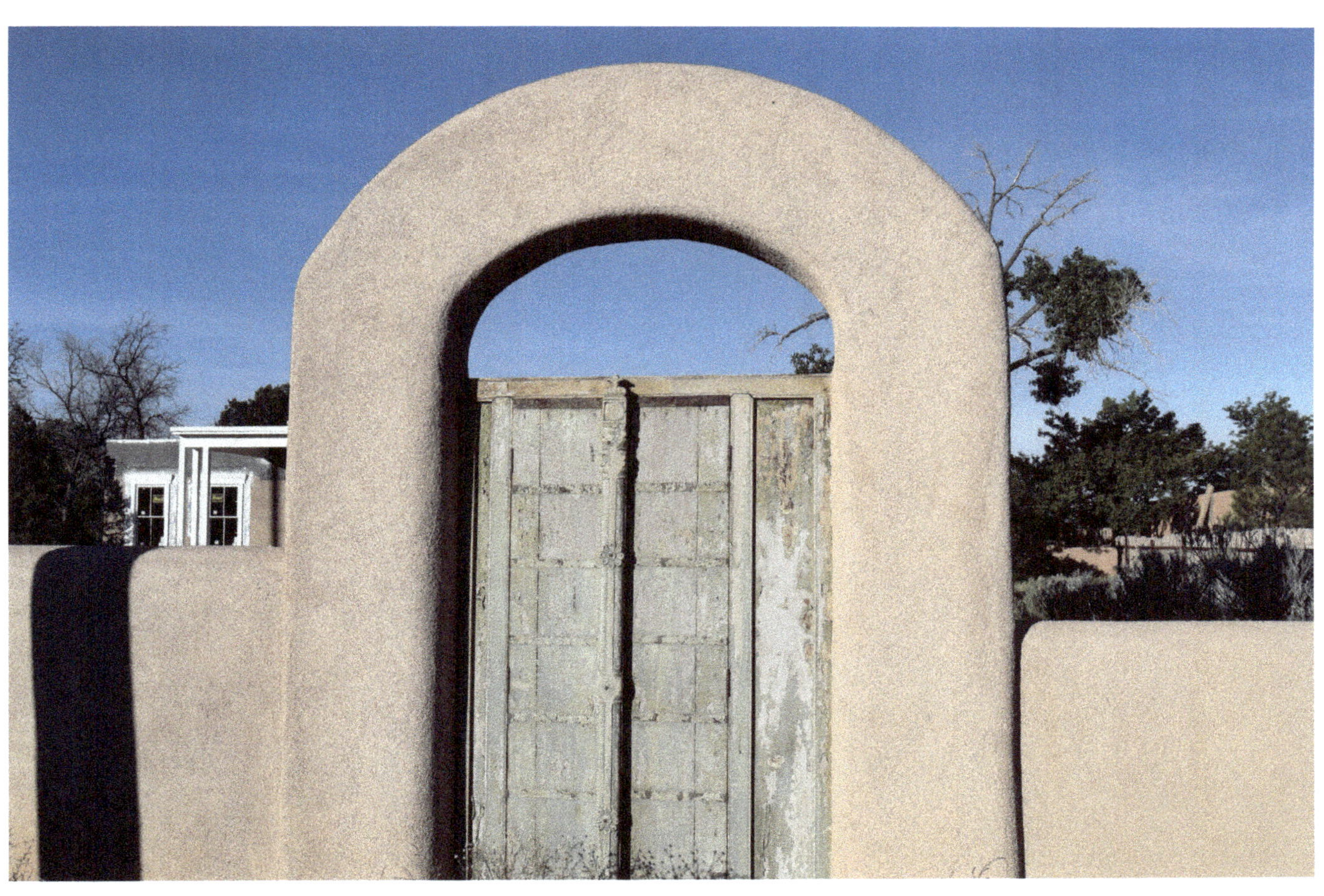

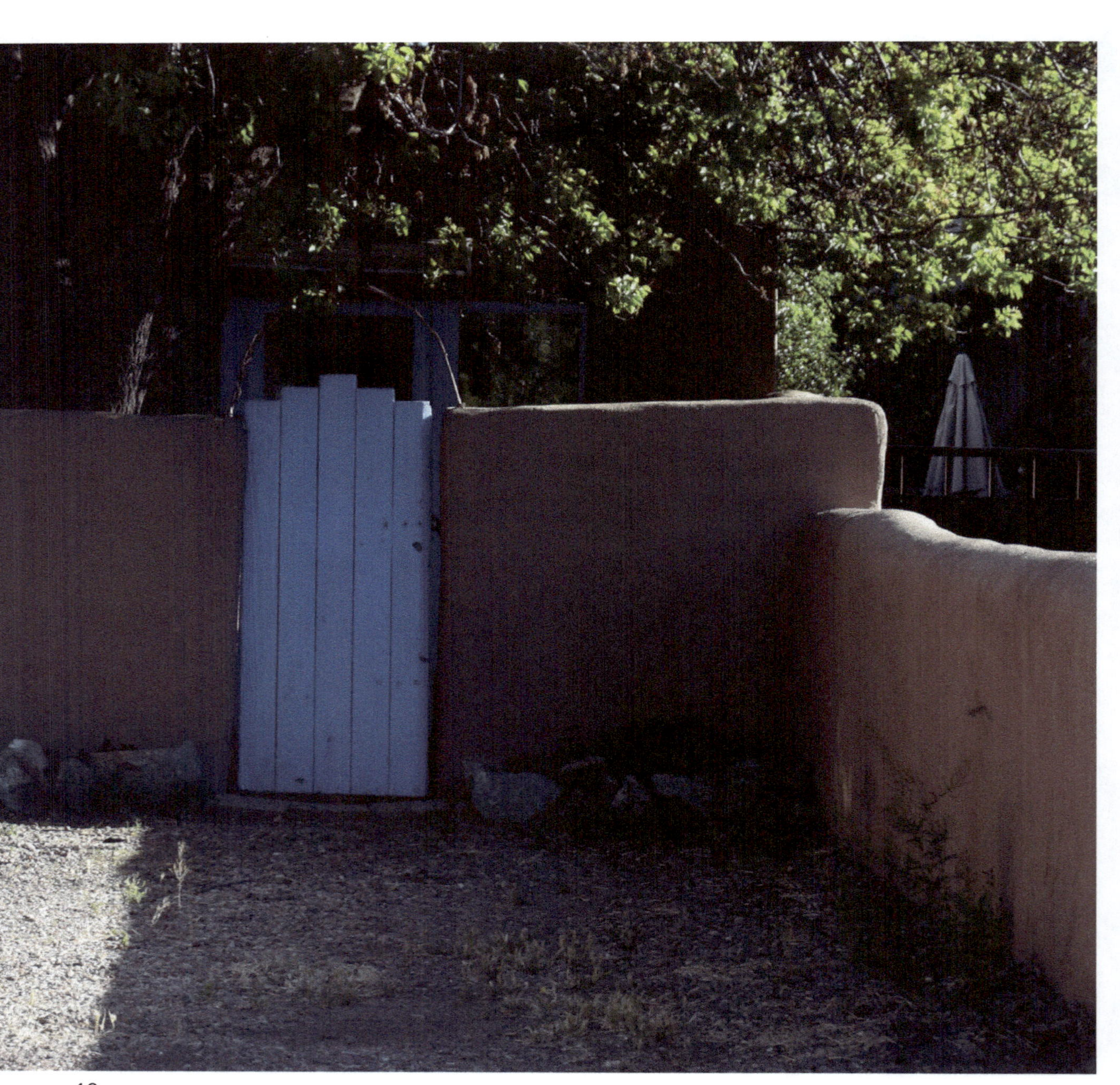

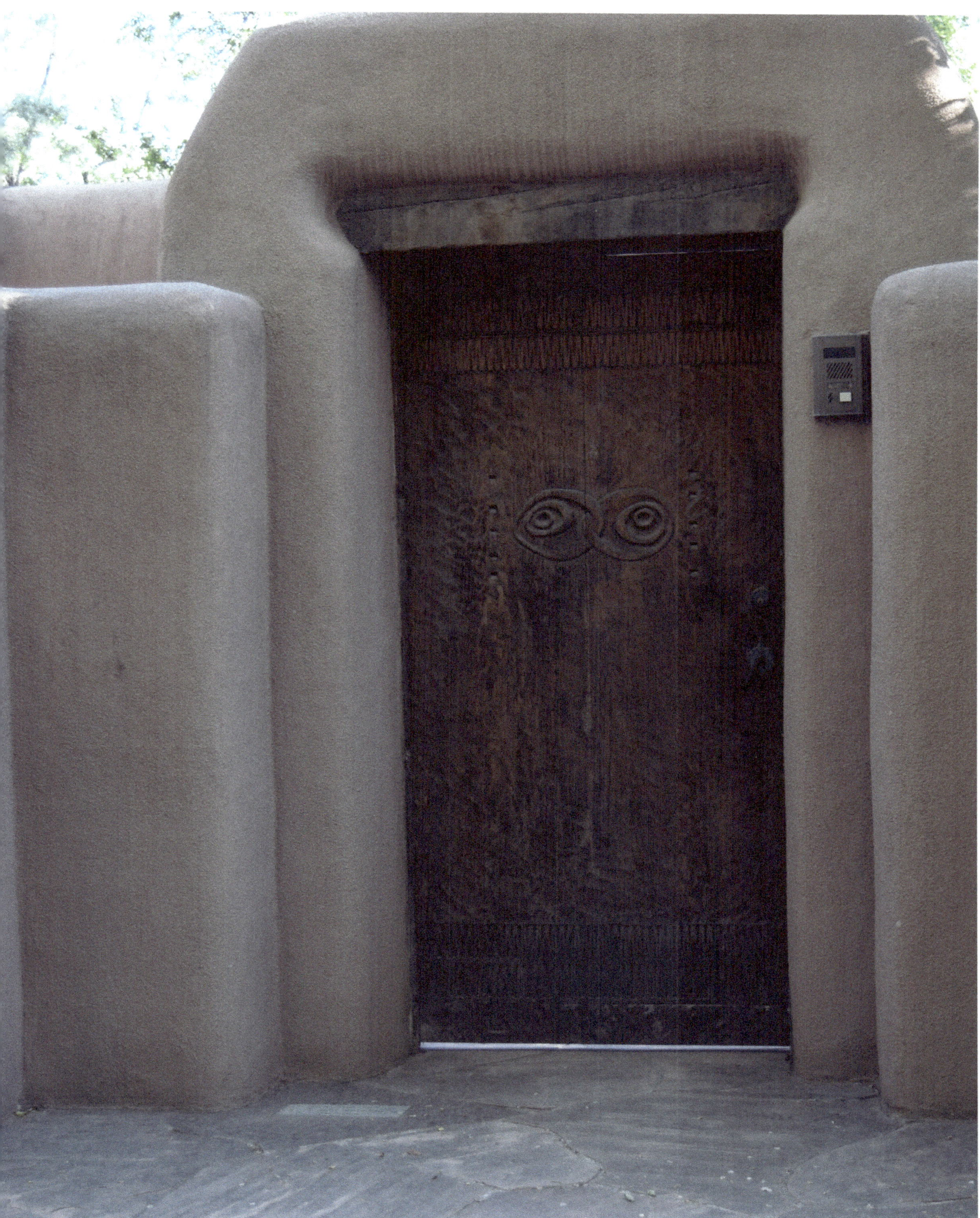

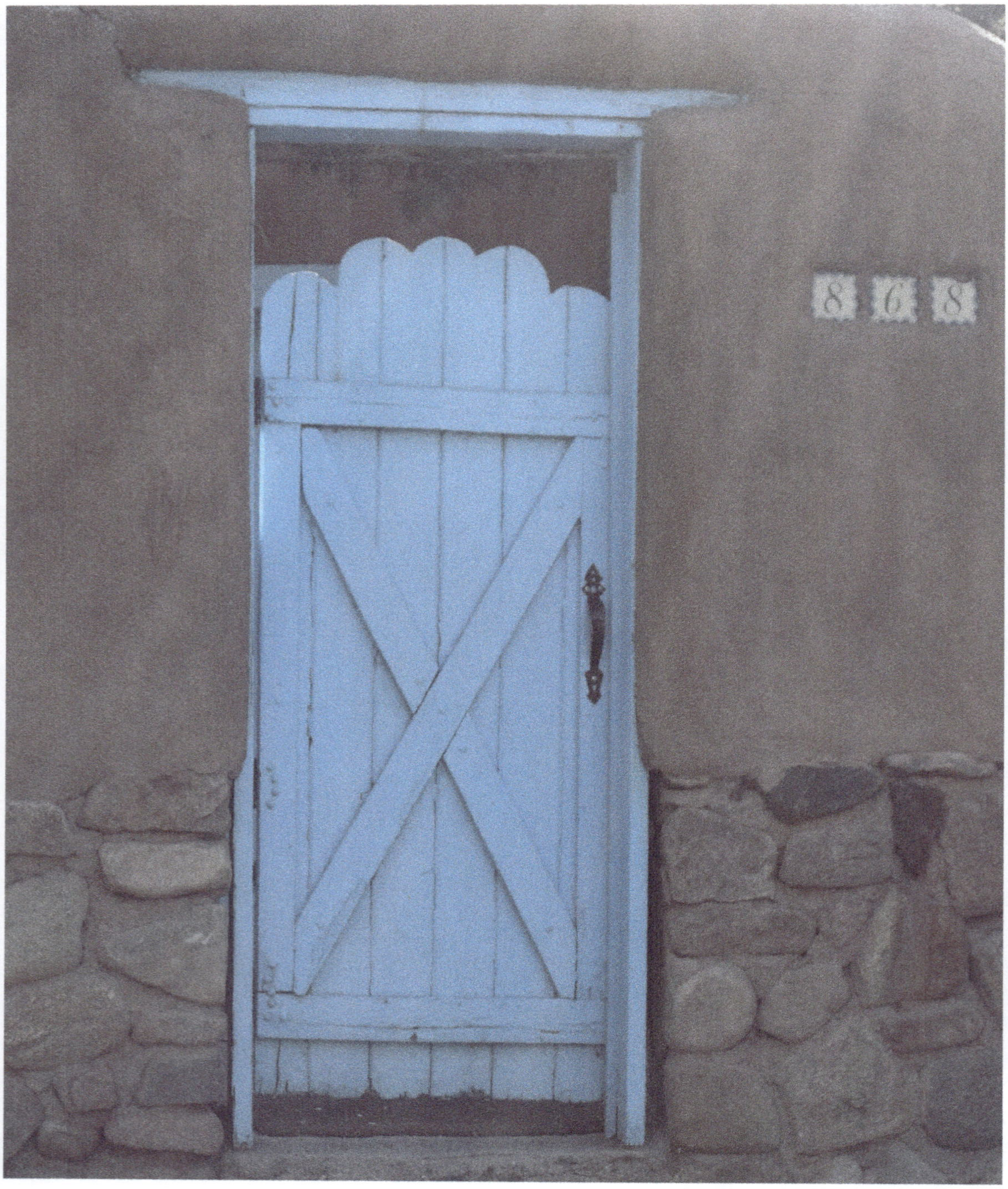

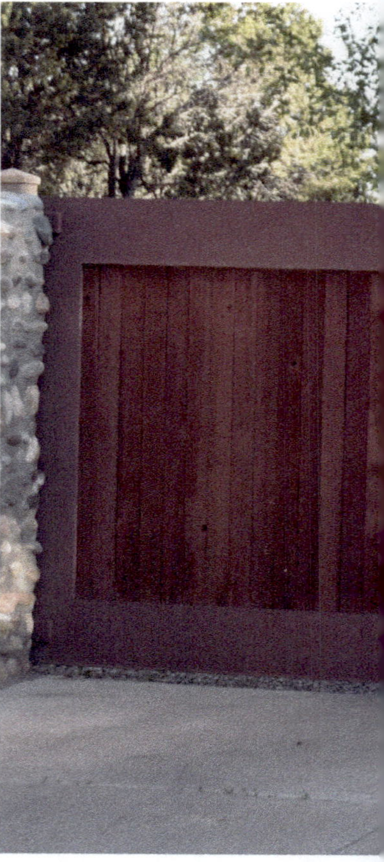

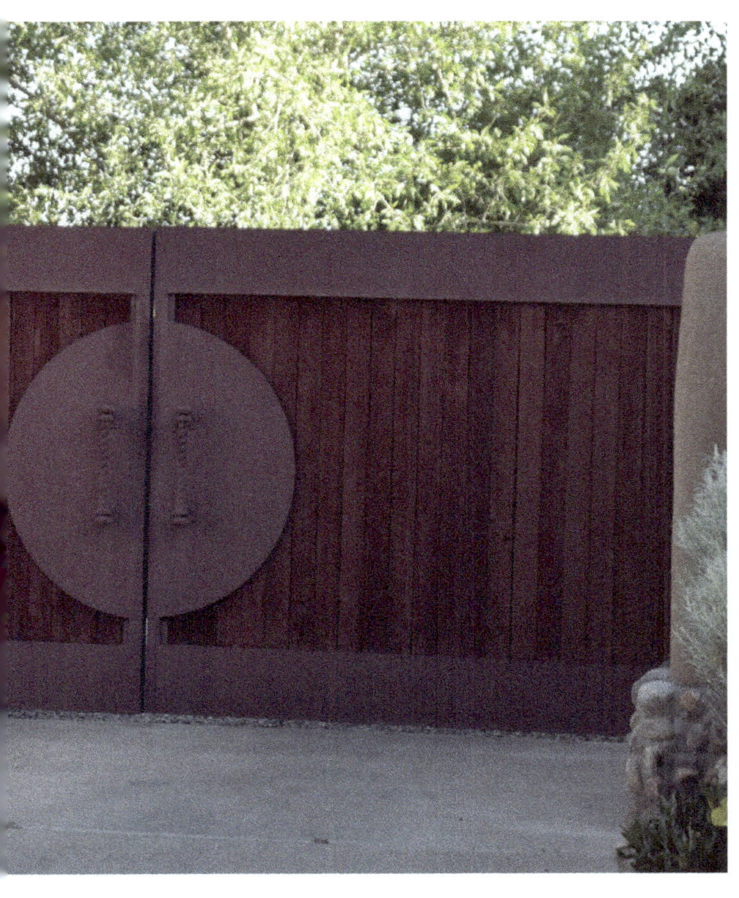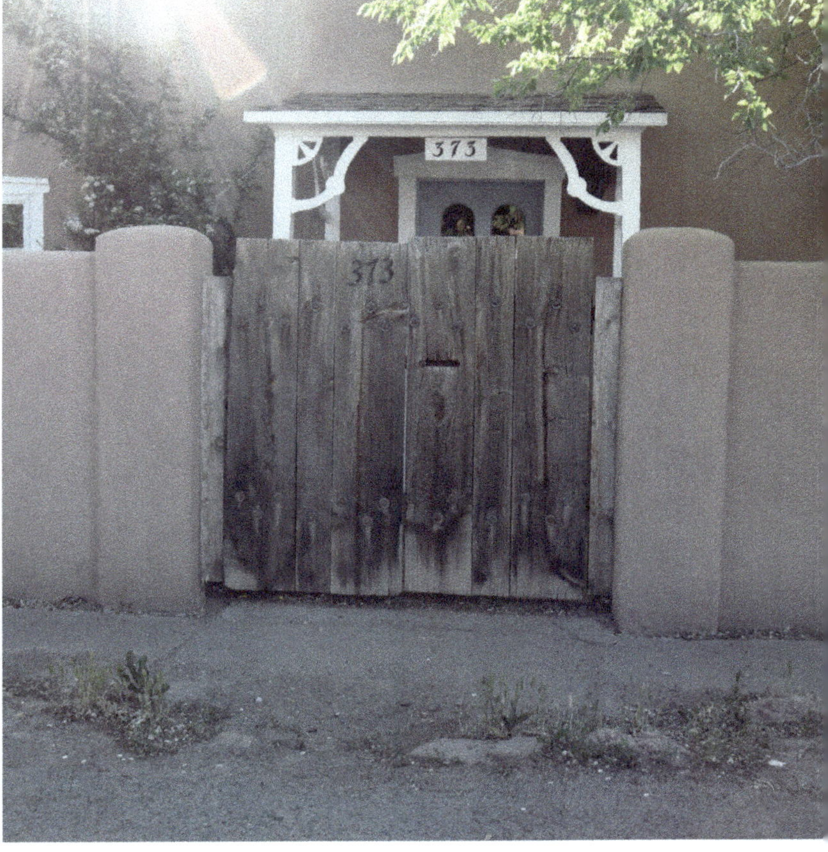

373

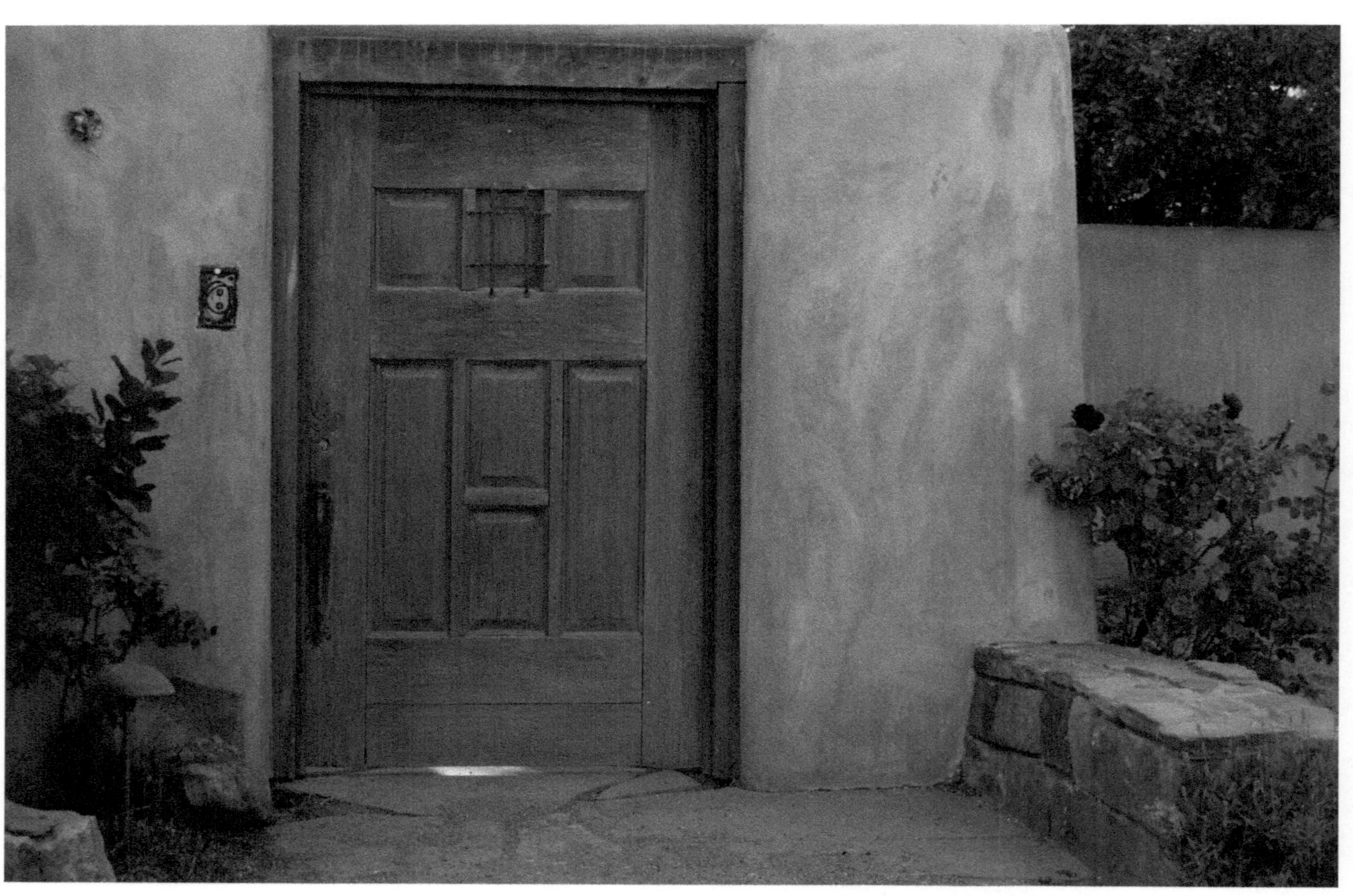

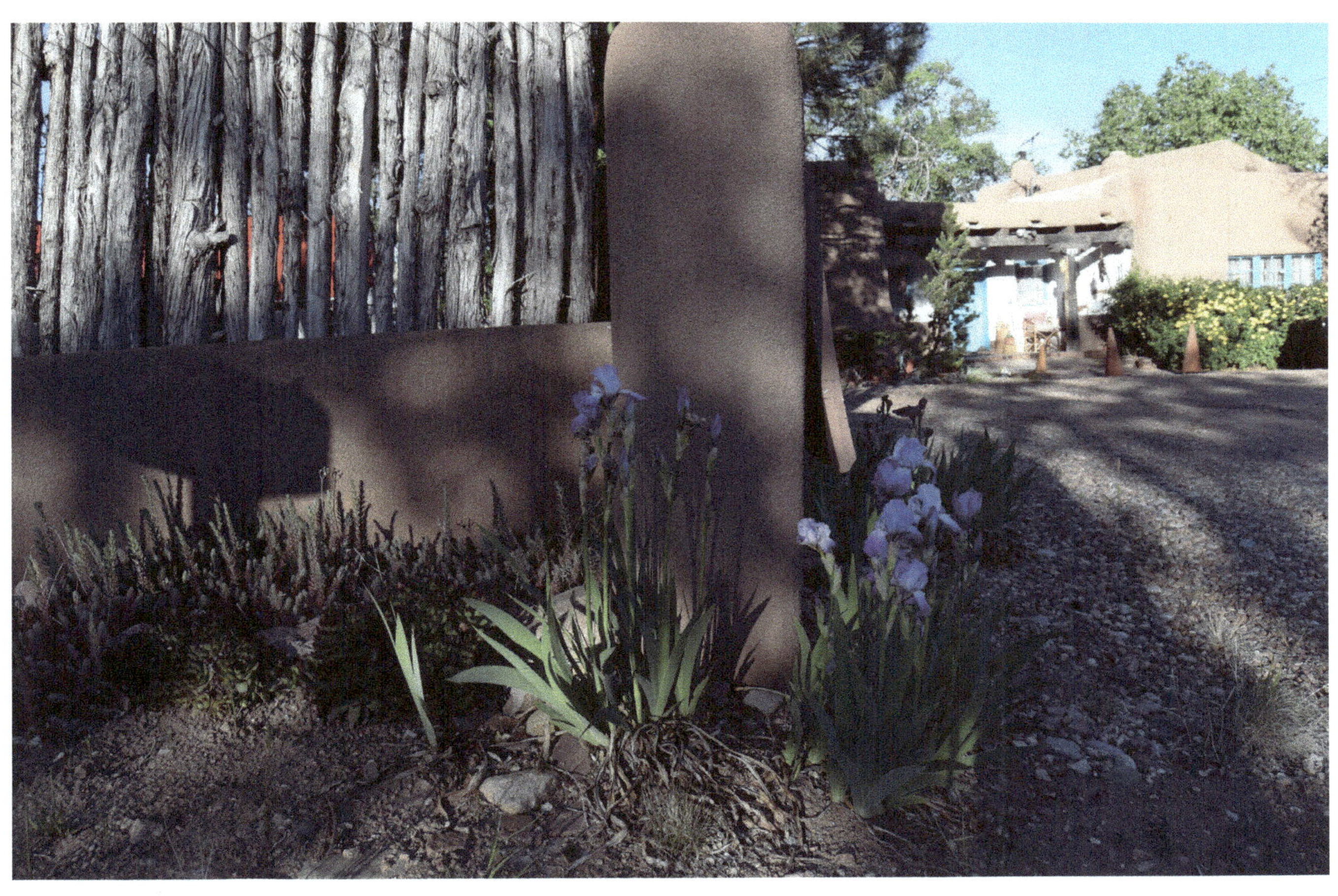

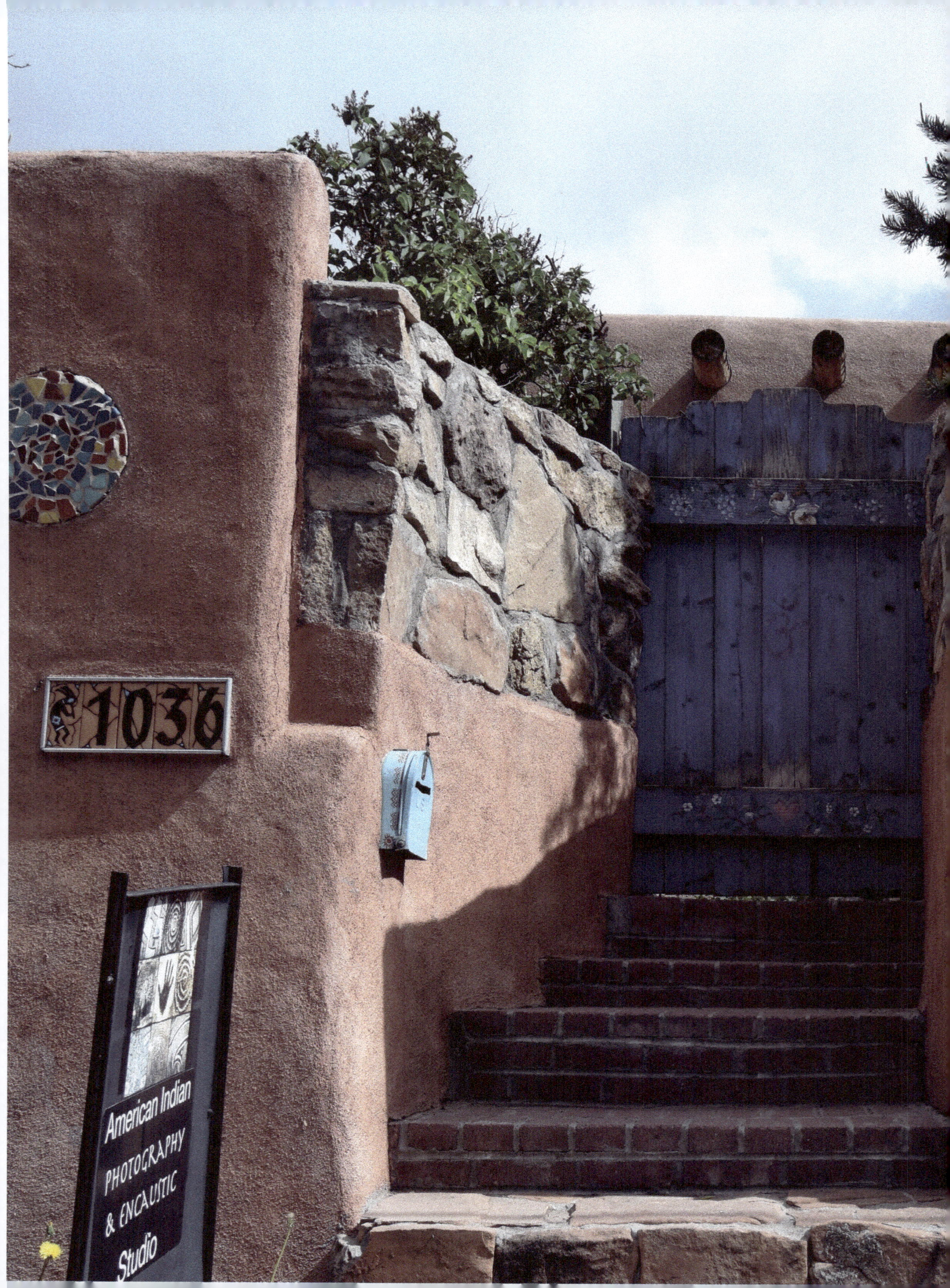

1036
American Indian
PHOTOGRAPHY
& ENCAUSTIC
Studio

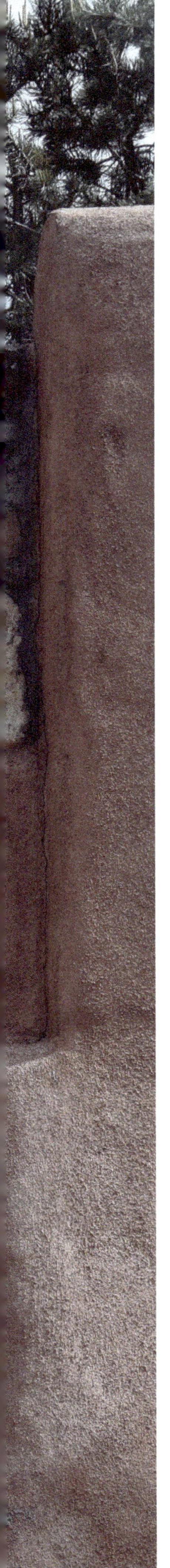
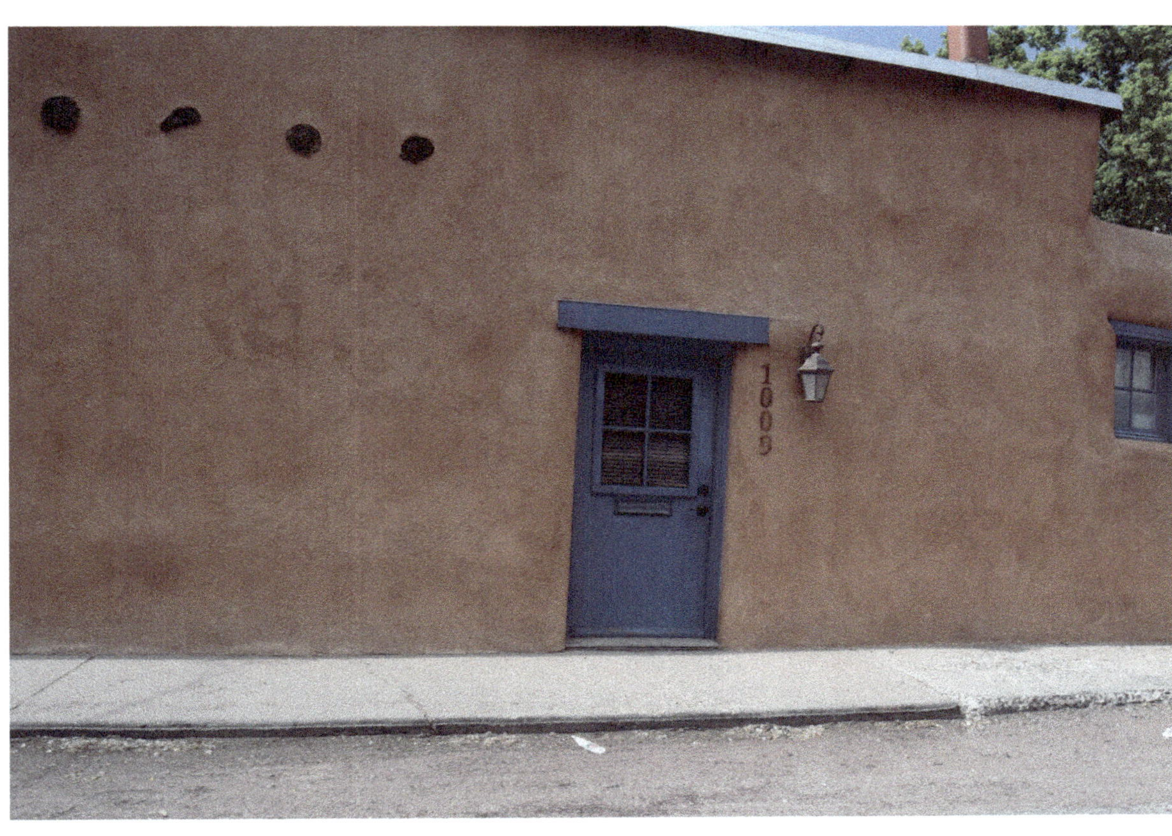

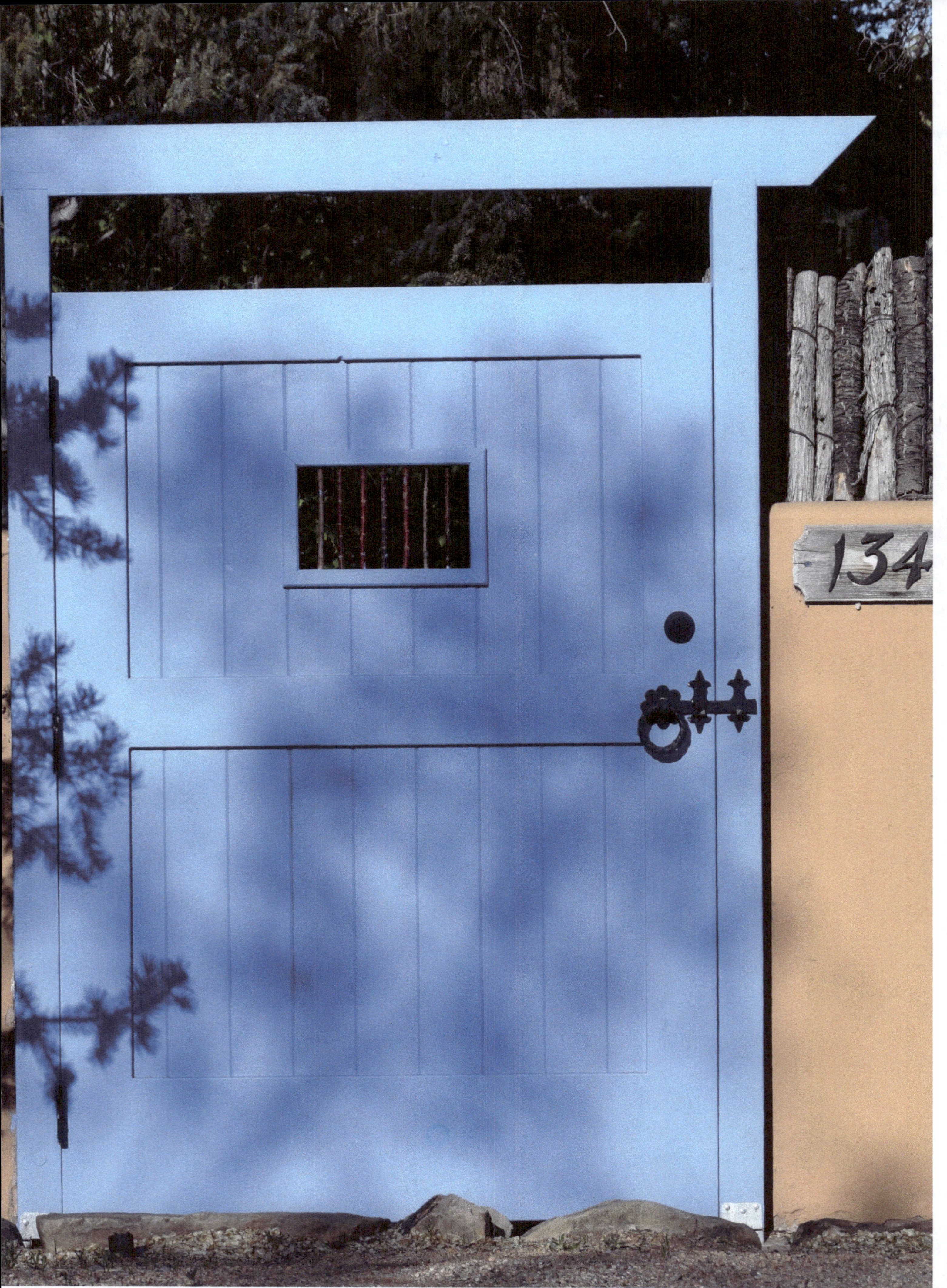
134

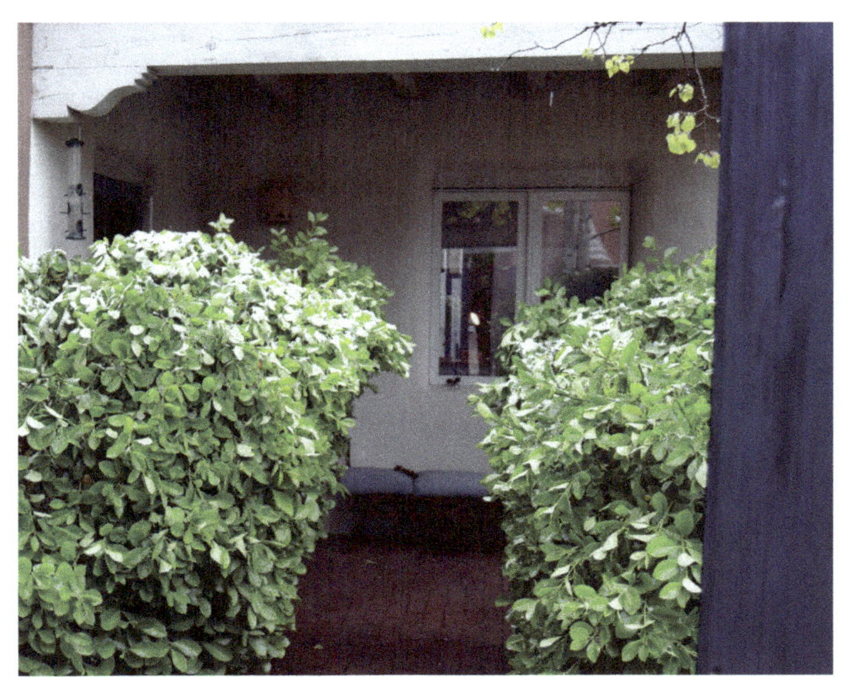
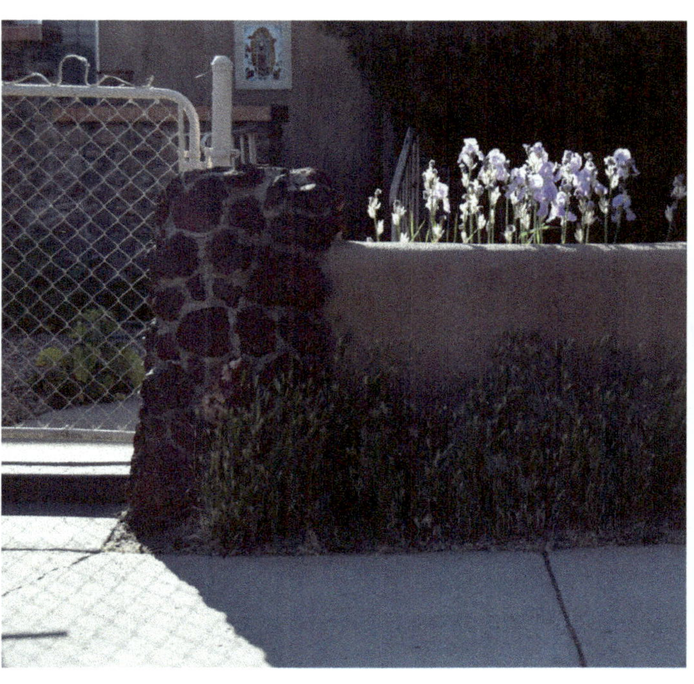

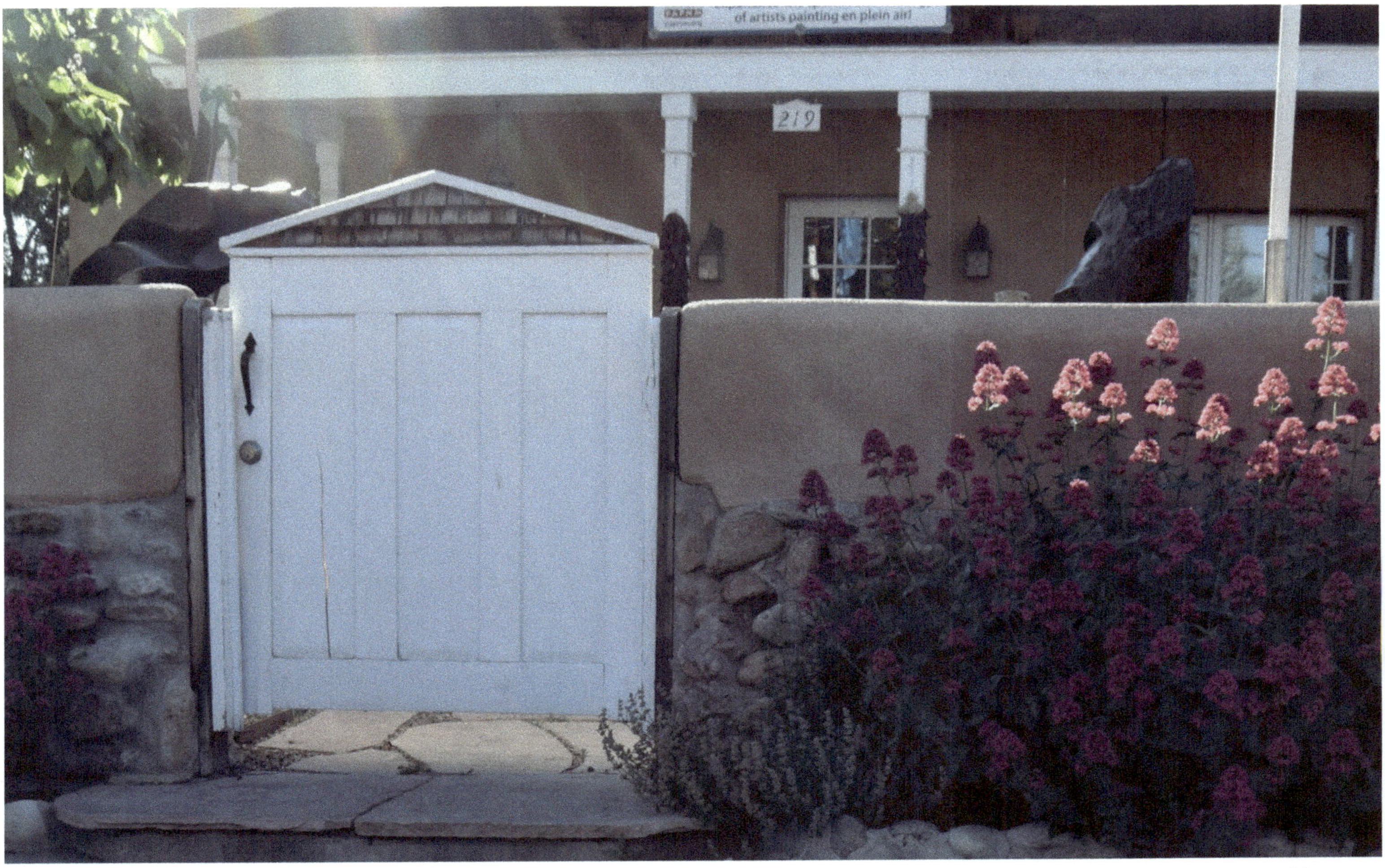

of artists painting en plein air
219

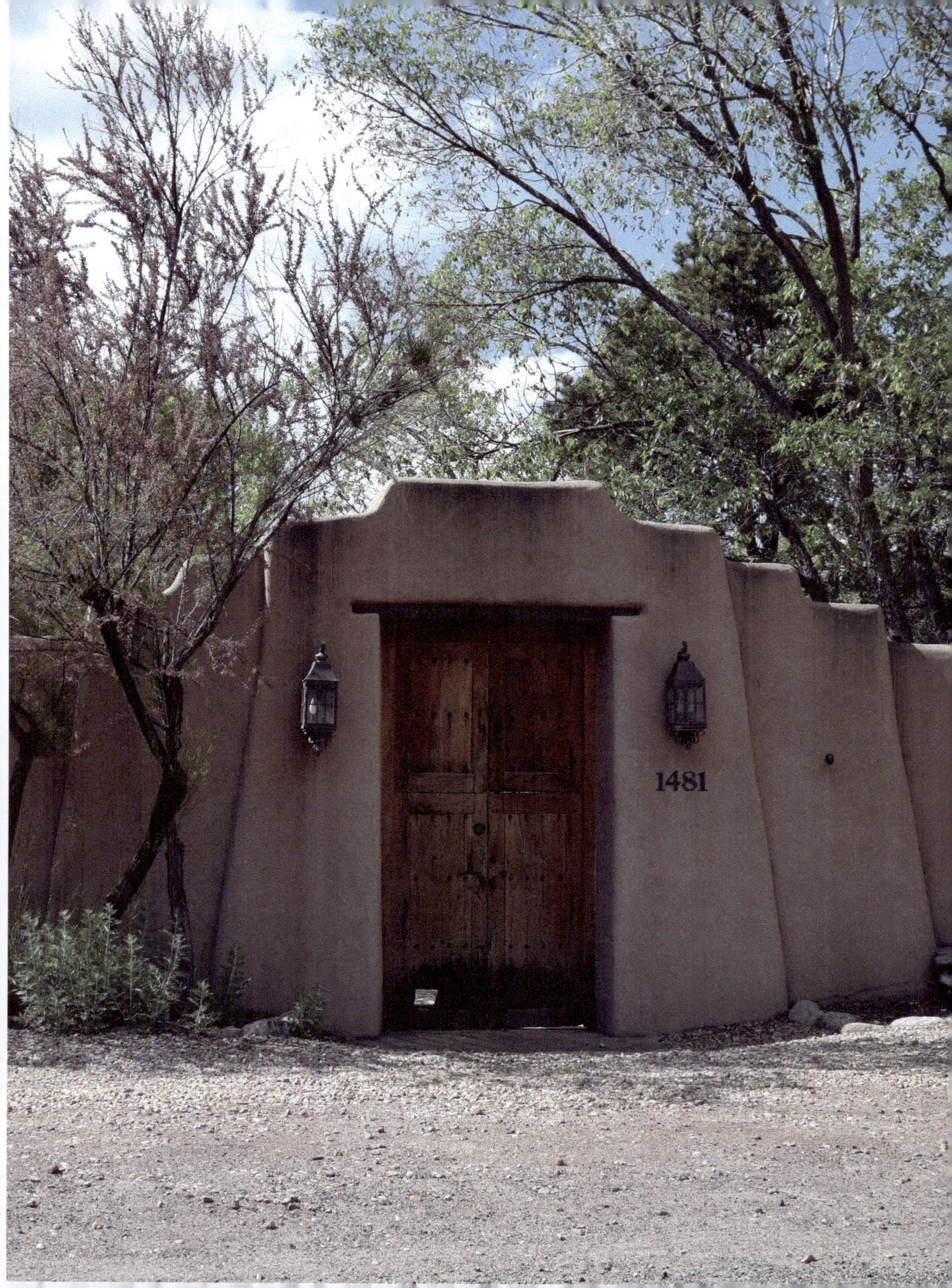
1481

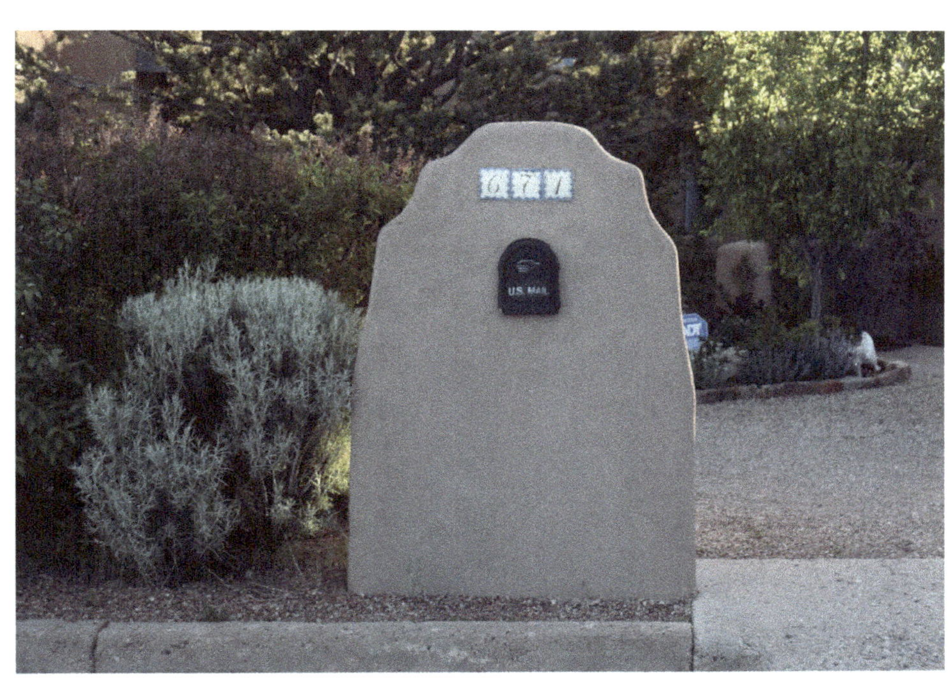
U.S. MAIL

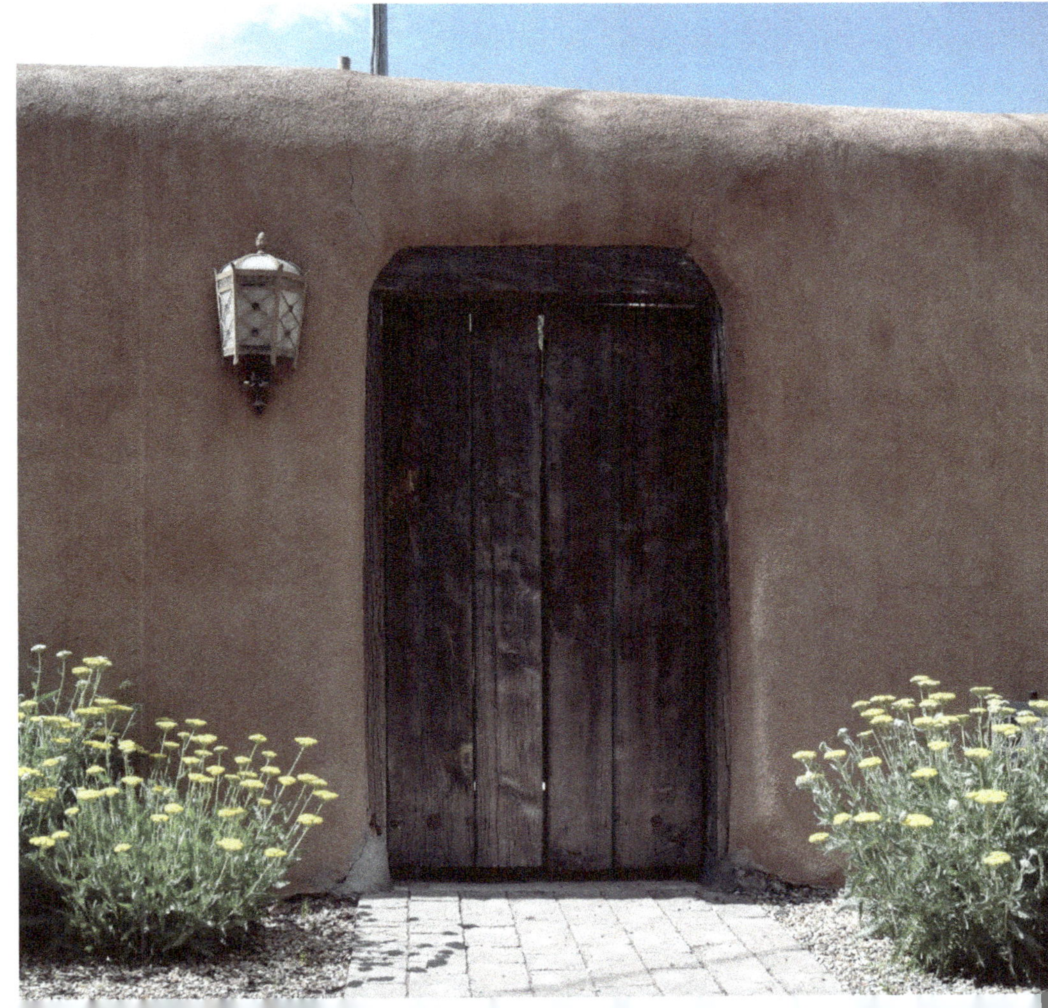

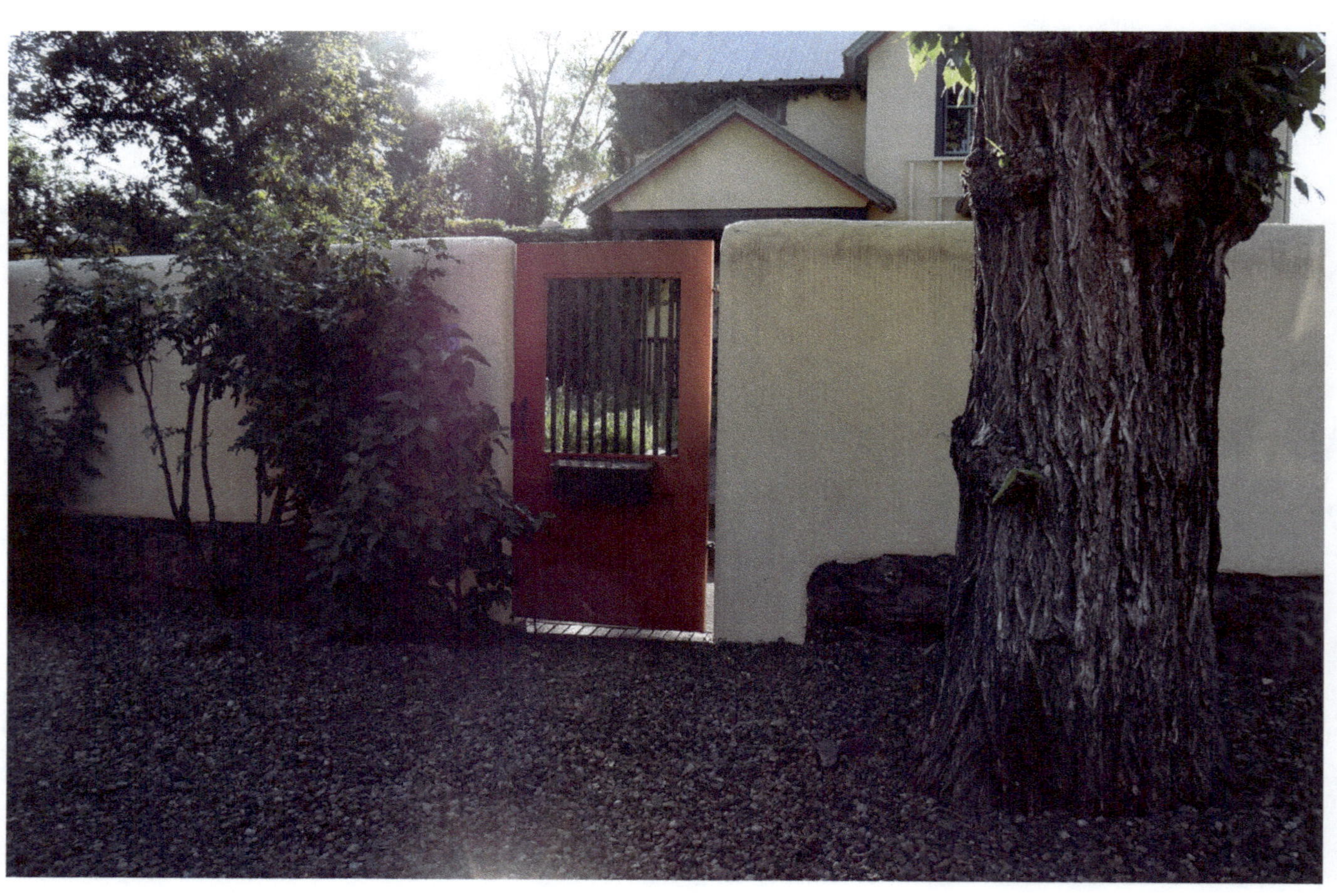

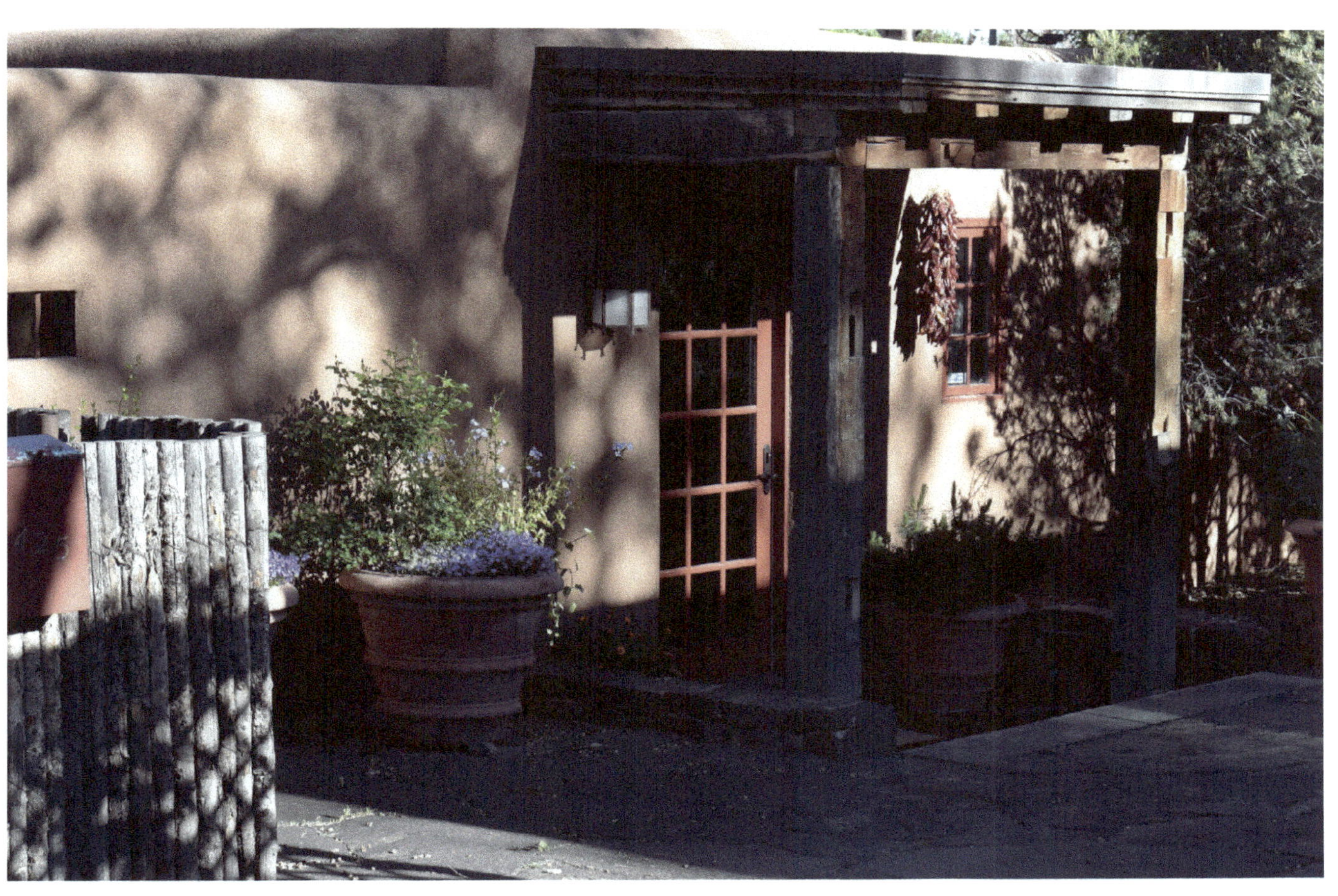

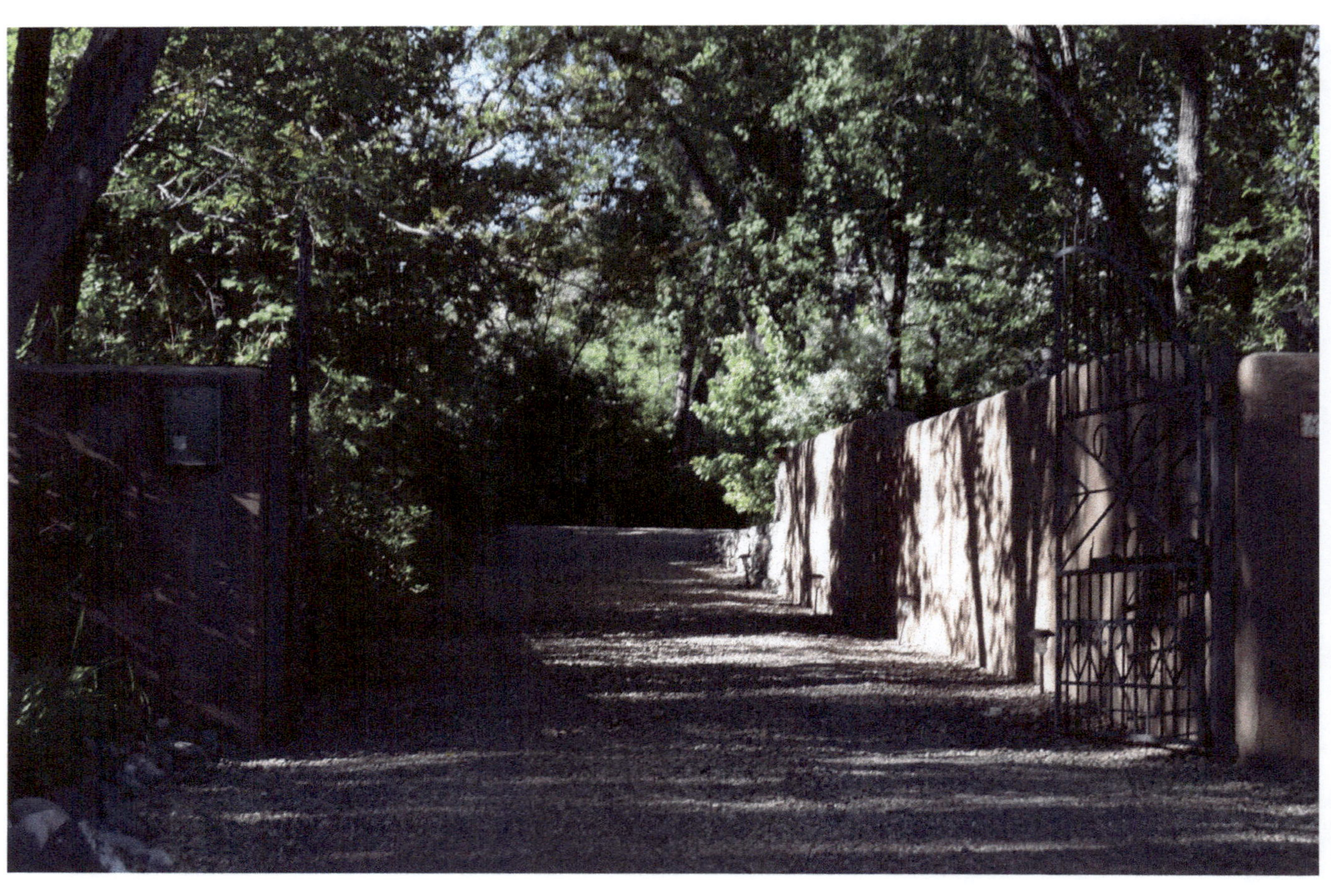

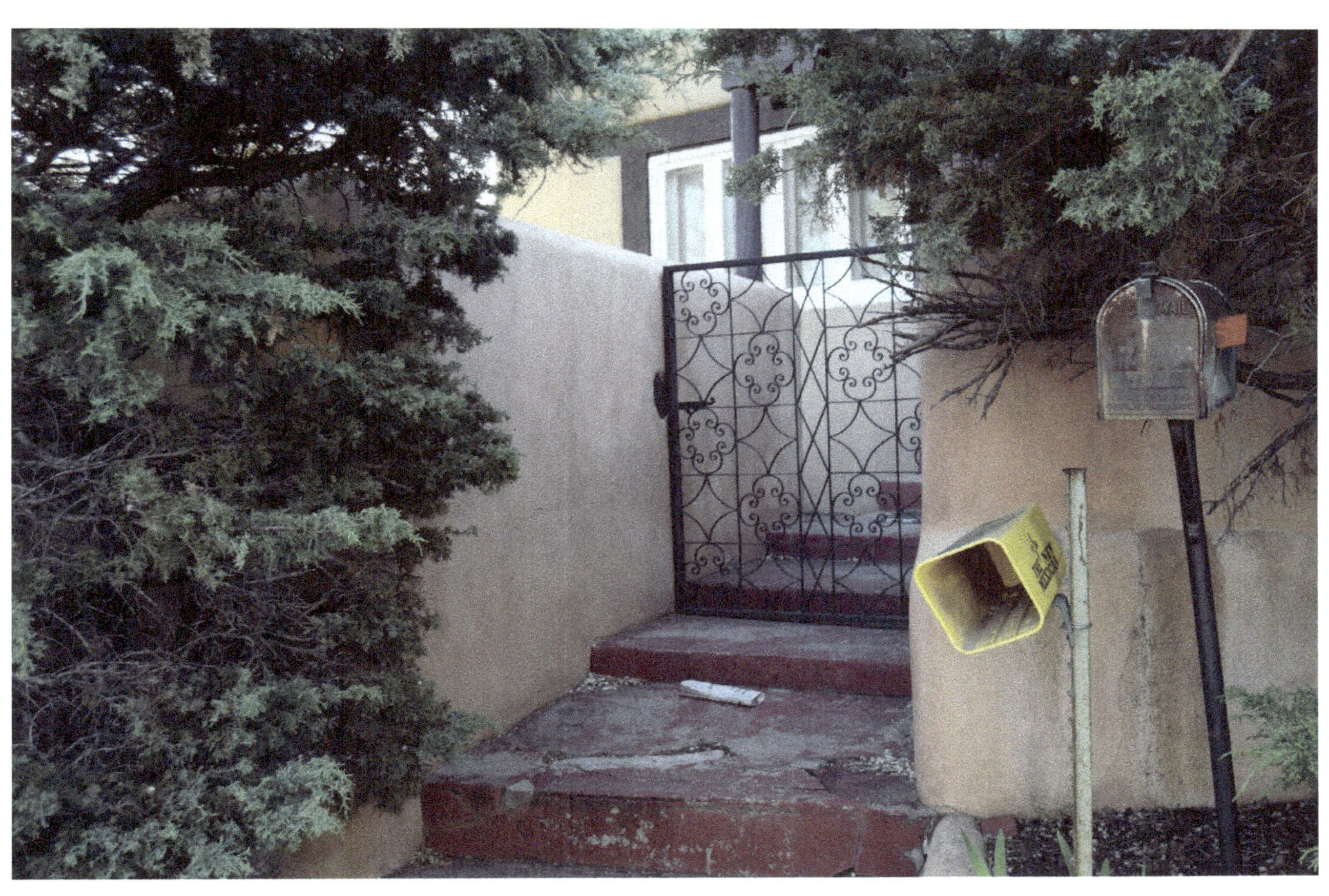

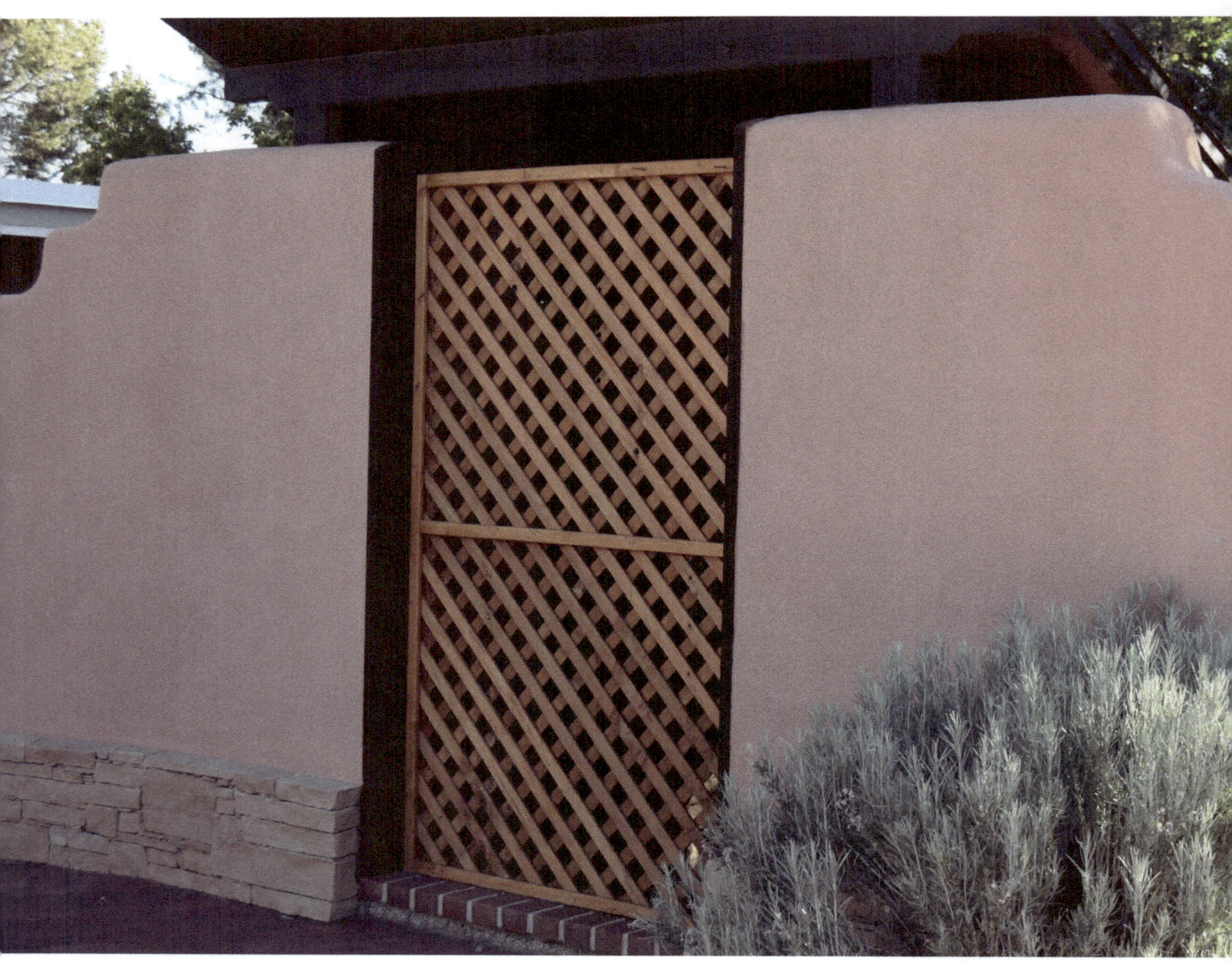

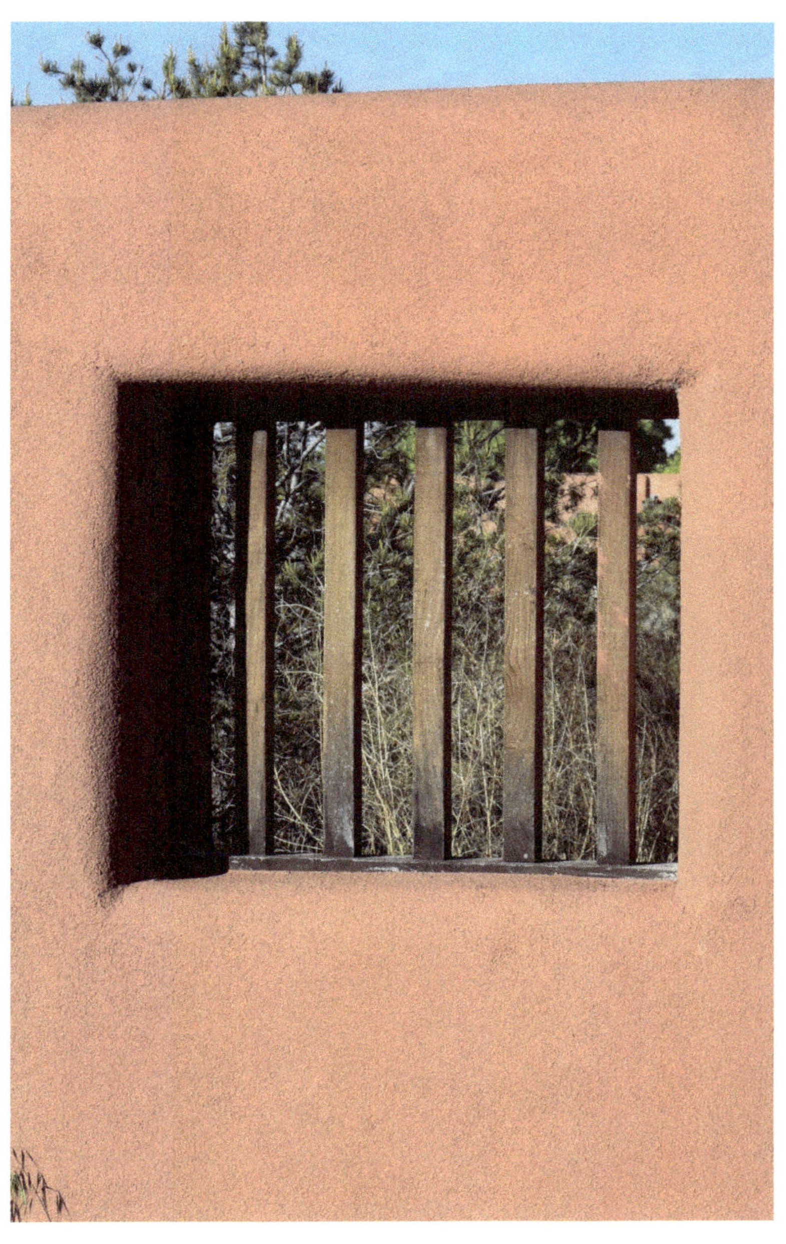
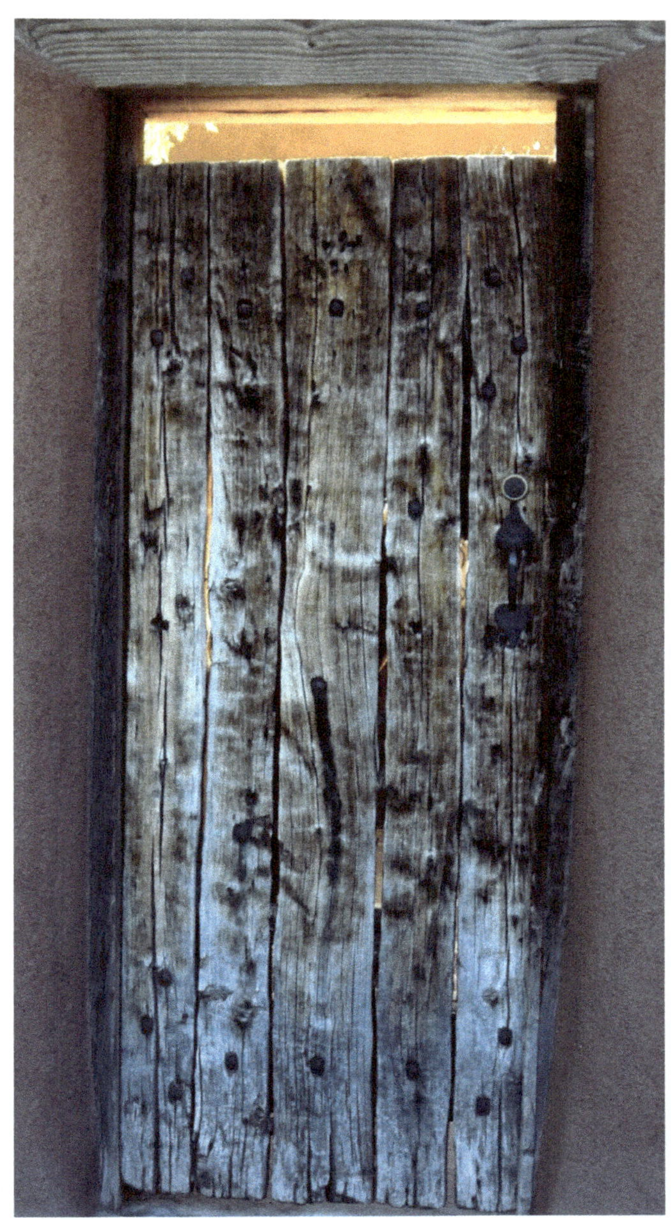

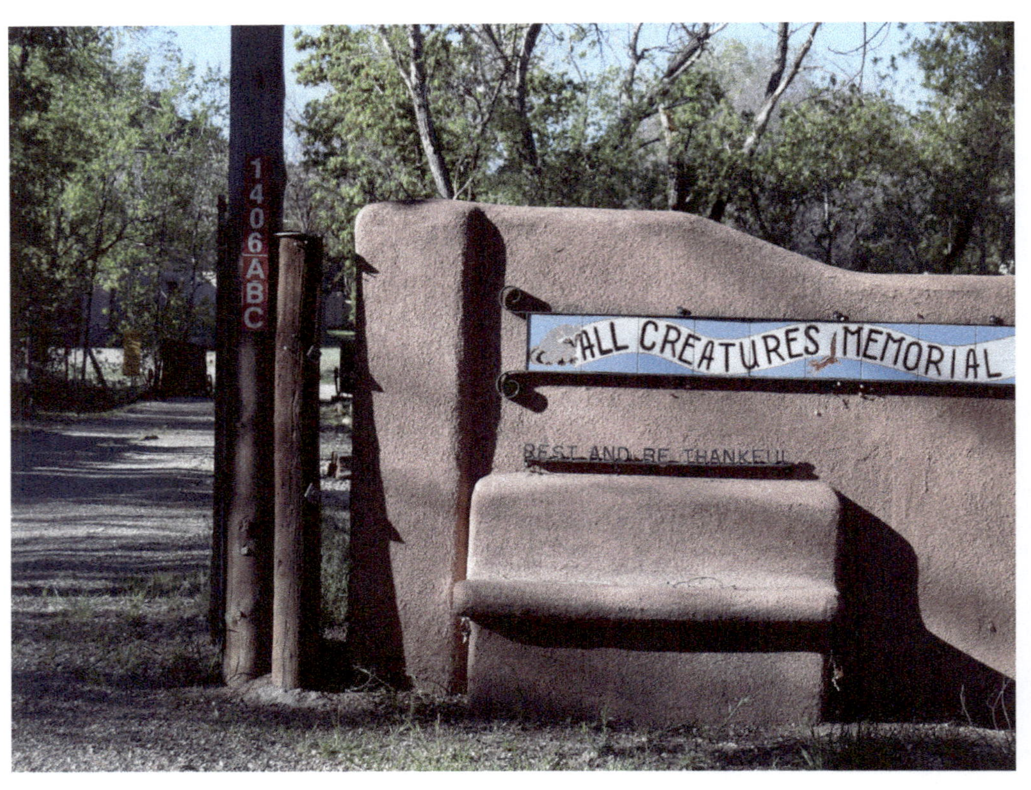
1406 ABC
ALL CREATURES MEMORIAL
REST AND BE THANKFUL

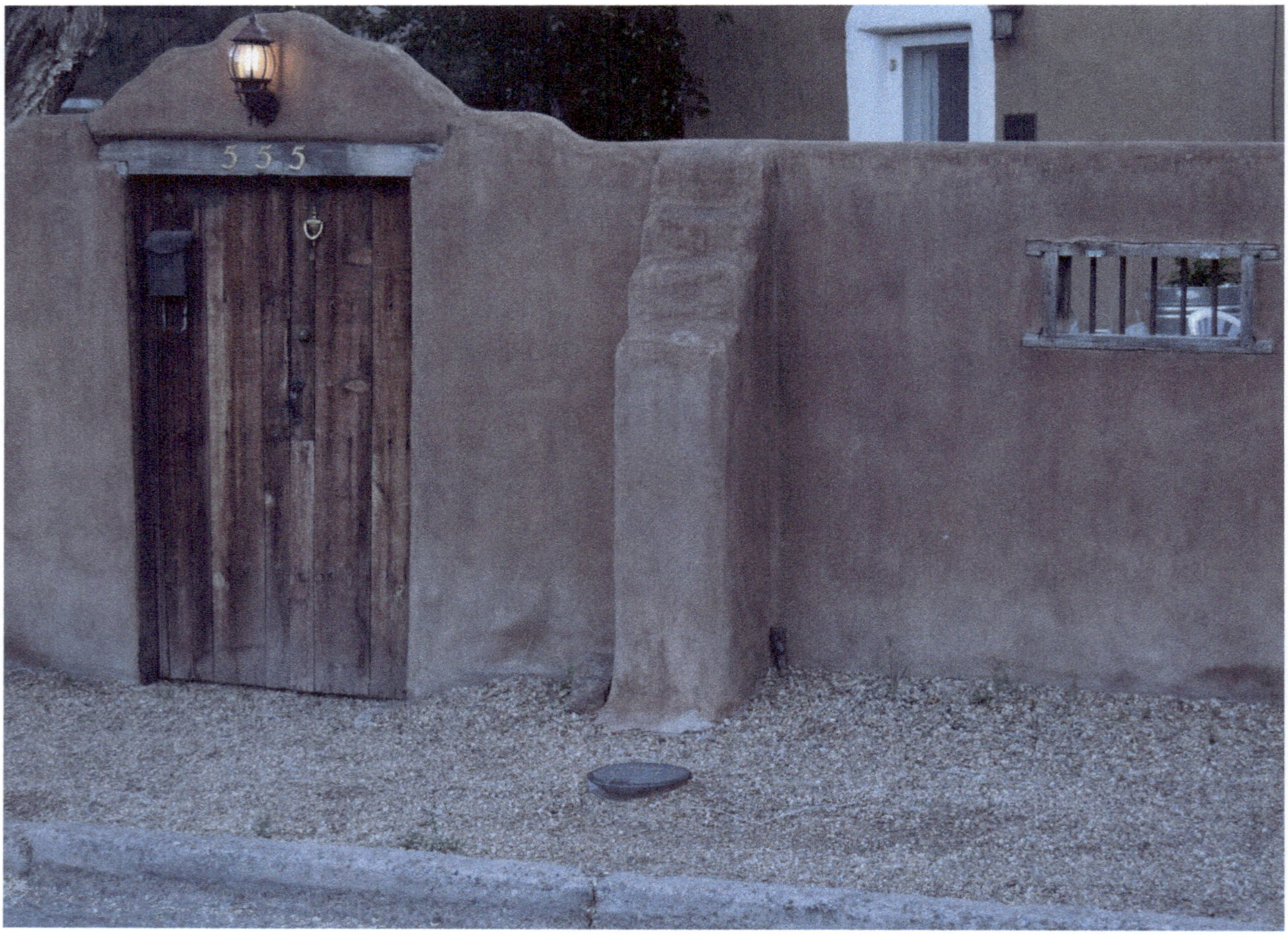

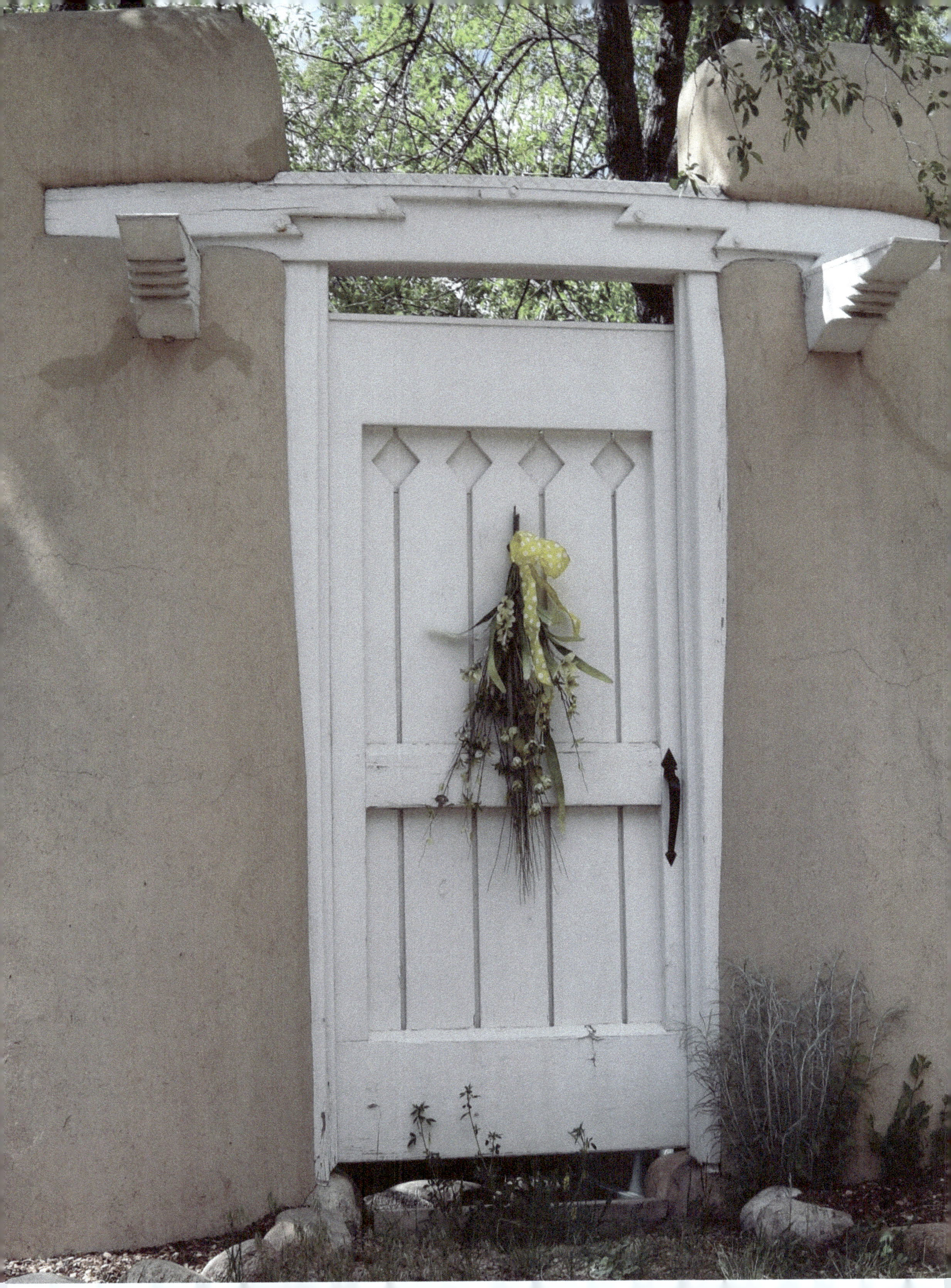

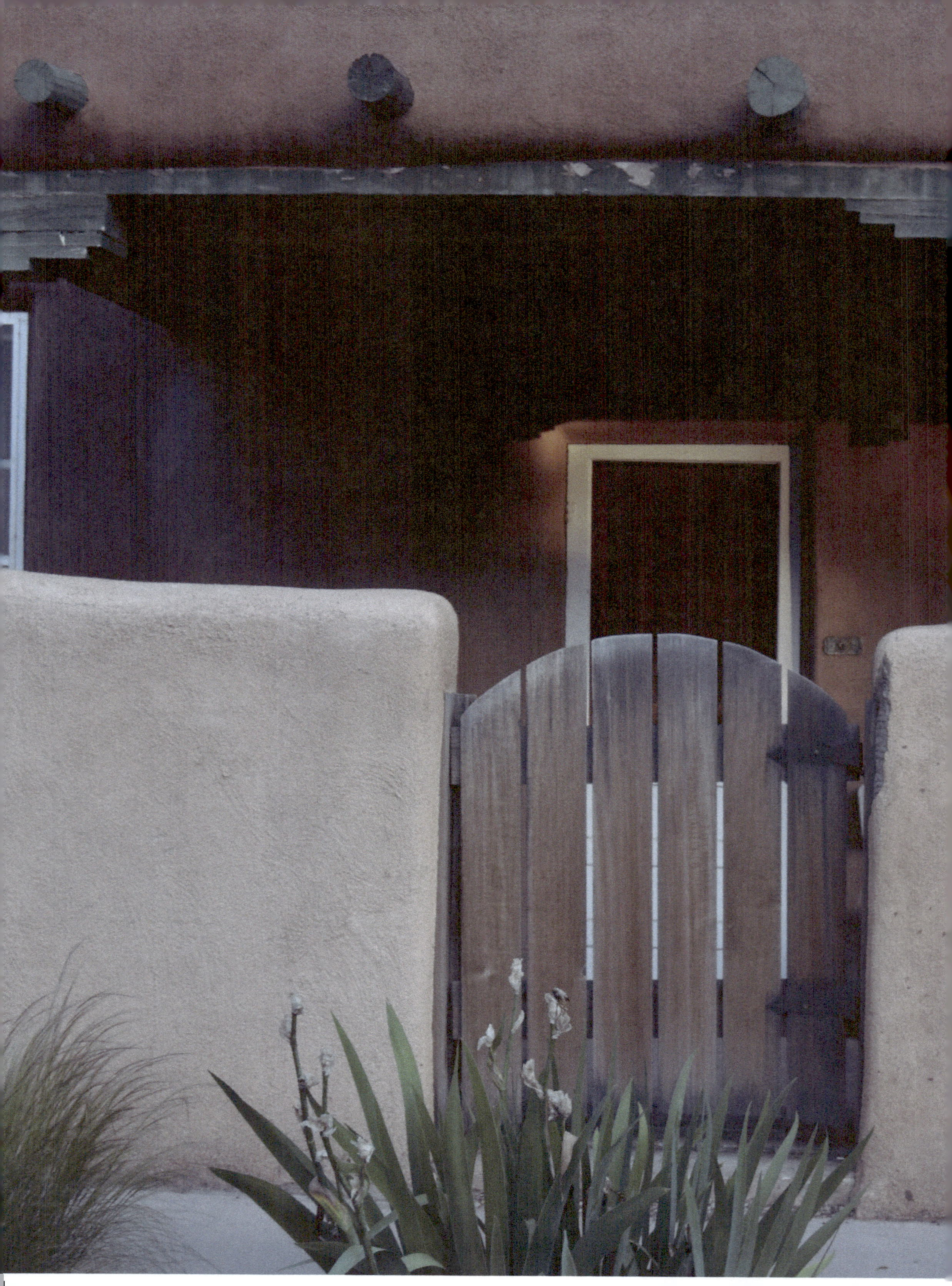

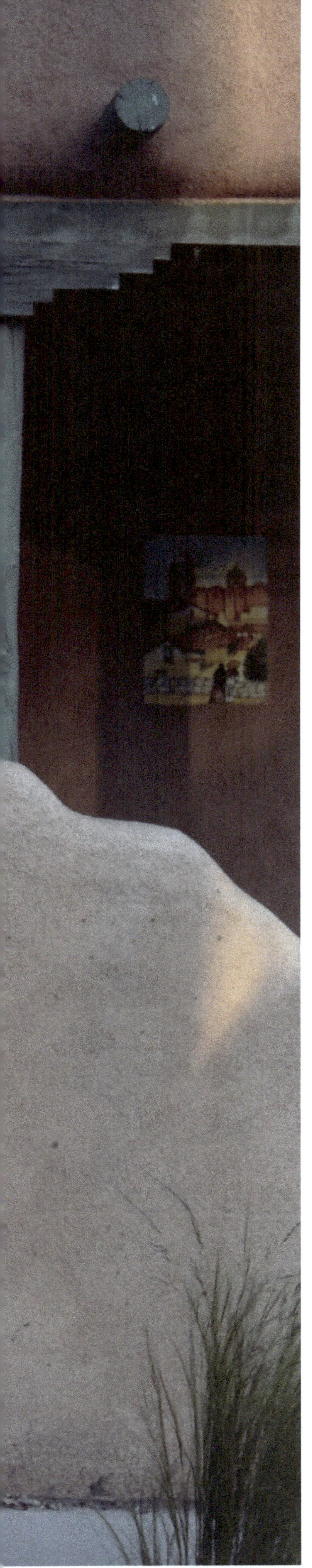

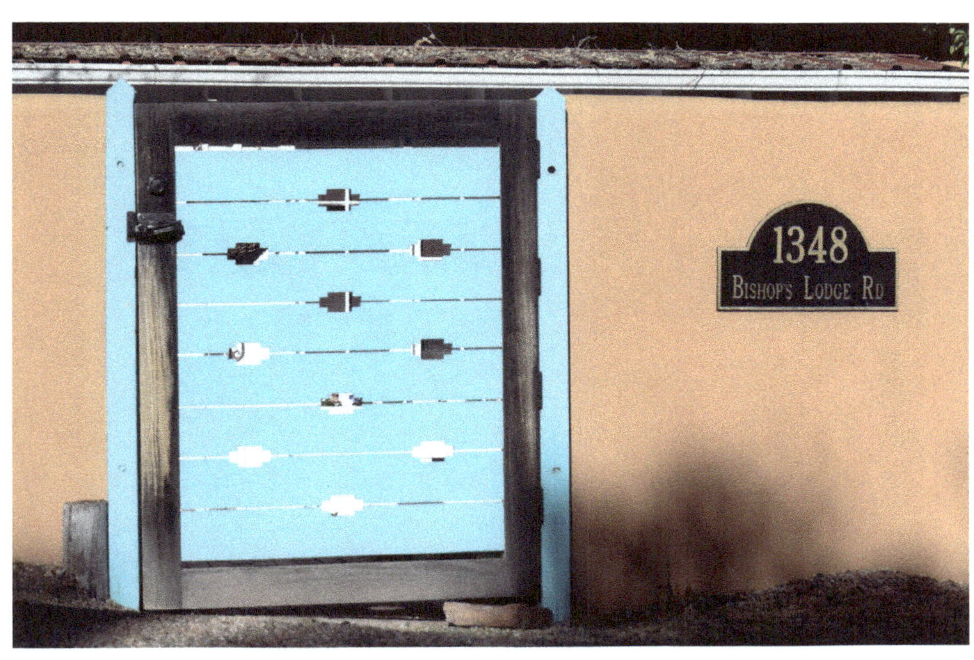
1348
BISHOP'S LODGE RD

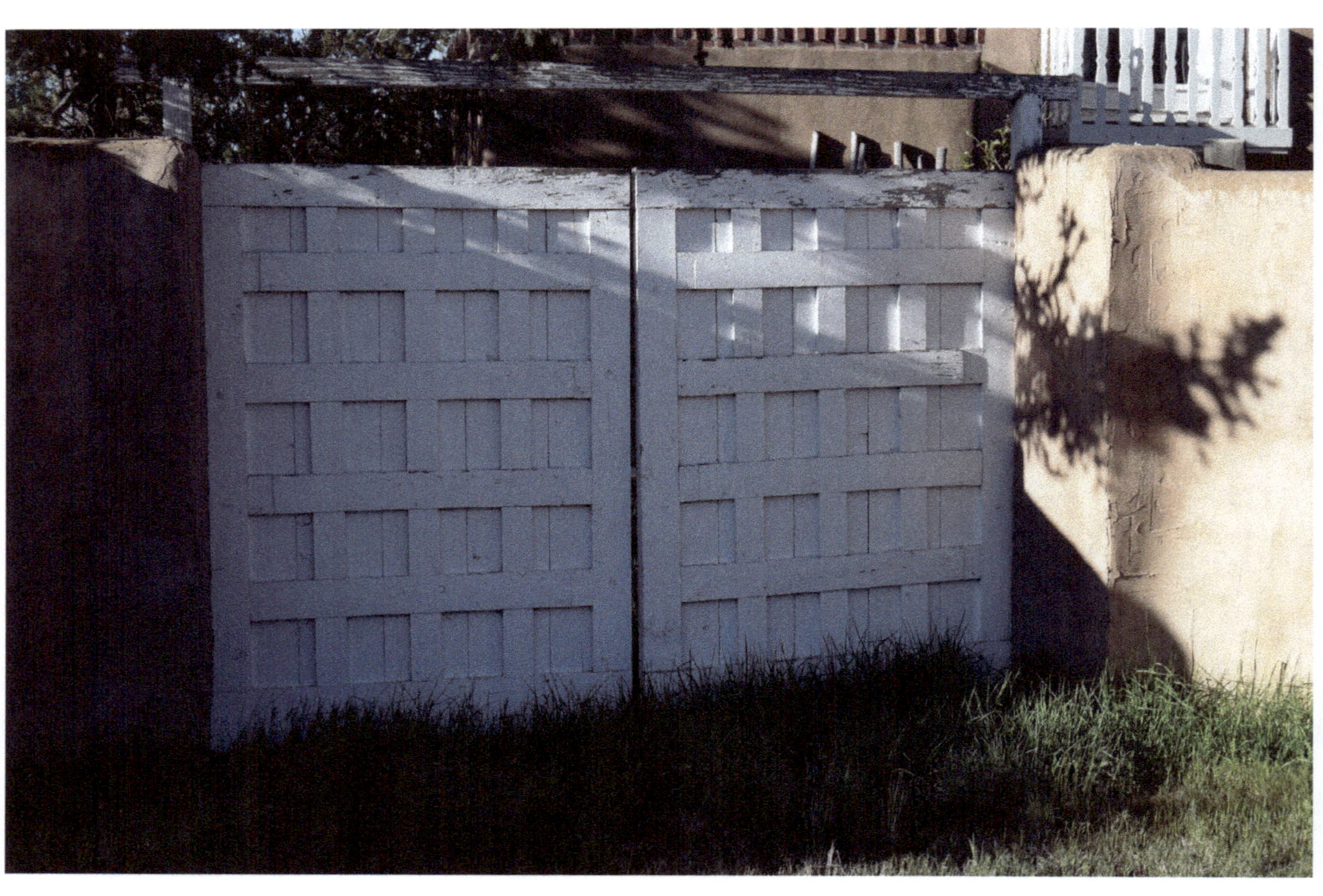

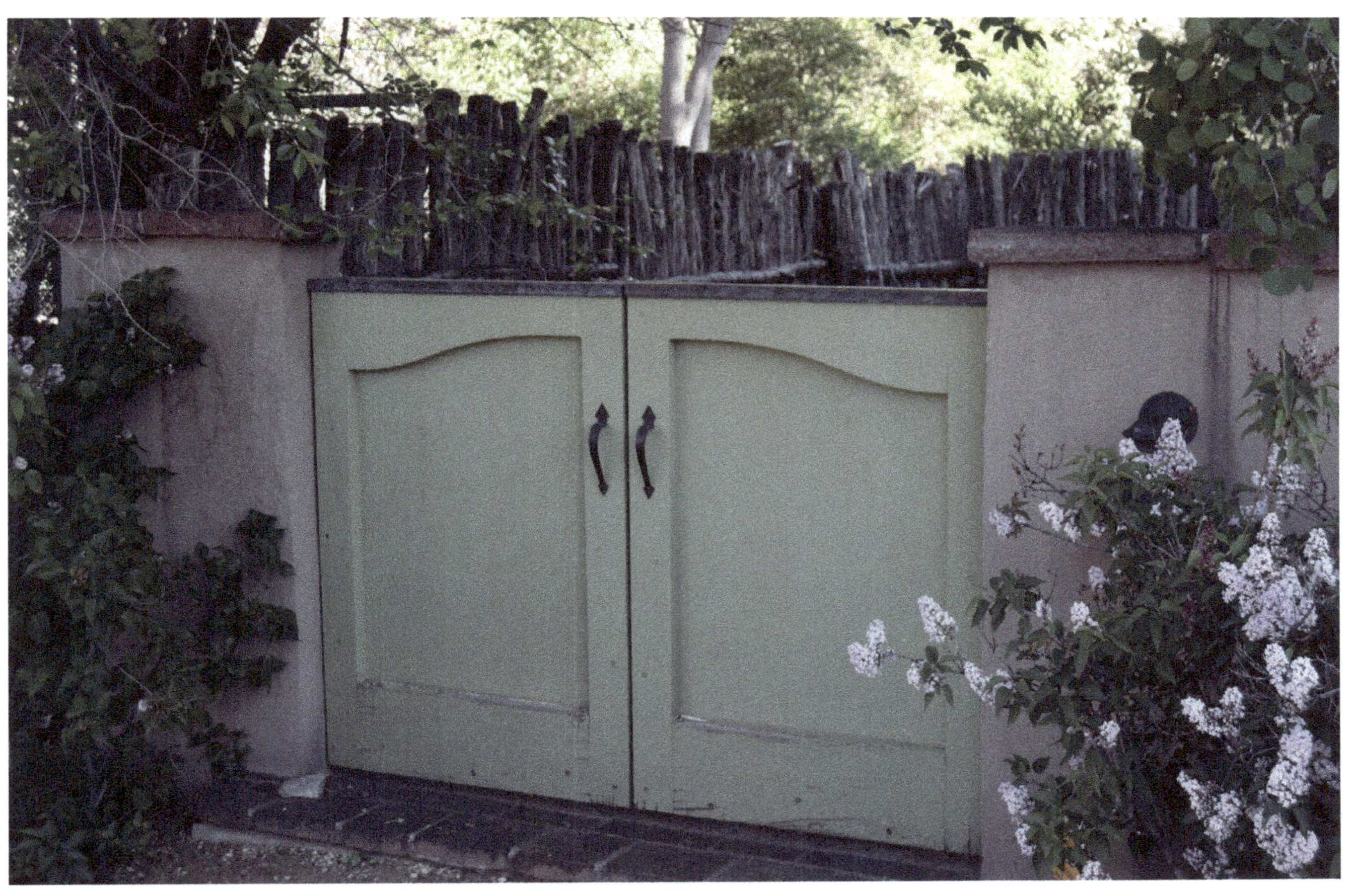

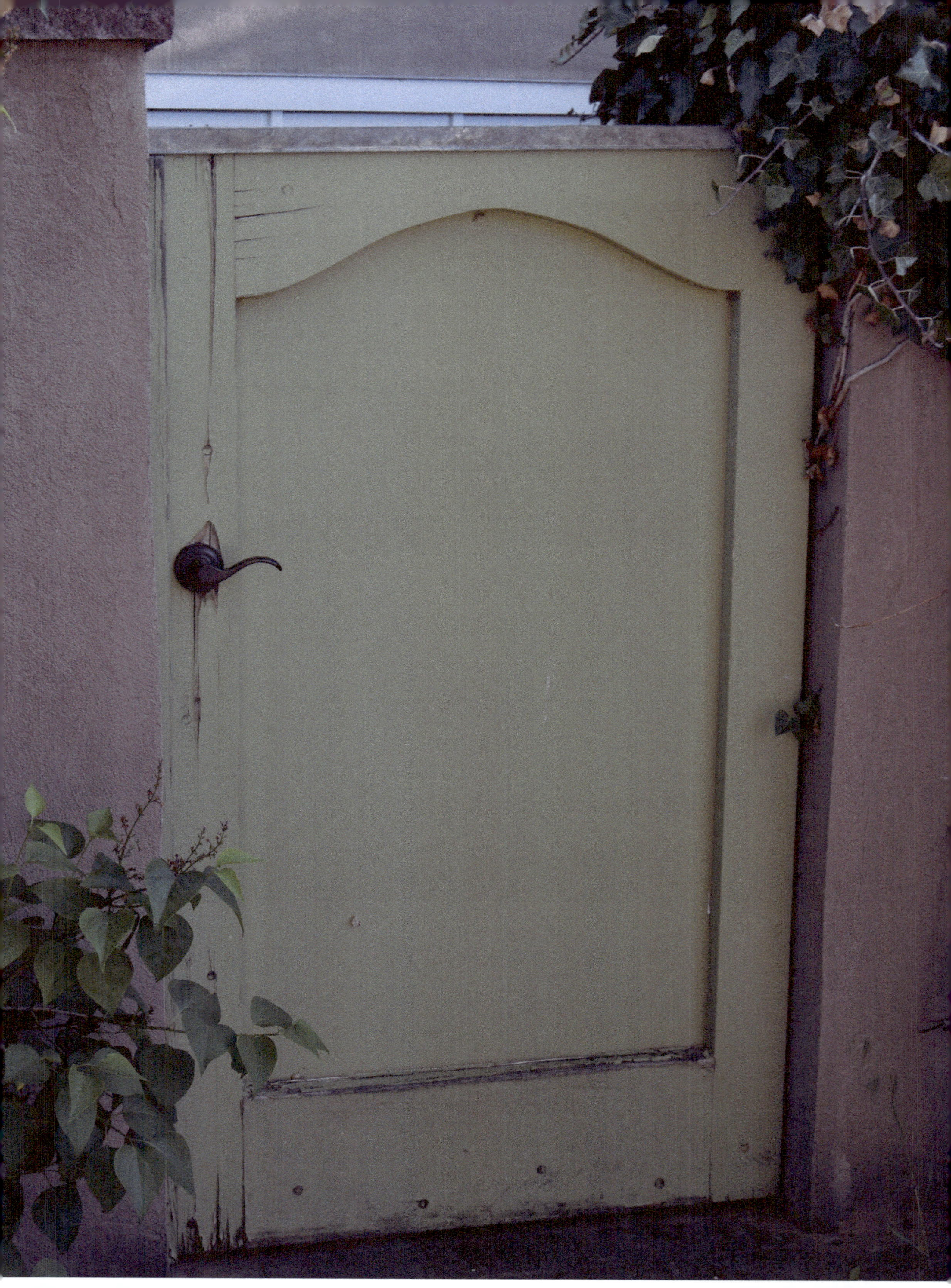

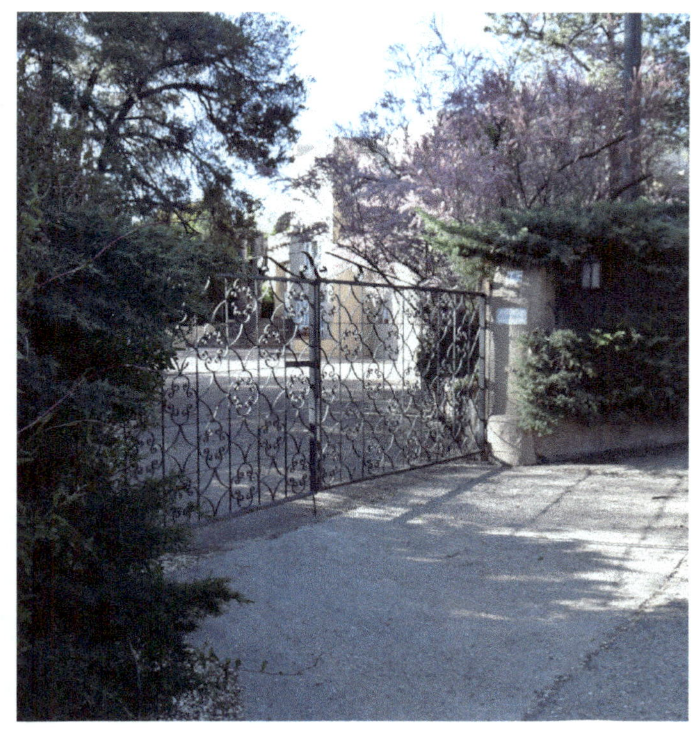

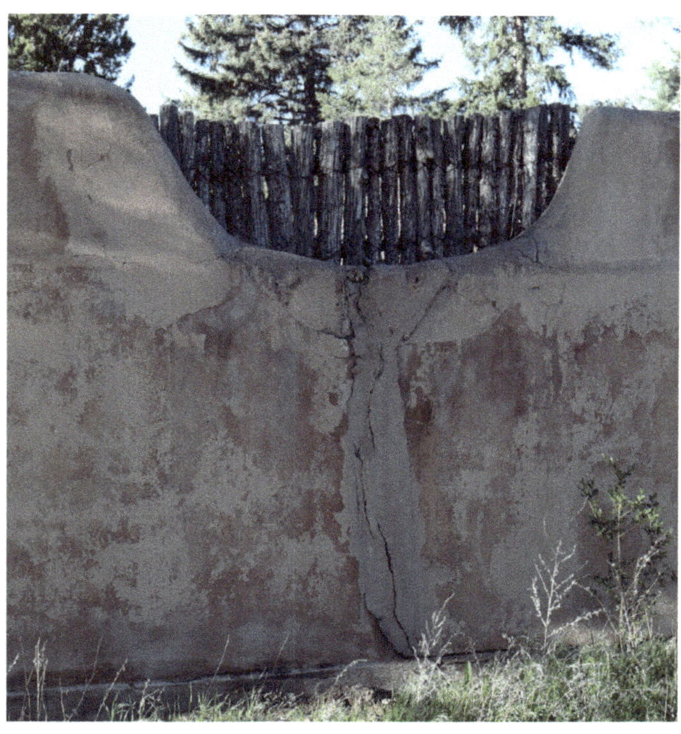

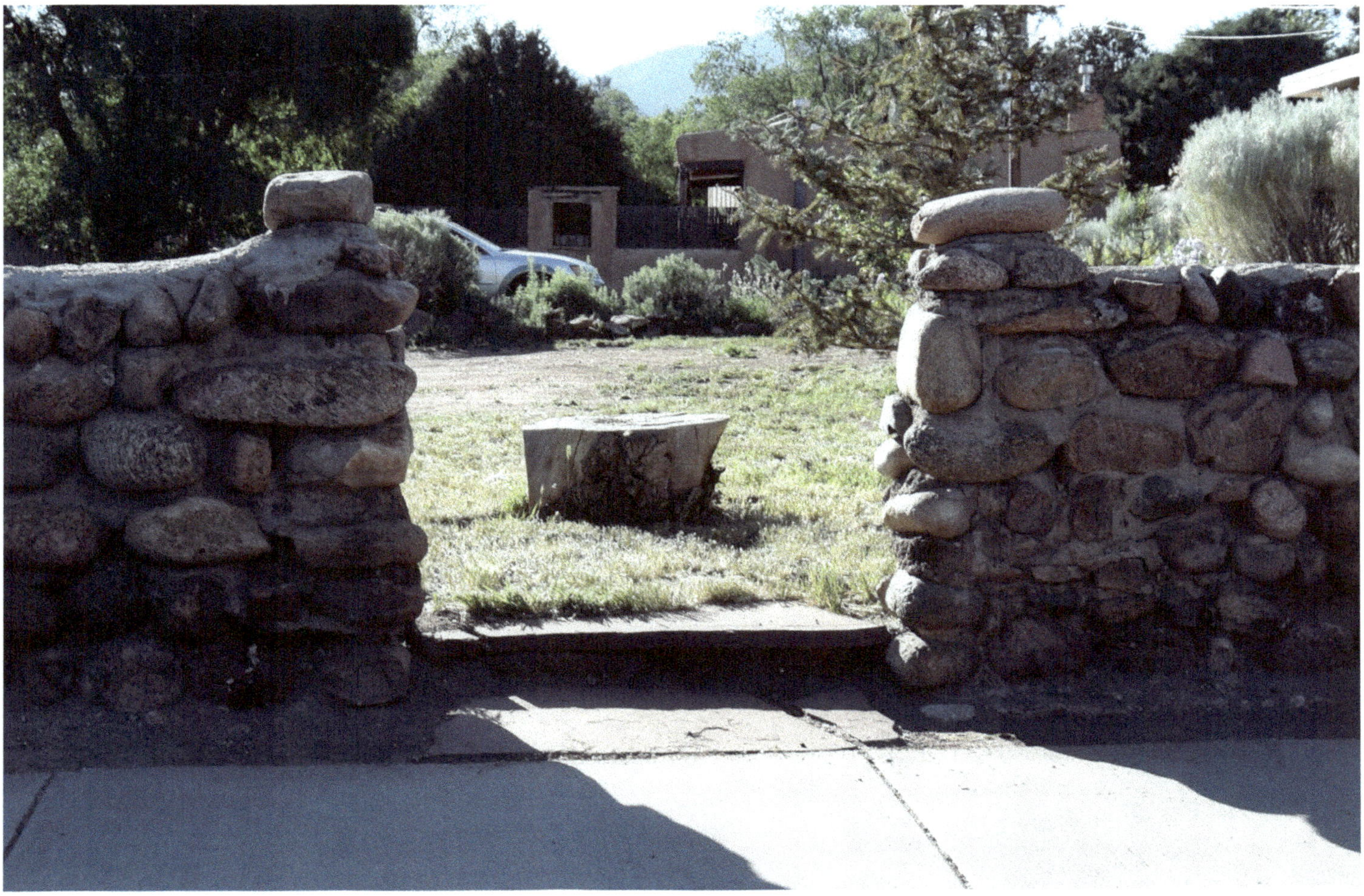

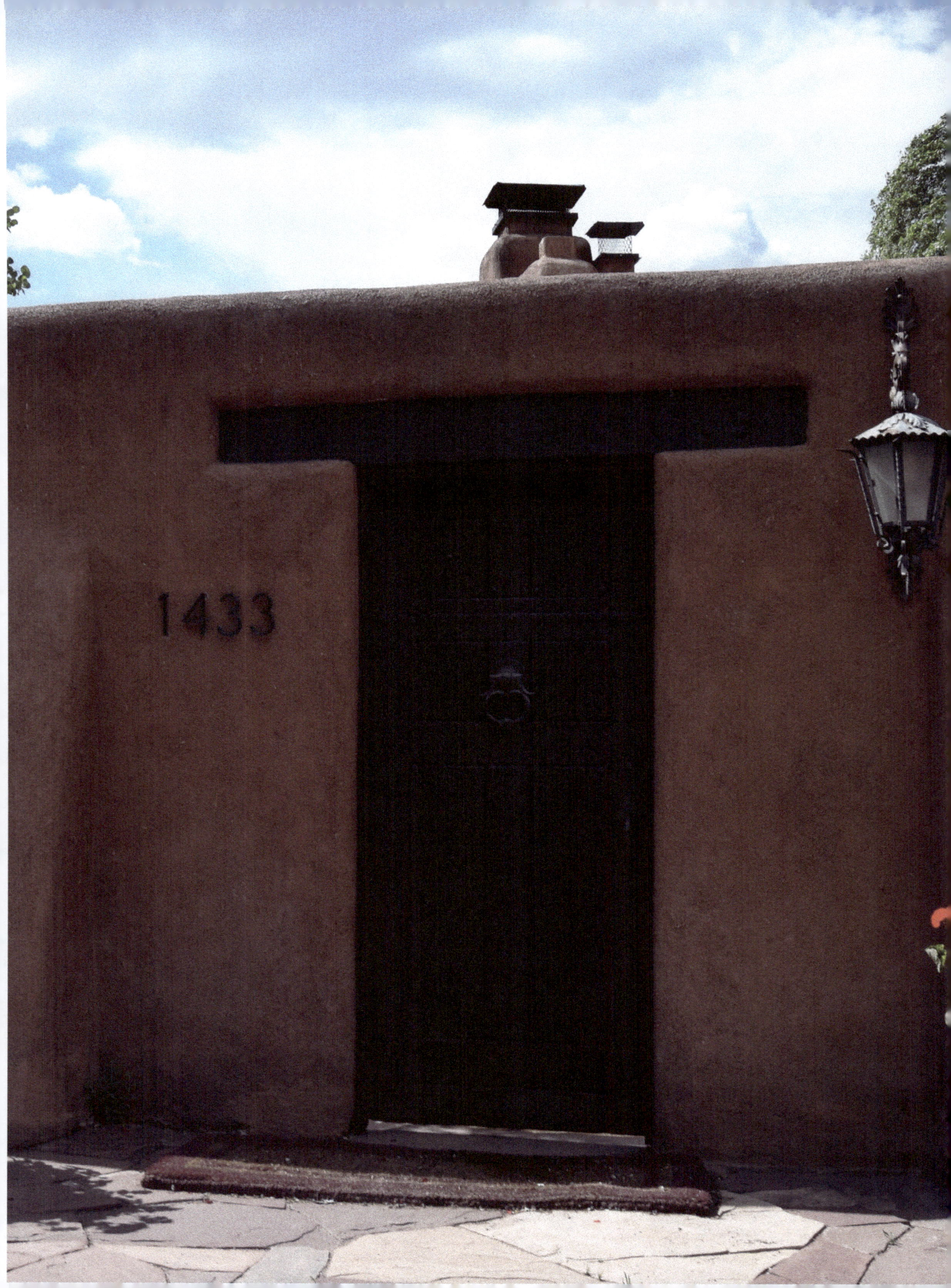

1433

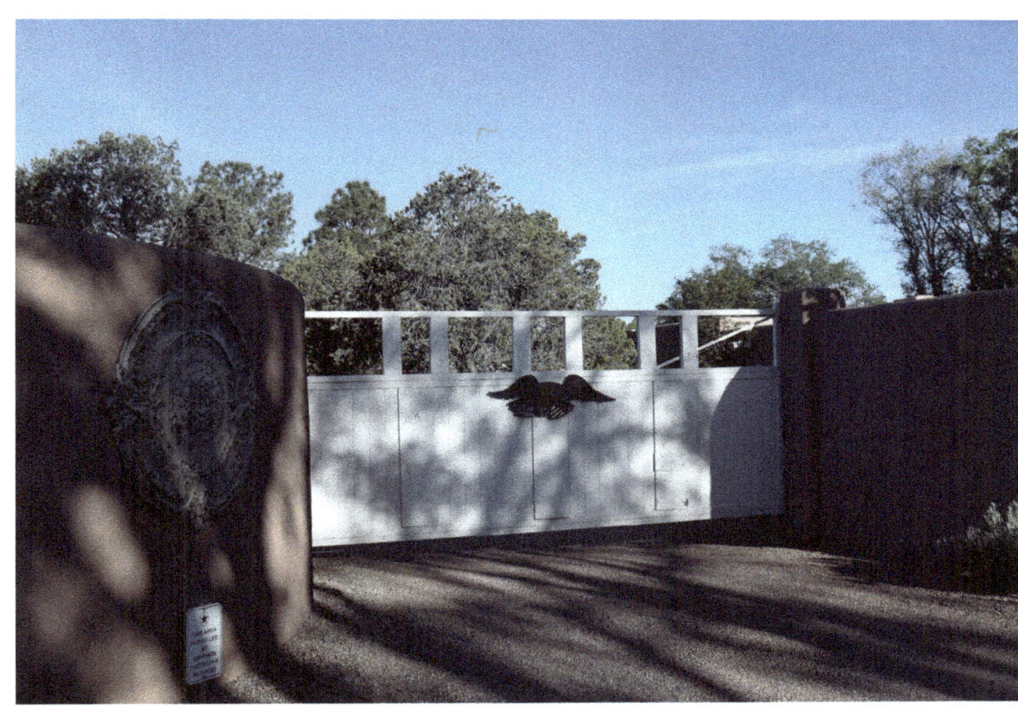

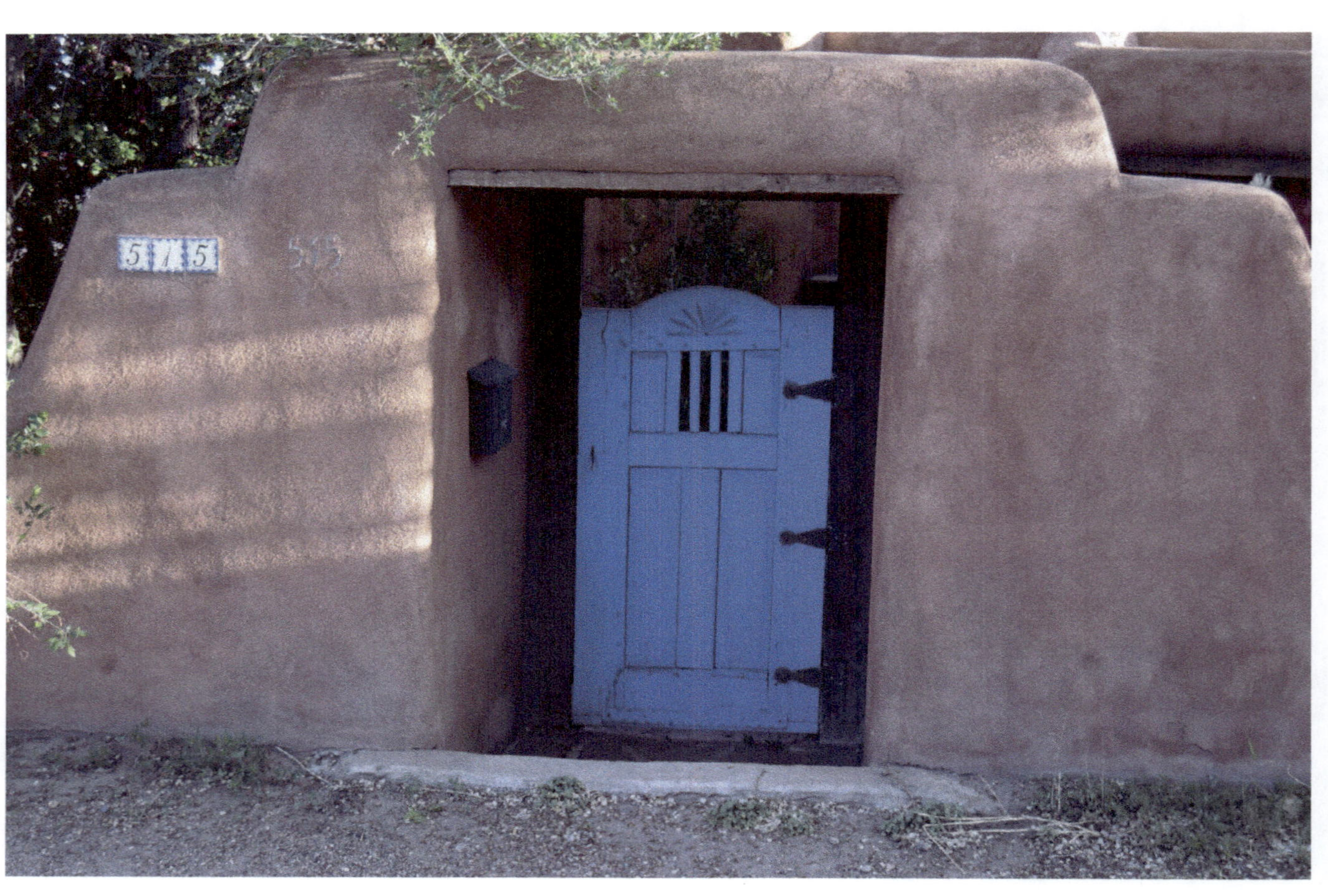

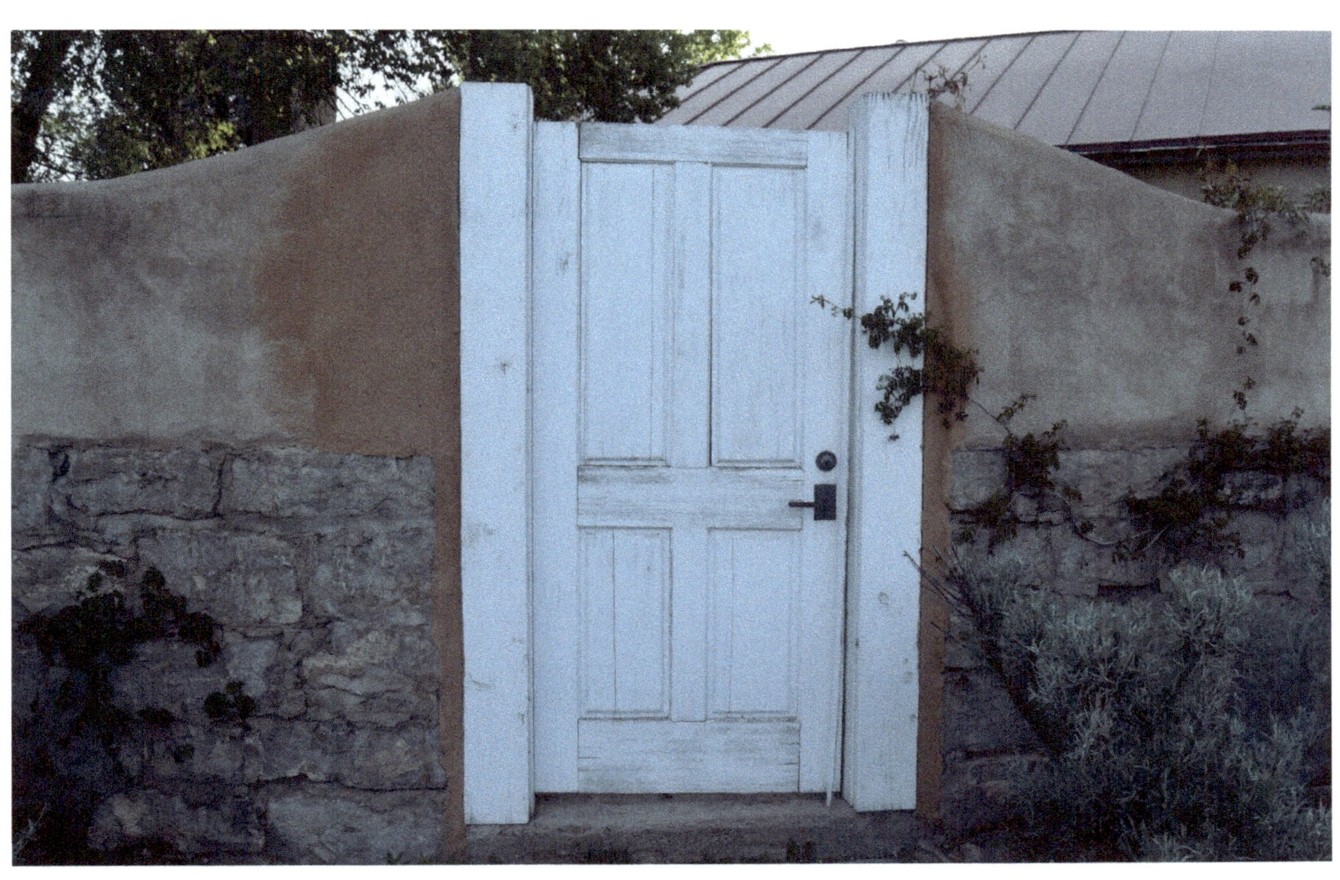

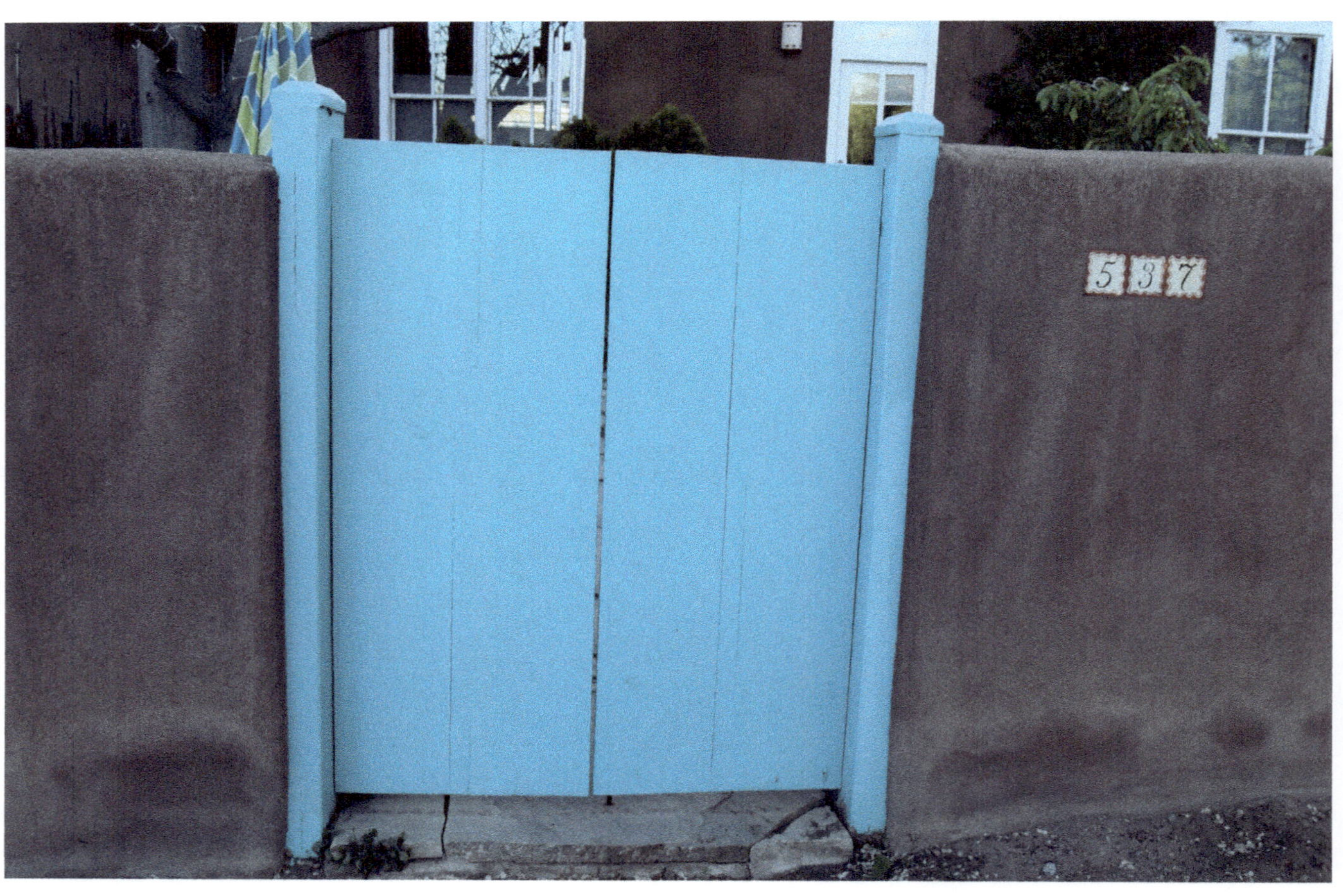

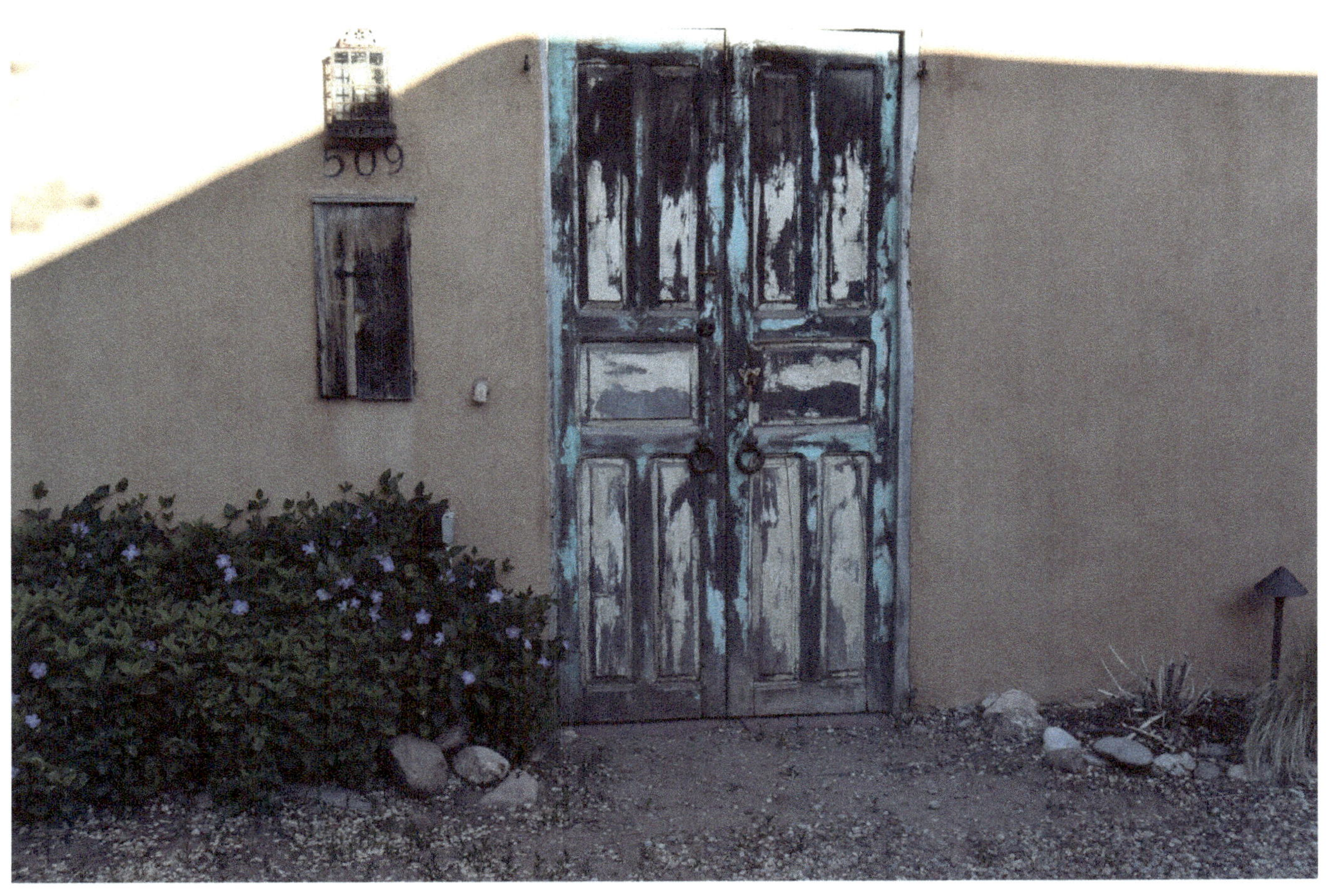

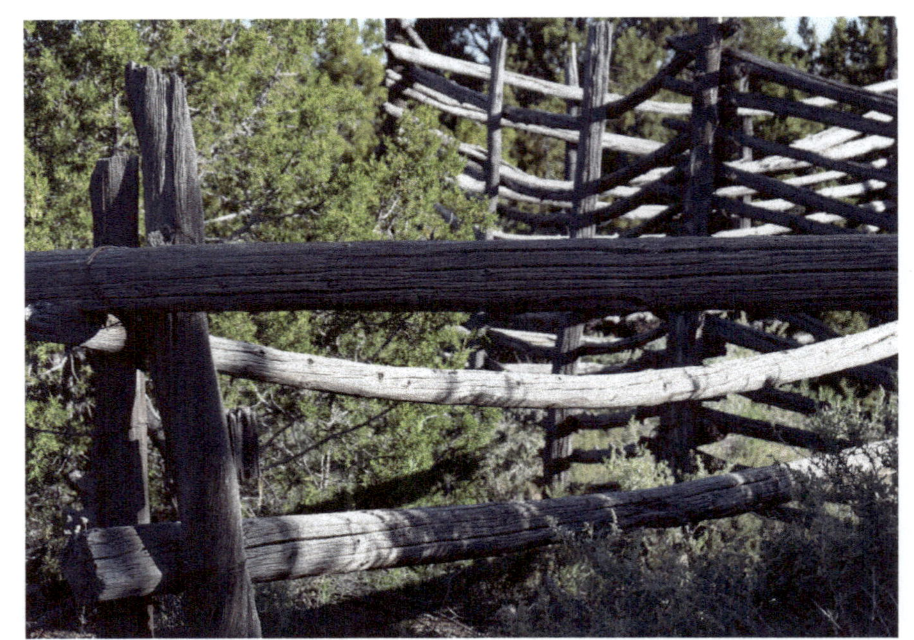

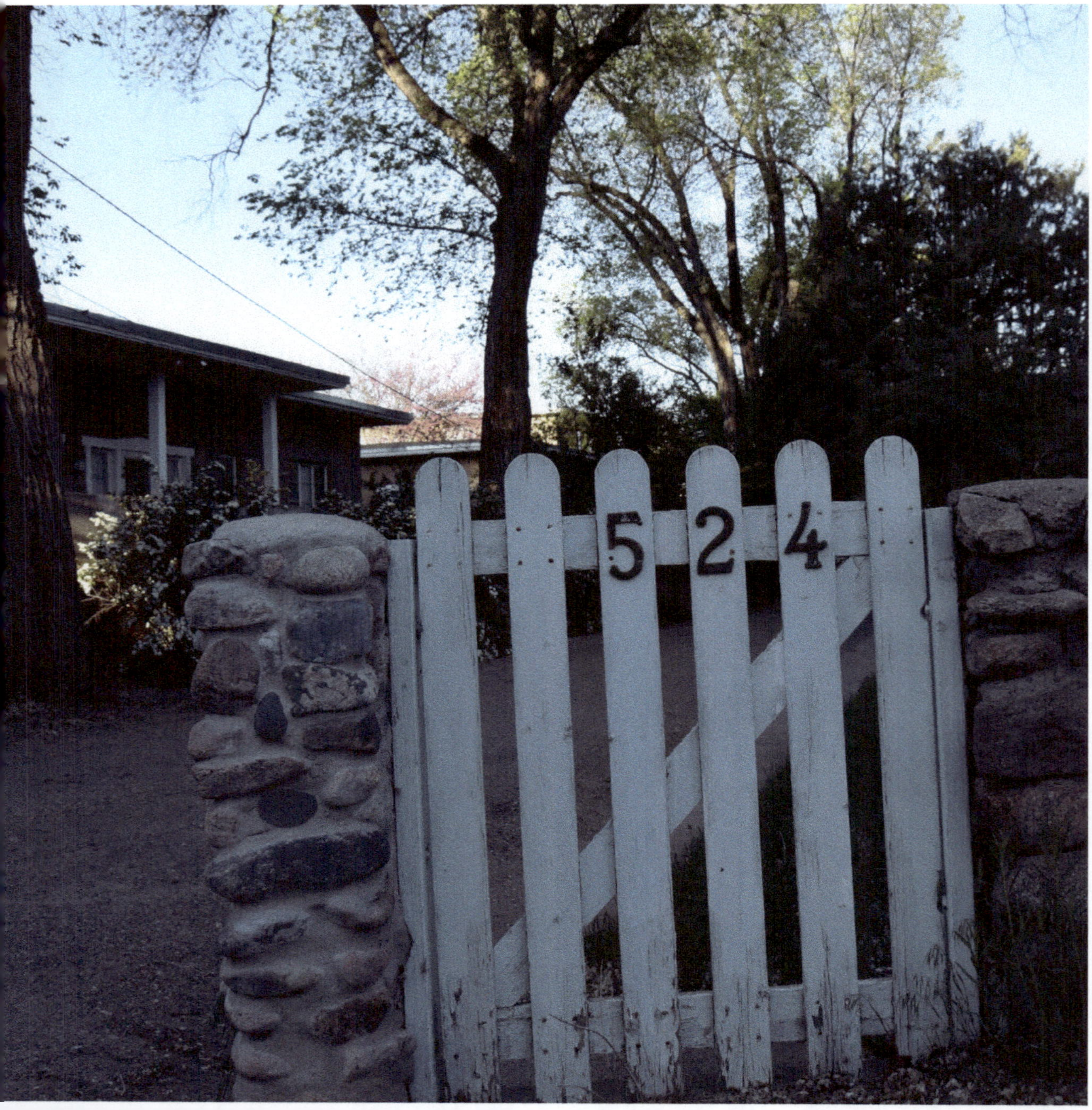

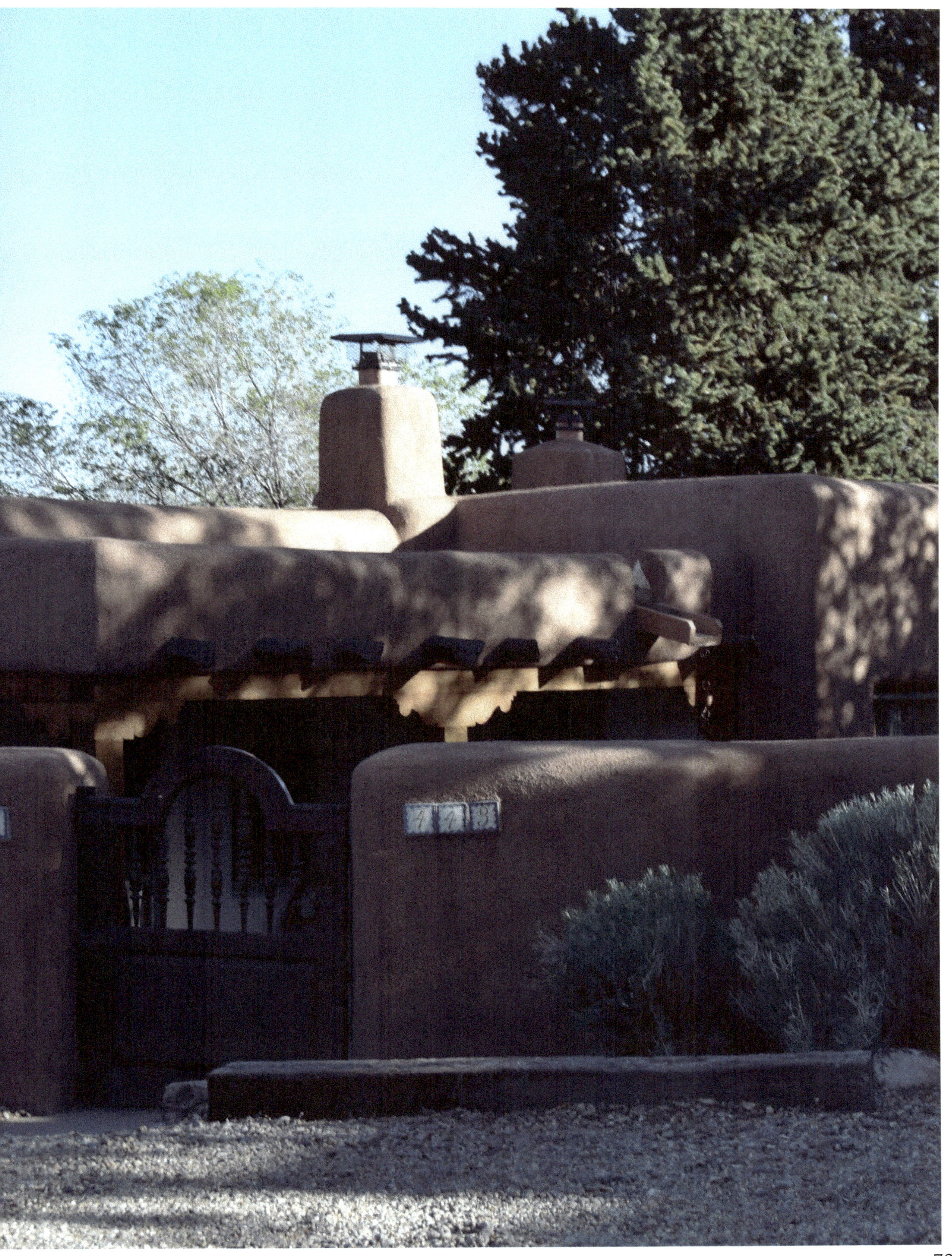

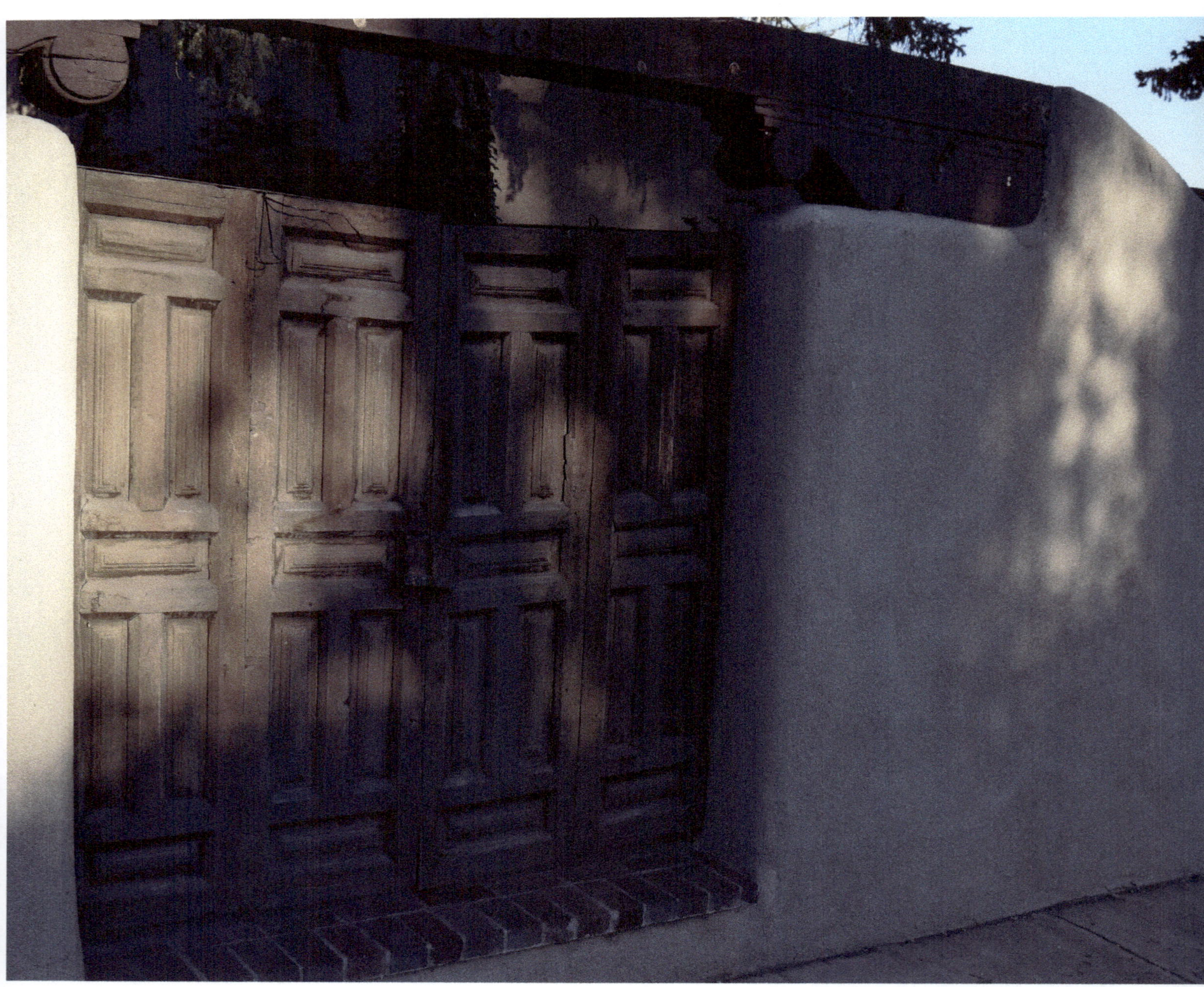

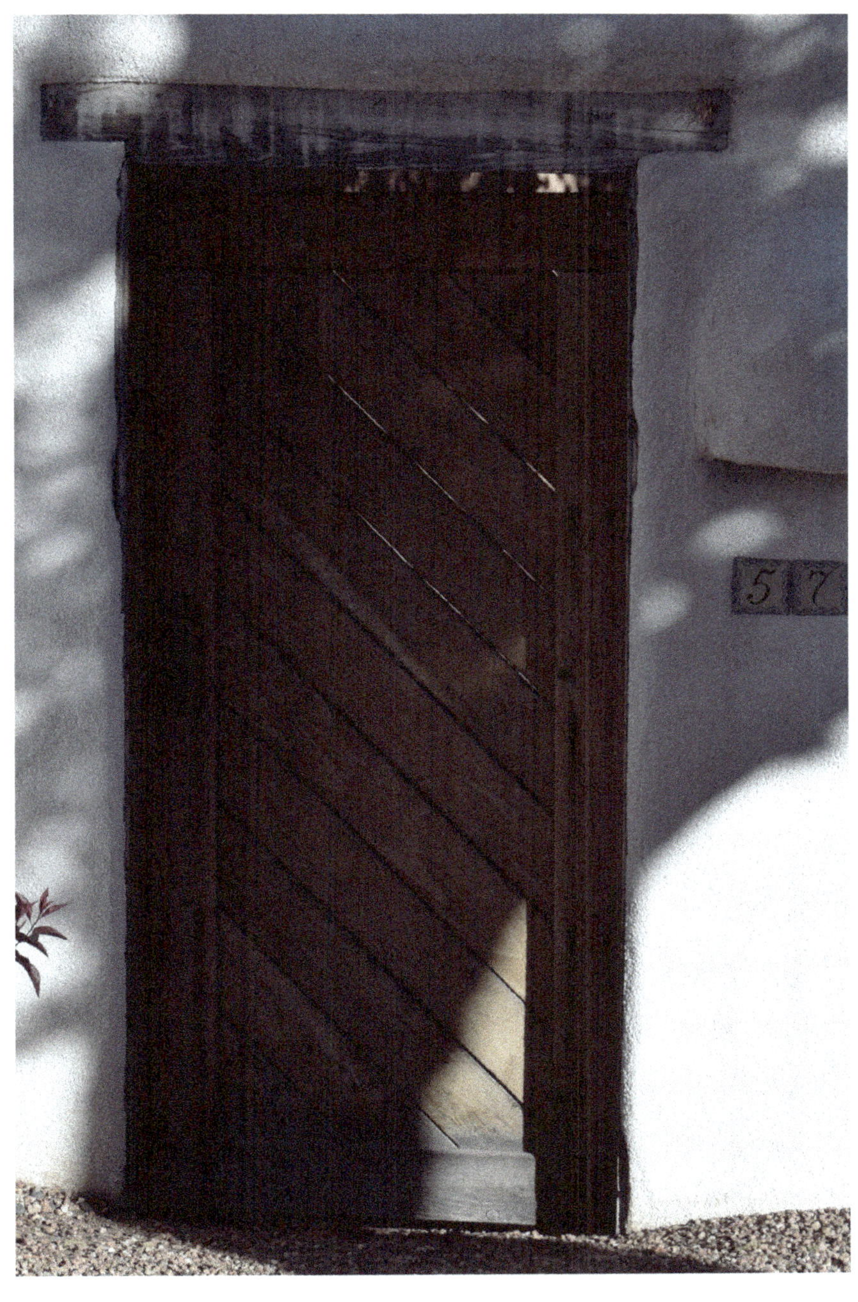

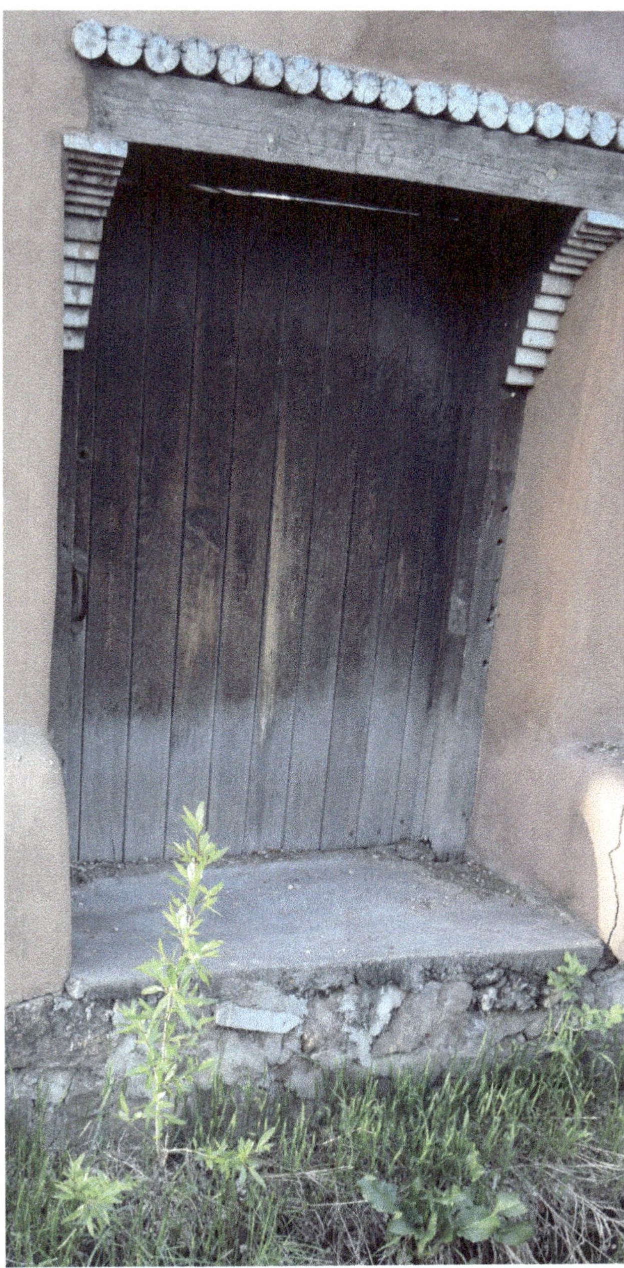

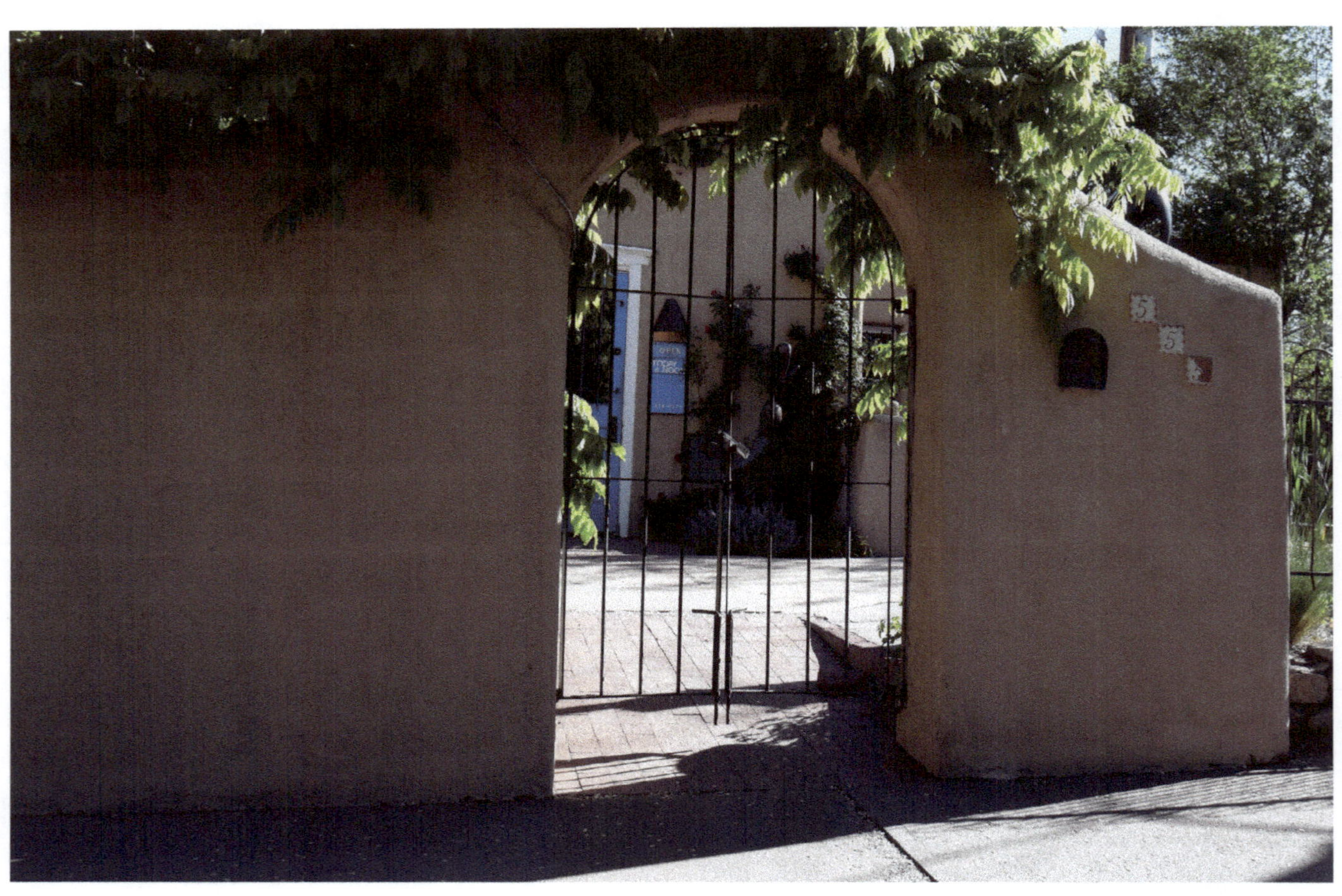

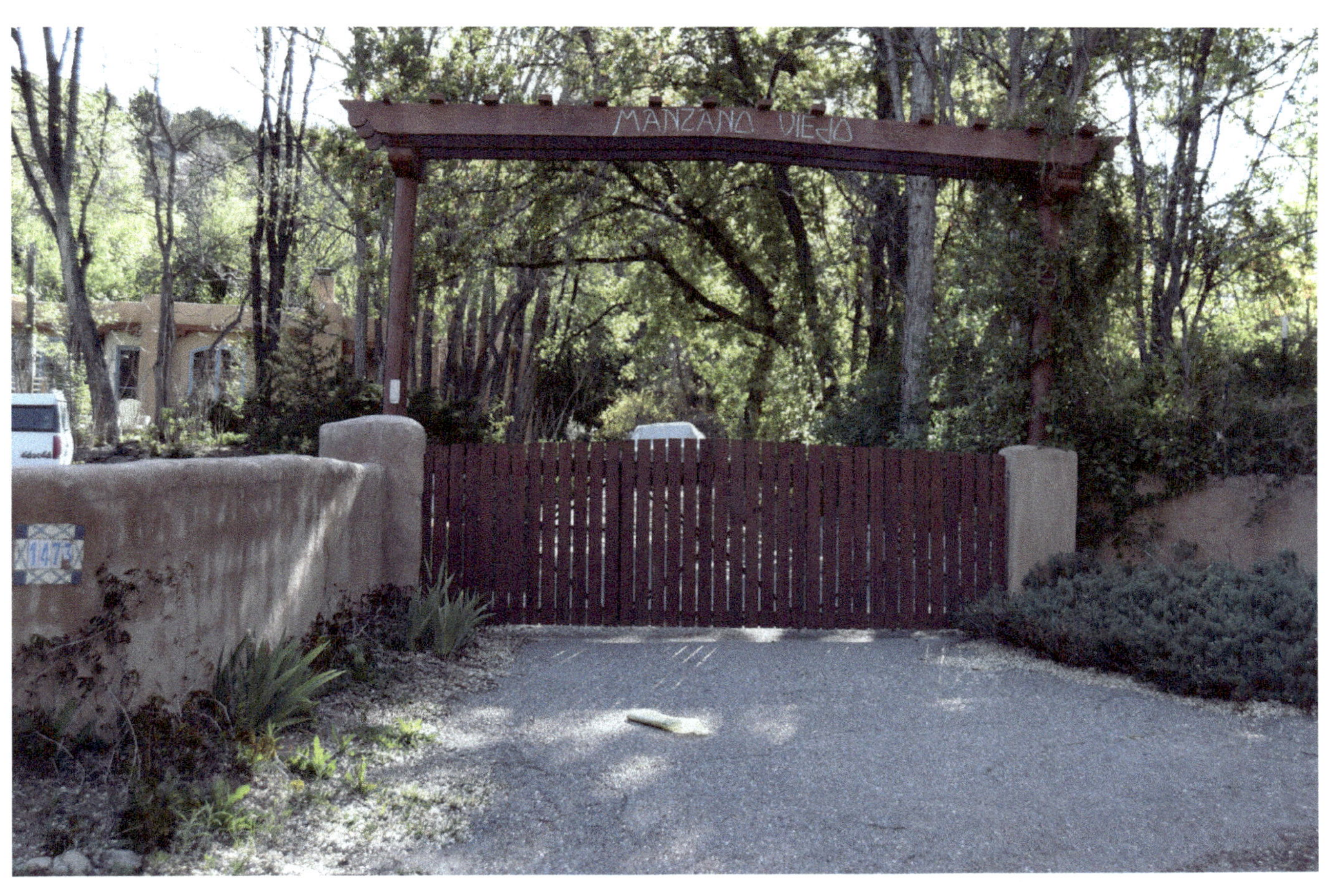
MANZANO VIEJO
1471

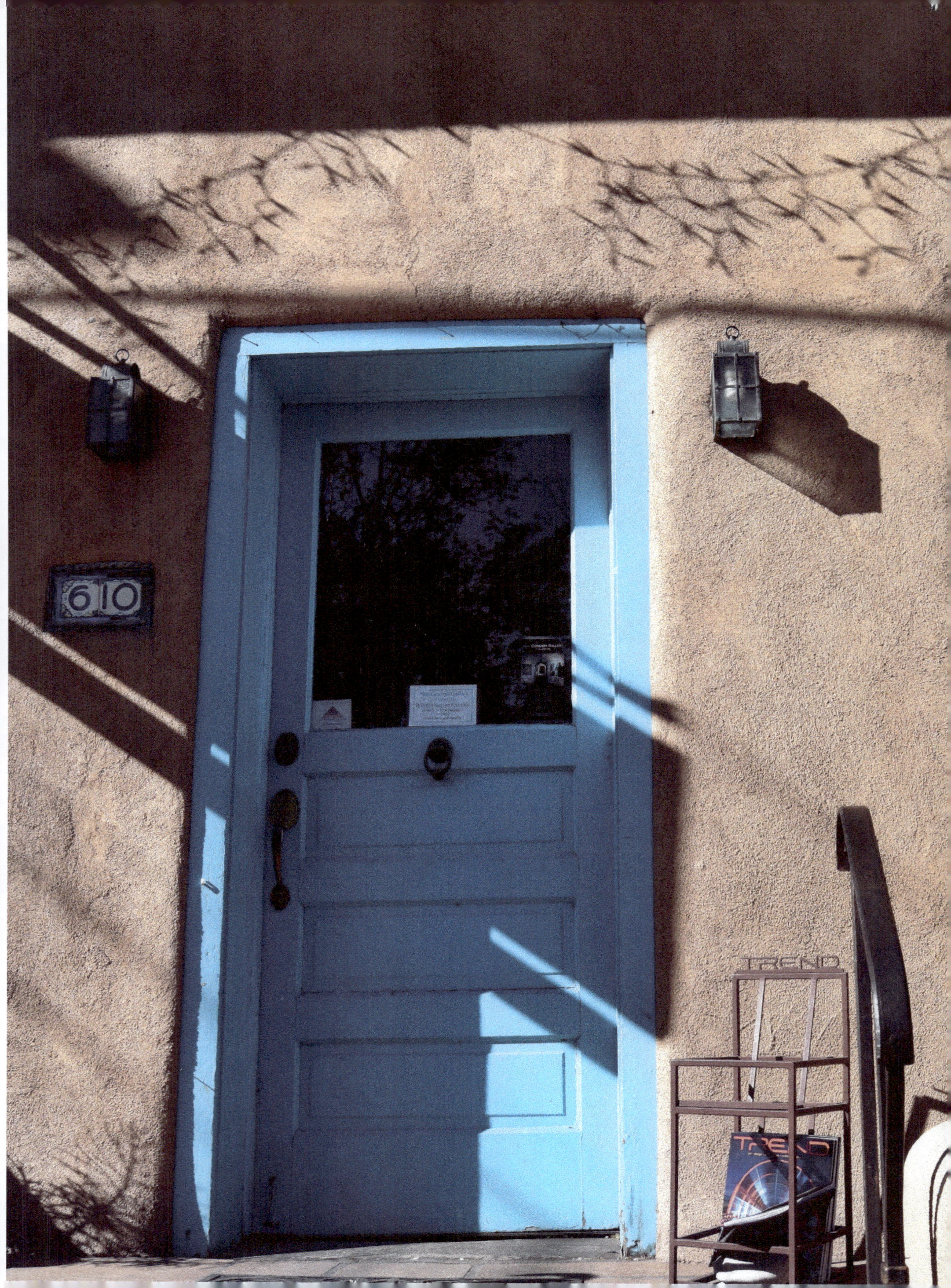

610
TREND
TREND

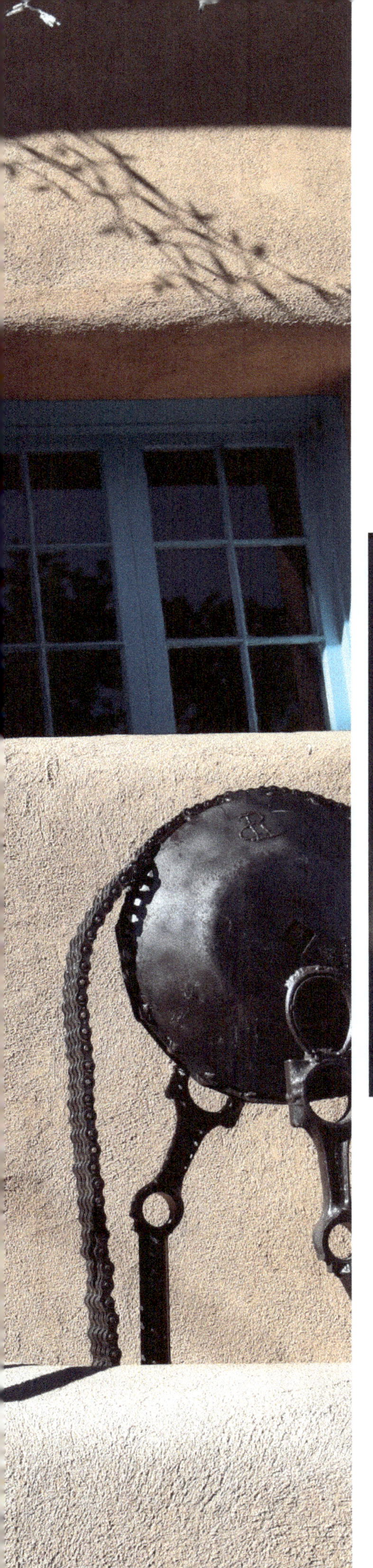

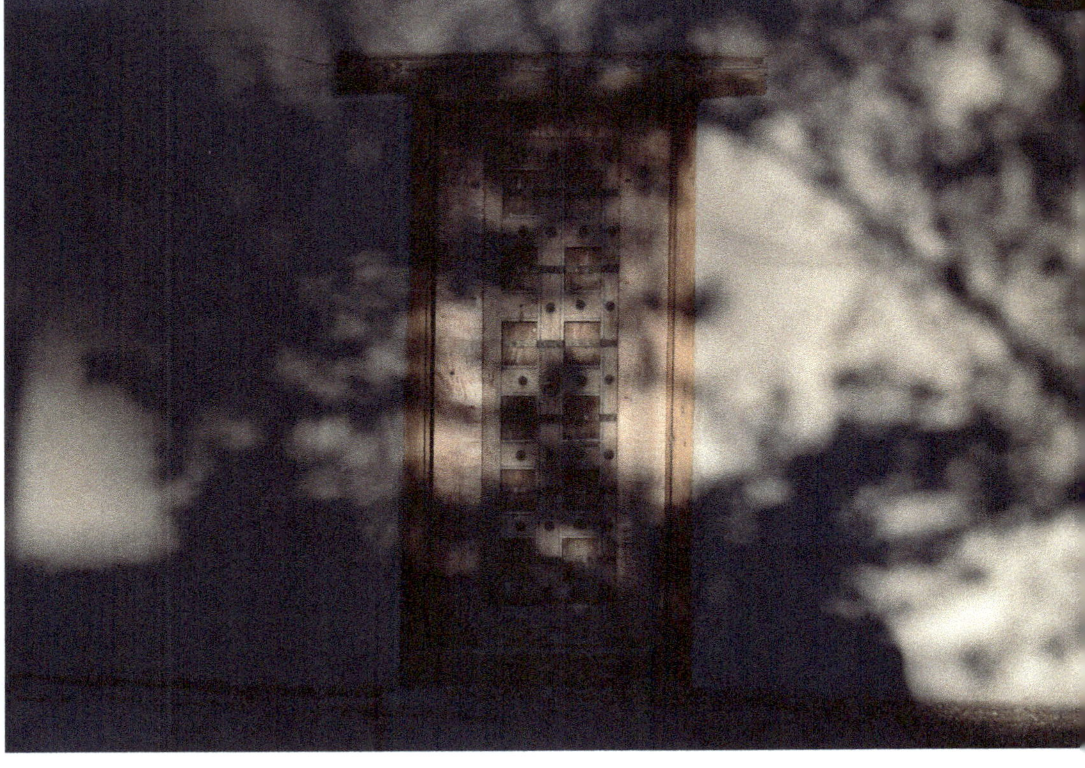

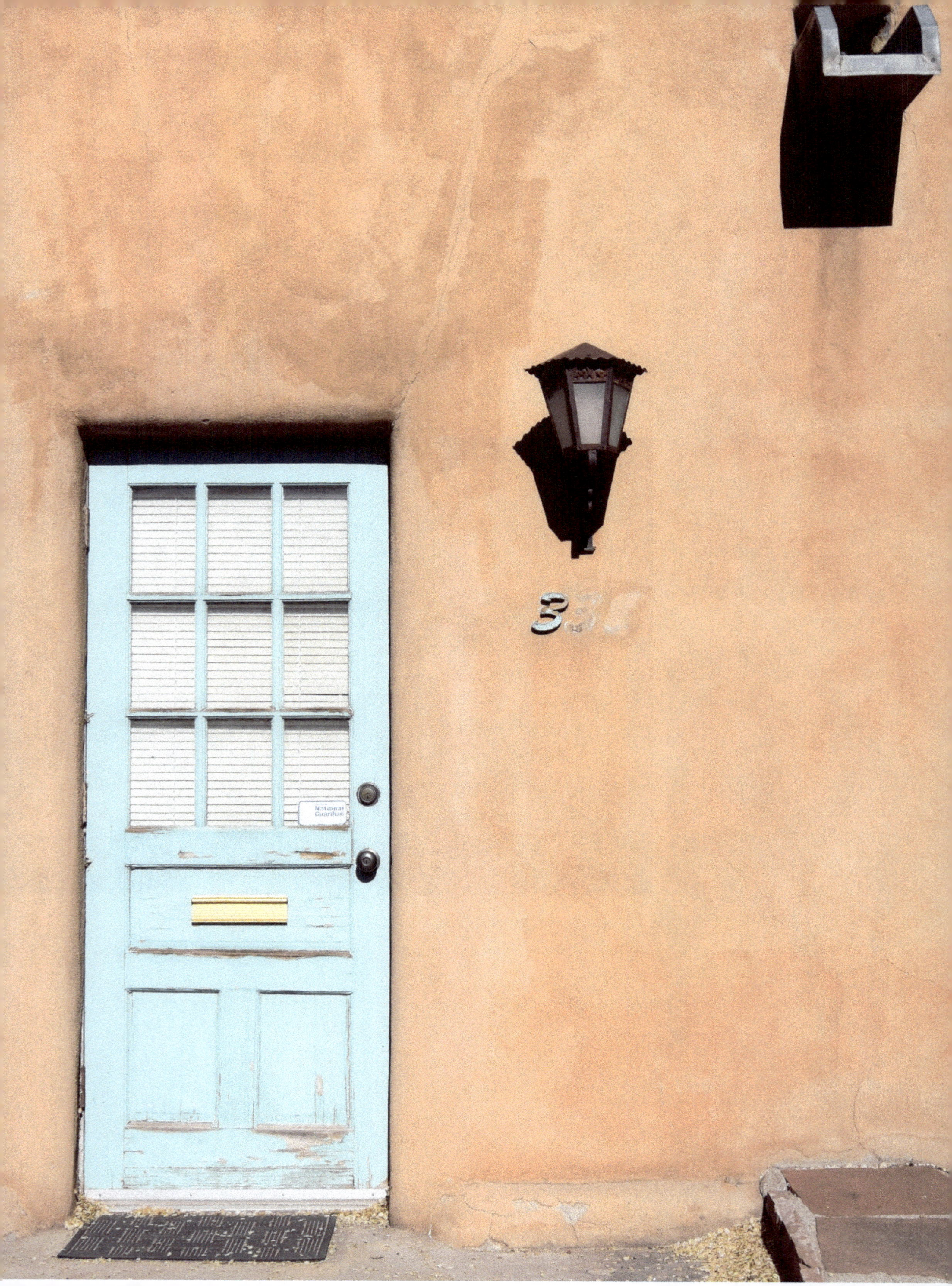

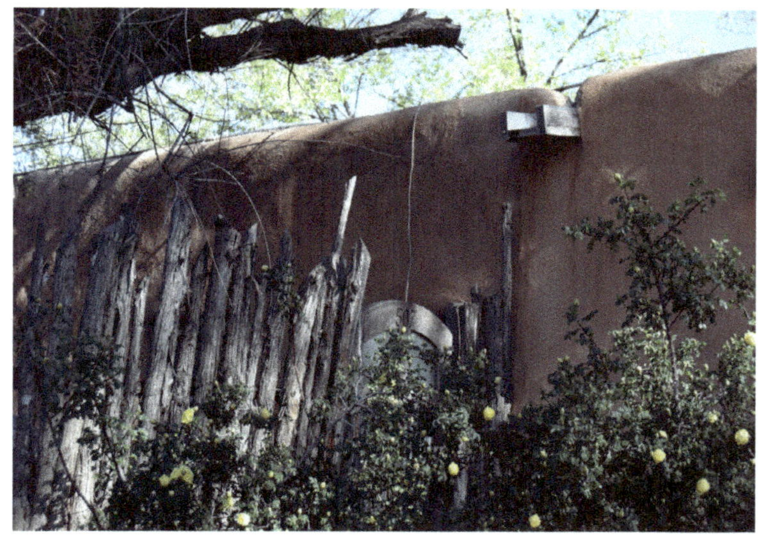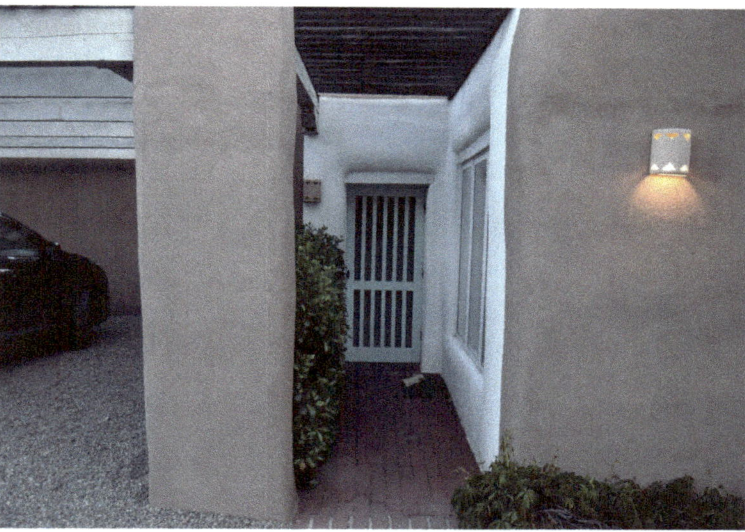

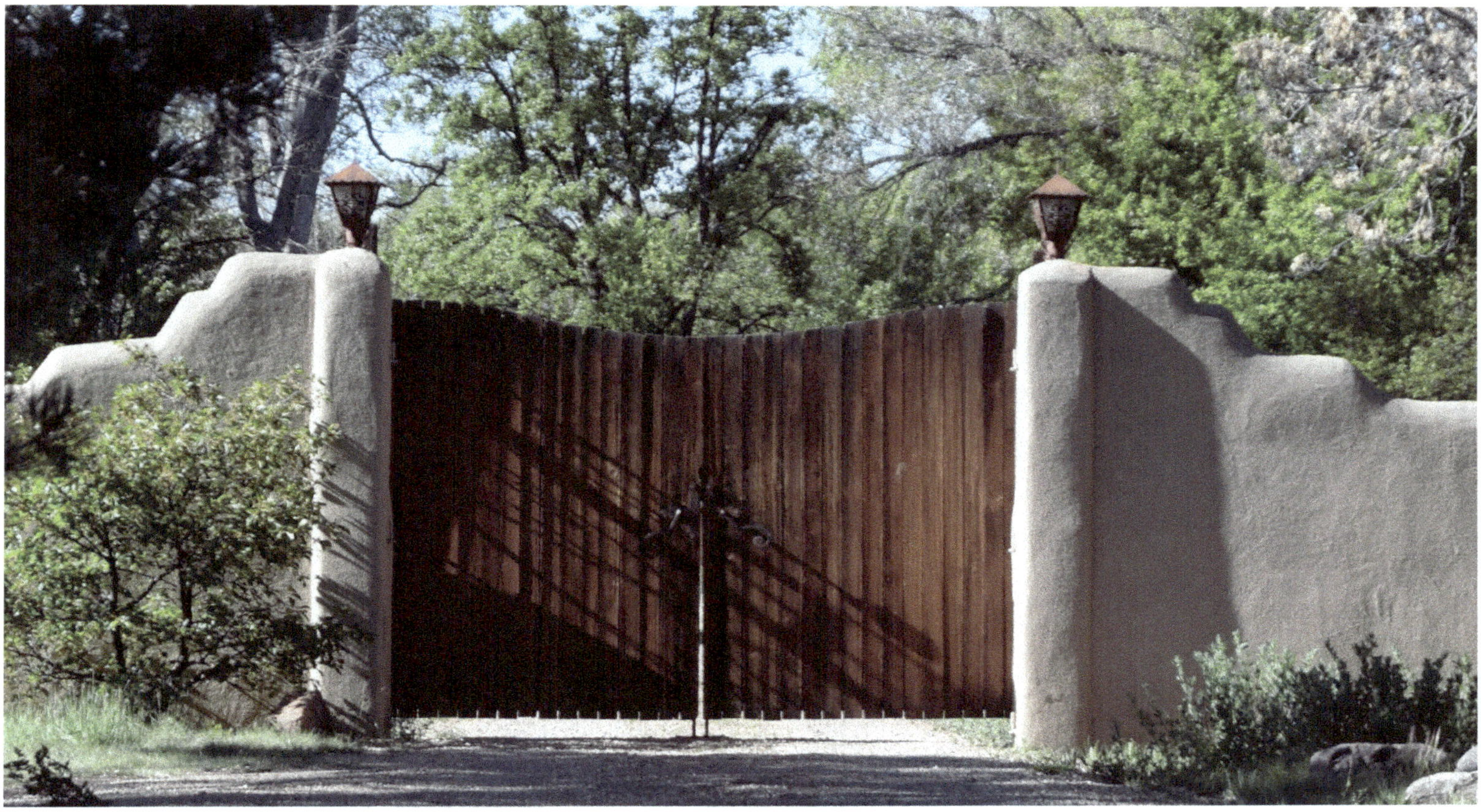

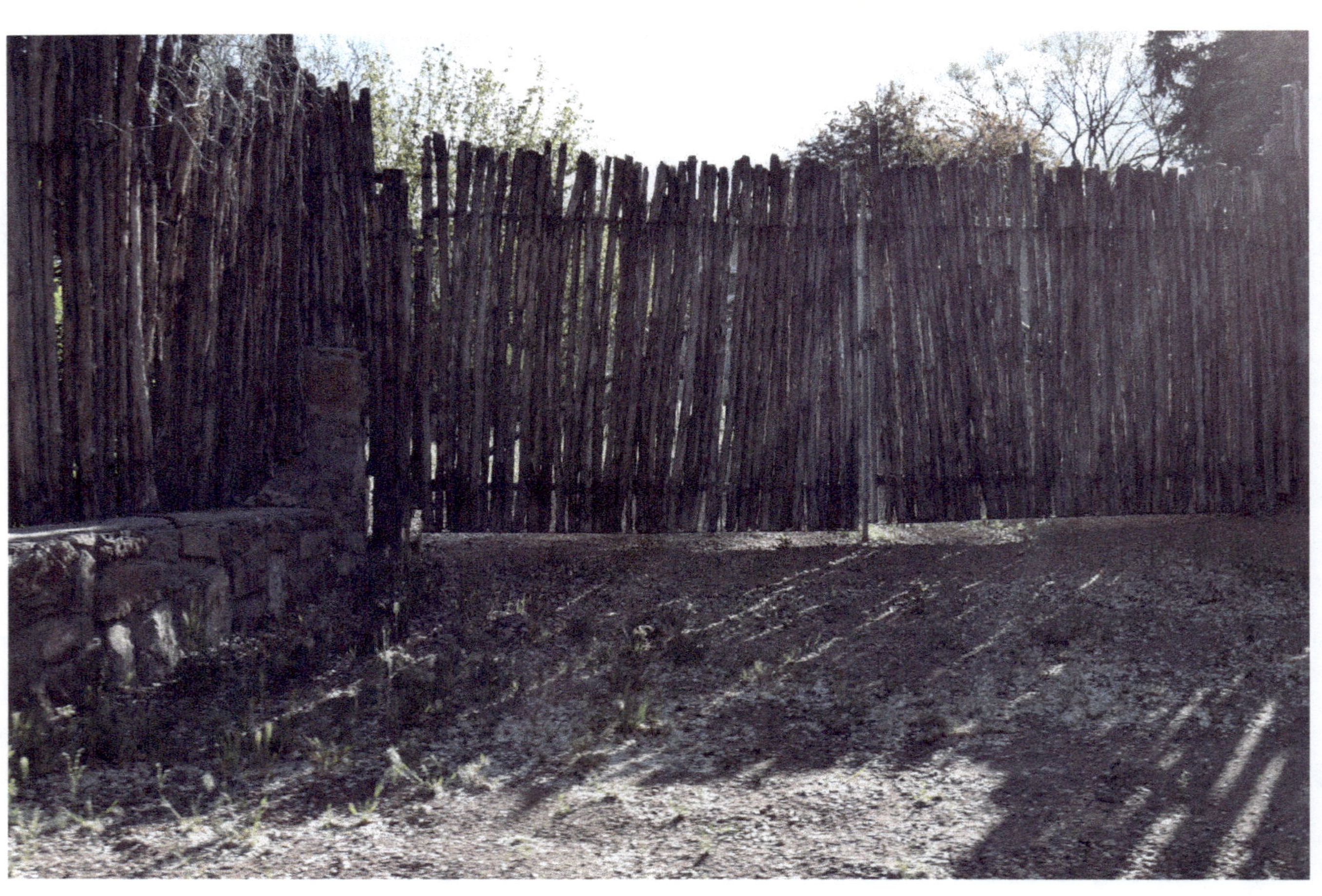

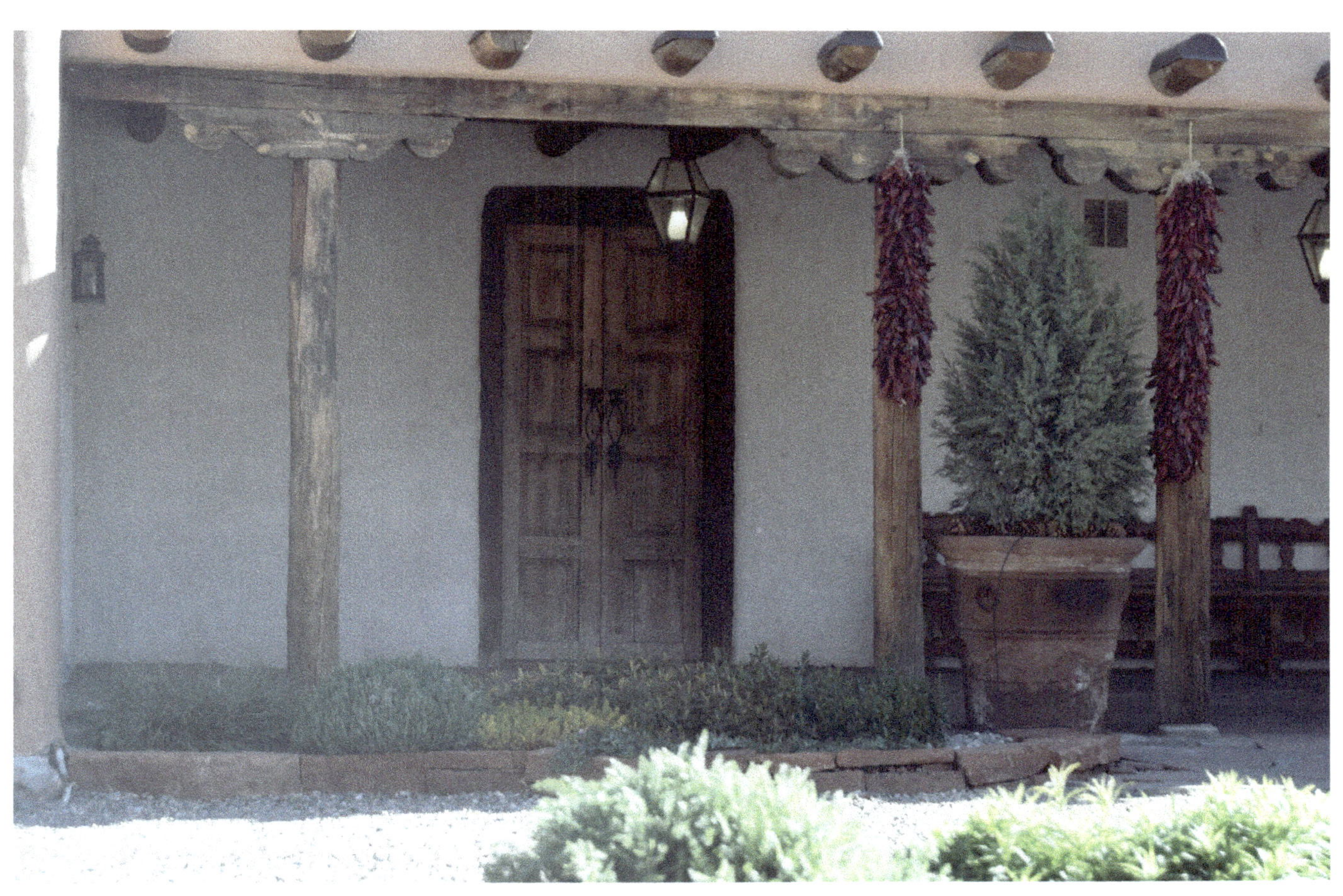

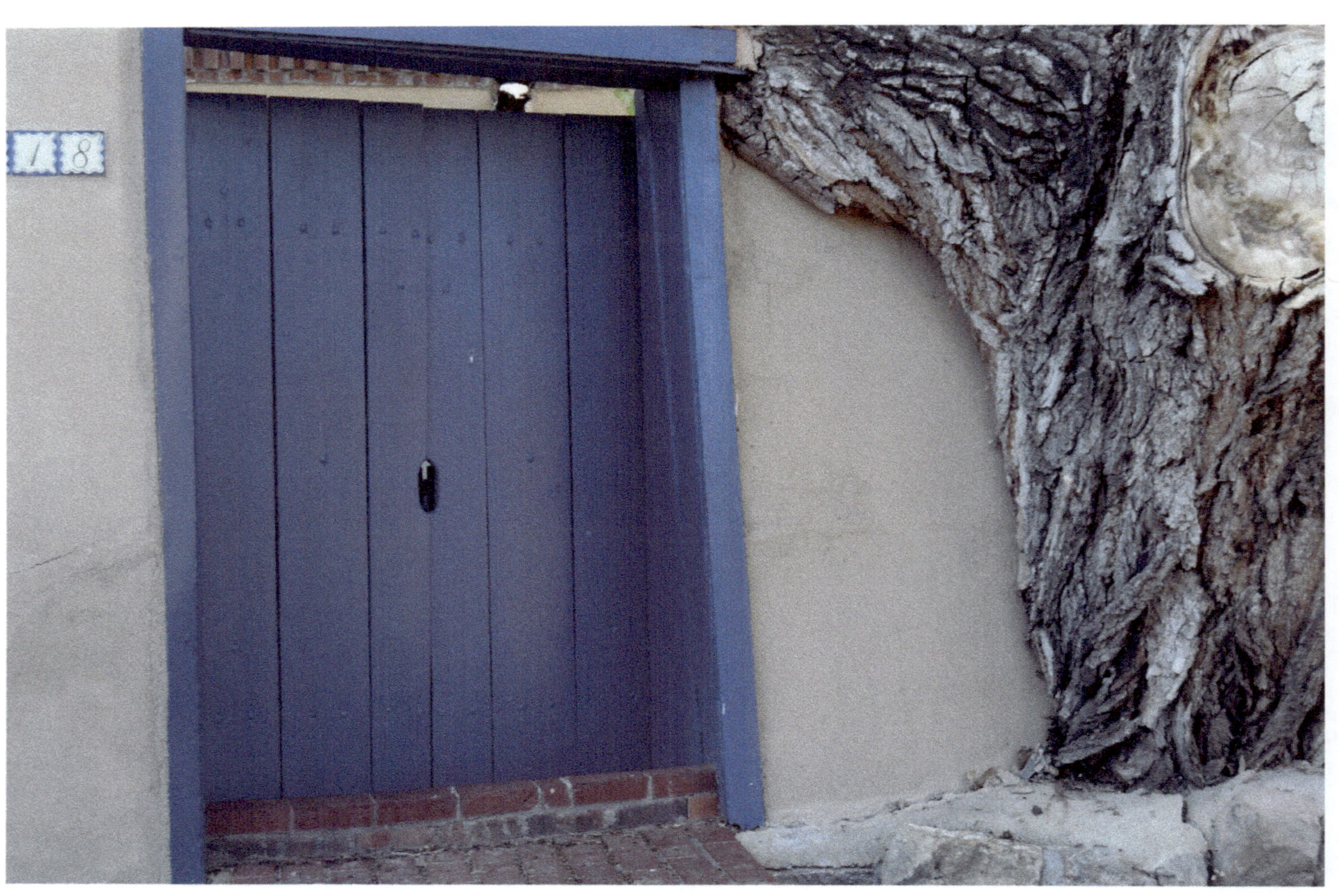

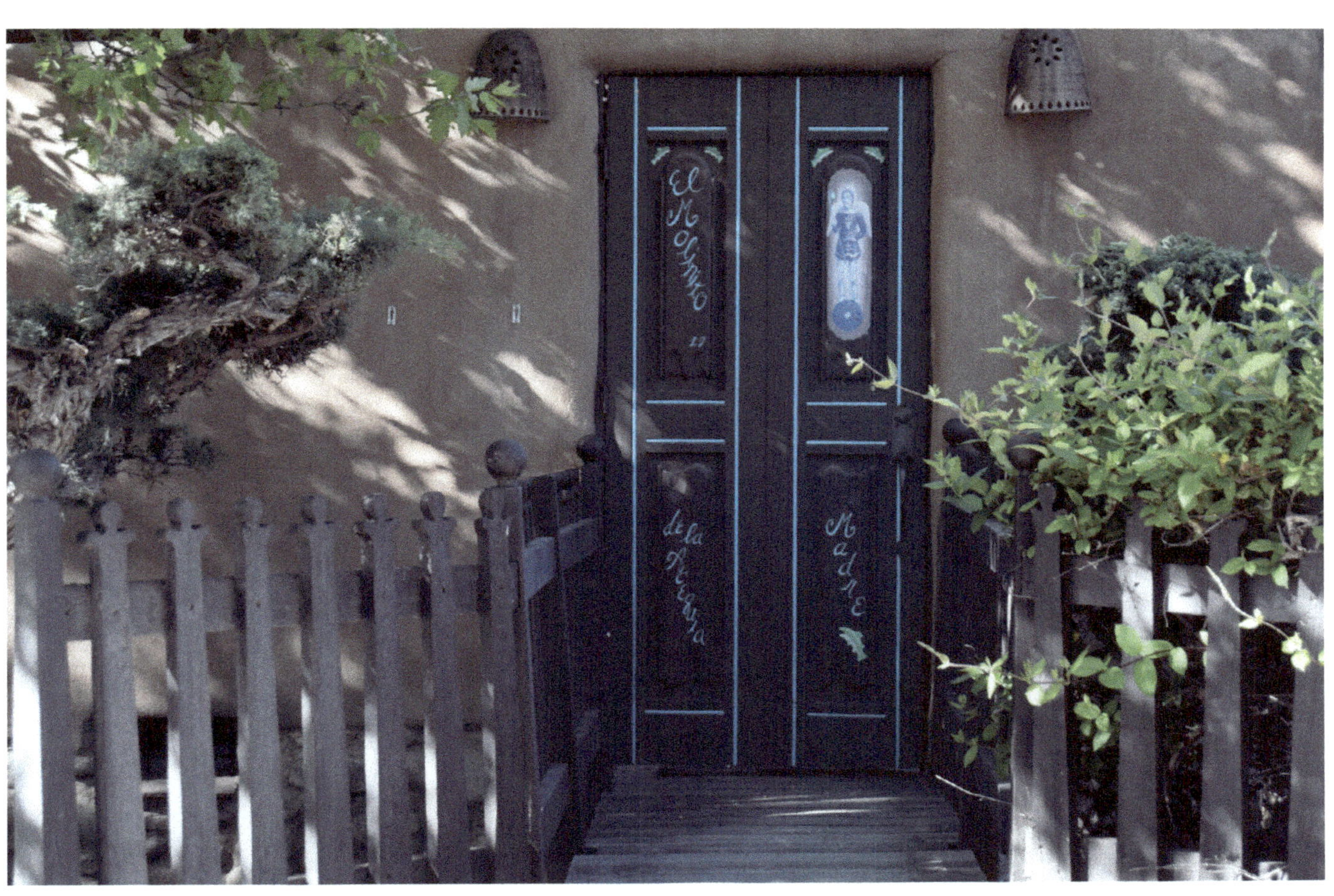

El
Molino
de la
Acequia
Madre

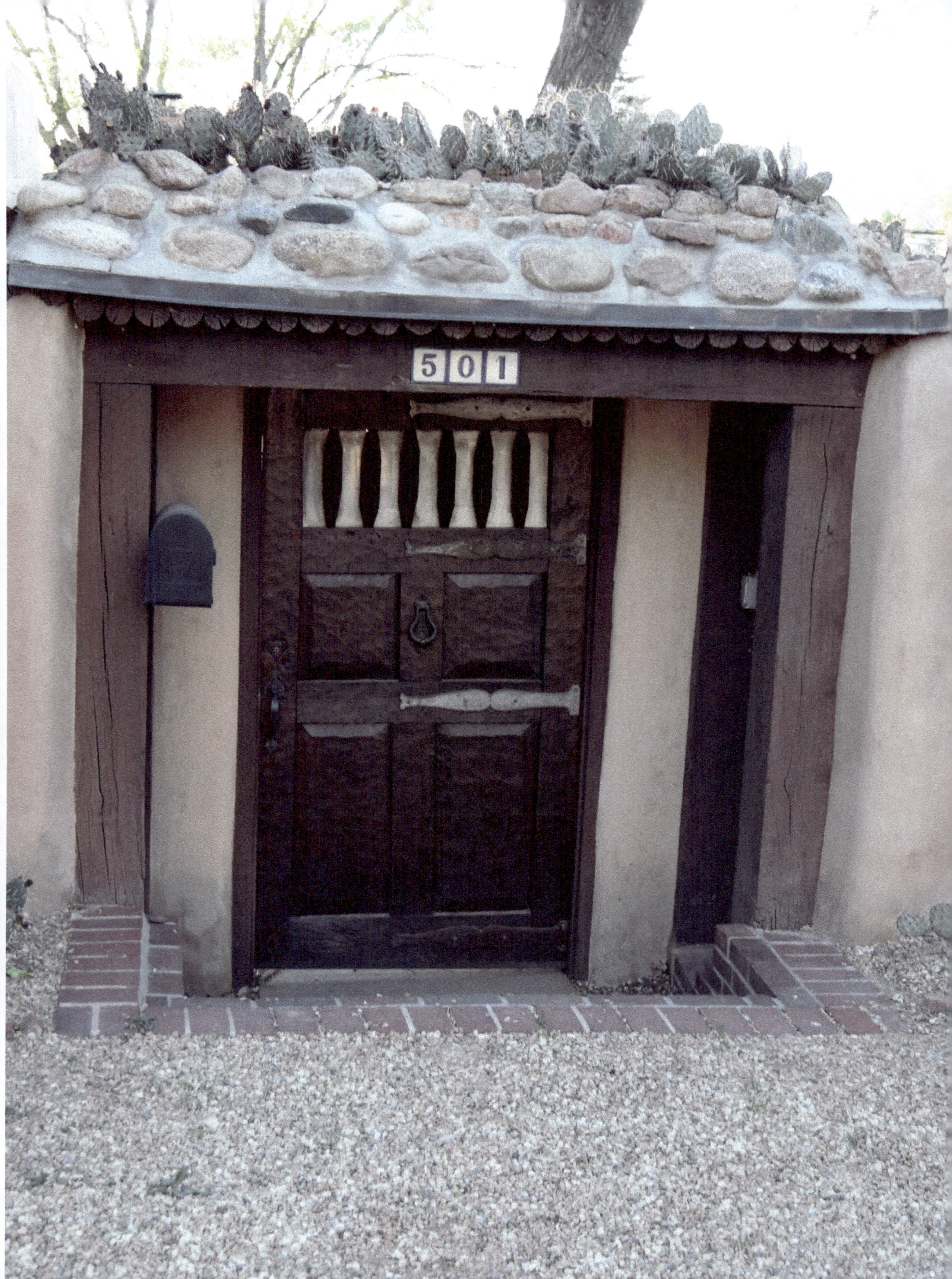

501

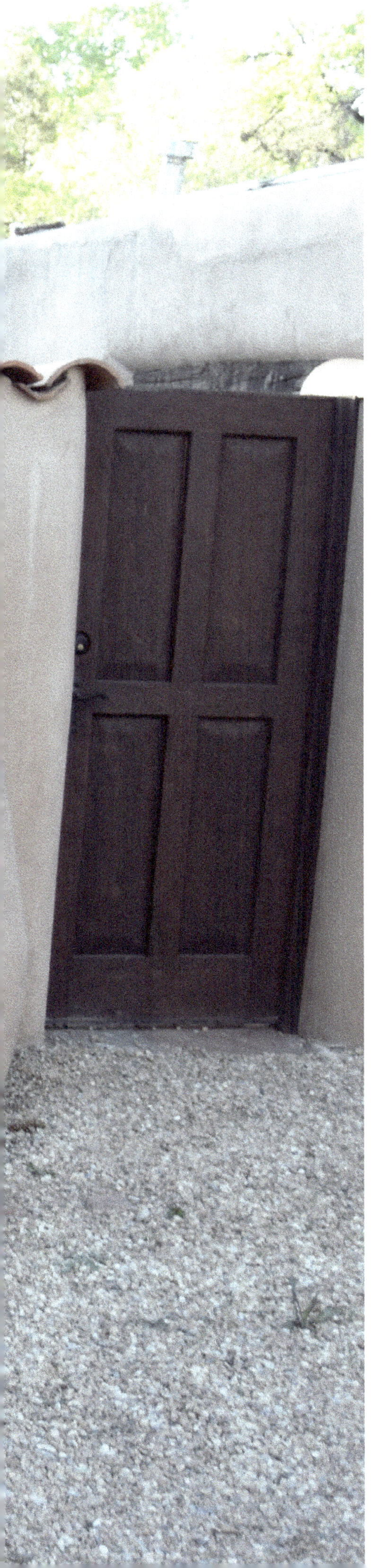

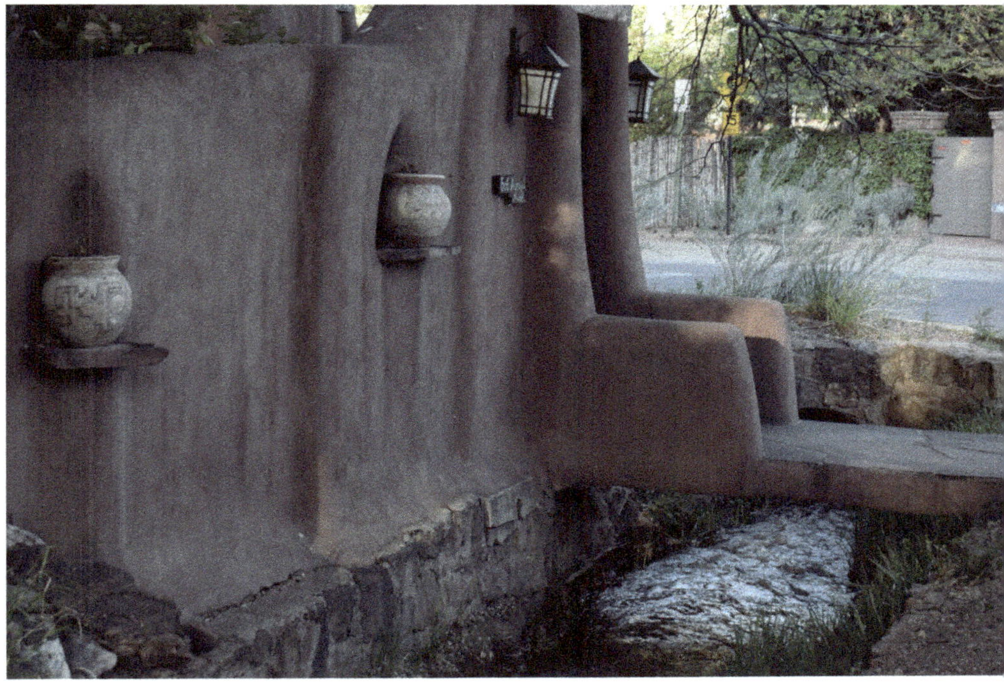

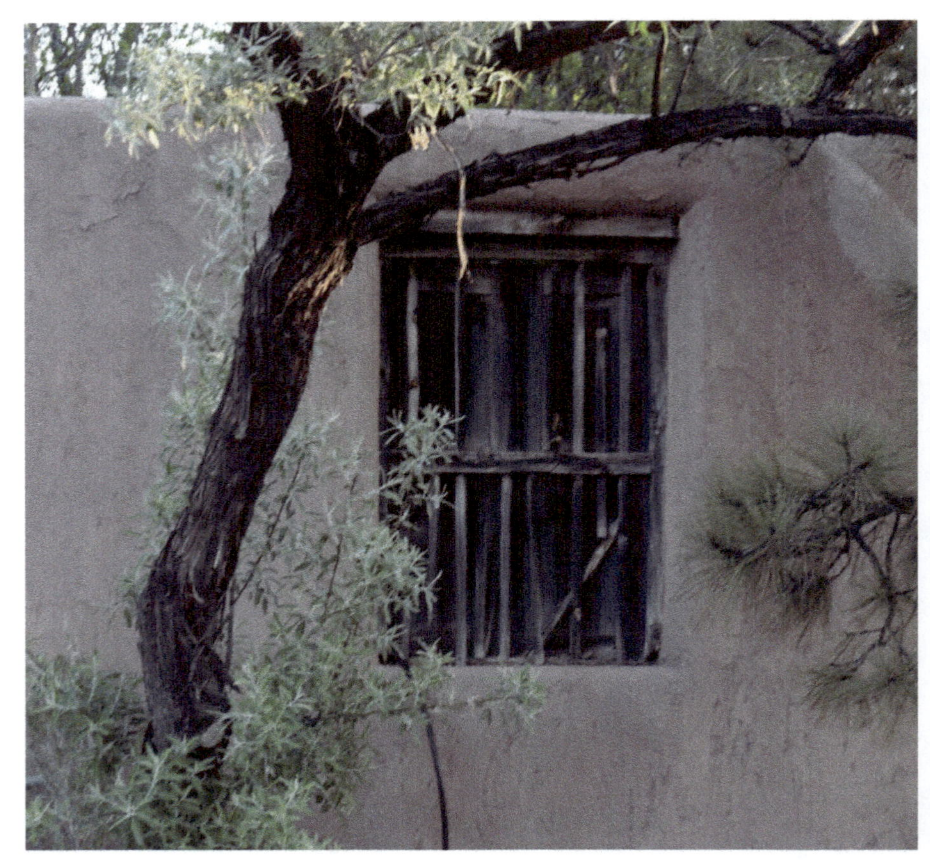

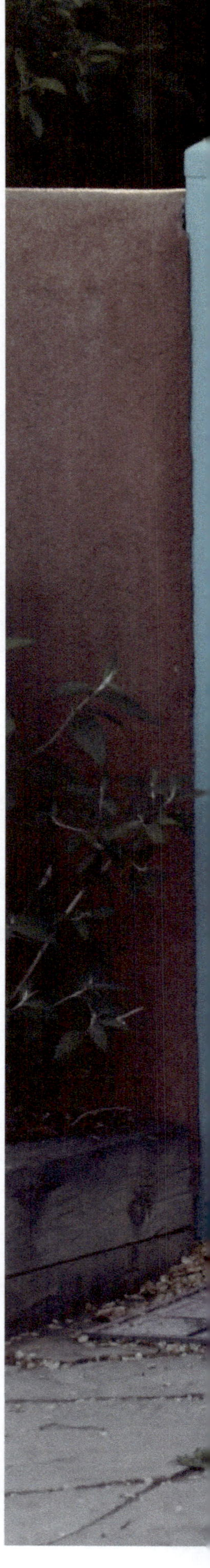

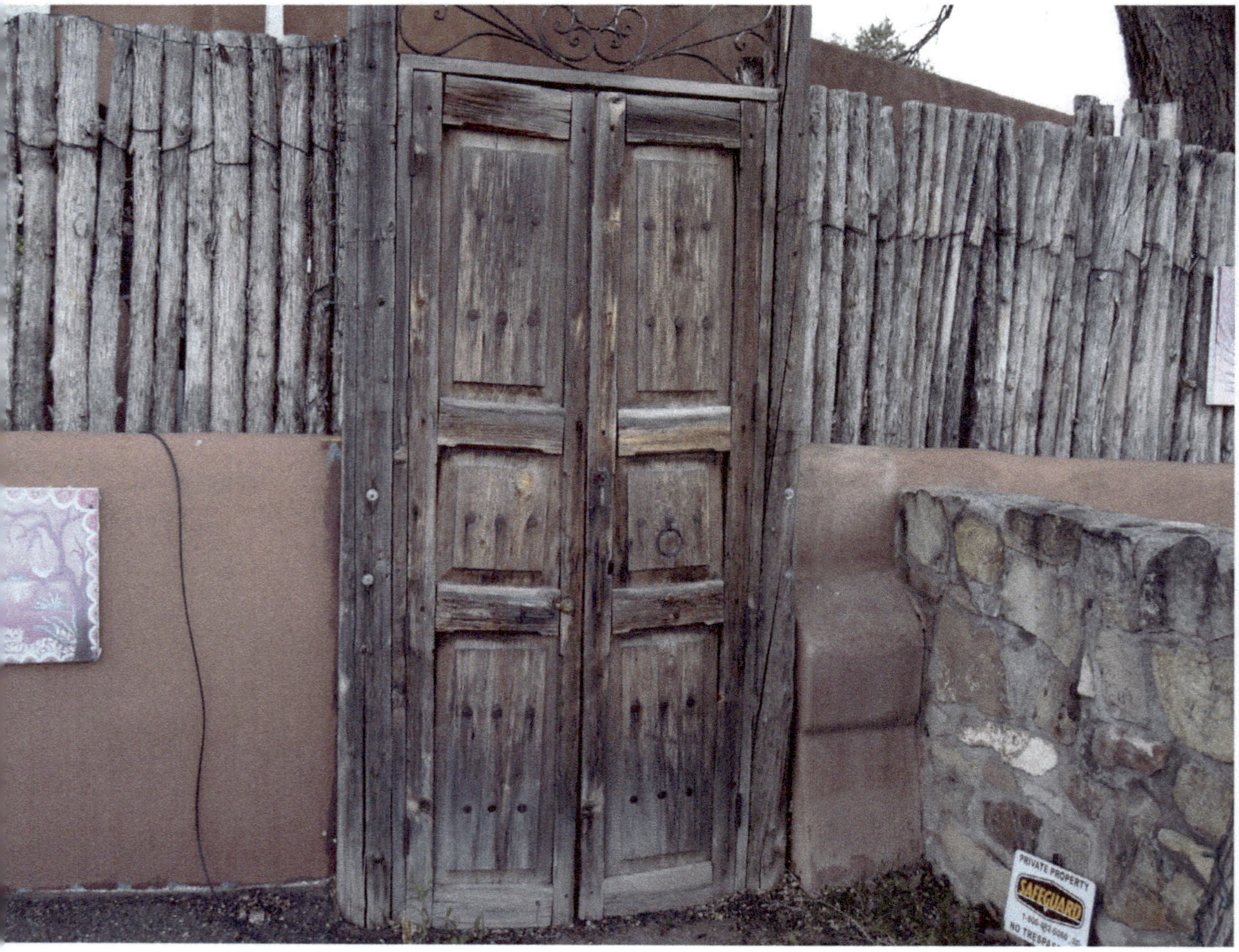

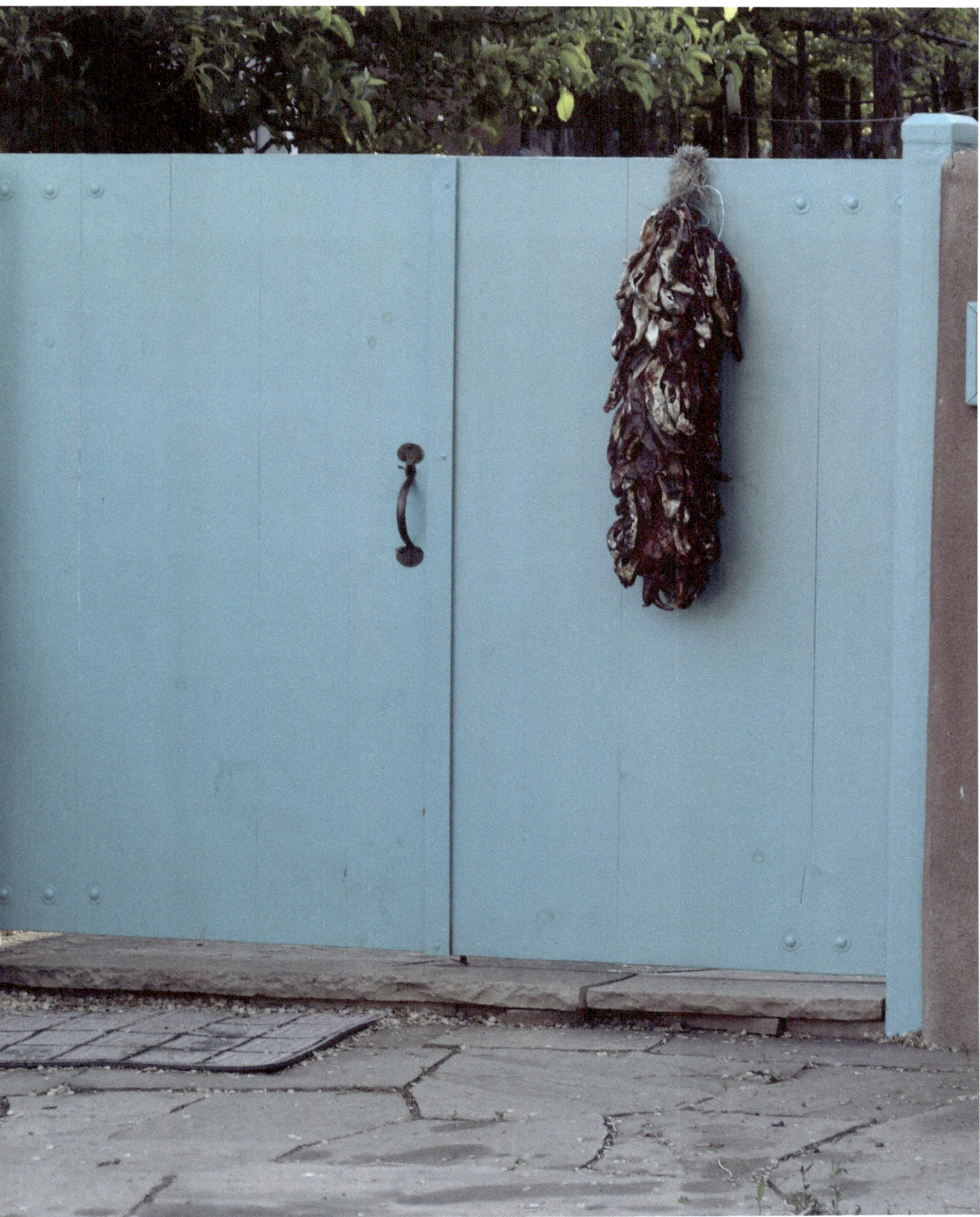

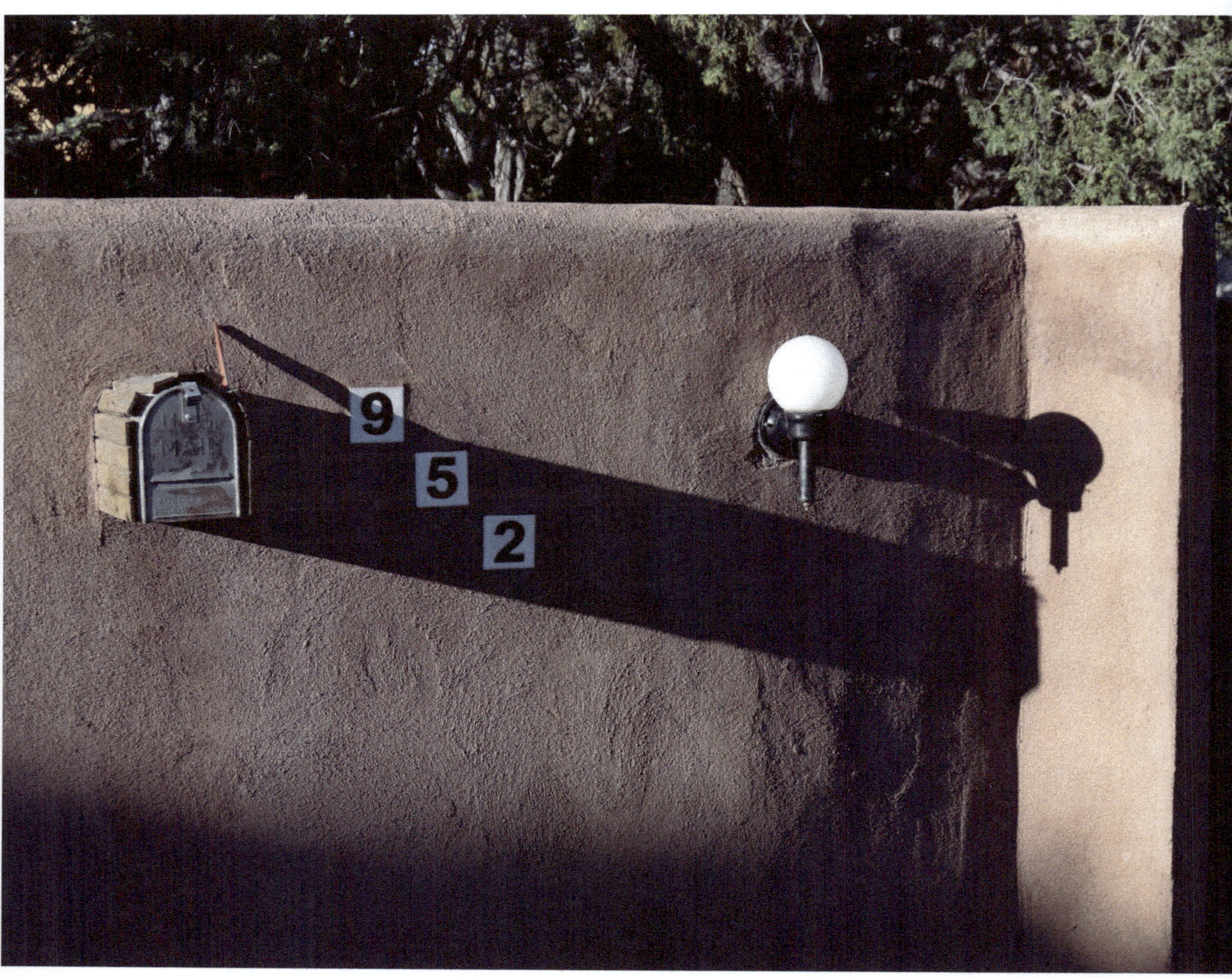

9
5
2

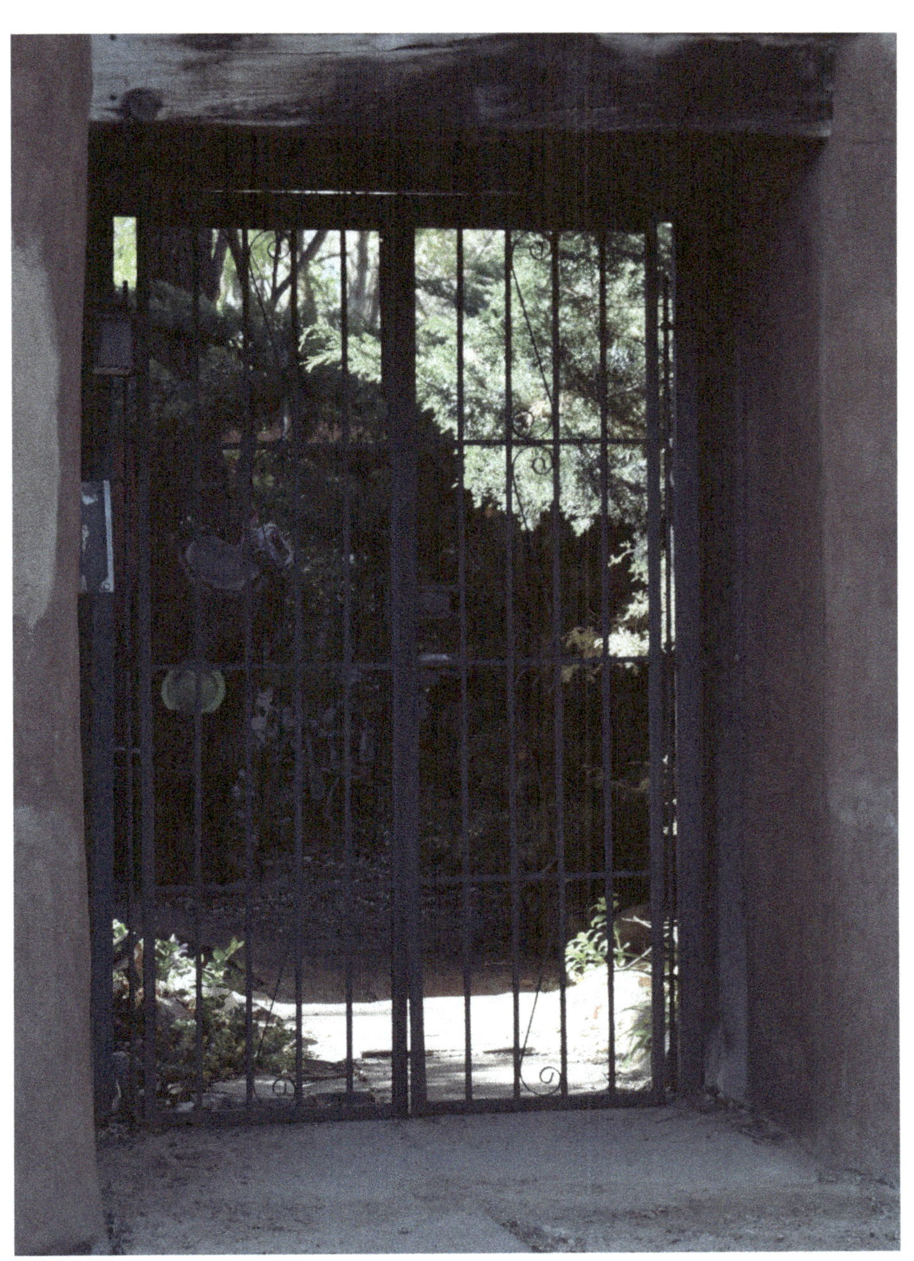

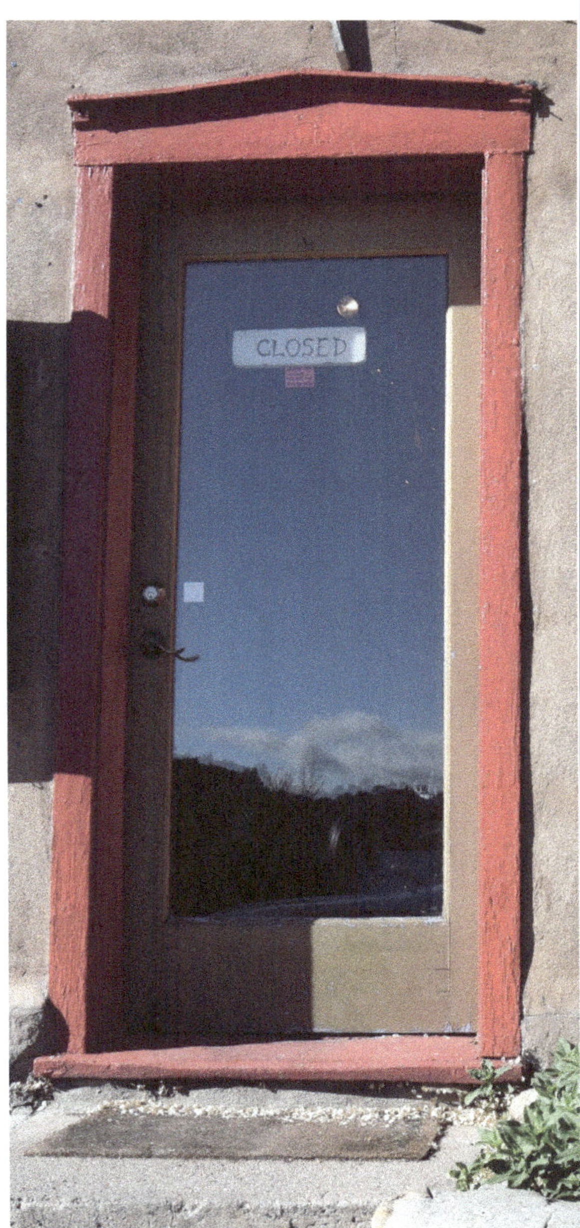
CLOSED

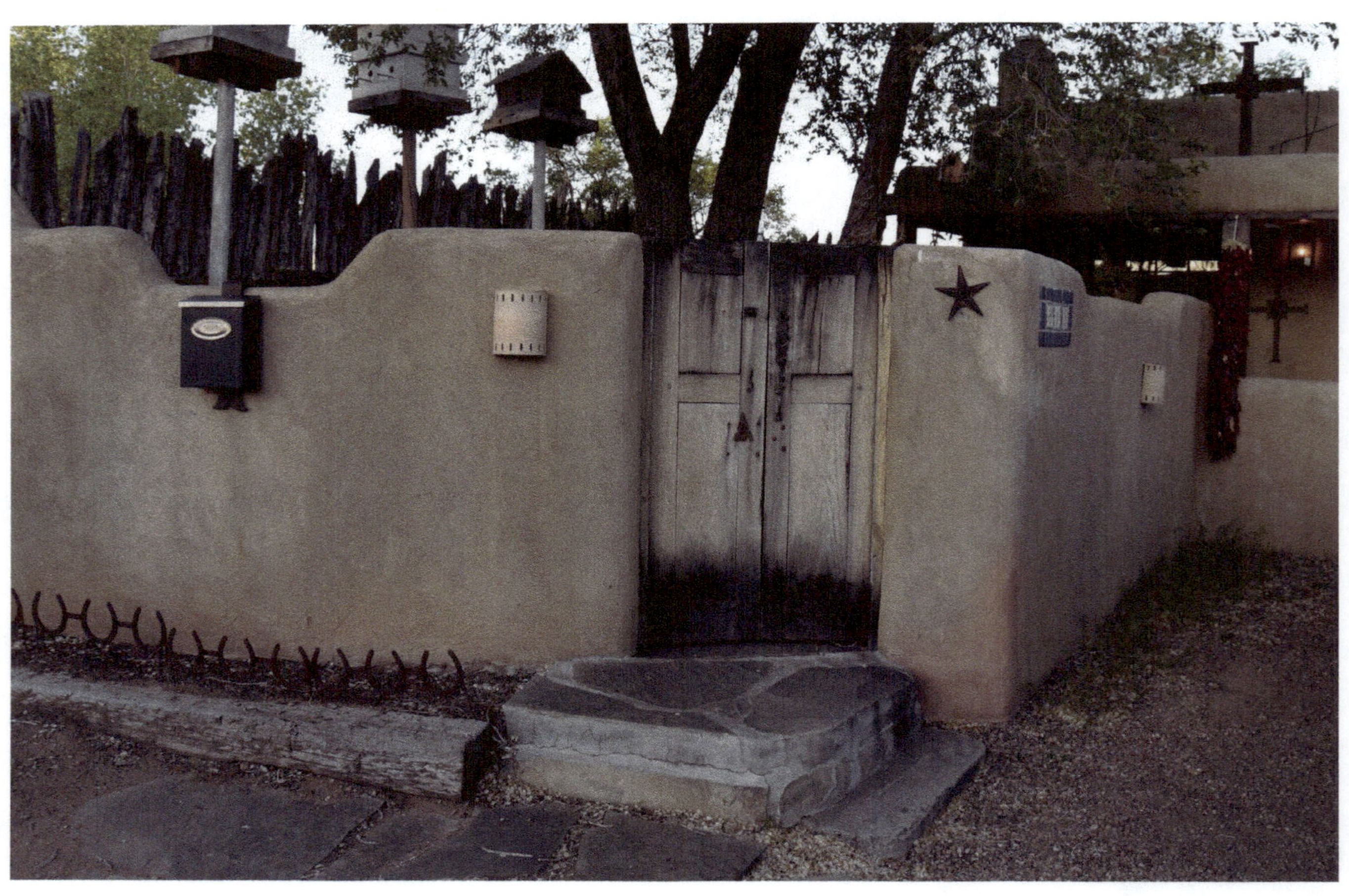

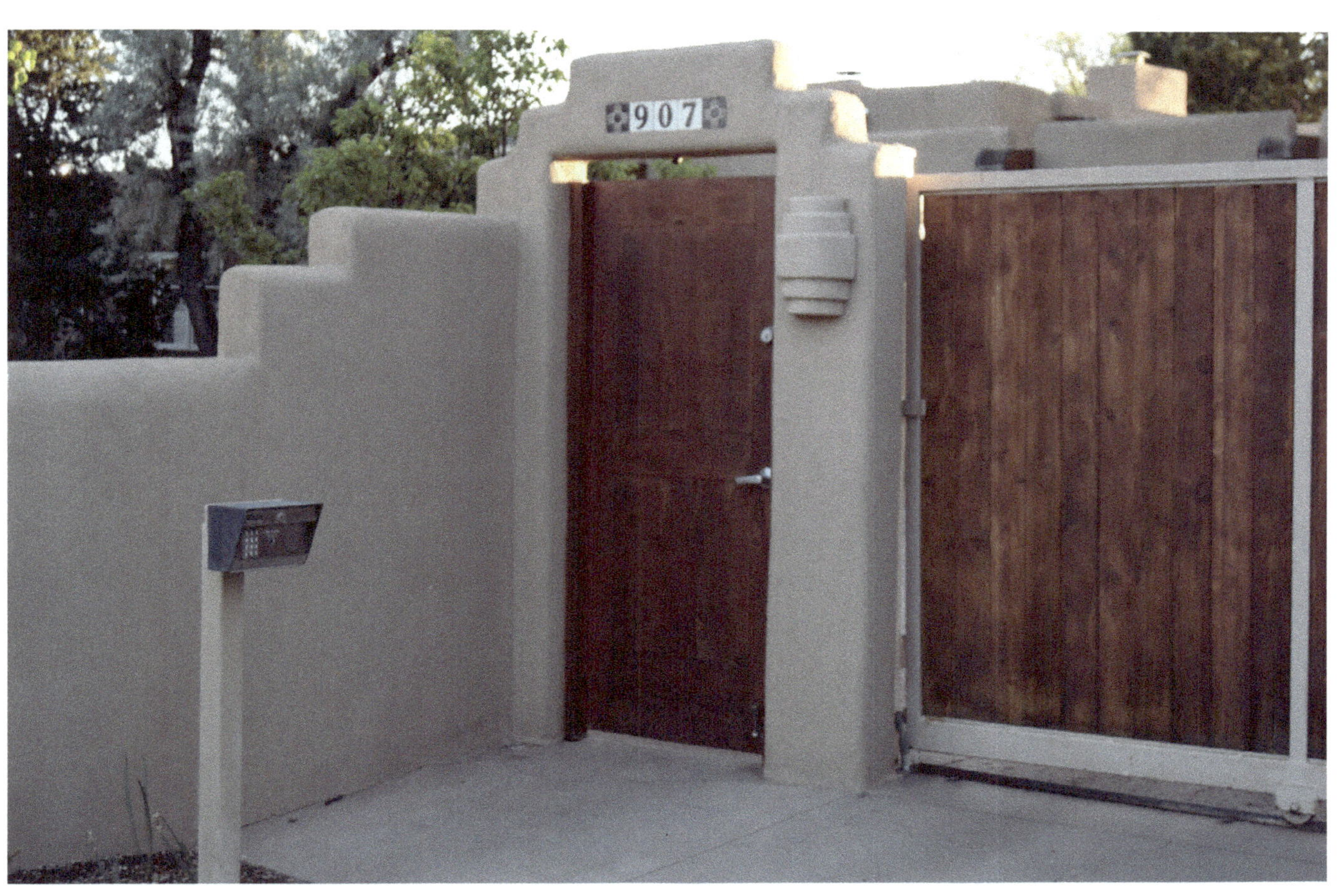

907

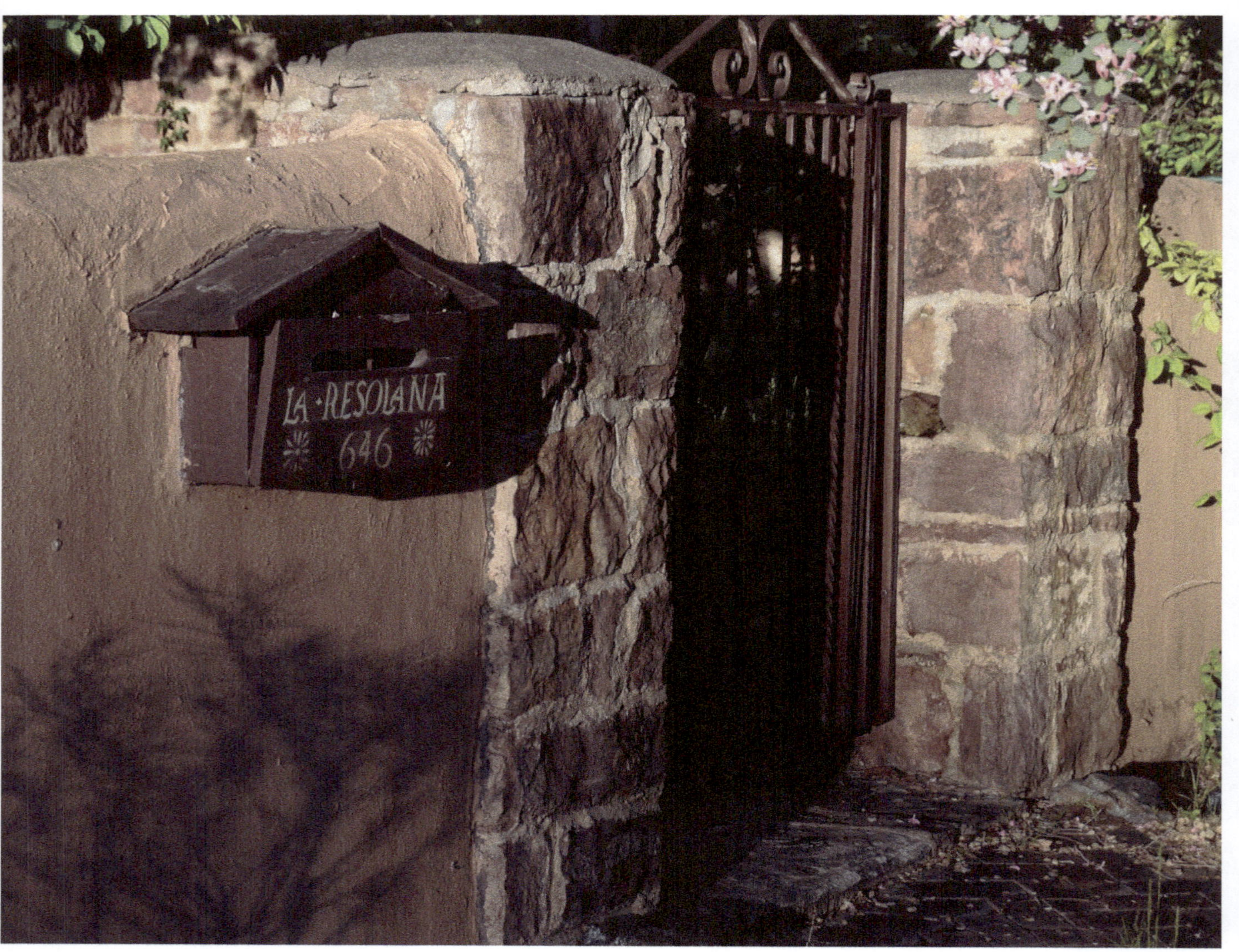
LA·RESOLANA
646

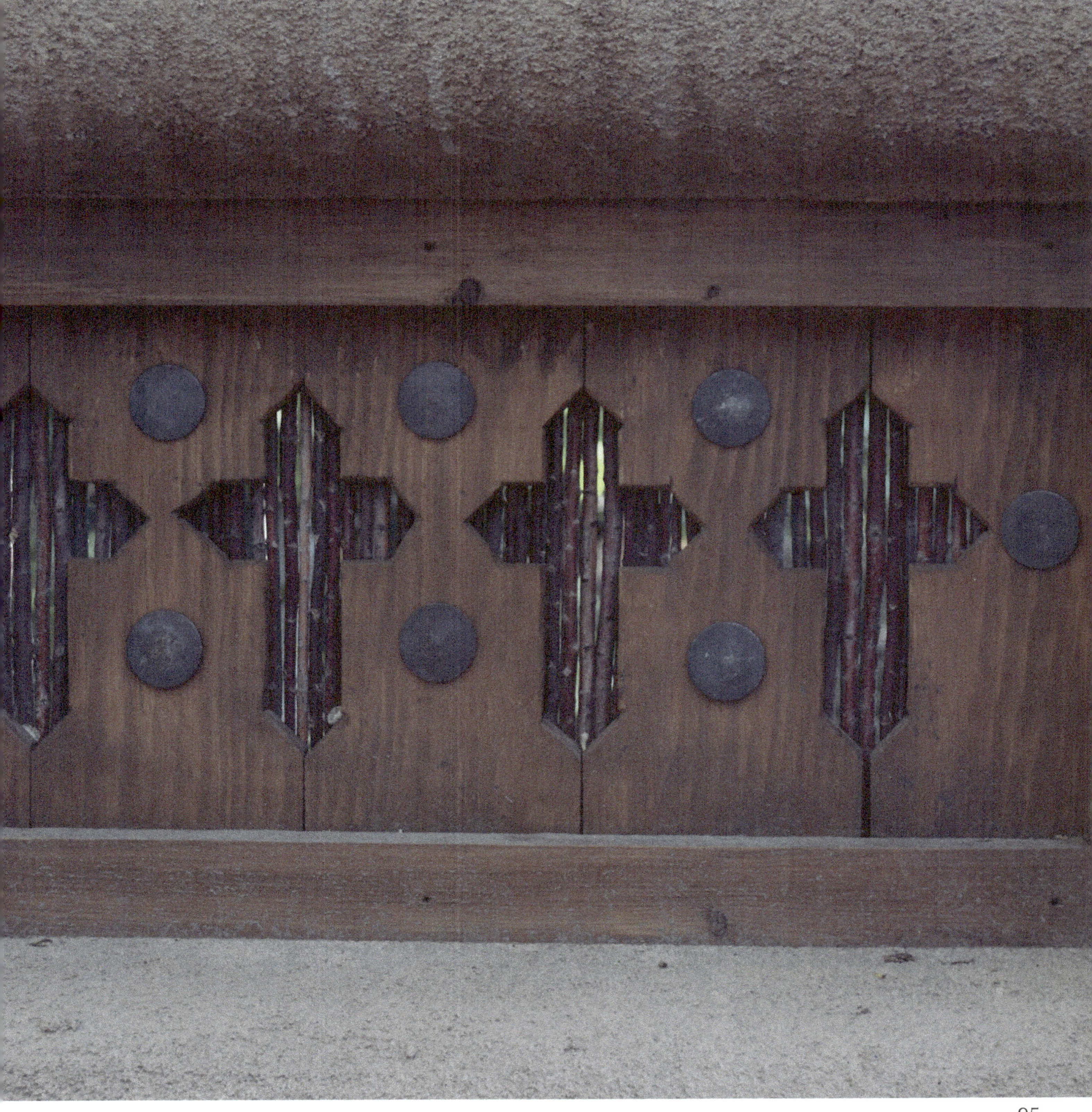

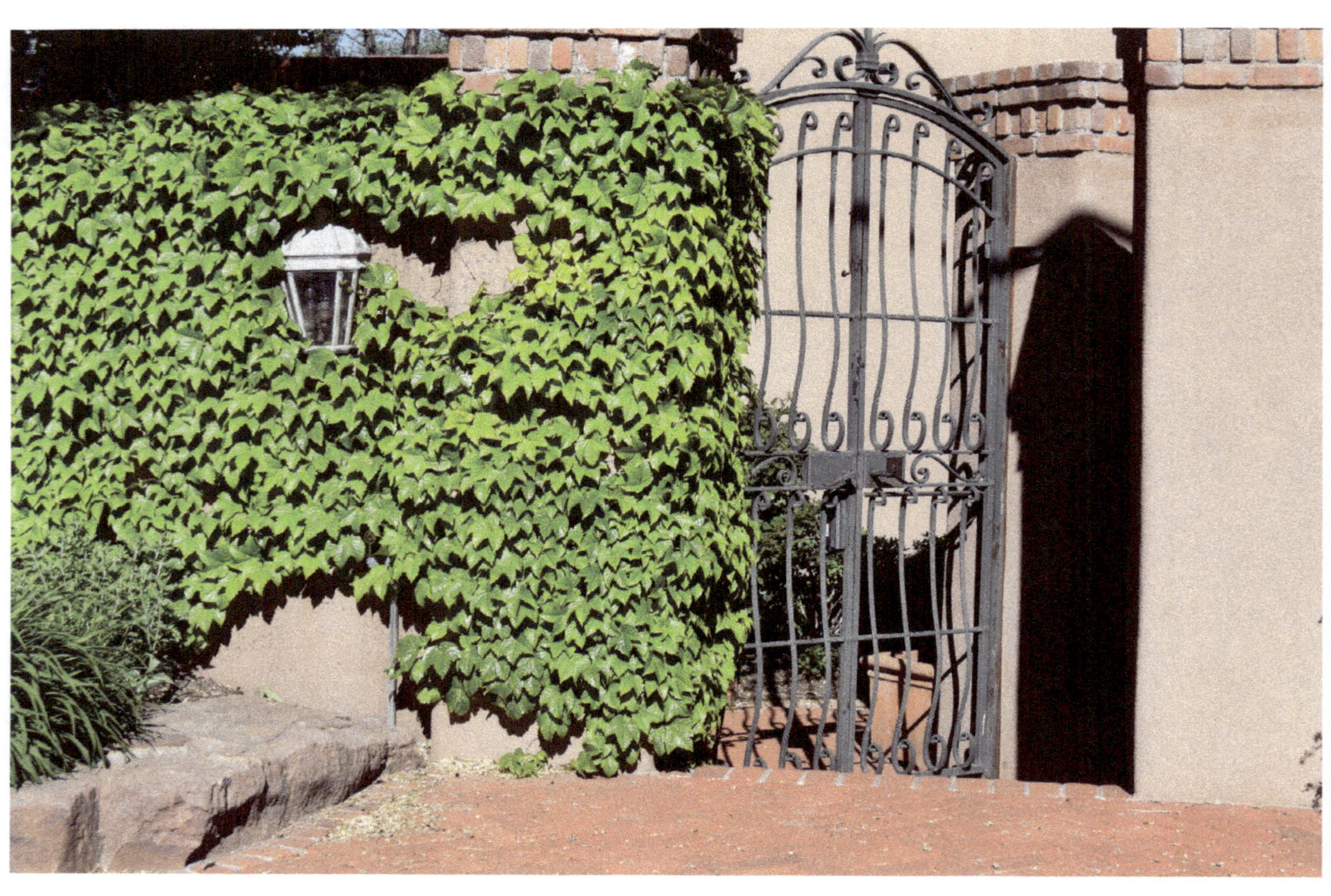

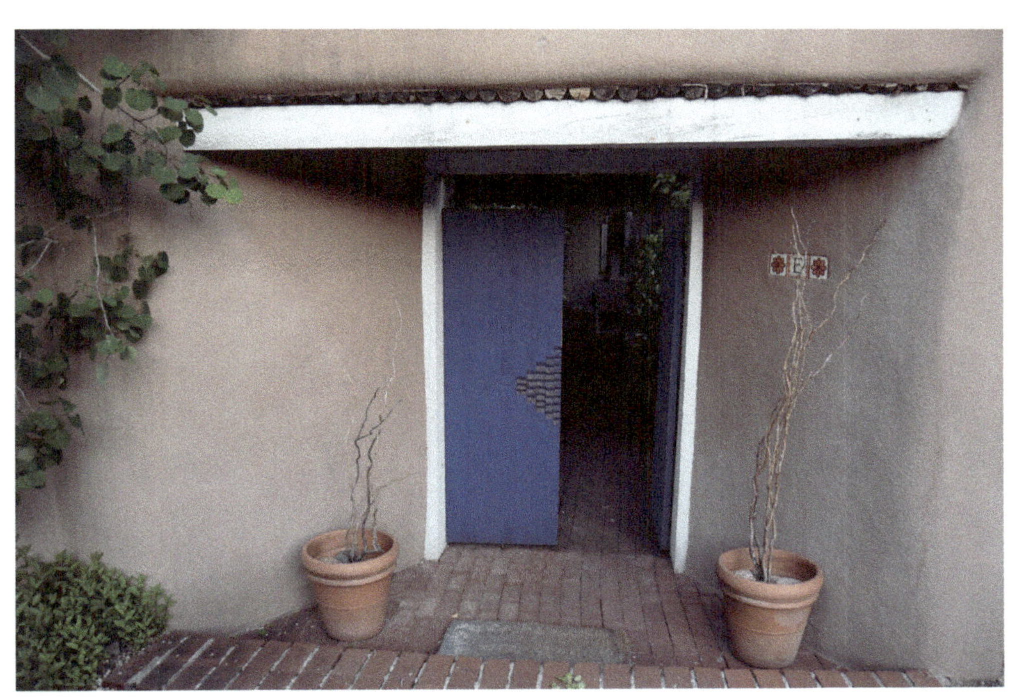

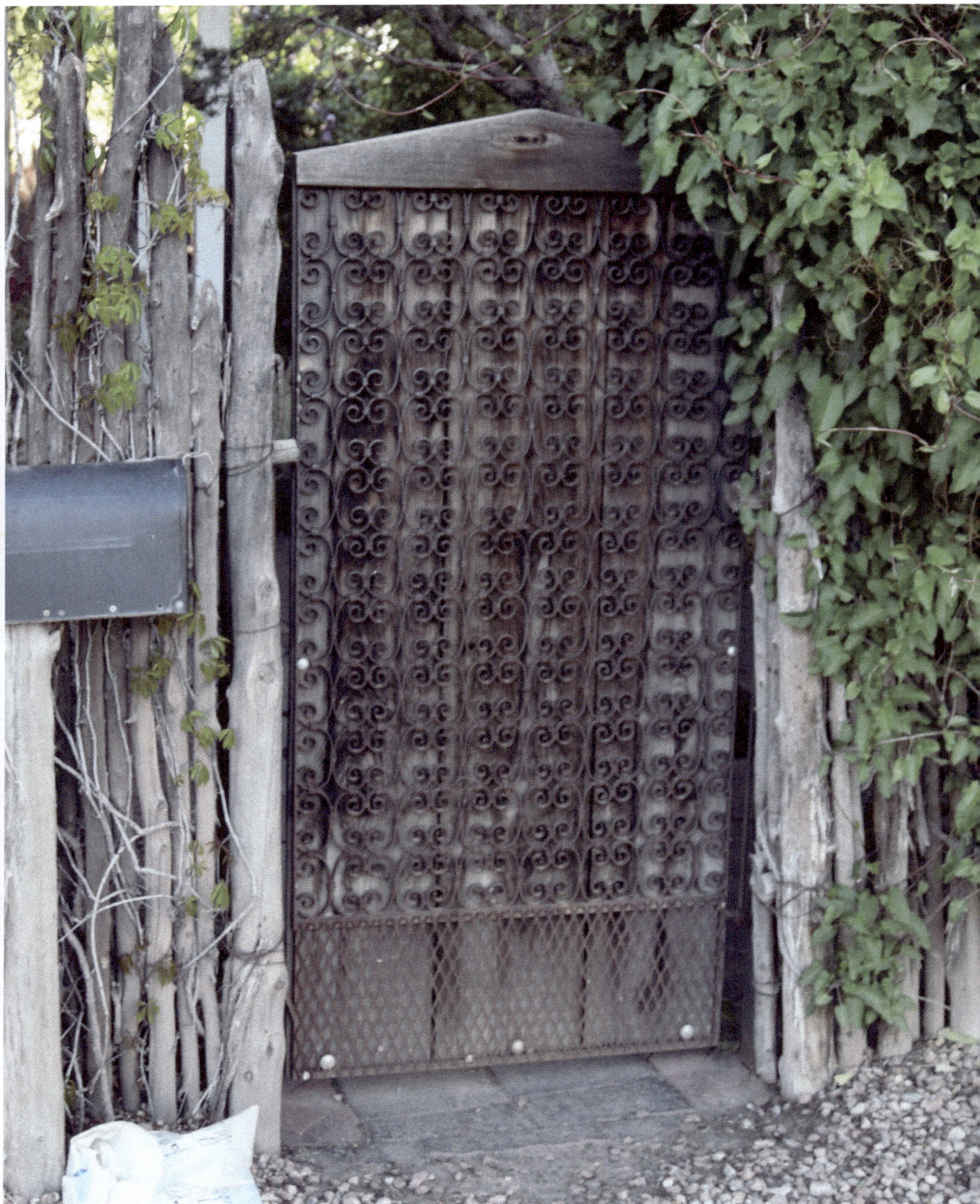

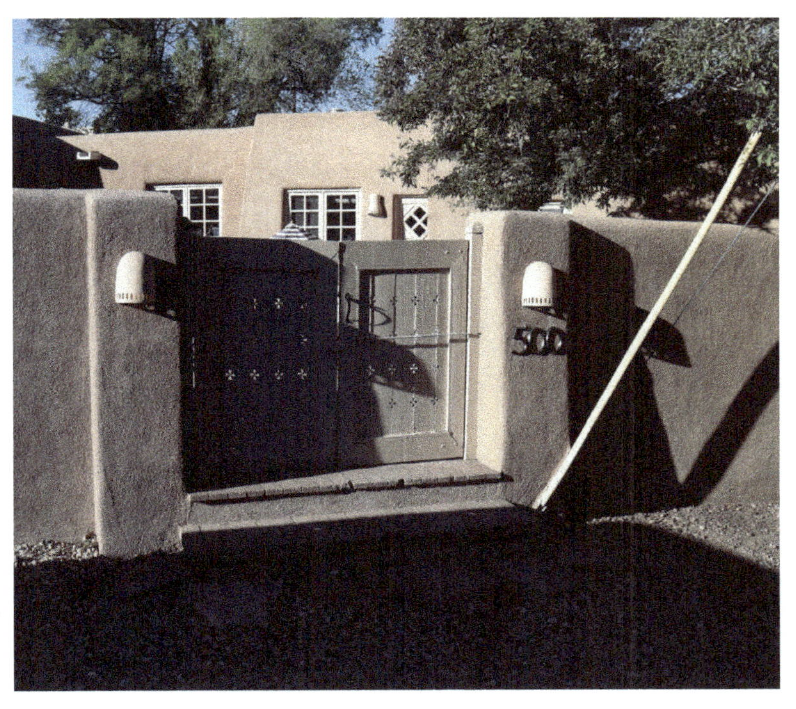
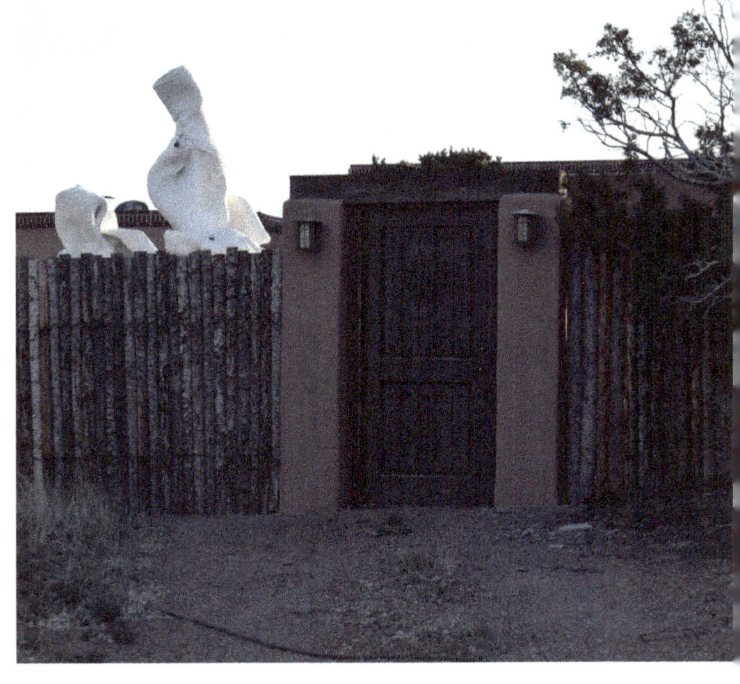
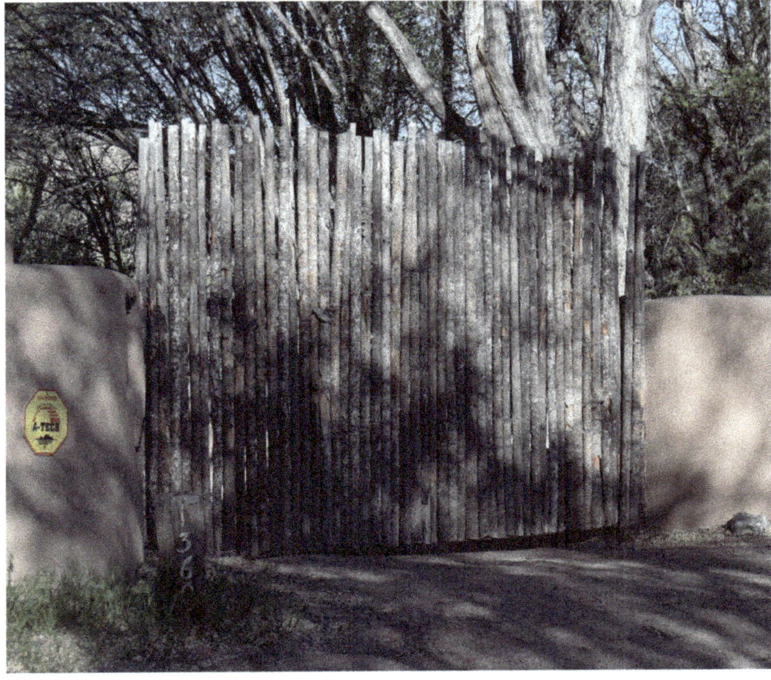
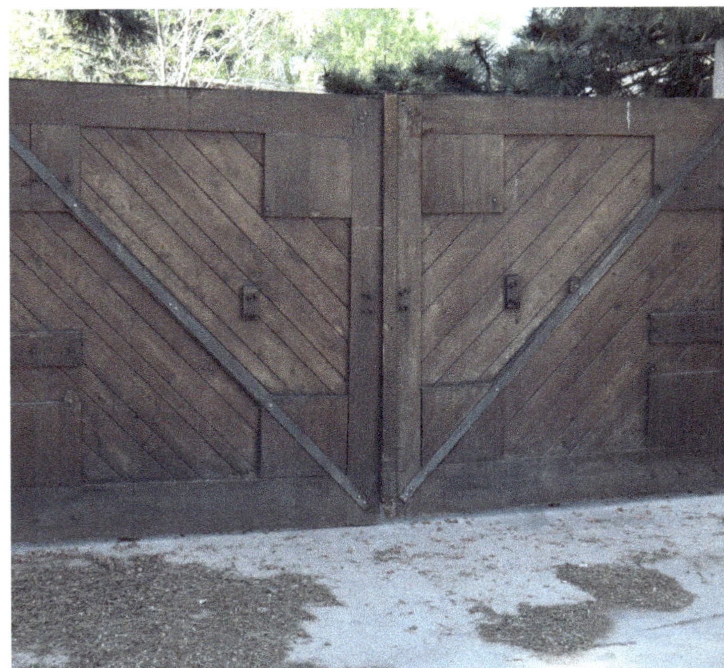

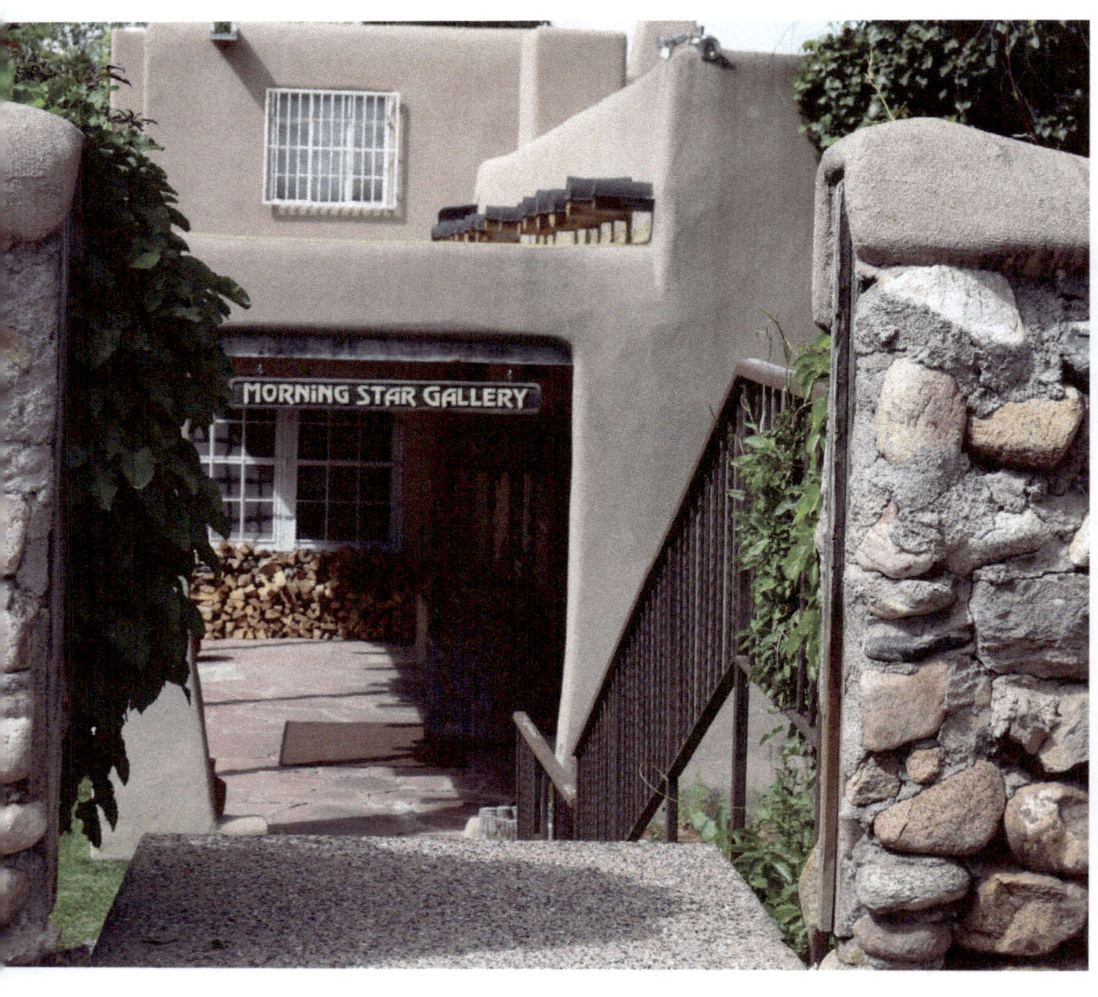

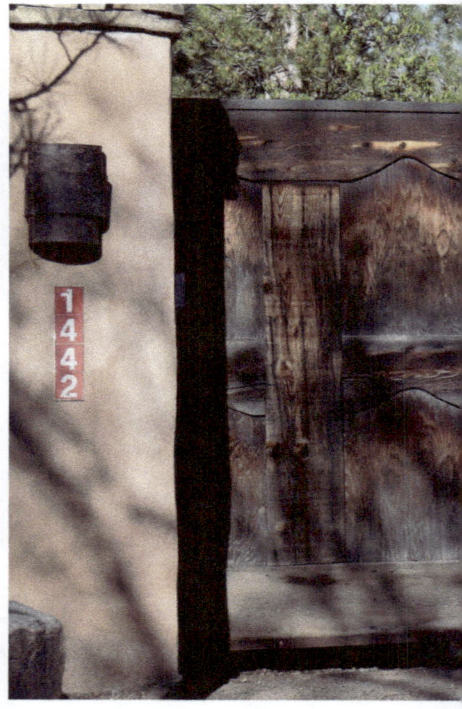

MORNING STAR GALLERY
1442

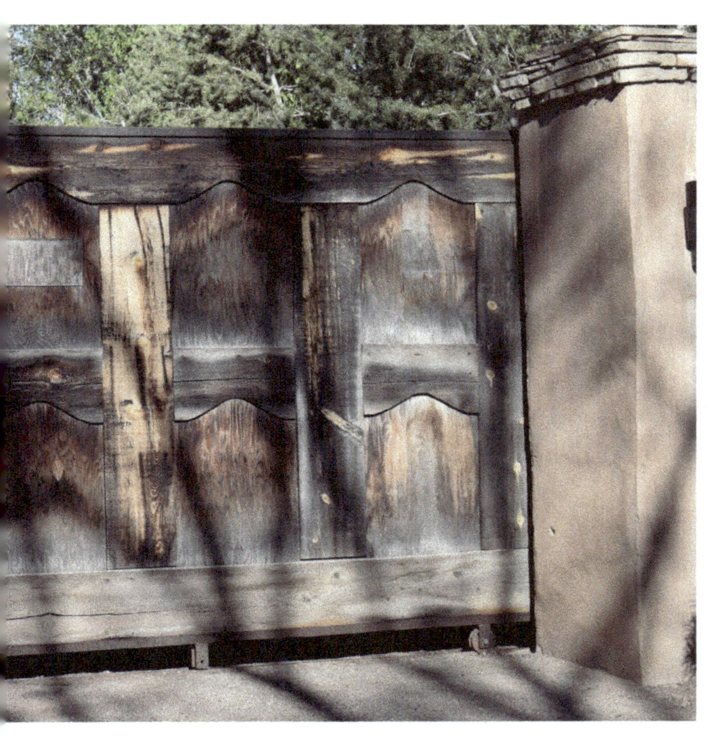

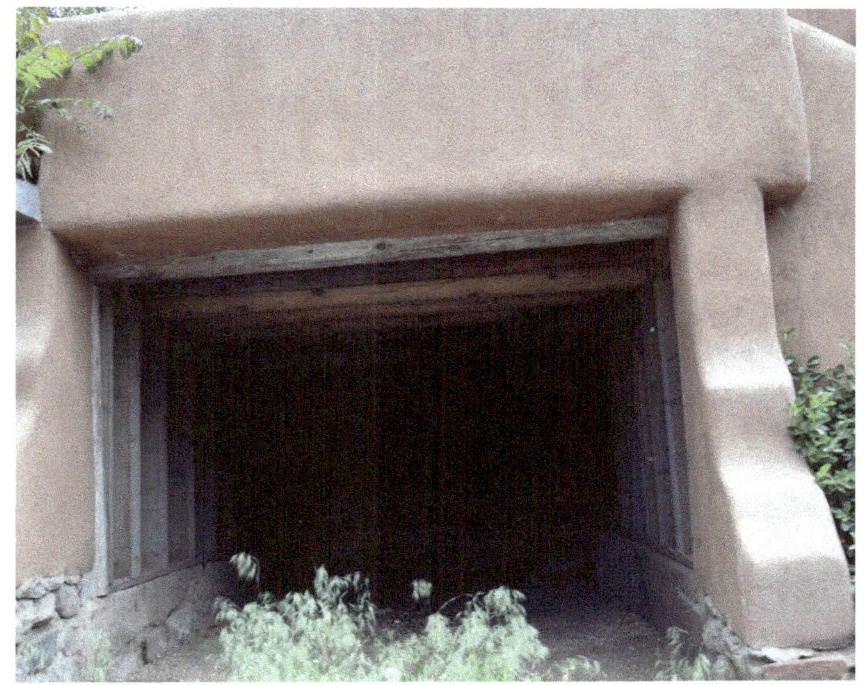

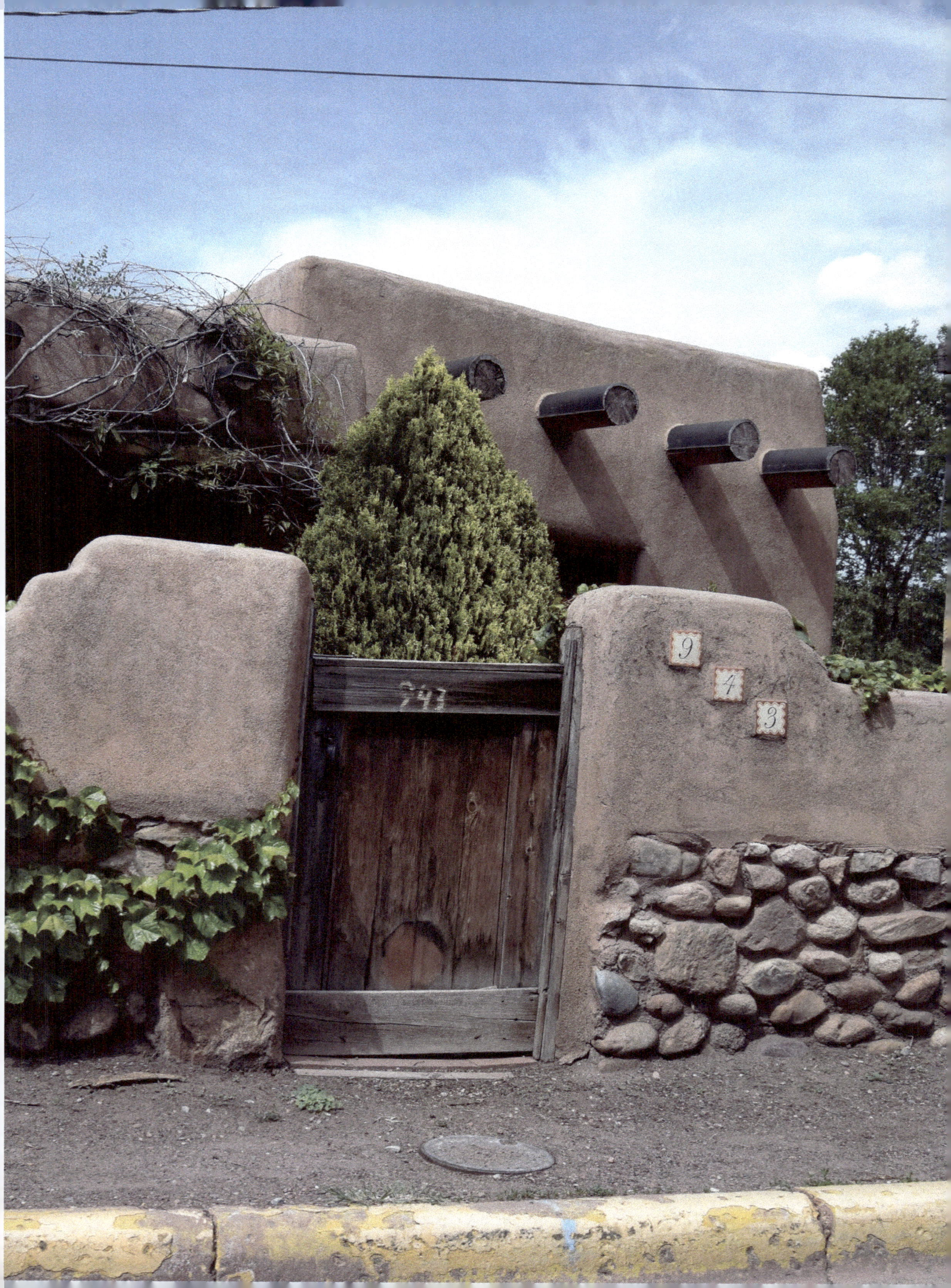
247
9
4
3

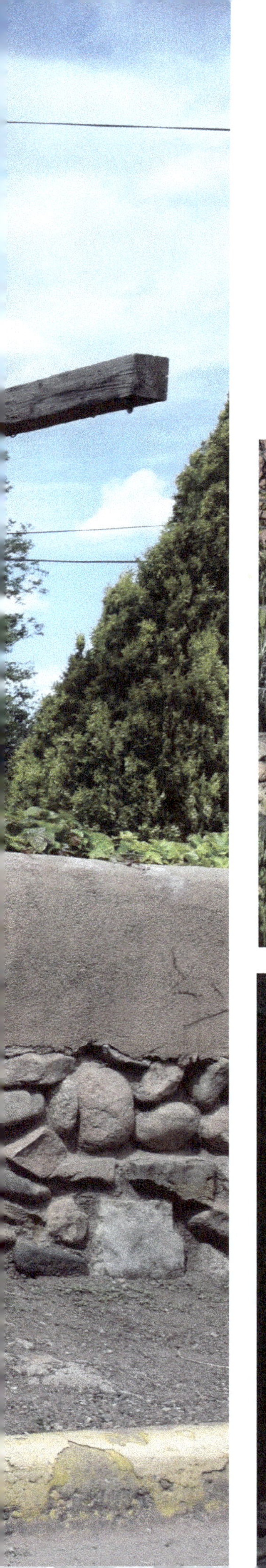

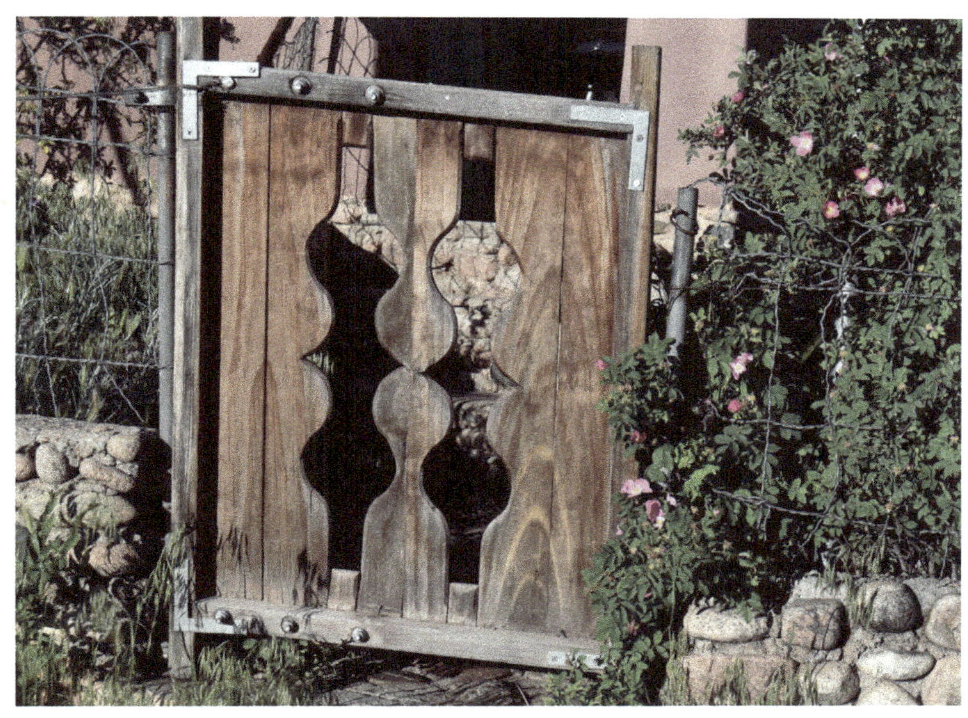

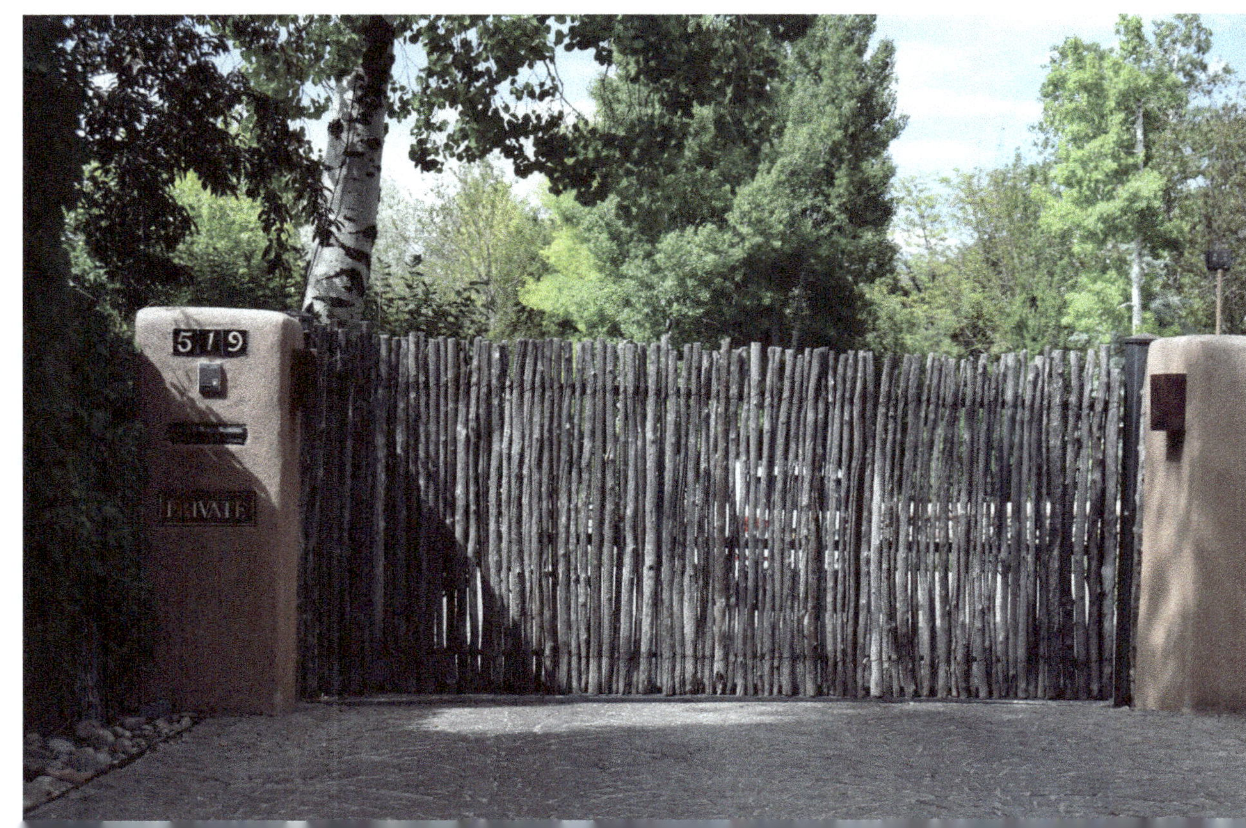

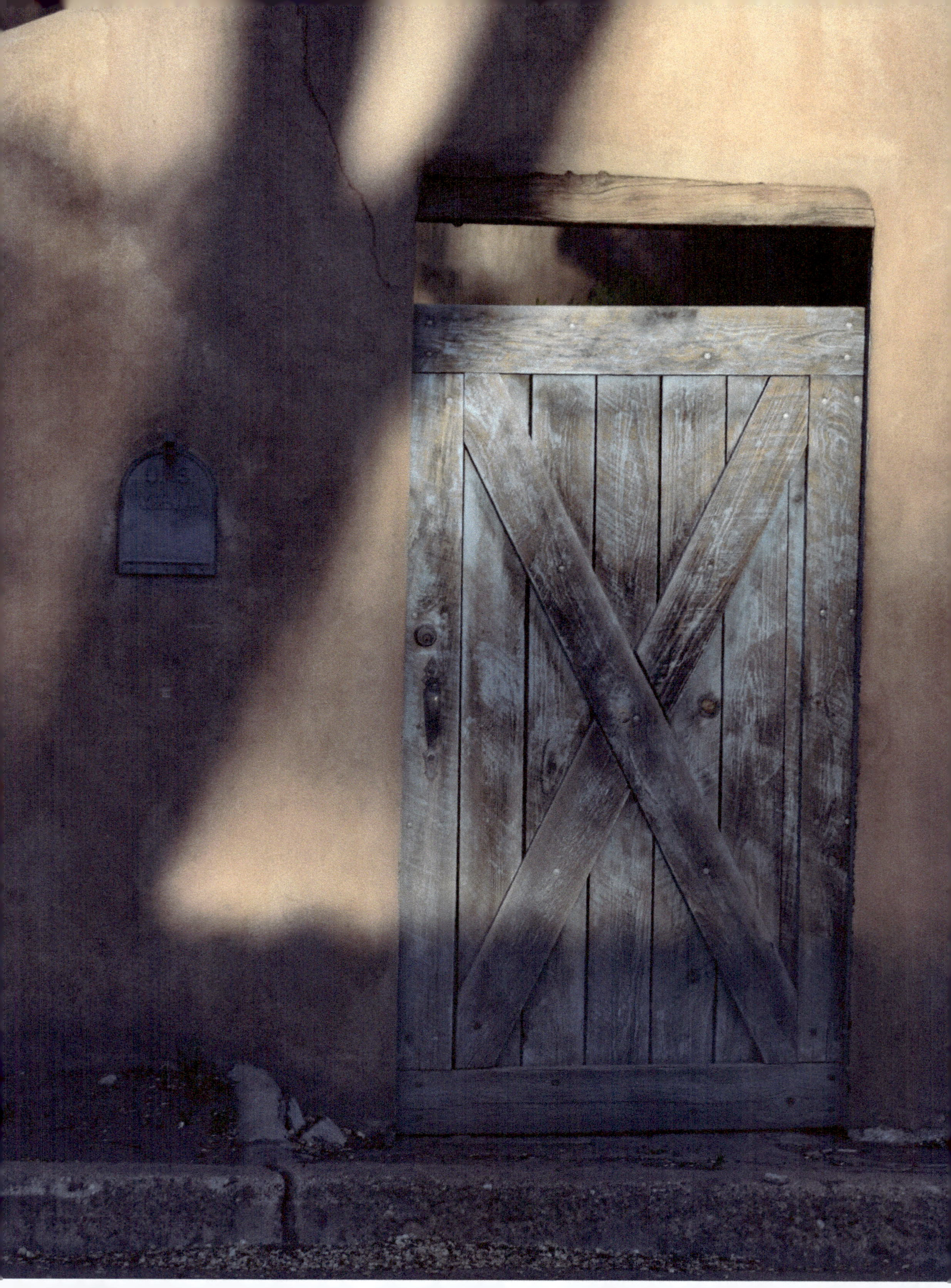

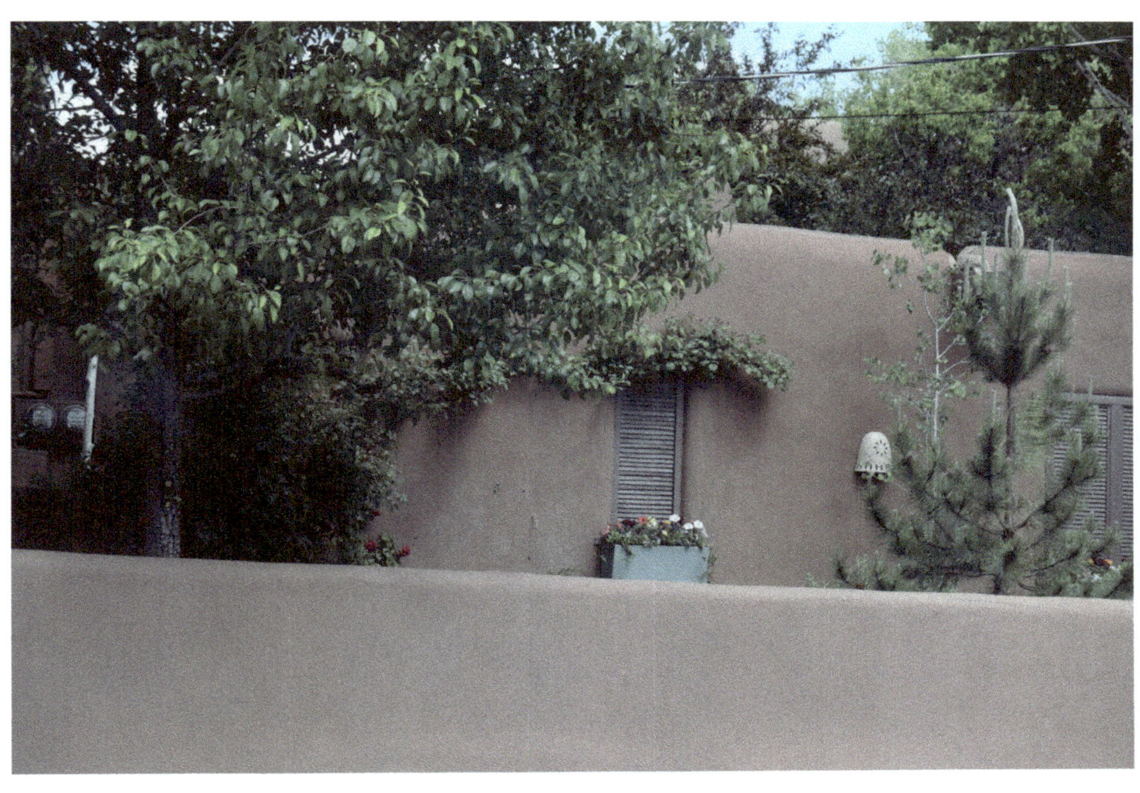

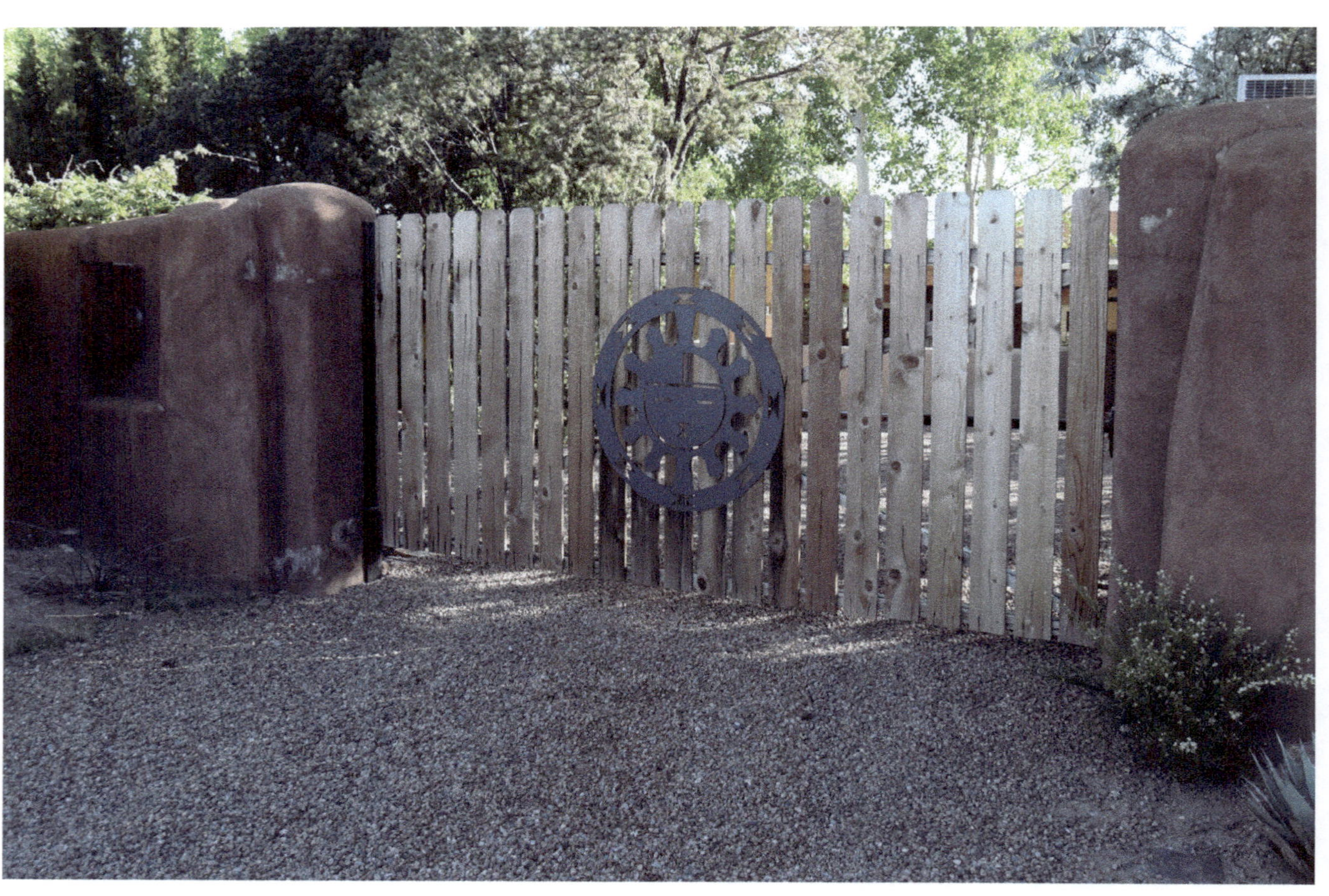

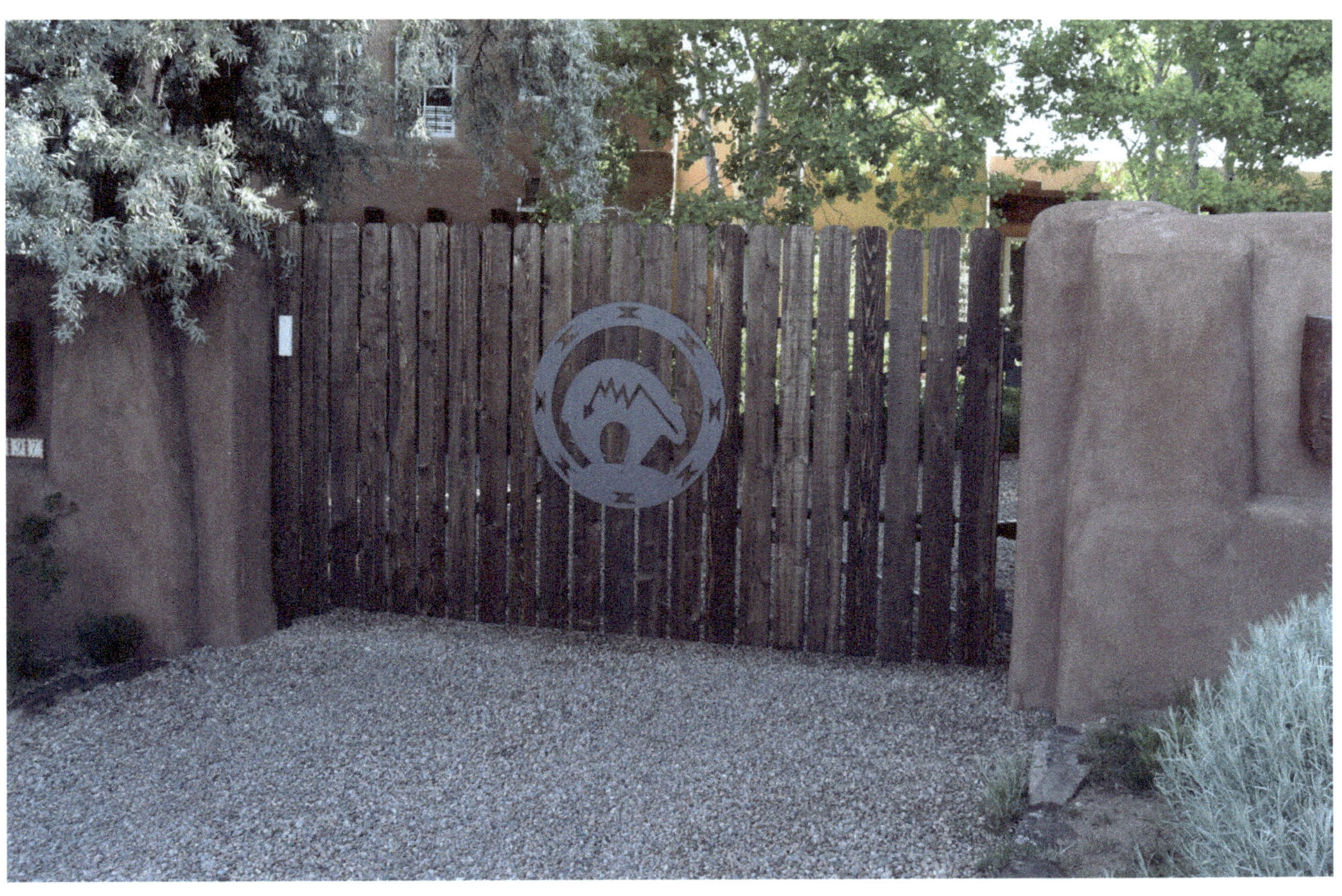

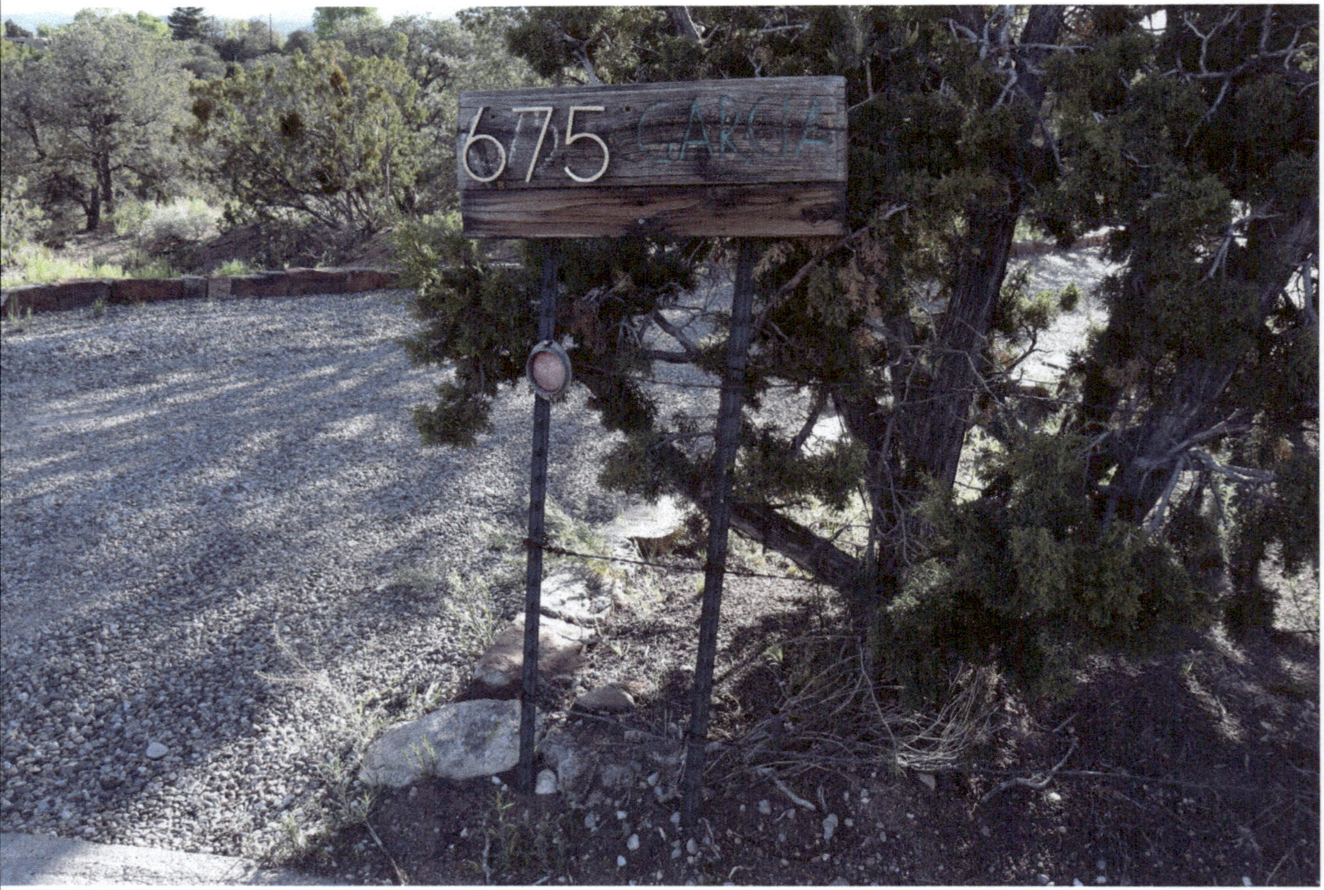

675 GARCIA

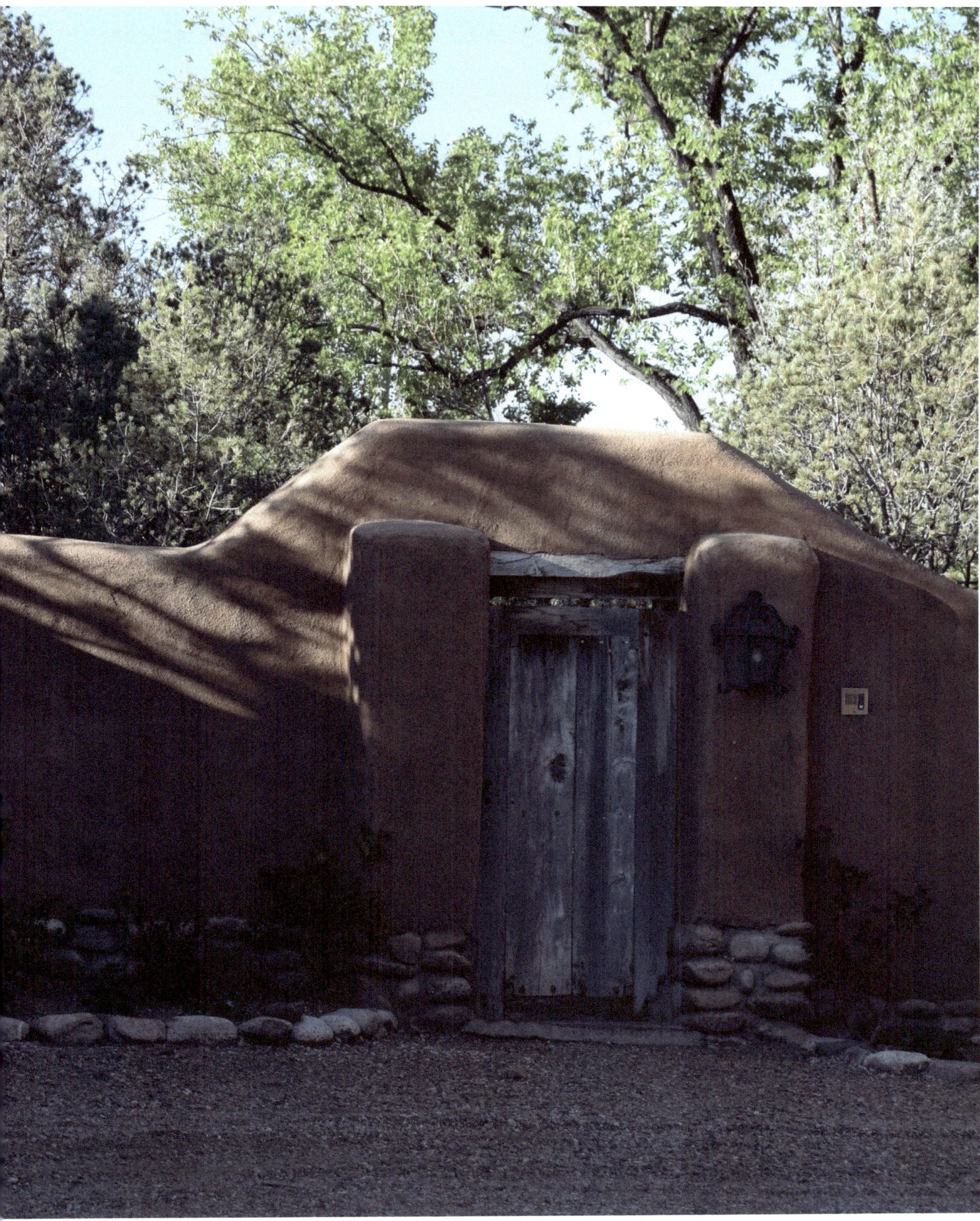

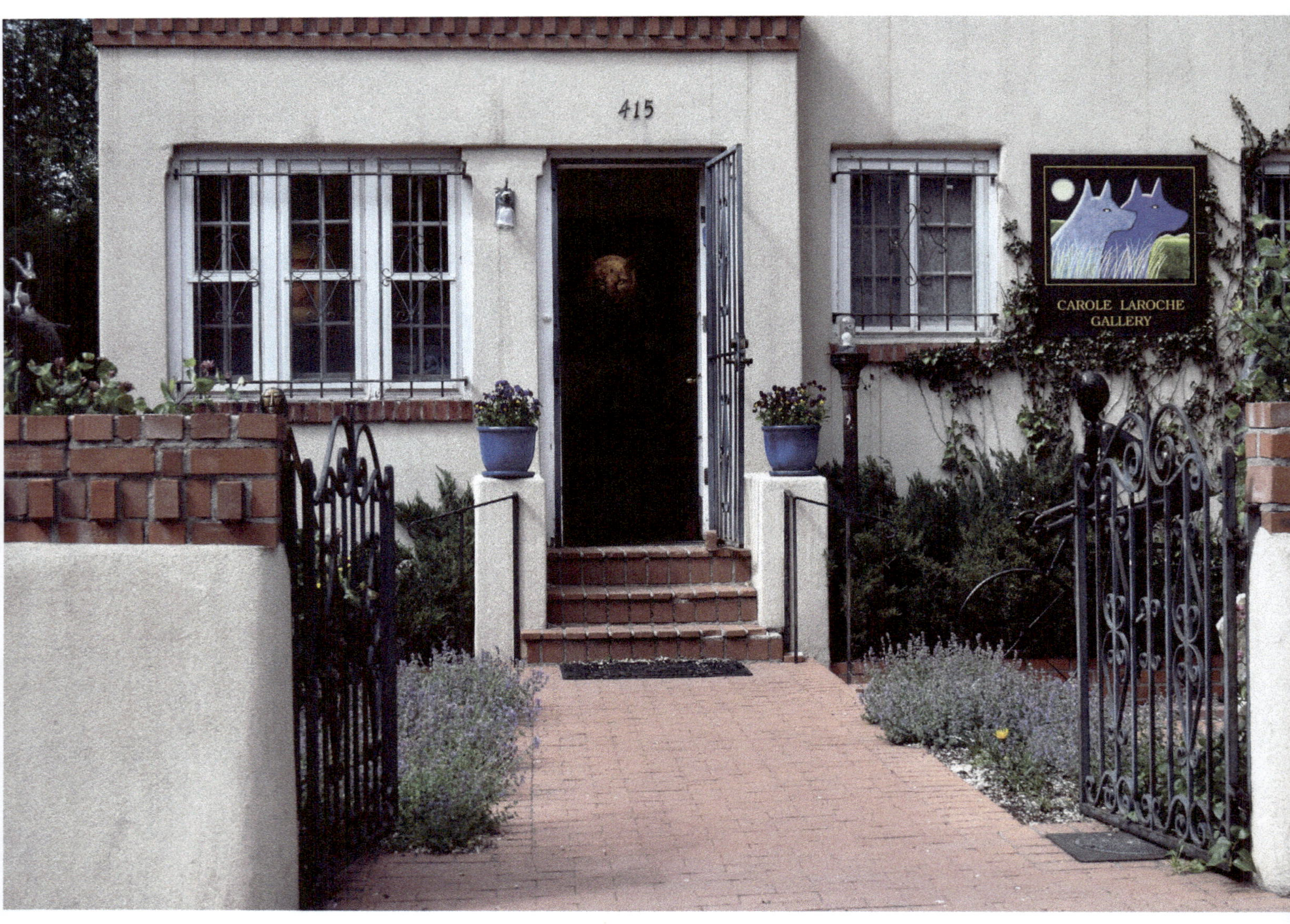
415
CAROLE LAROCHE
GALLERY

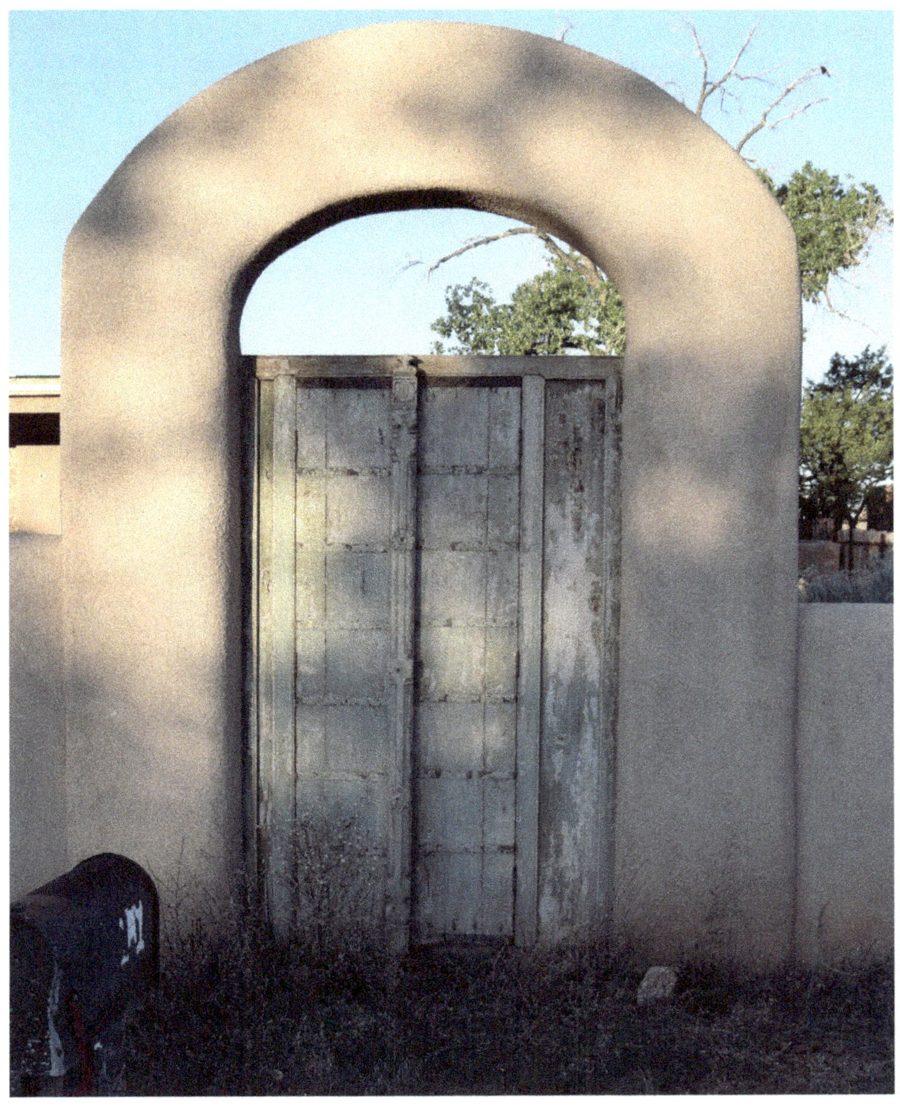

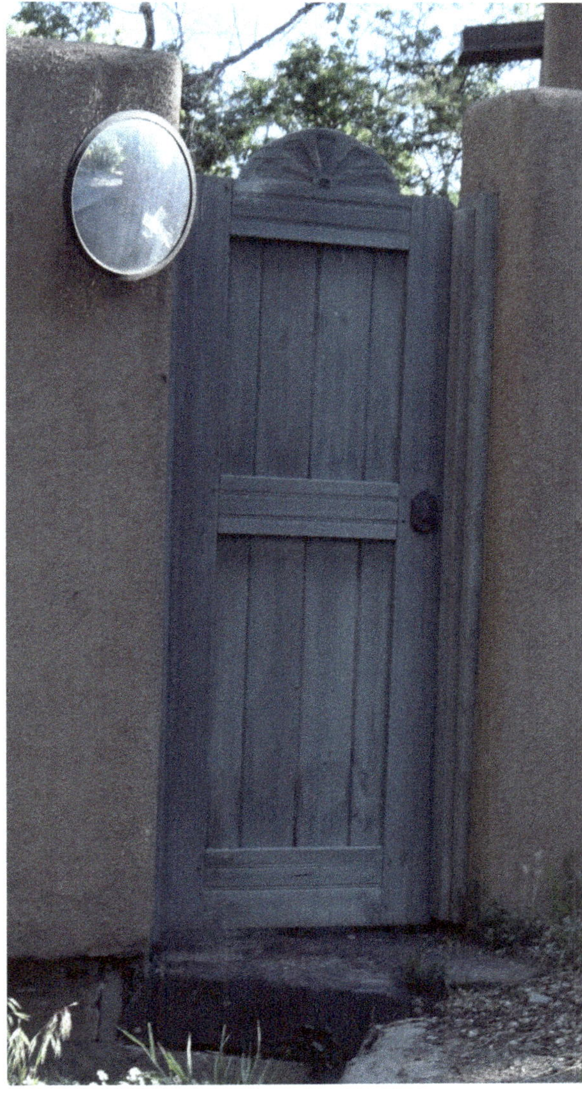

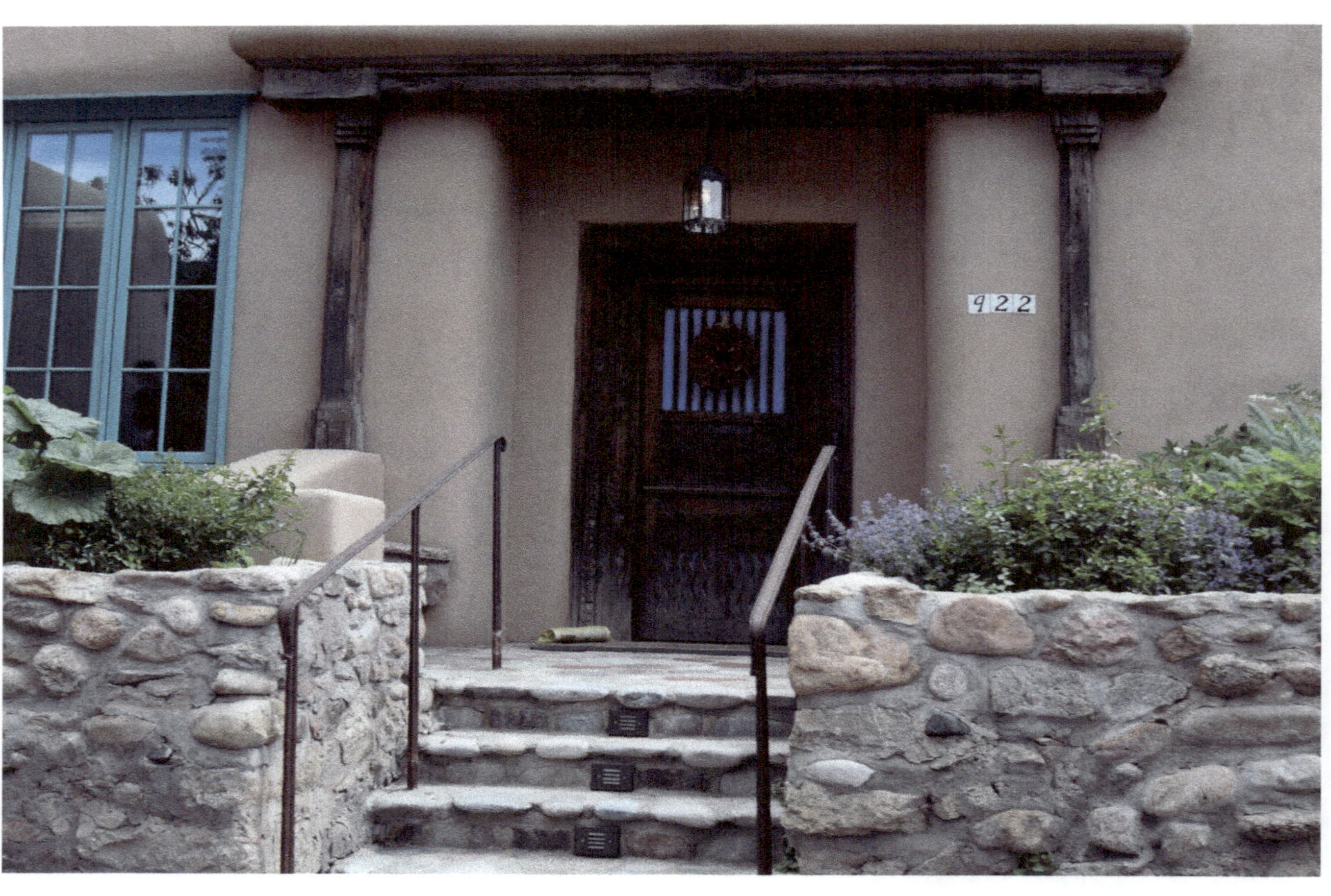

922

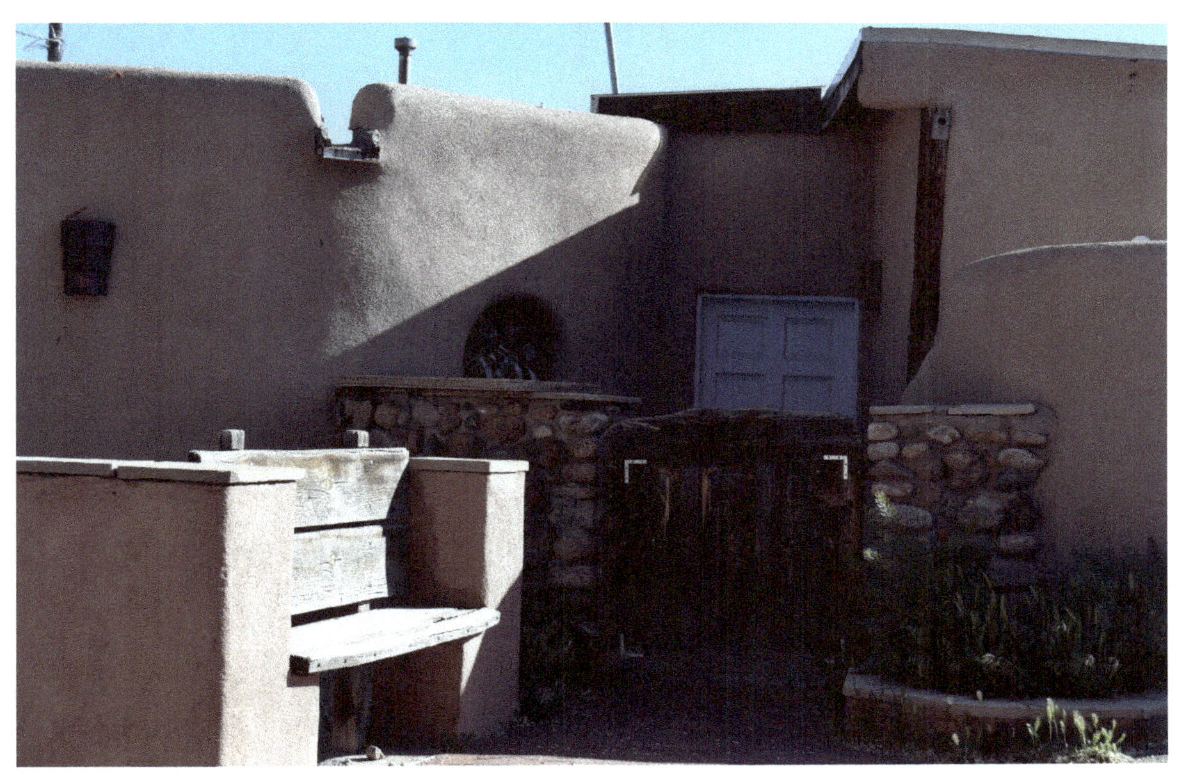

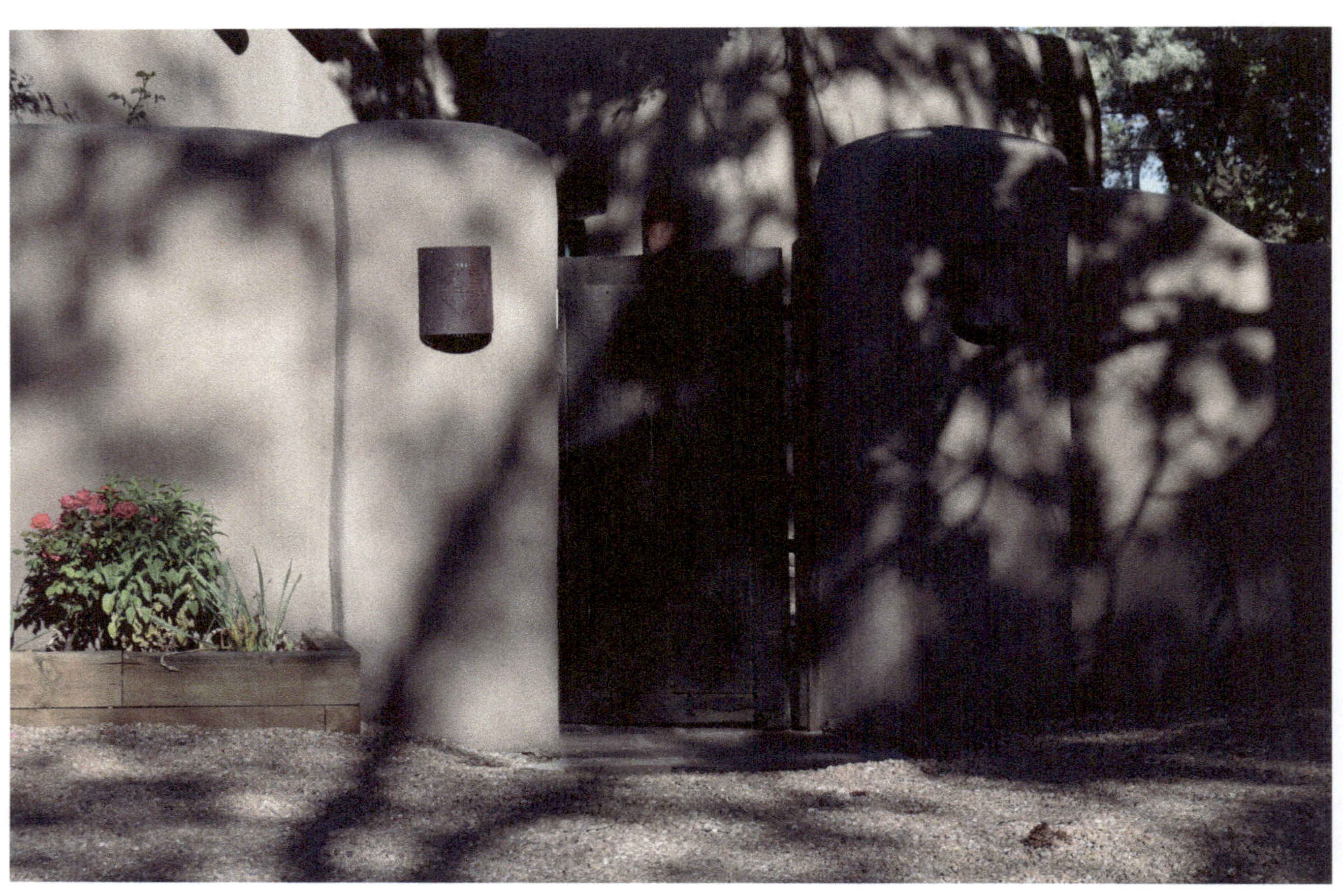

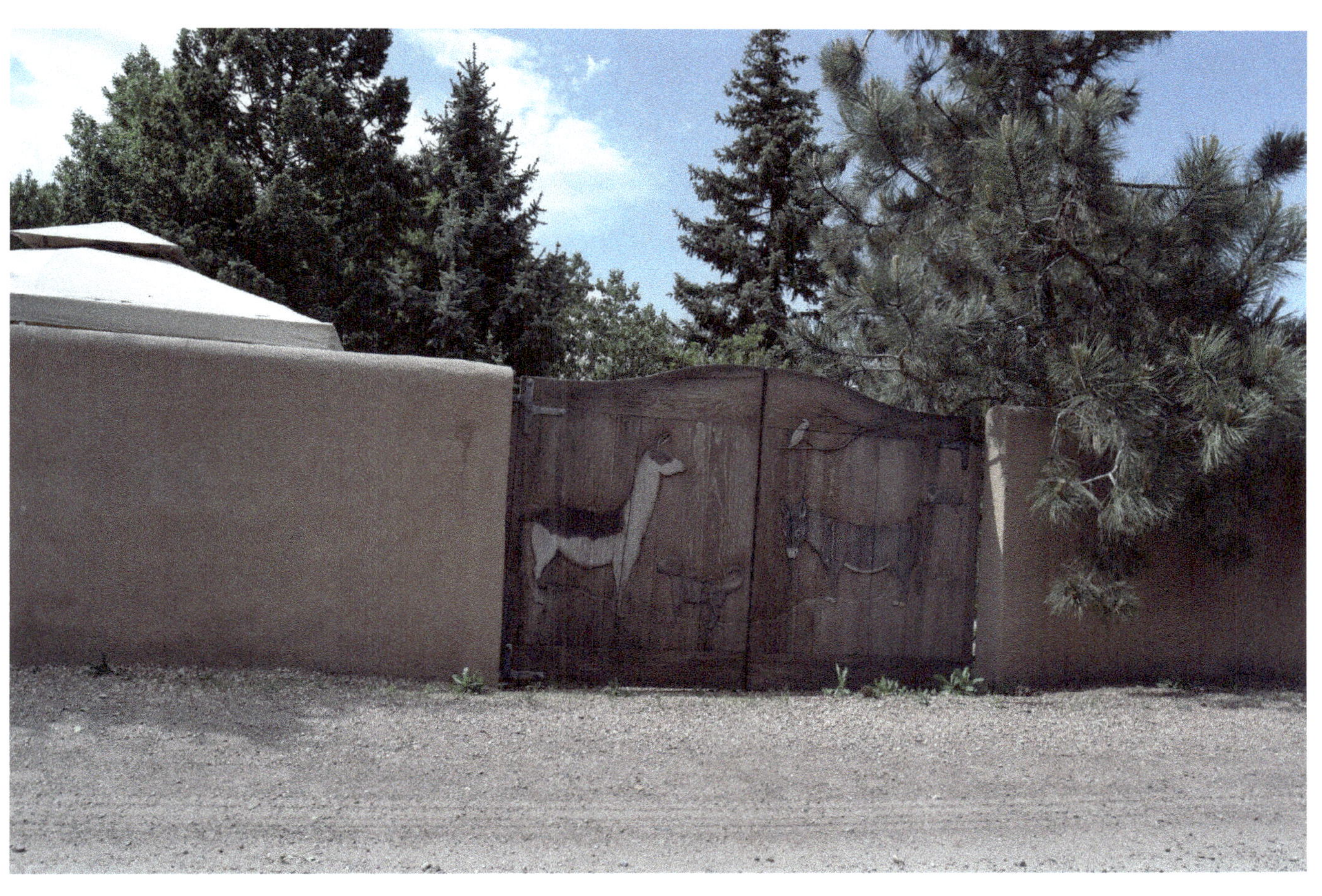

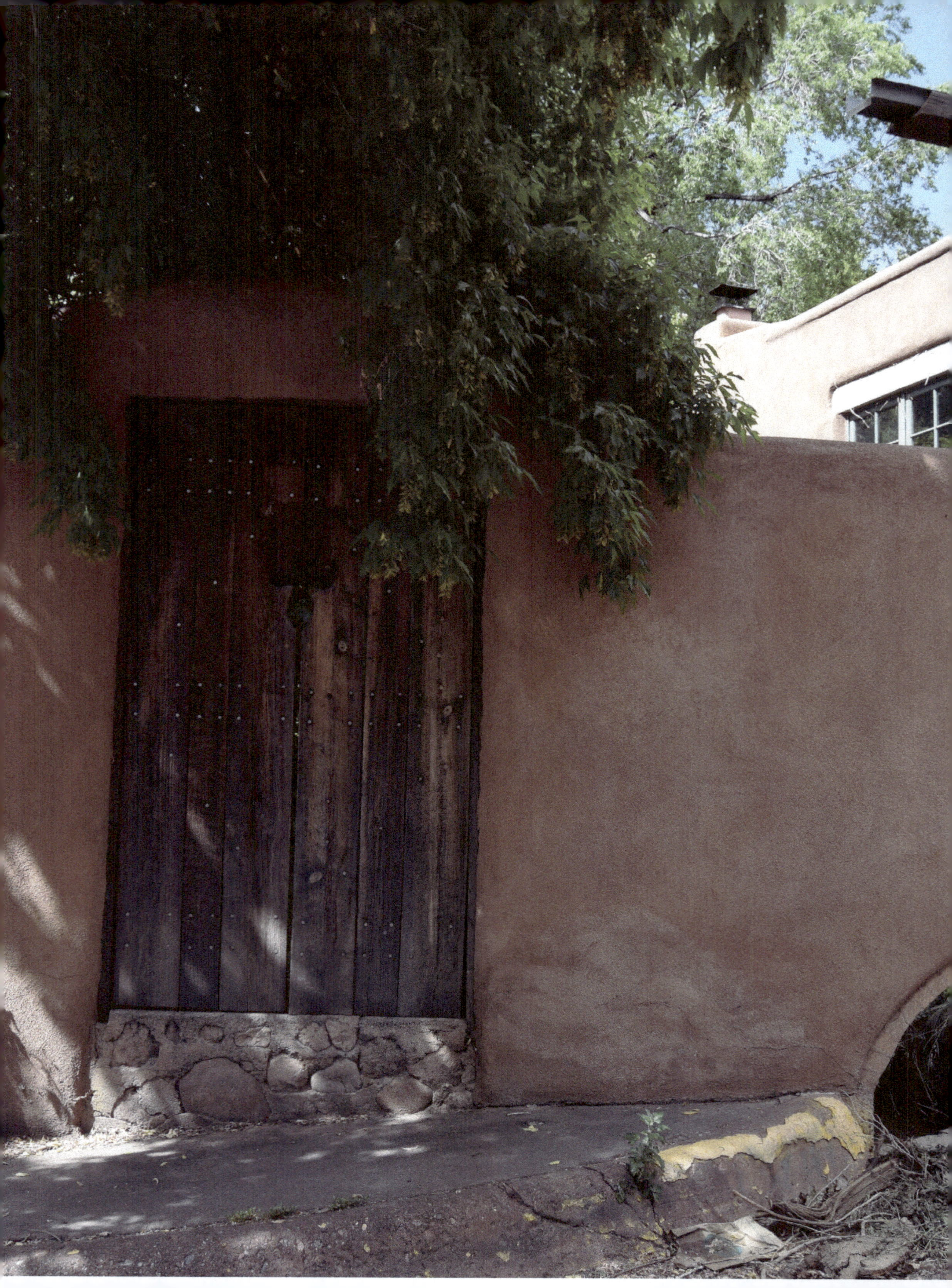

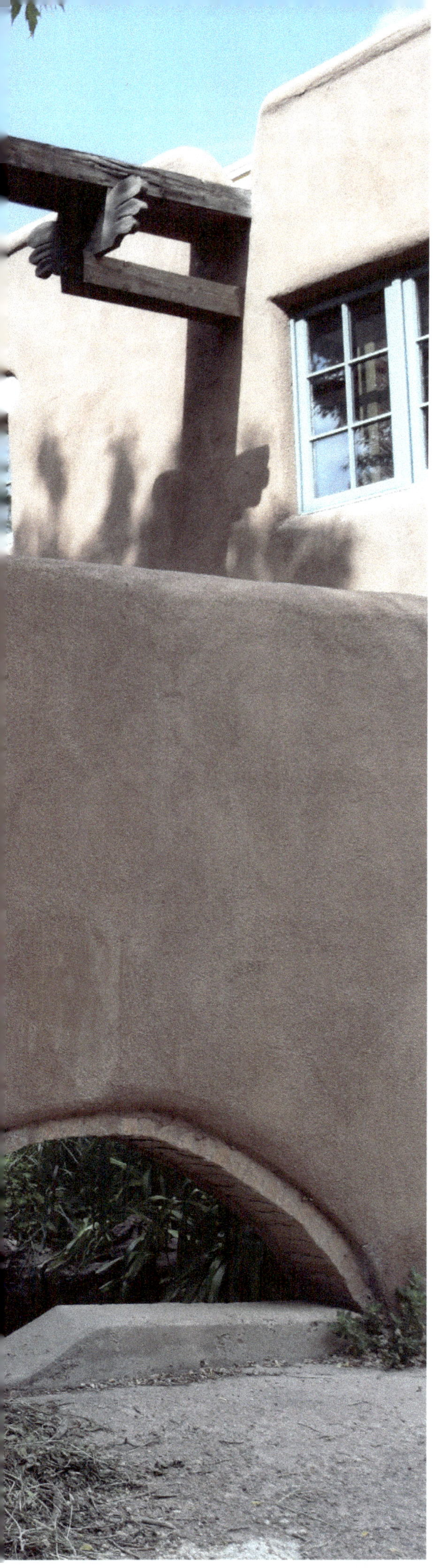

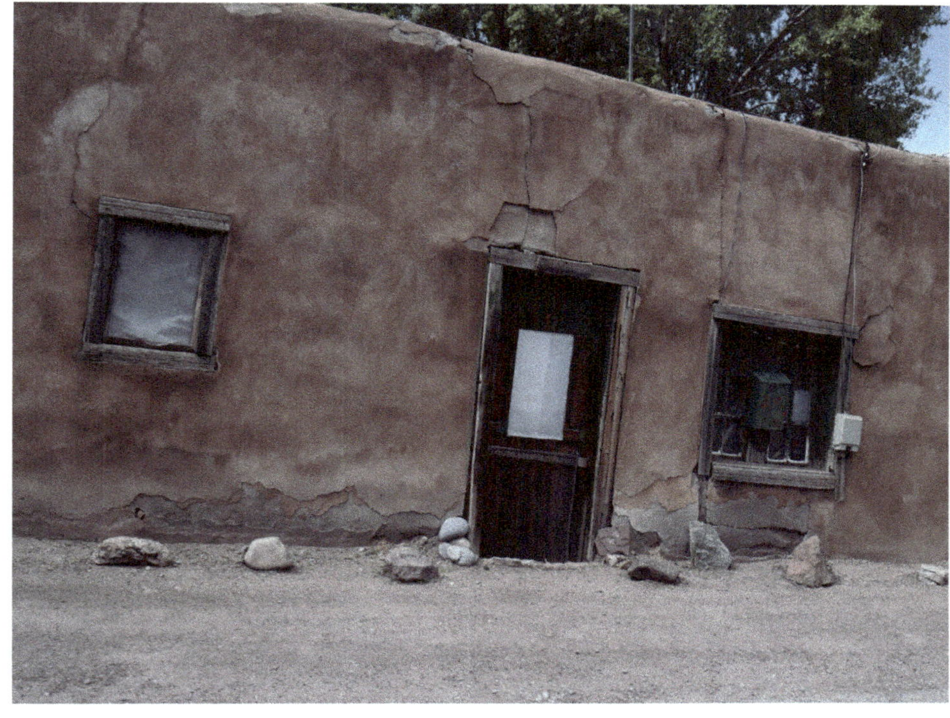

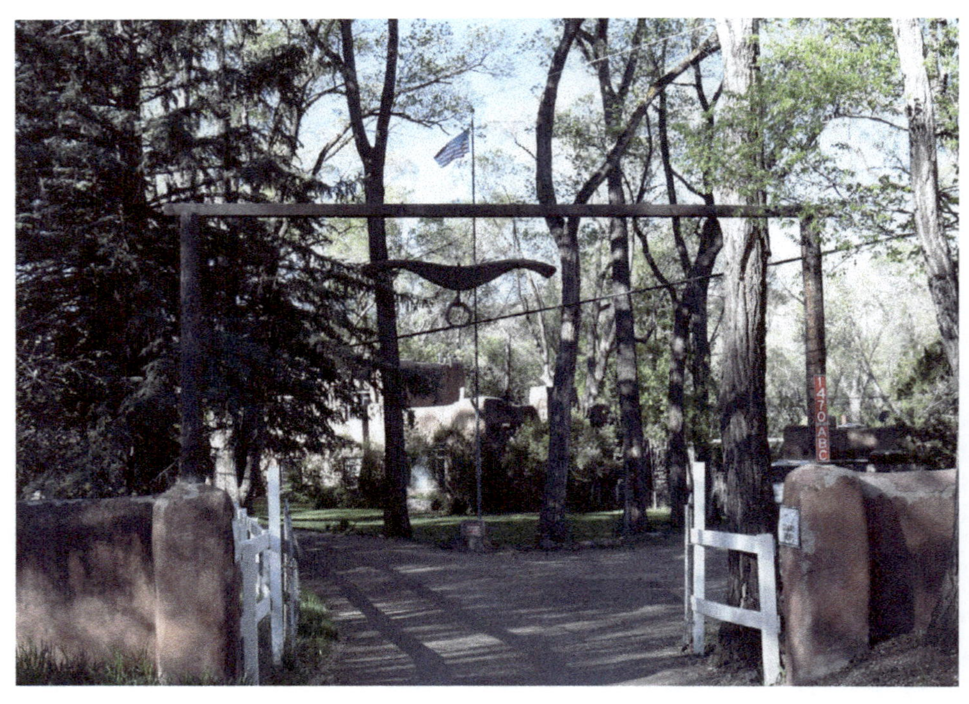

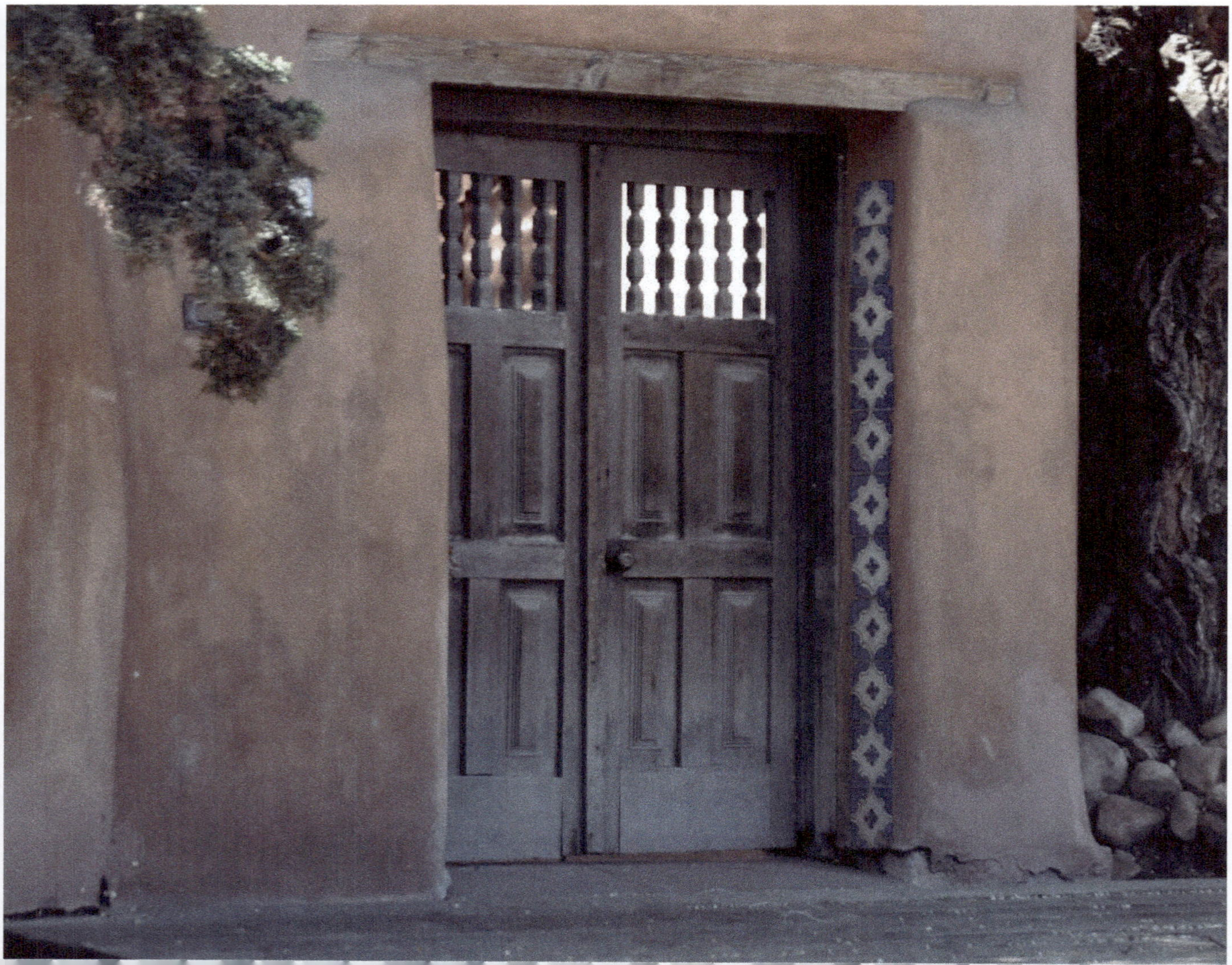

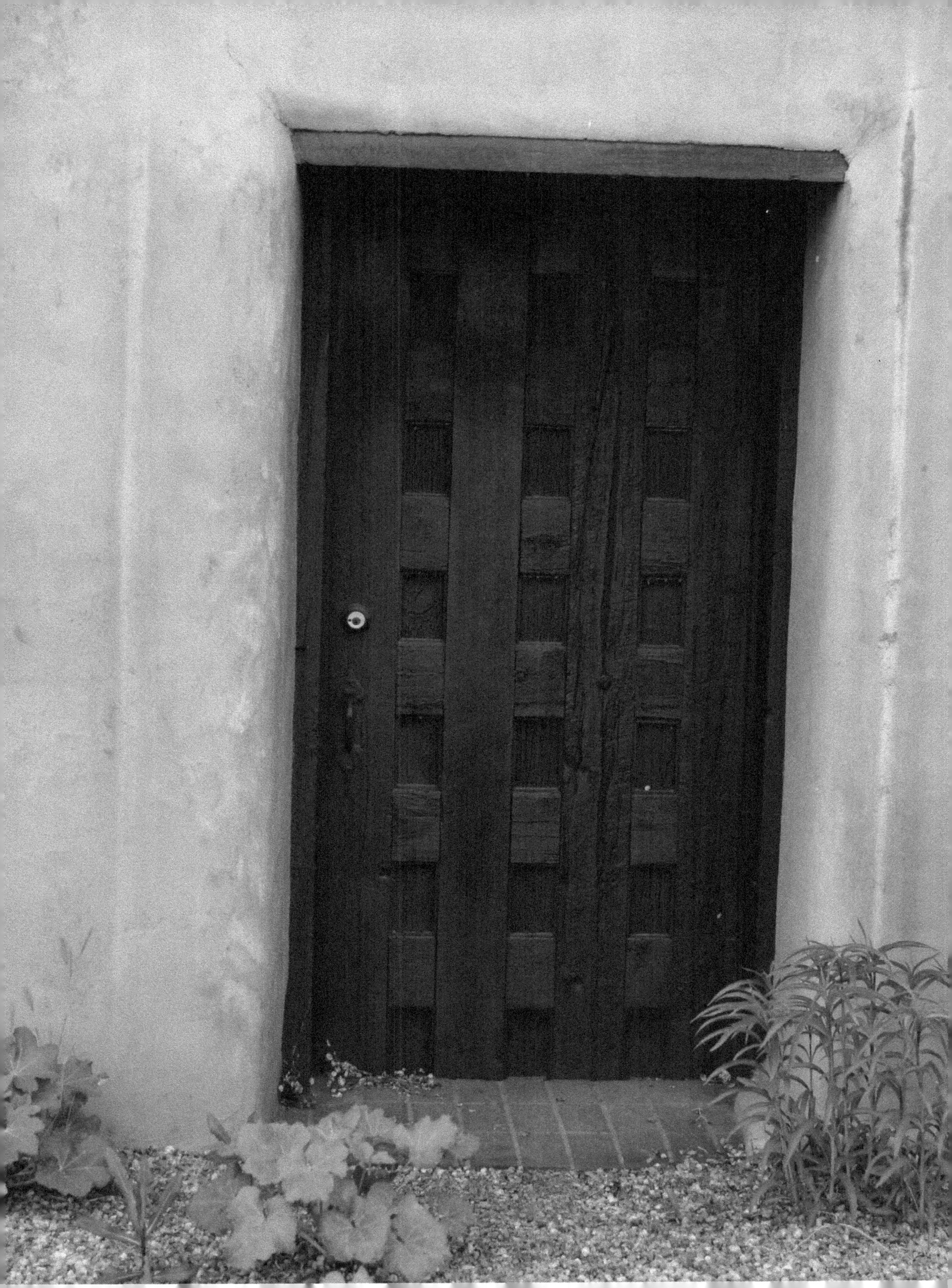

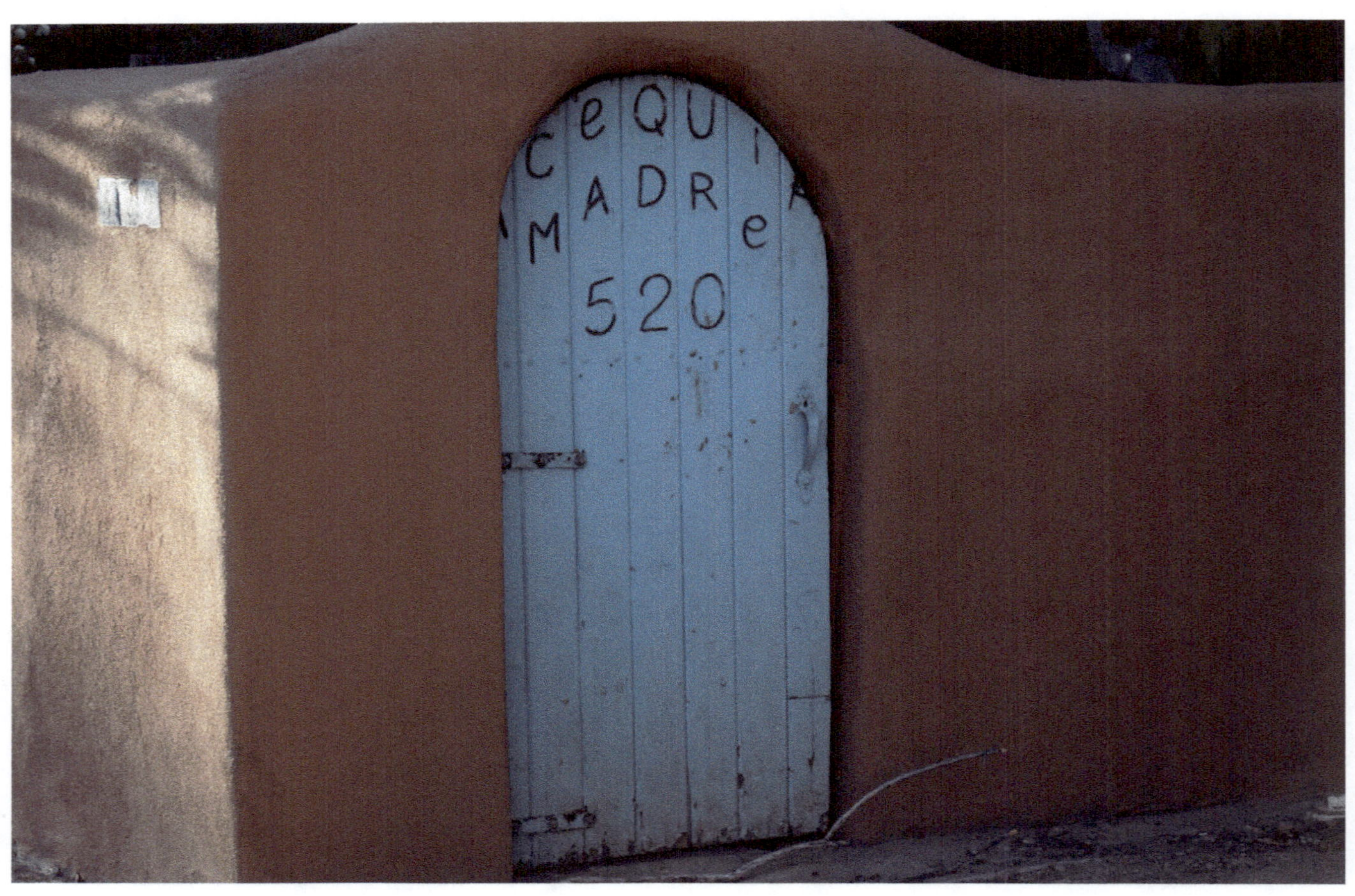
ACeQUIA
MADRe
520

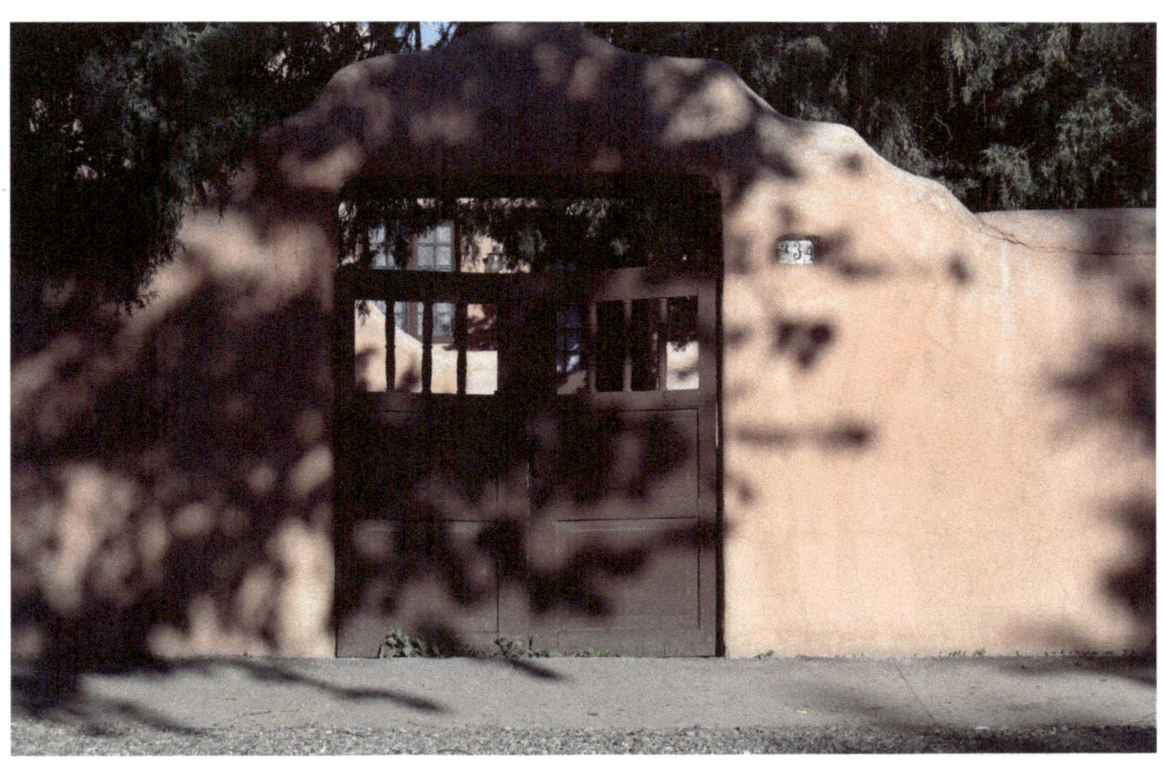

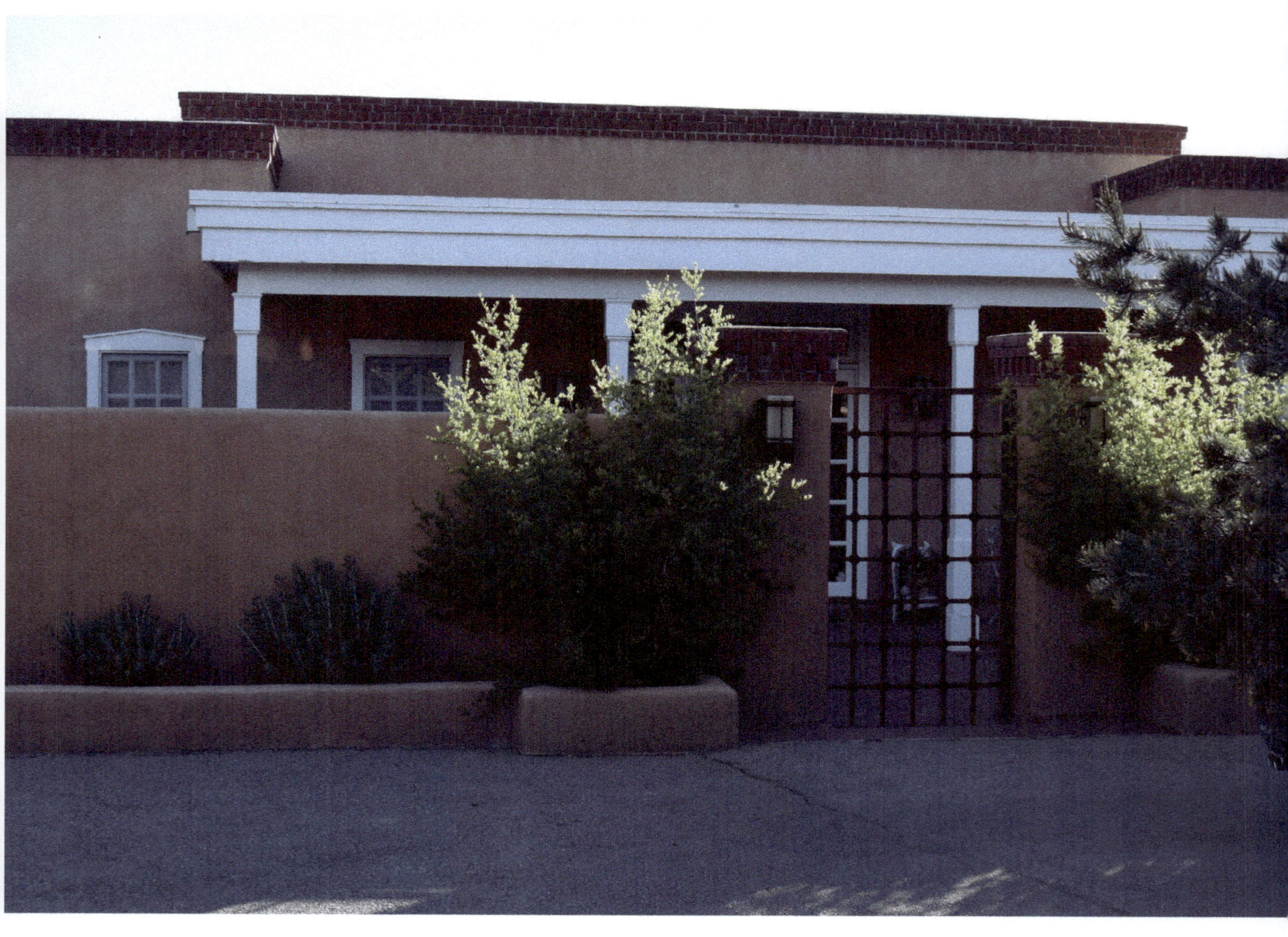

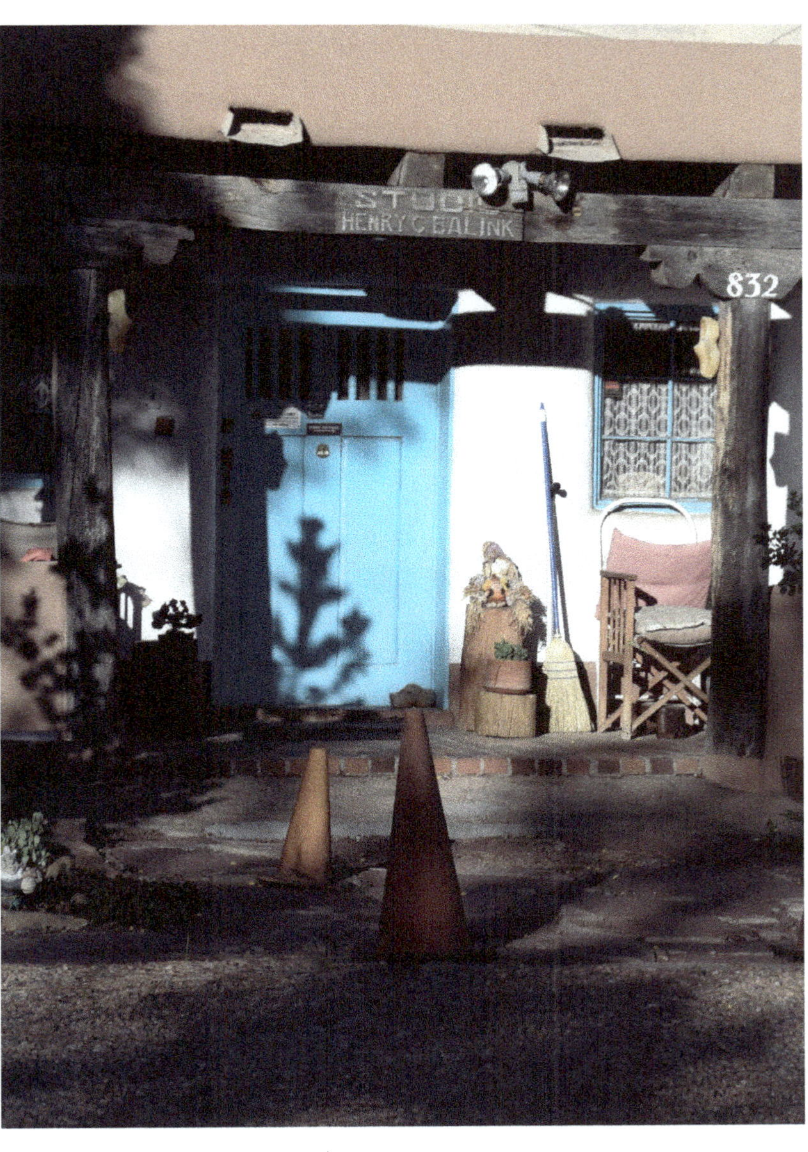
STUDIO
HENRY C BALINK
832

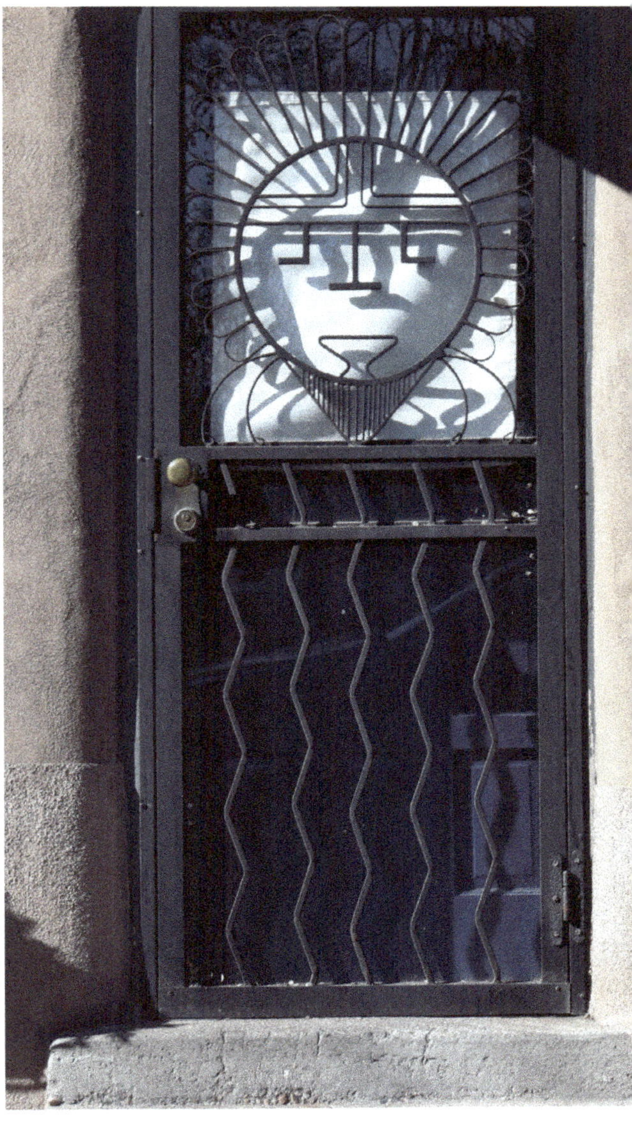

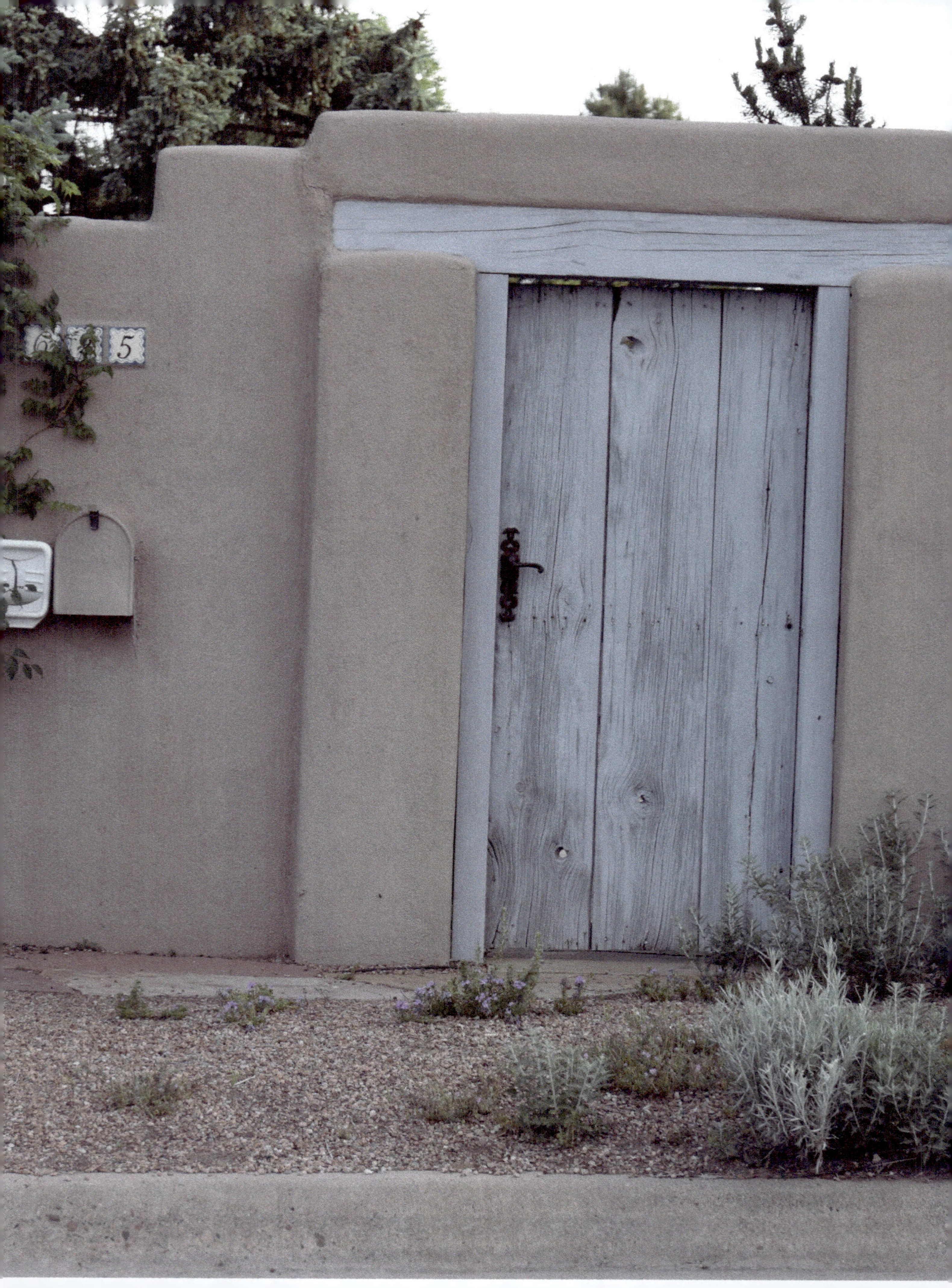

5

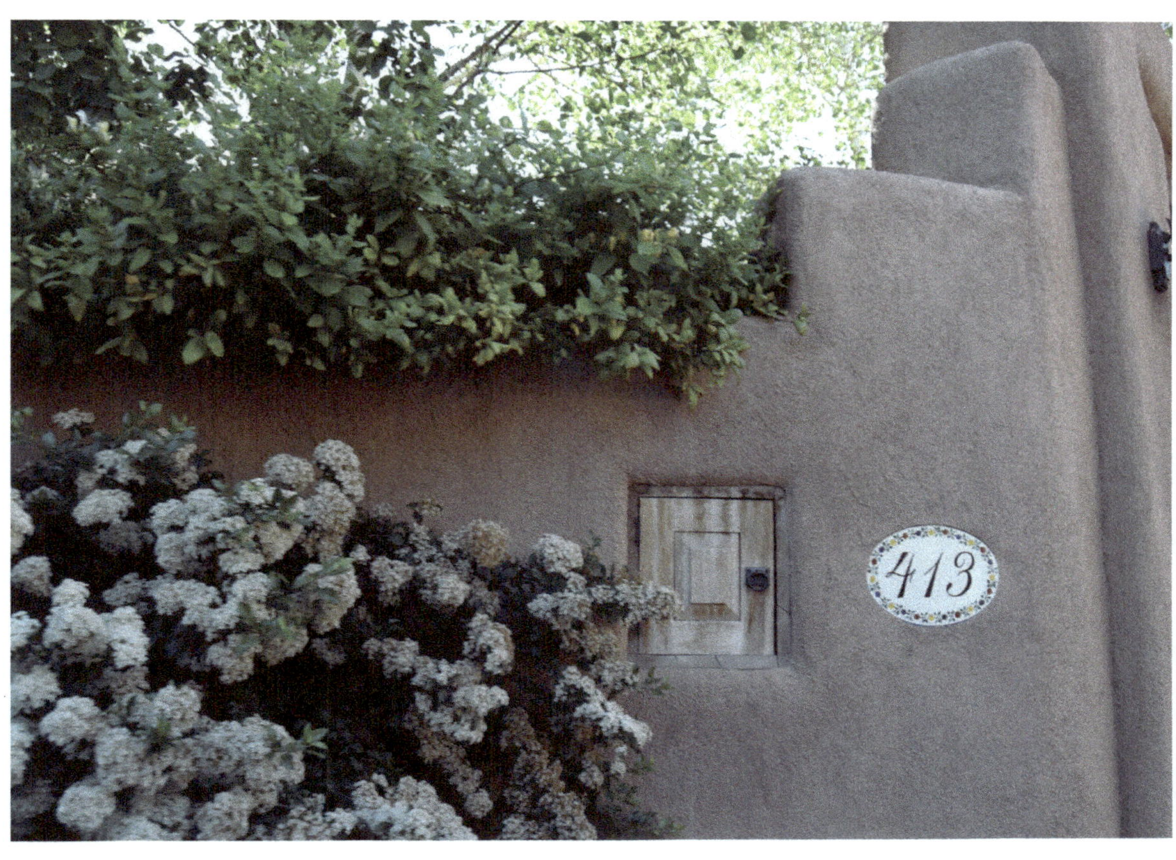
413

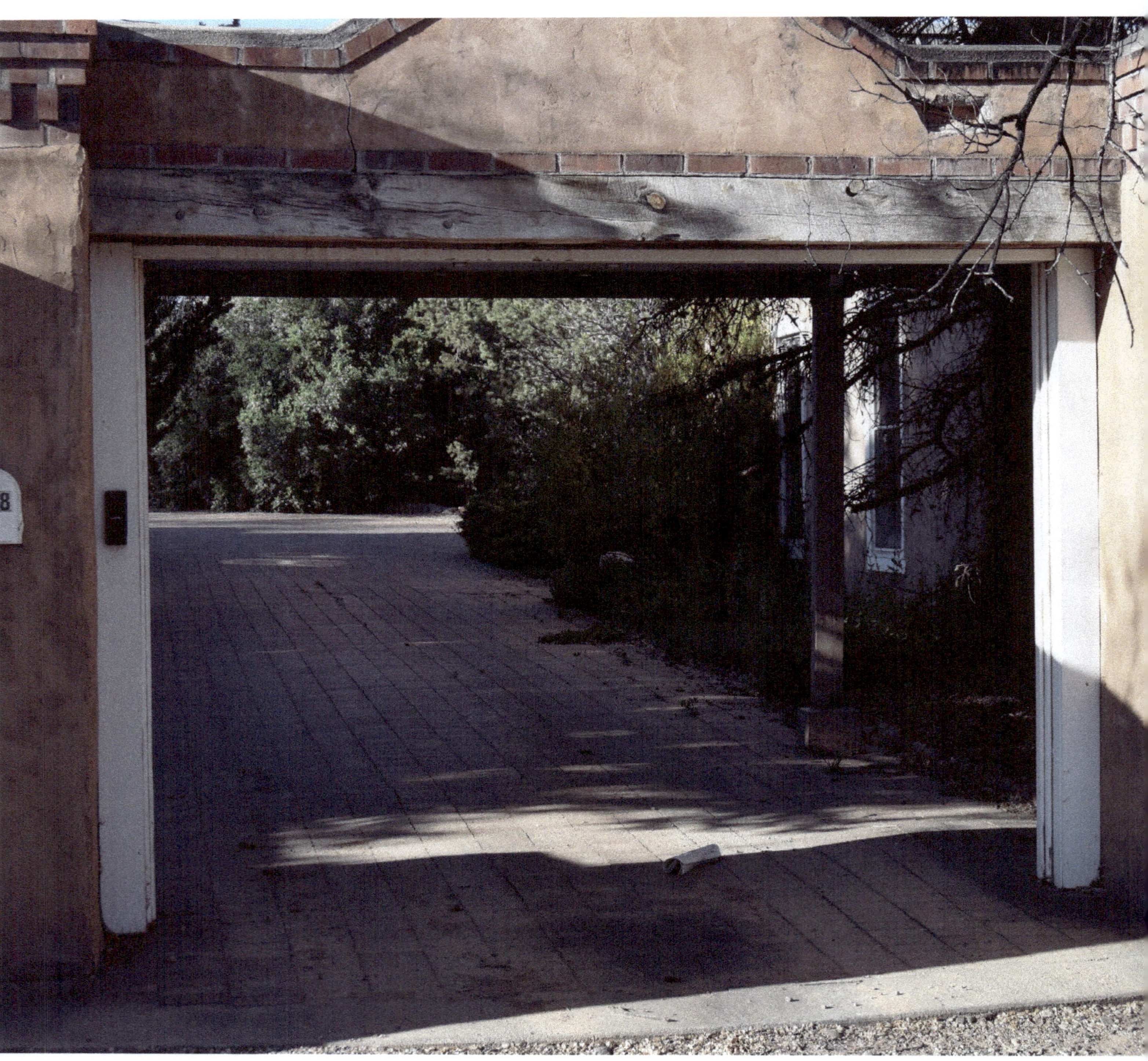

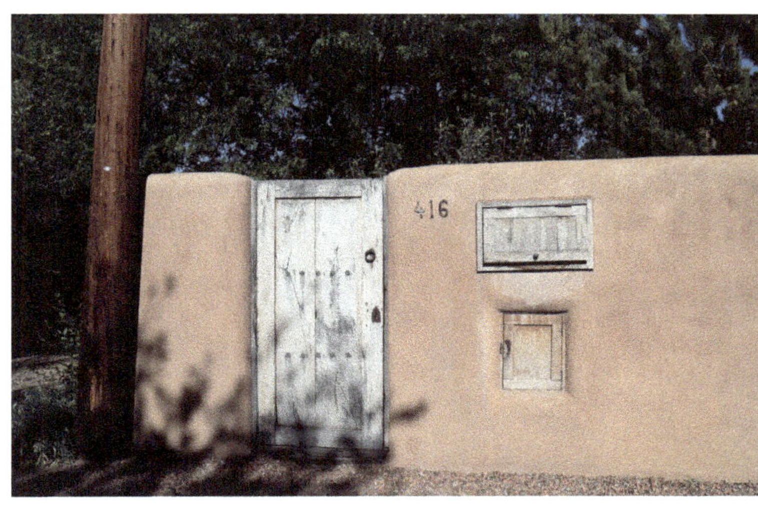
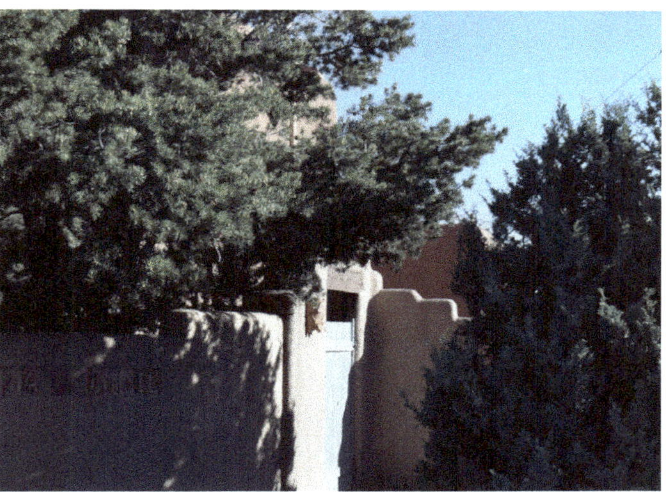
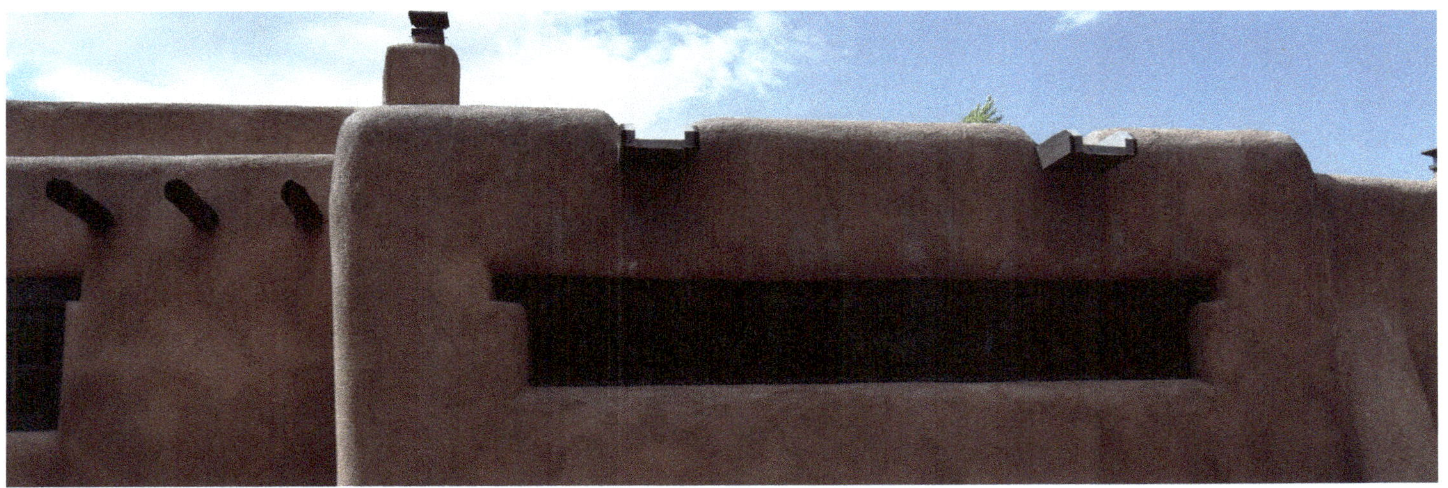

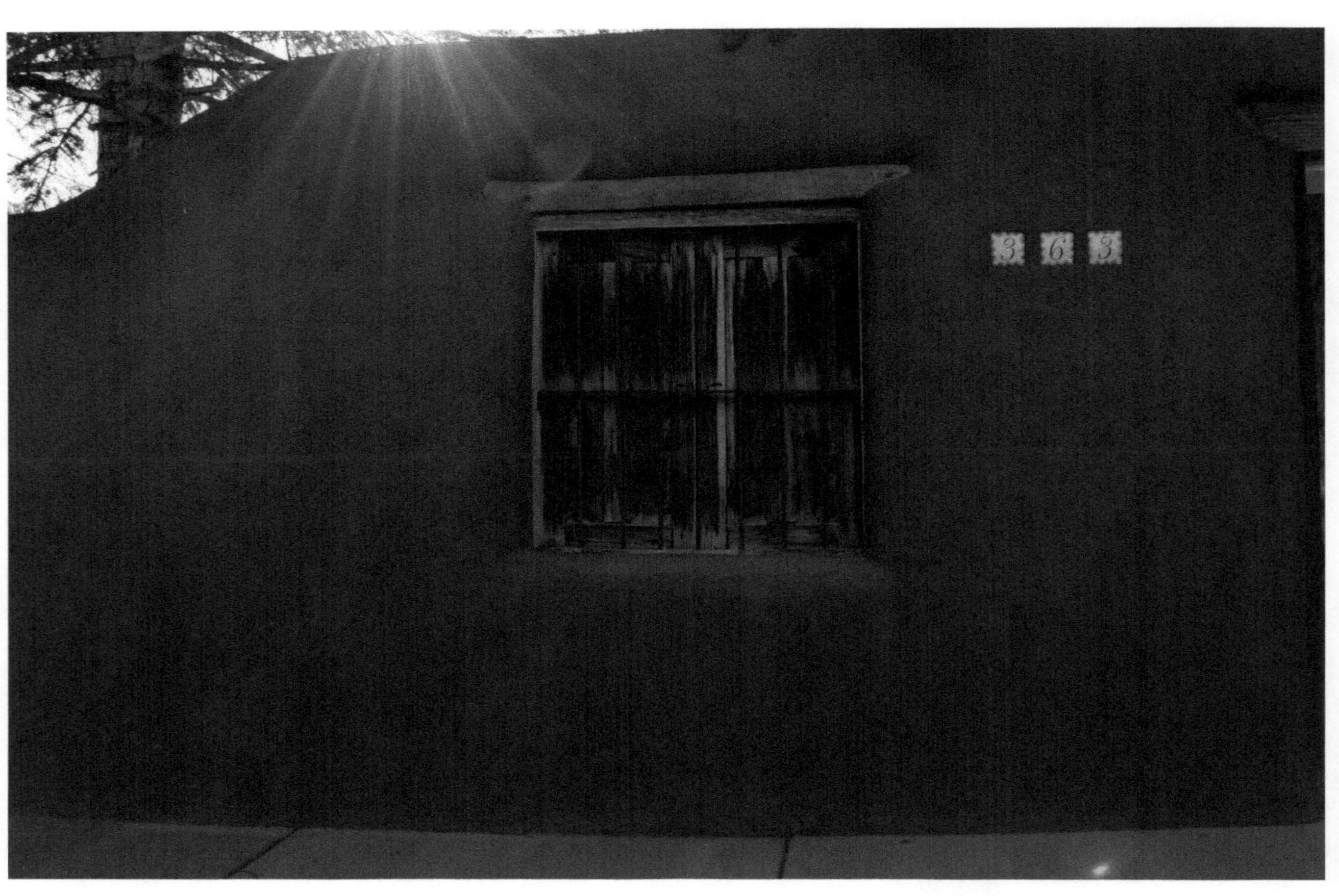

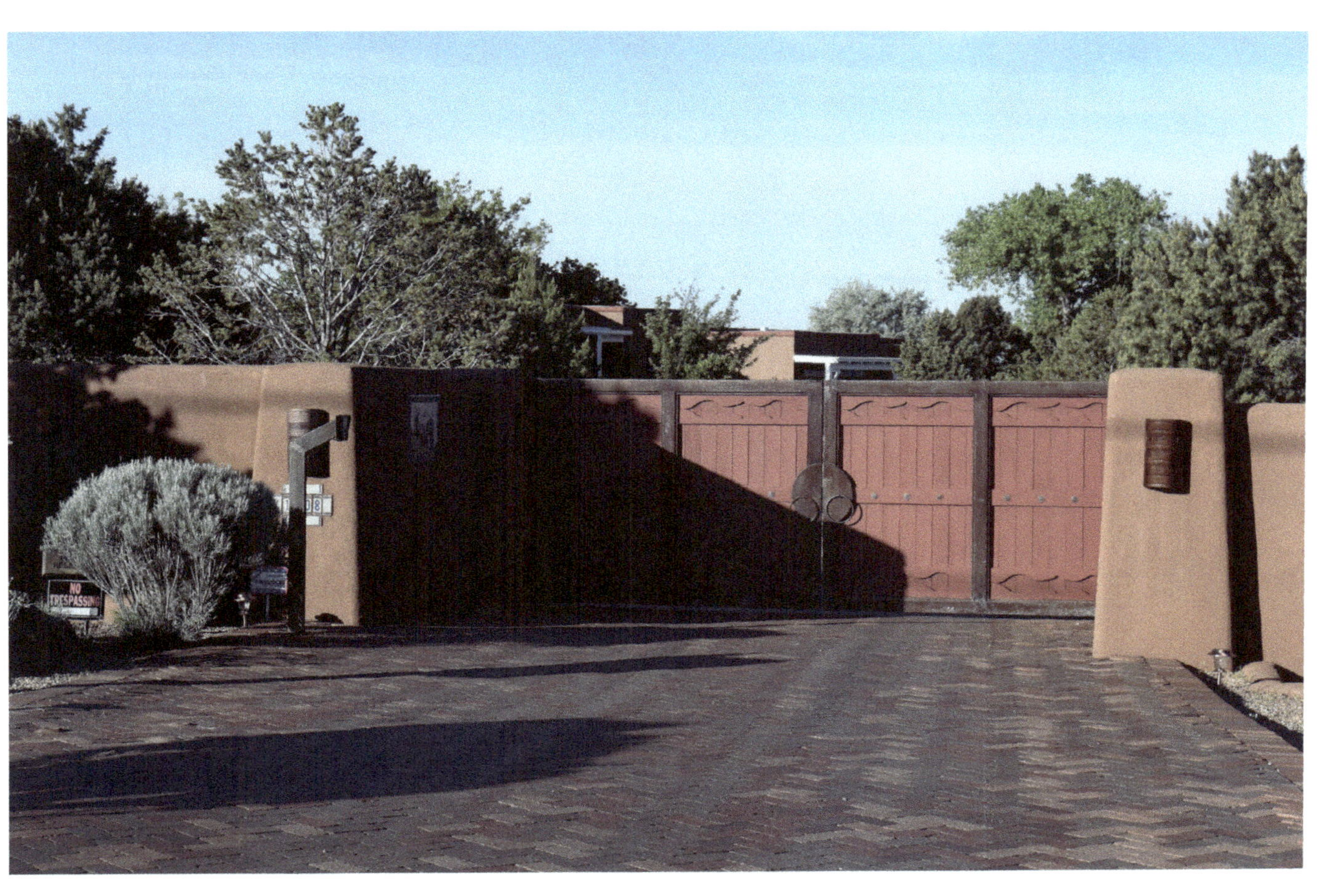

NO
TRESPASSING

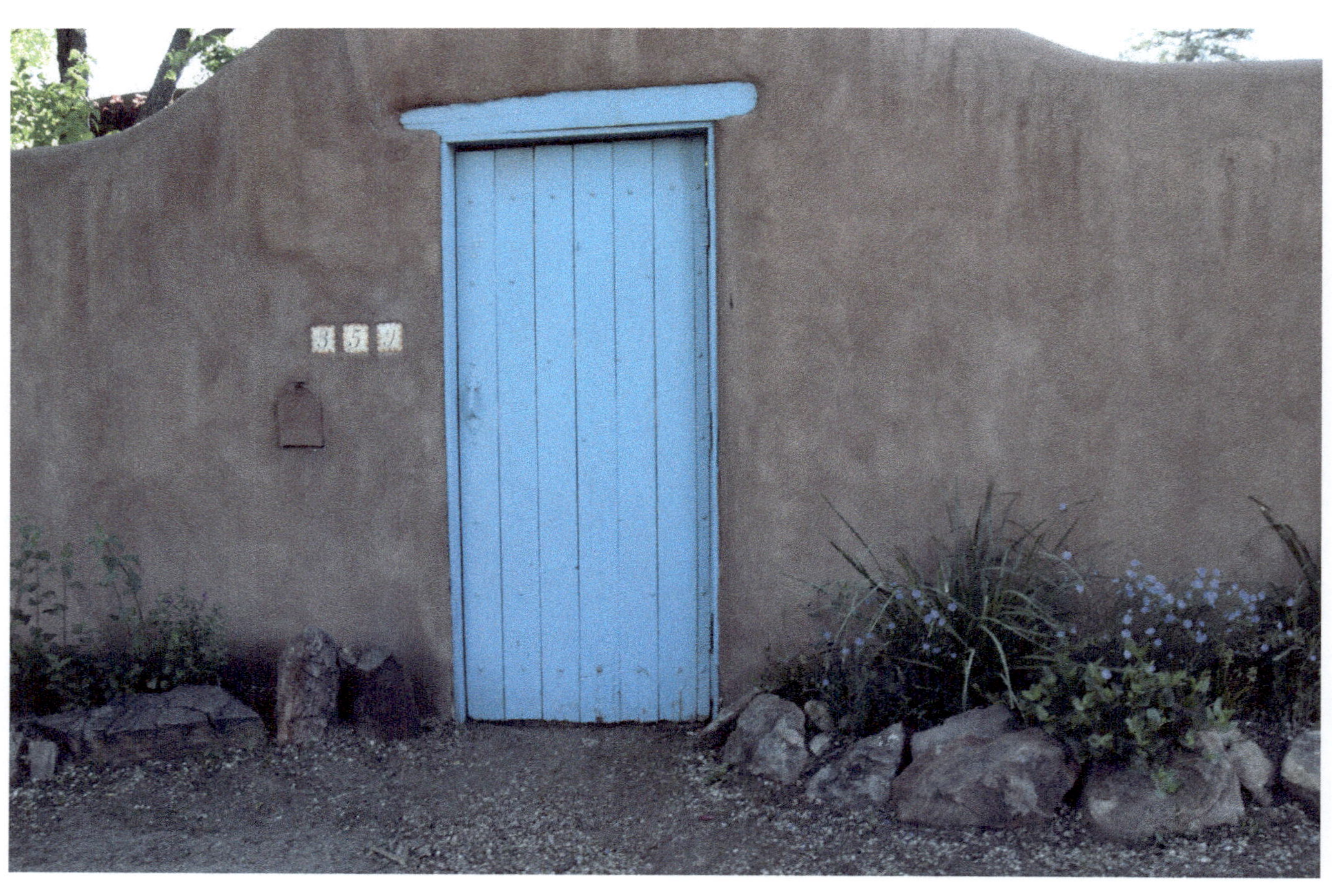

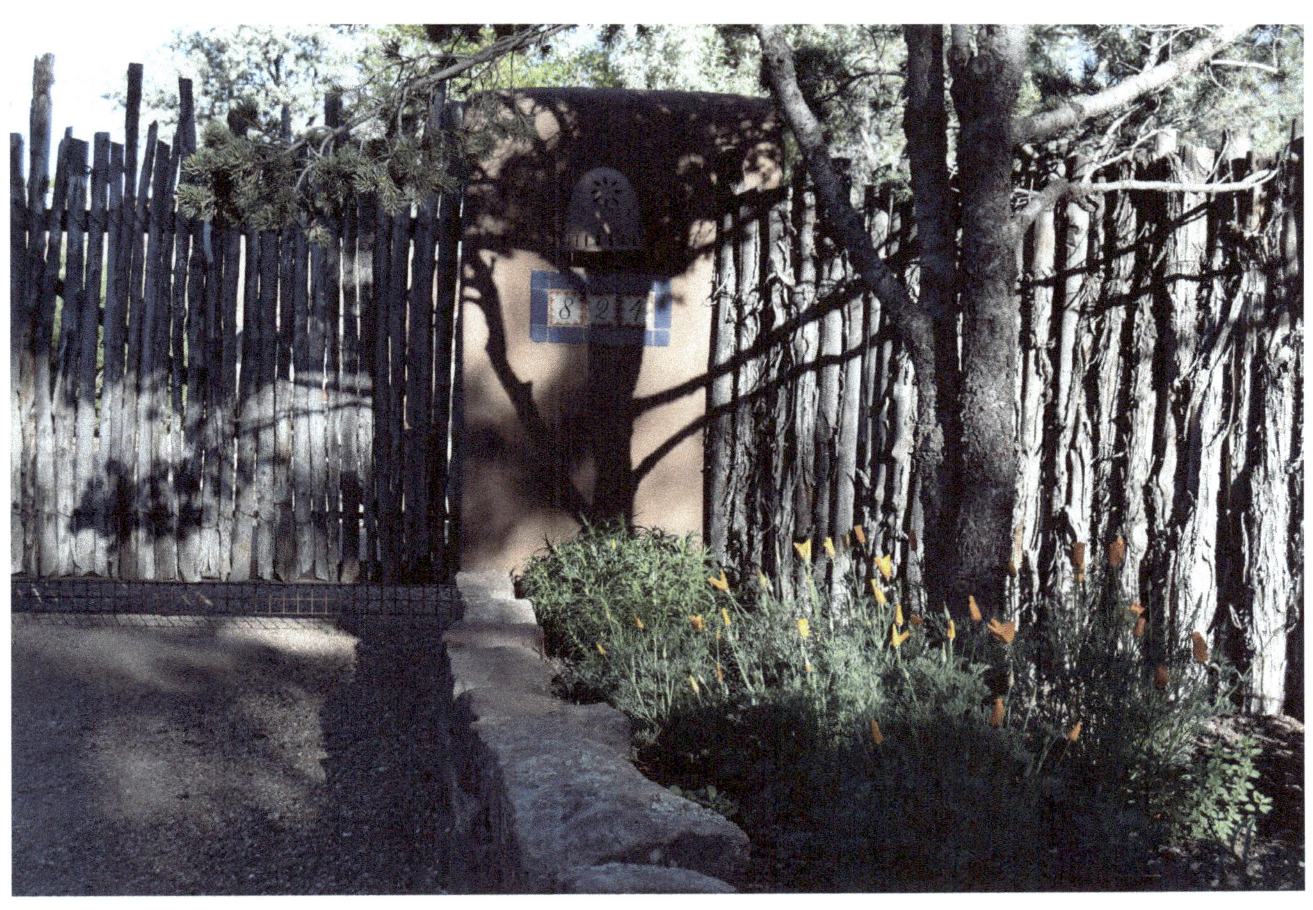

8 2 2

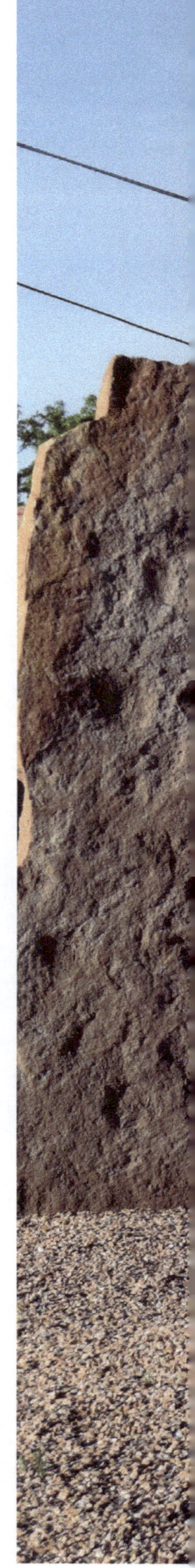
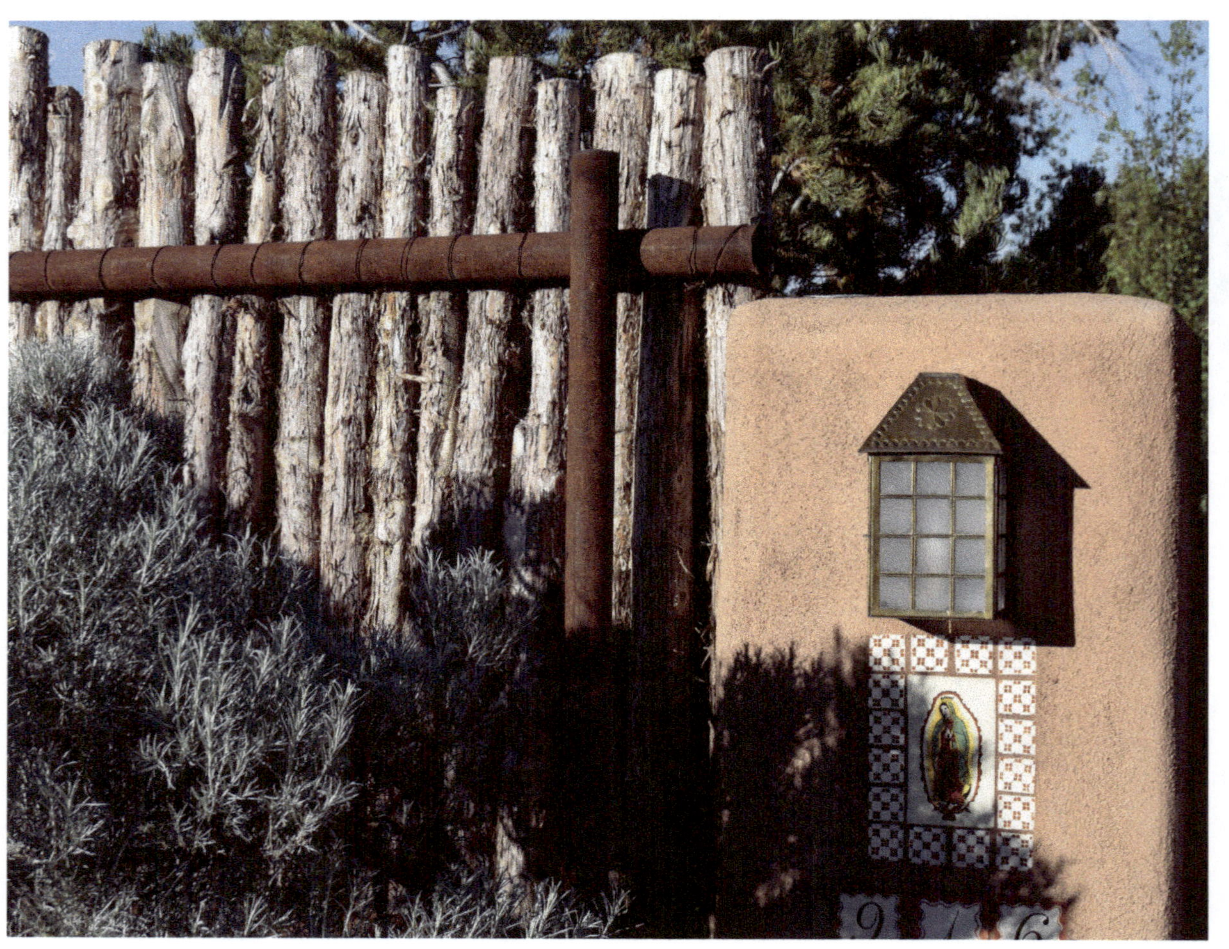

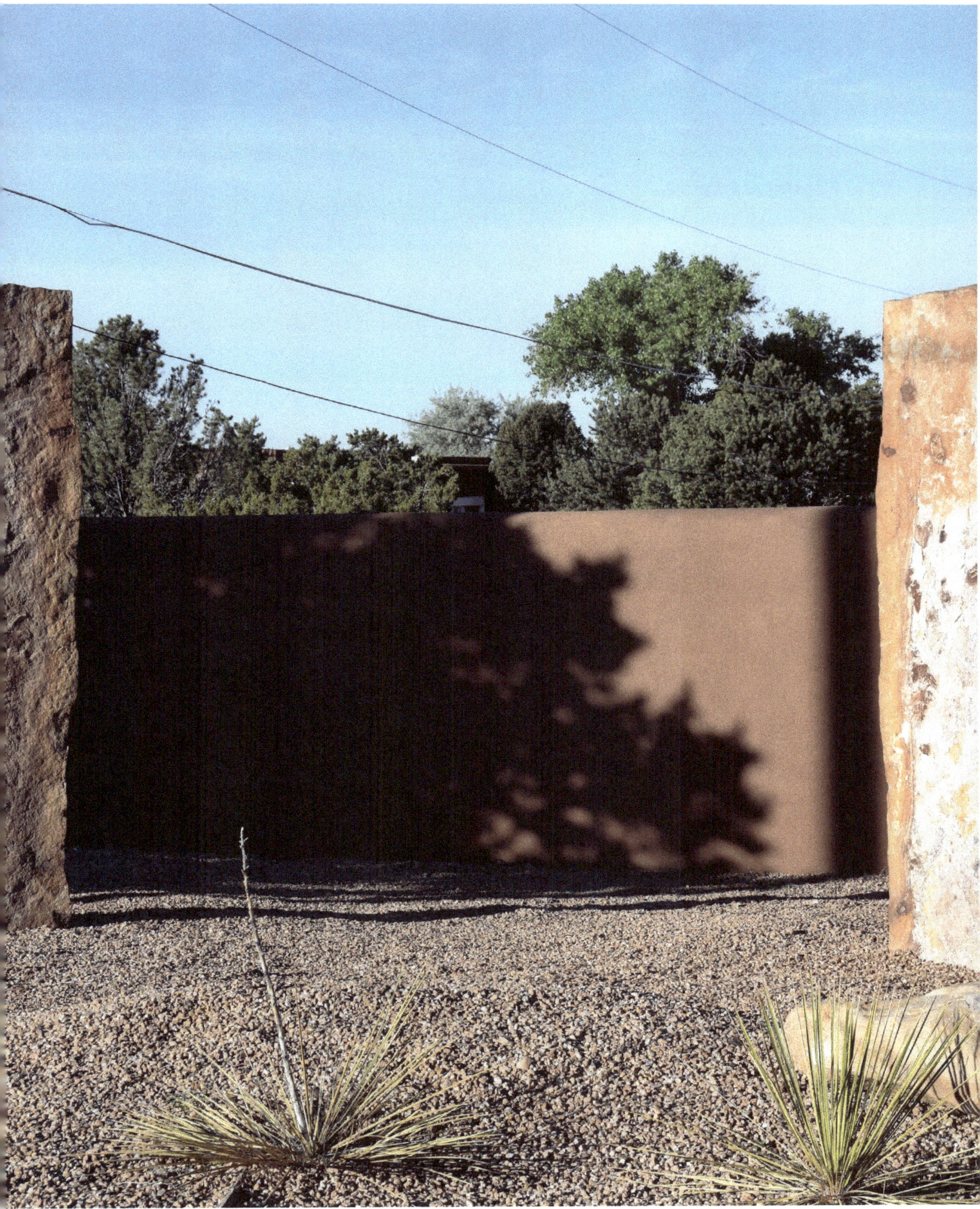

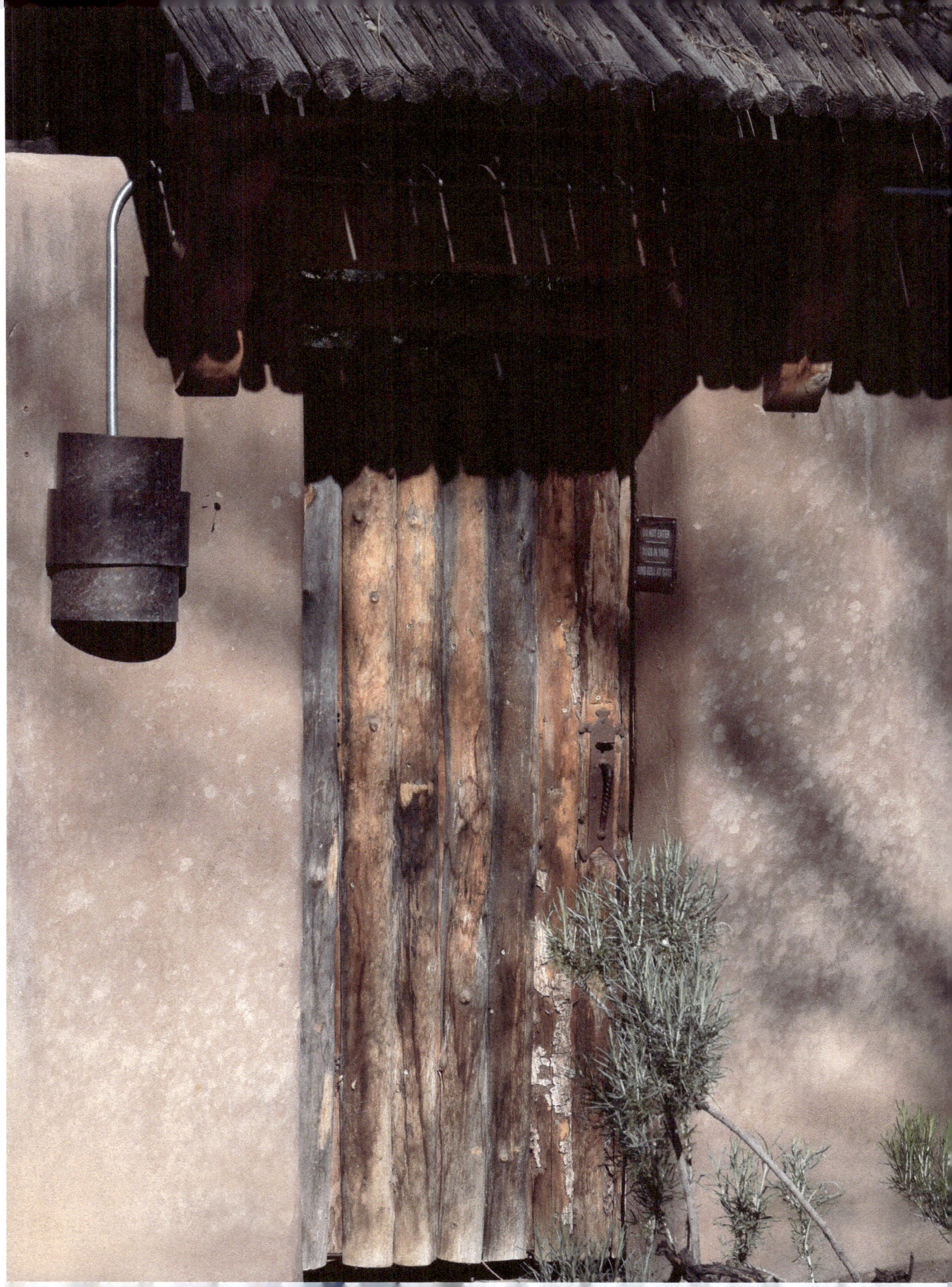

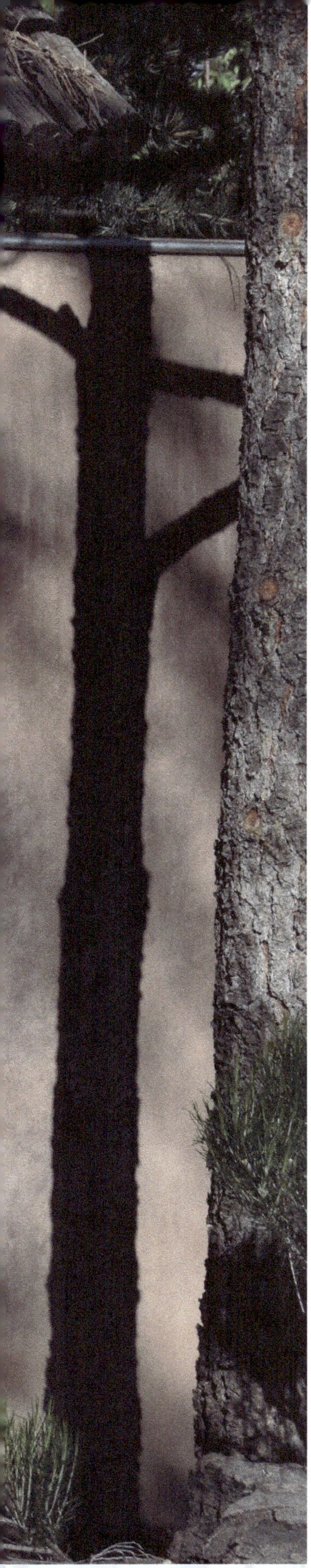

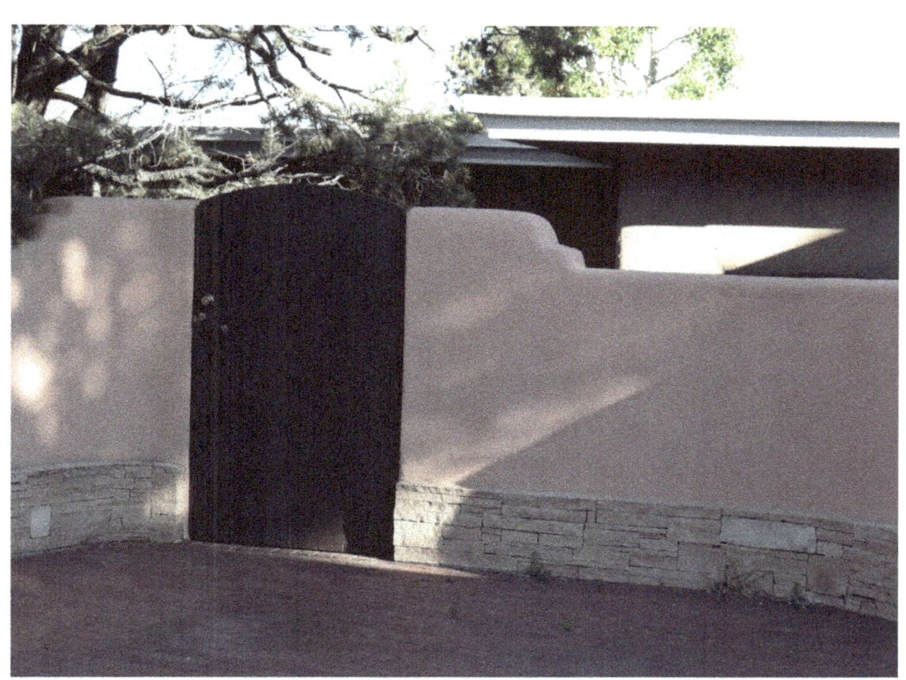

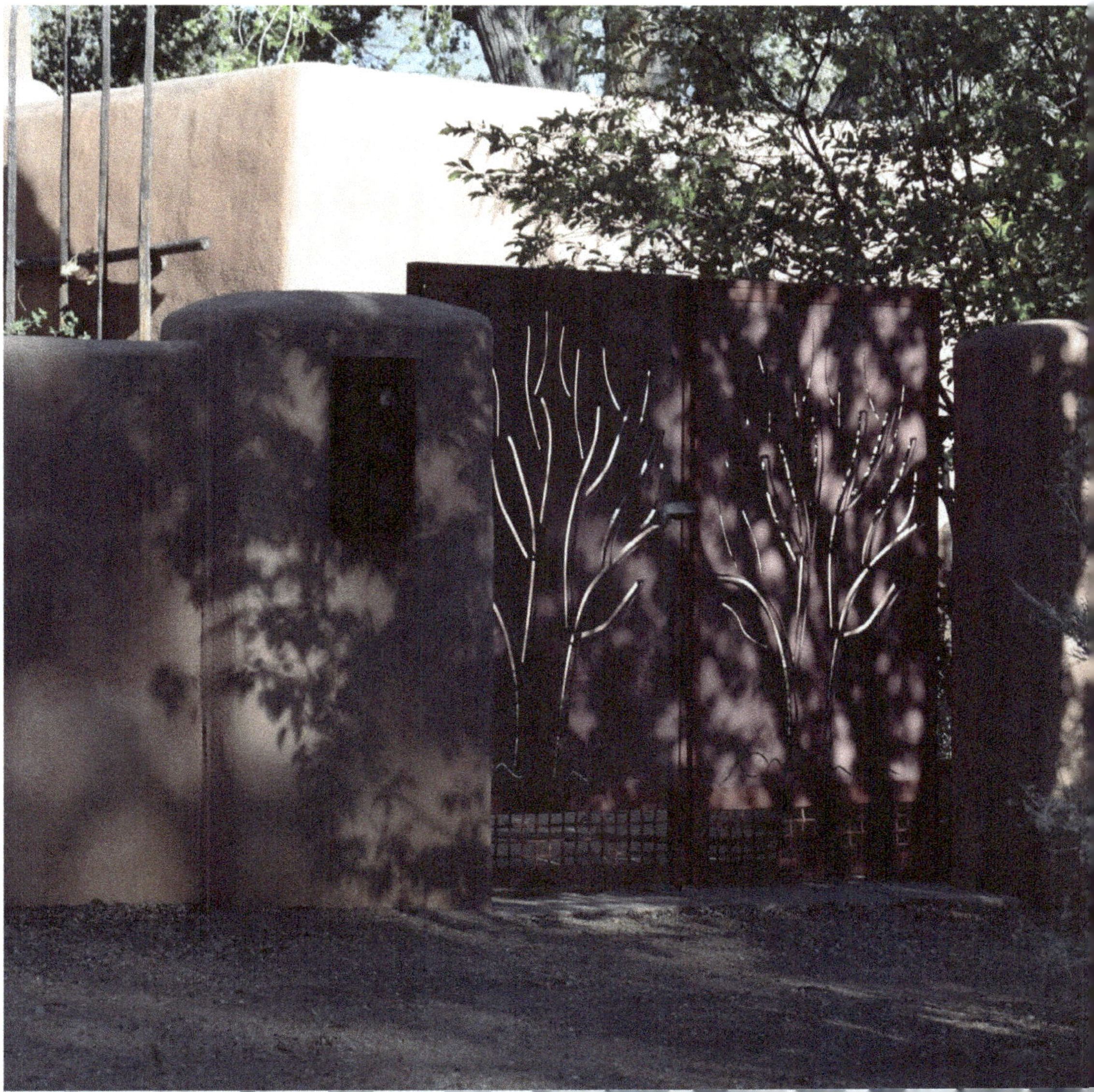

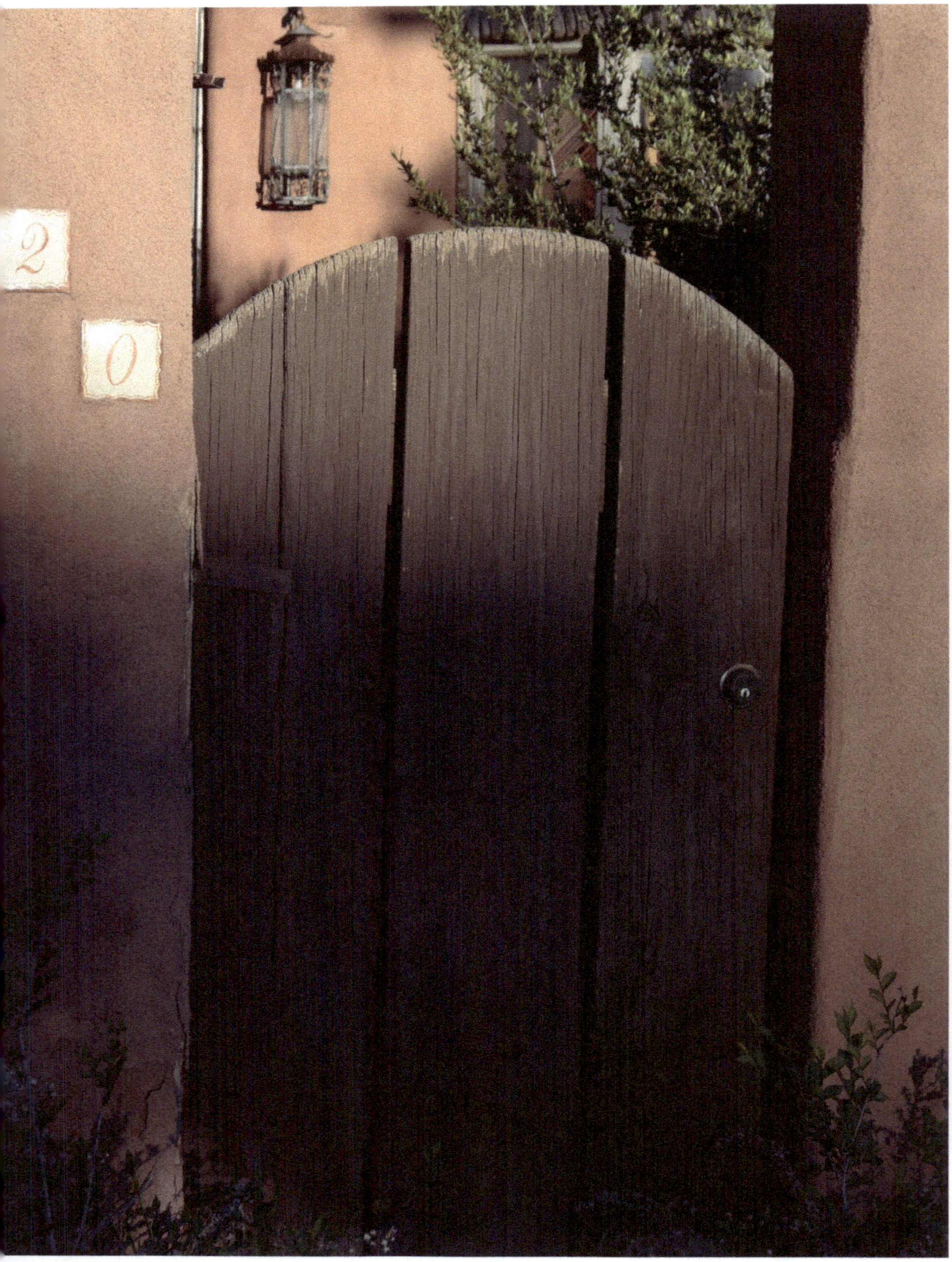

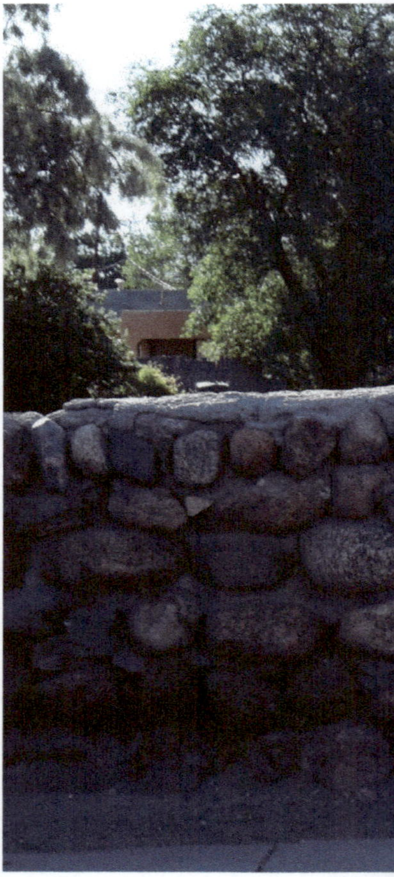

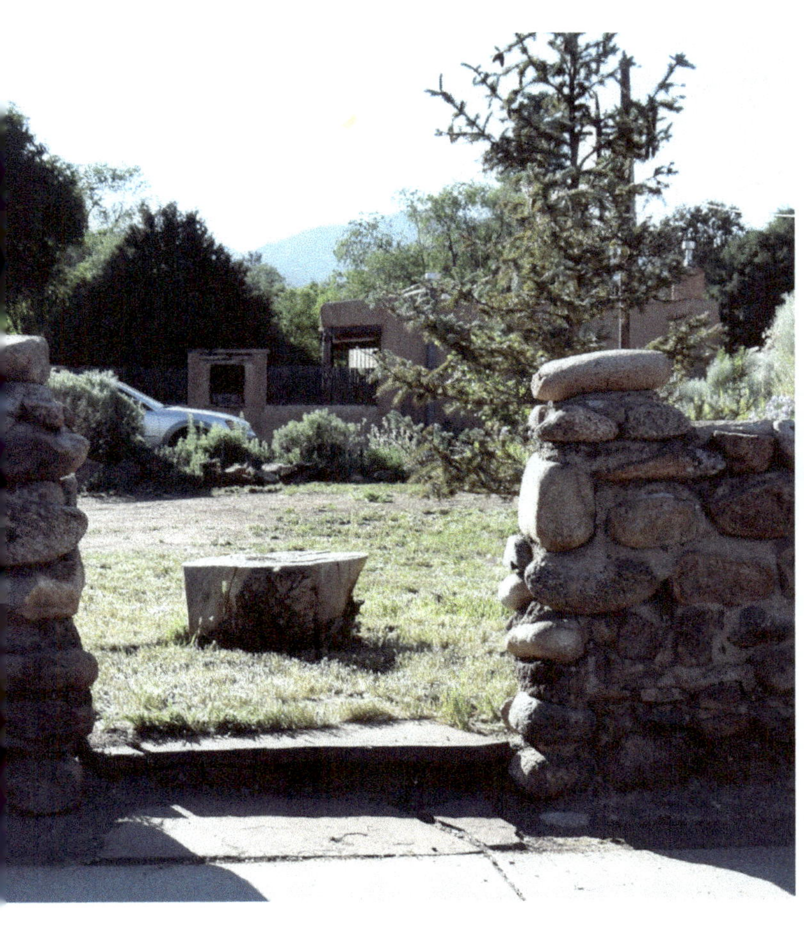

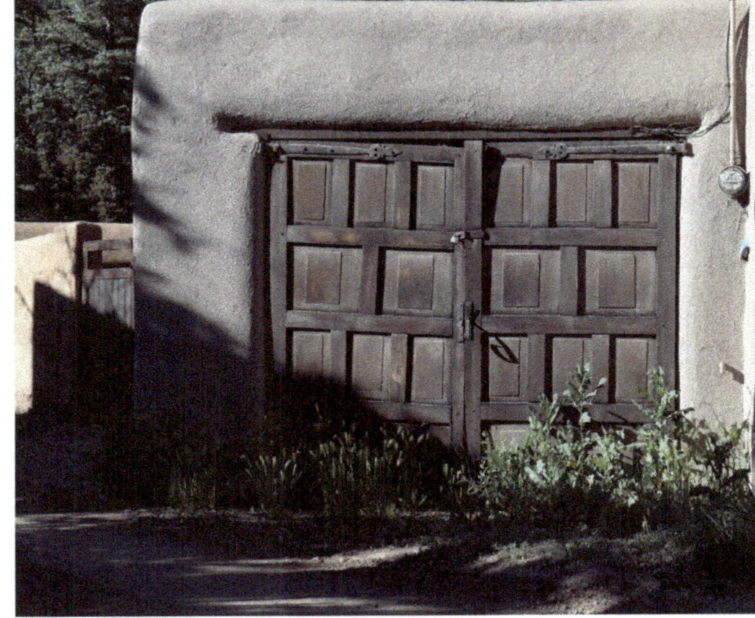

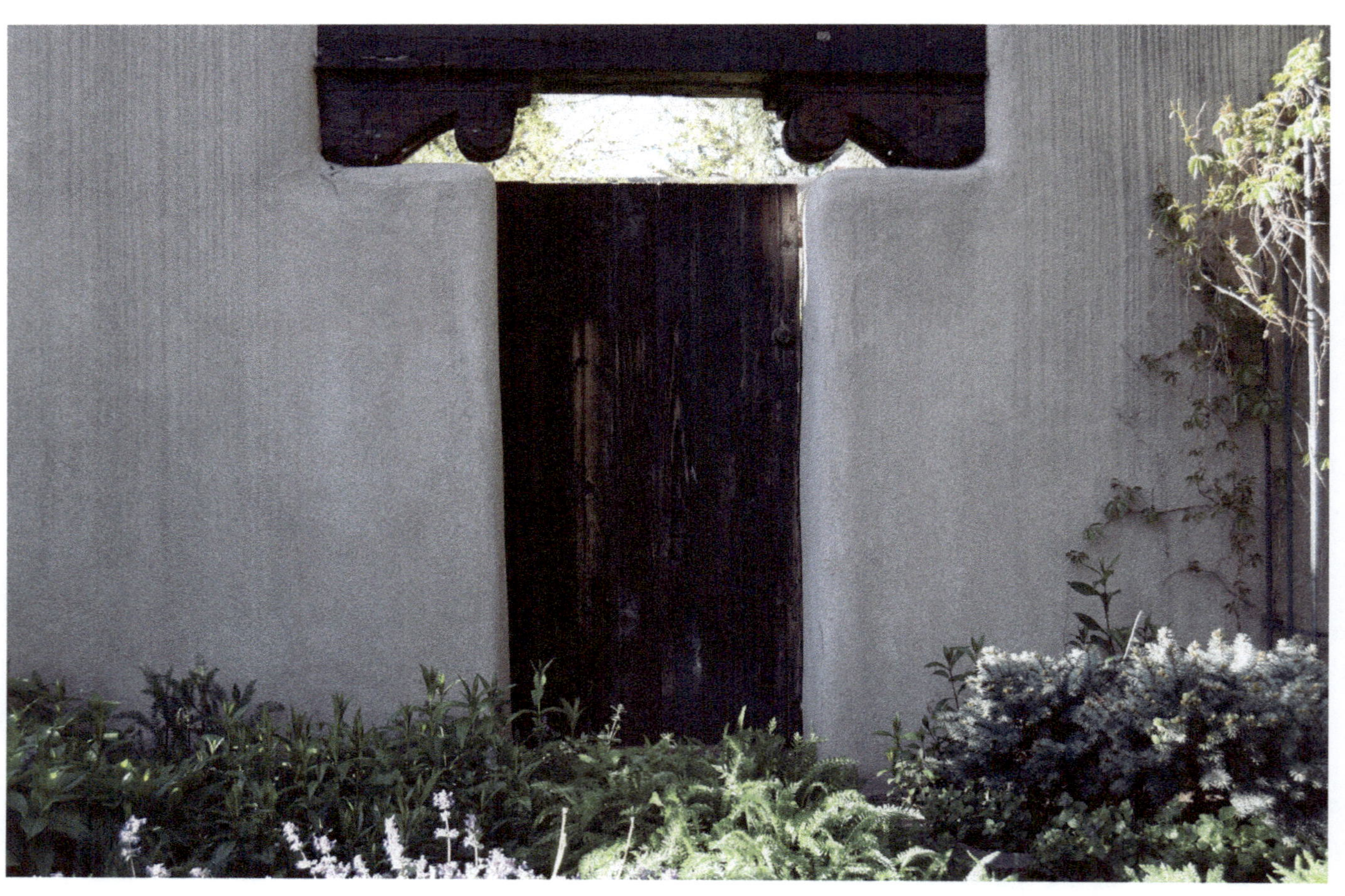

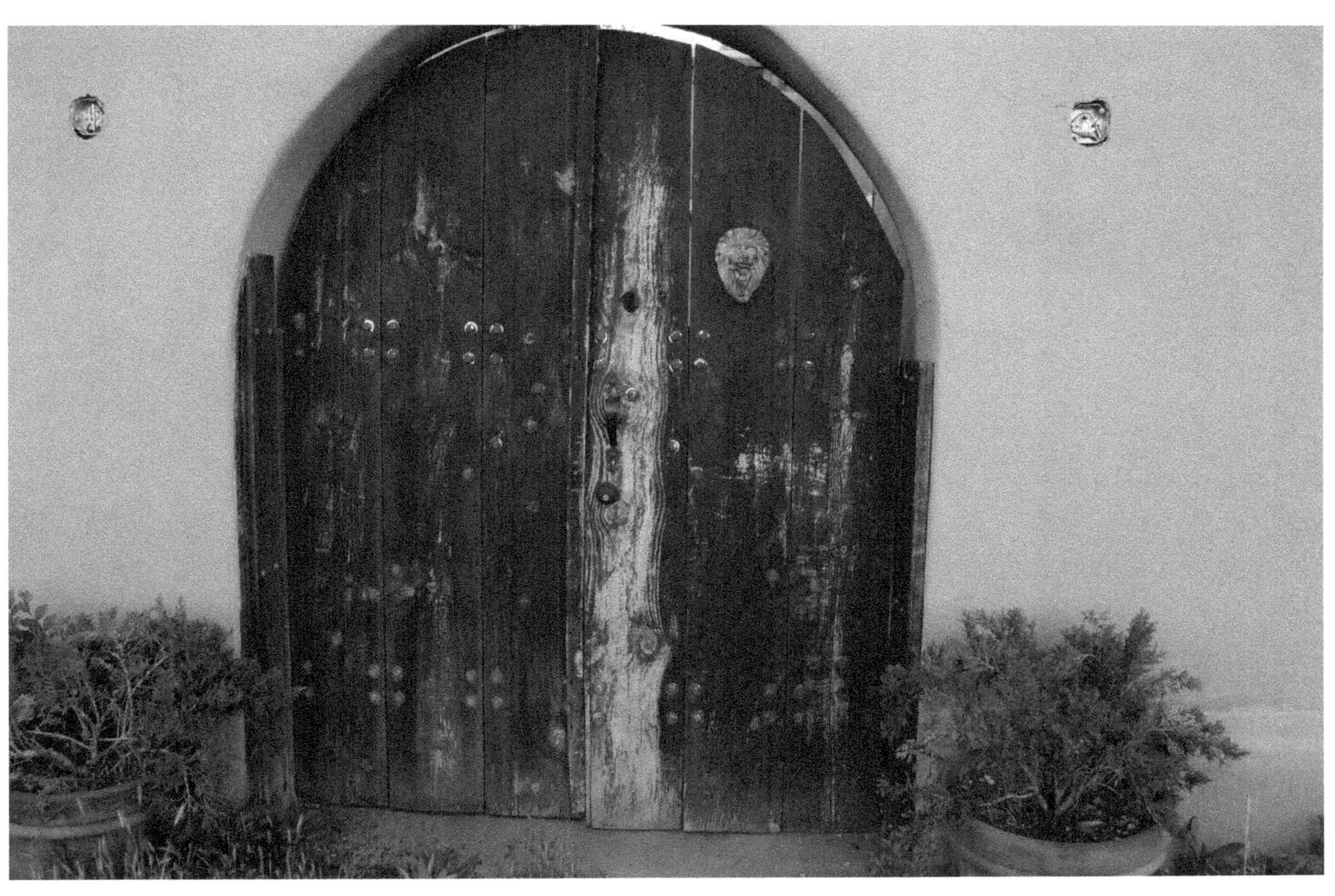

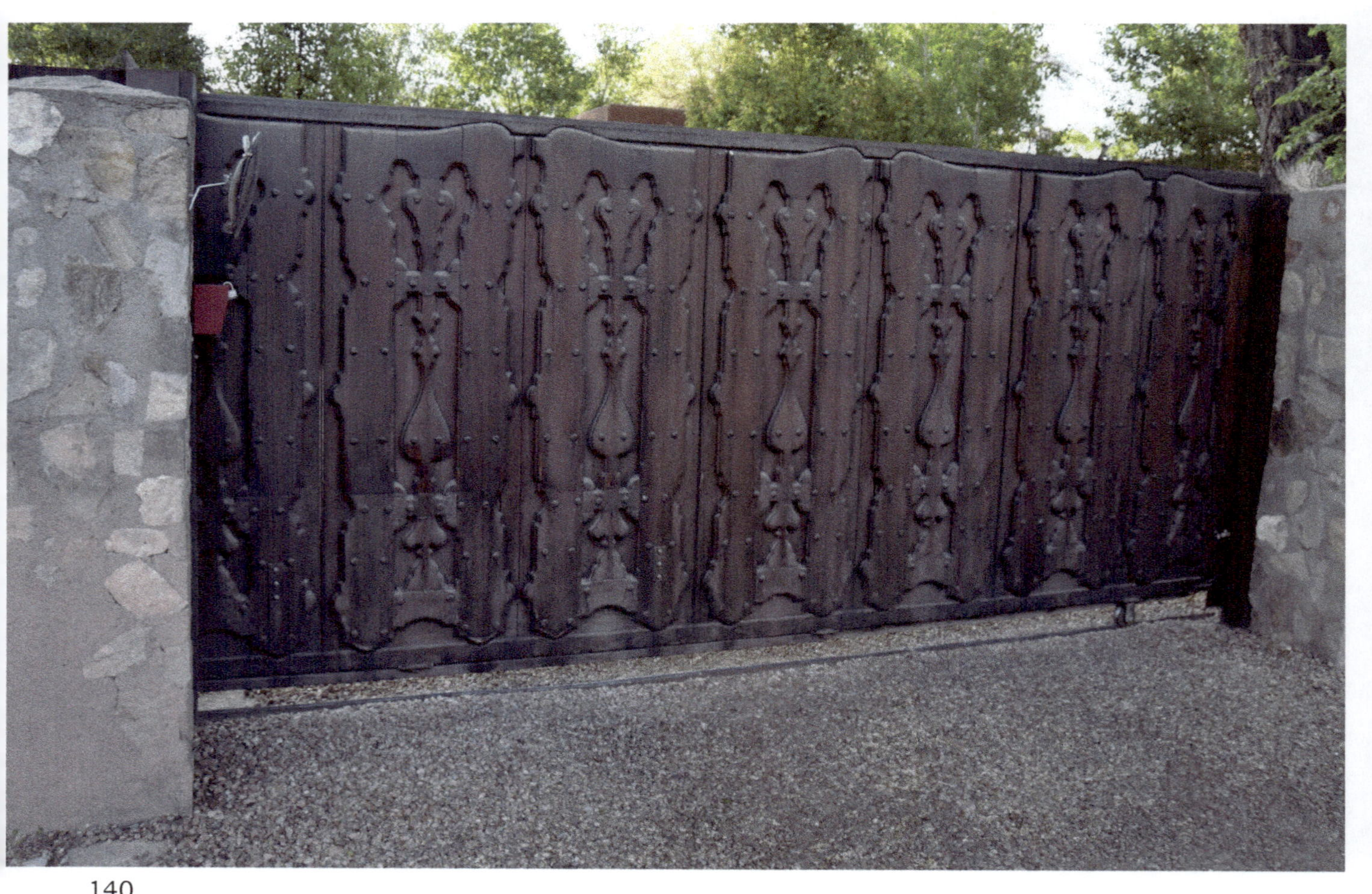

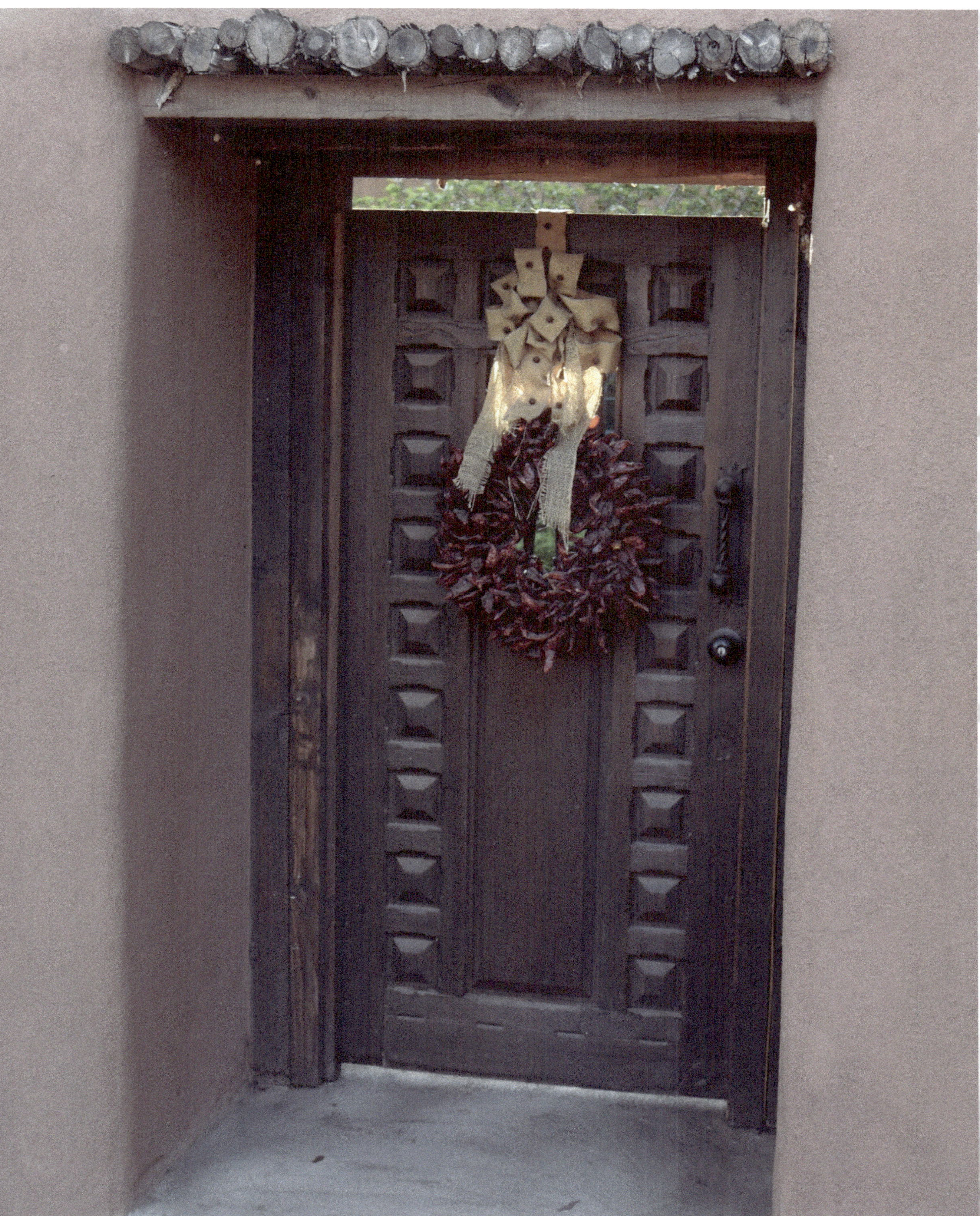

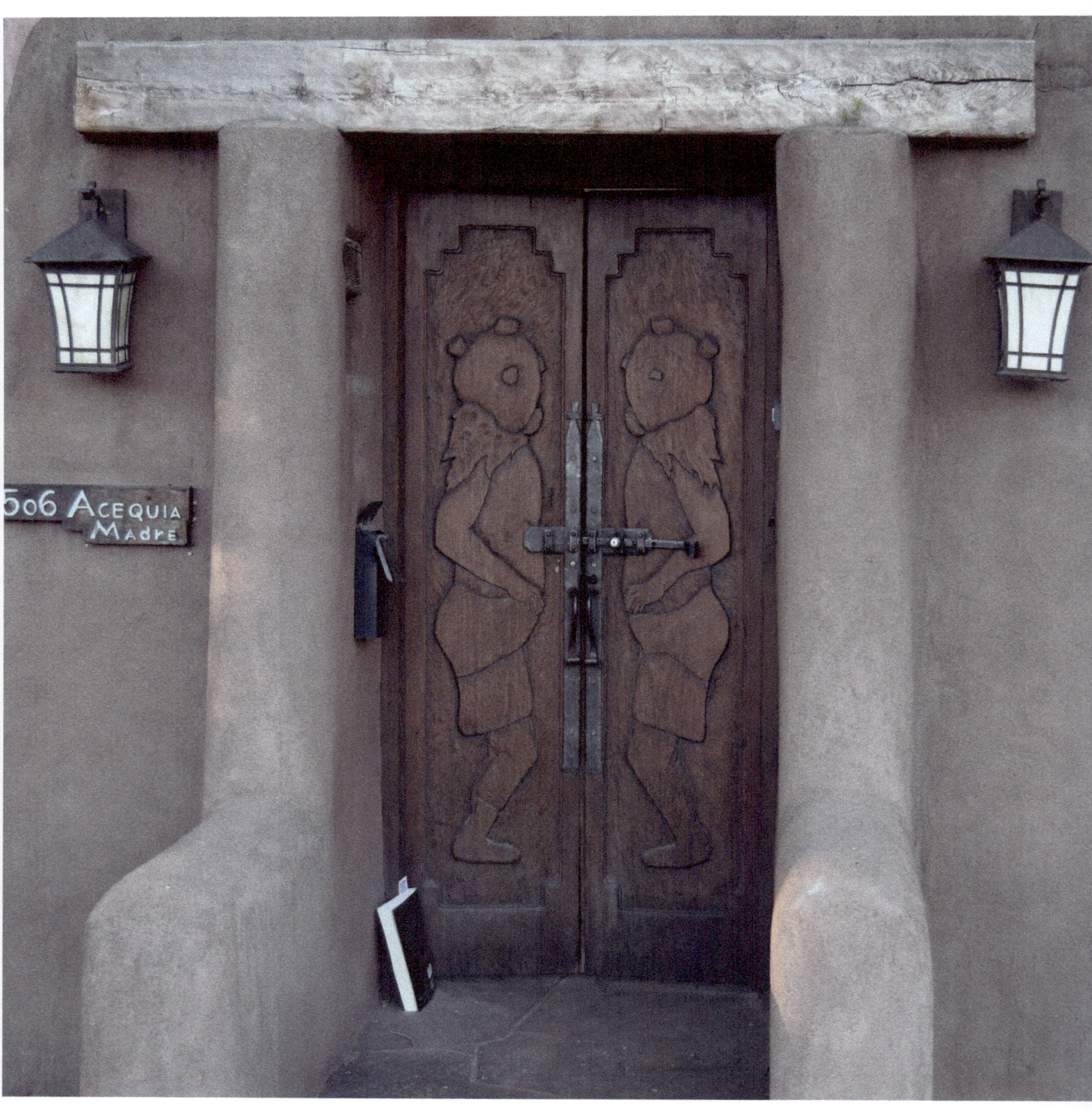
506 ACEQUIA MADRE

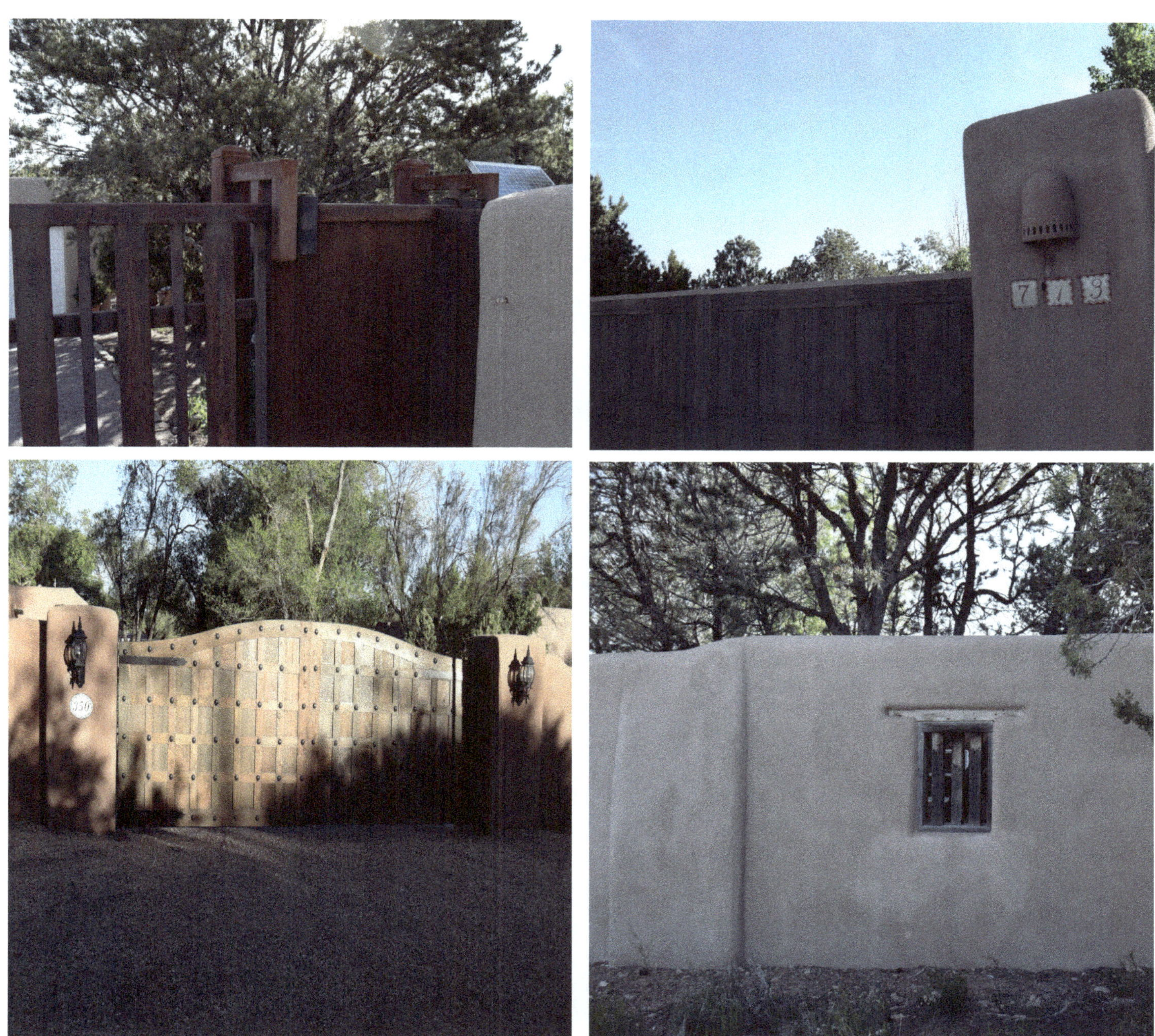

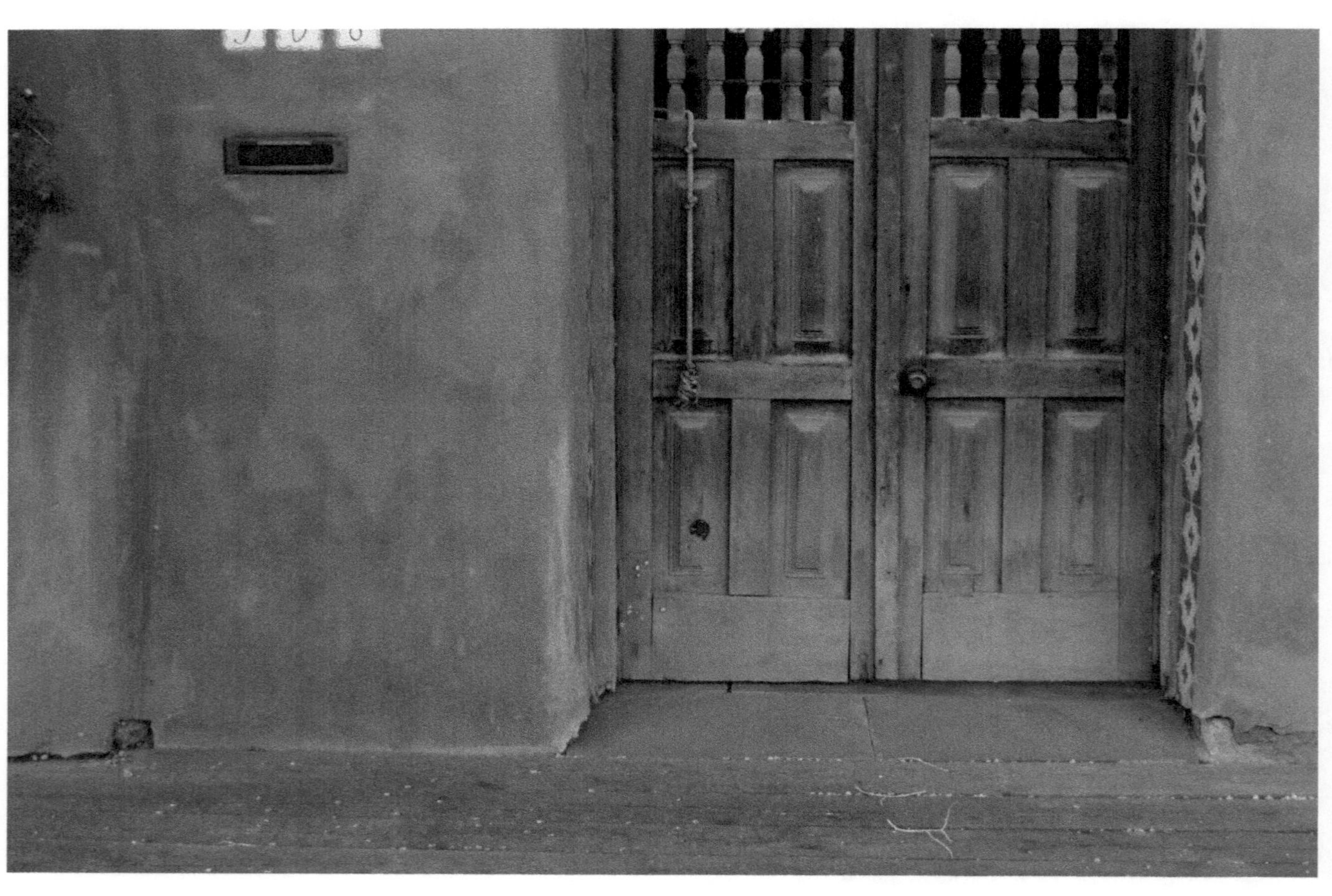

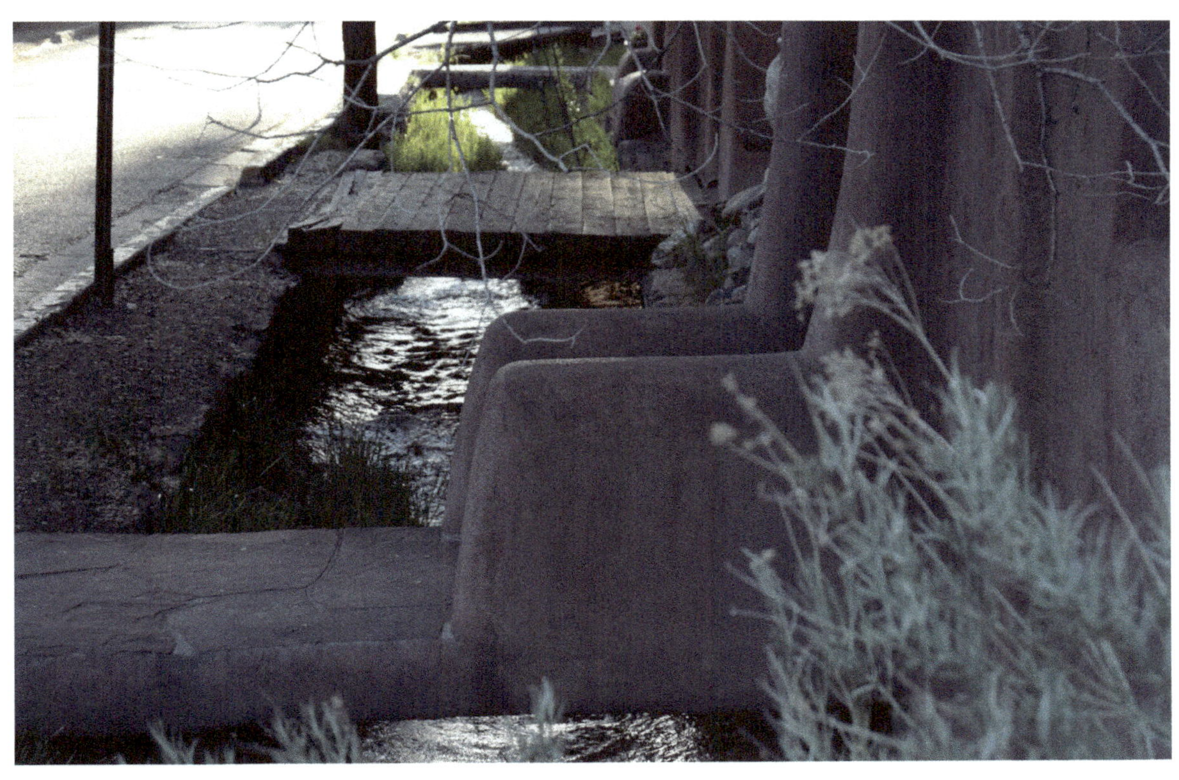

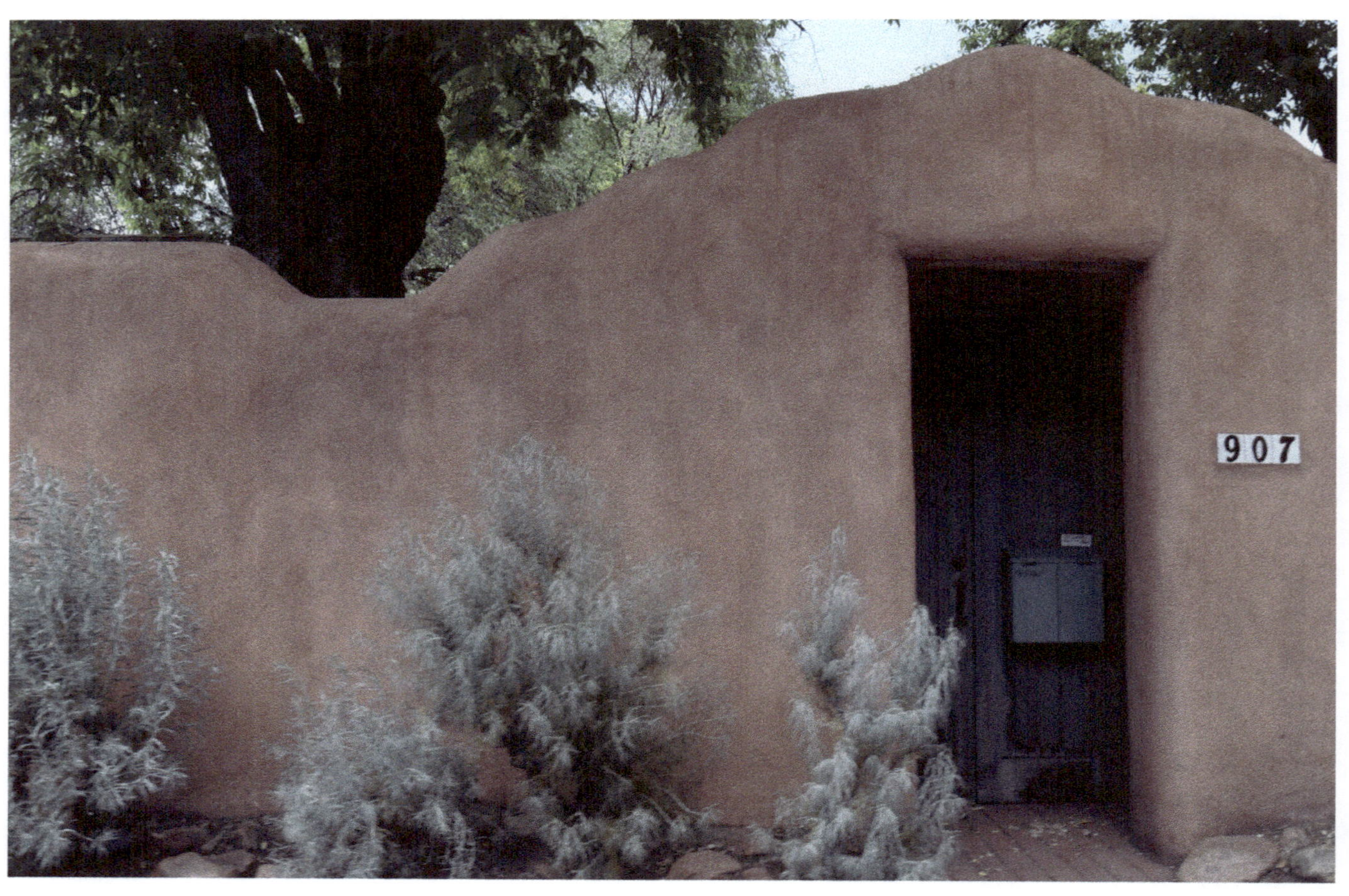

907

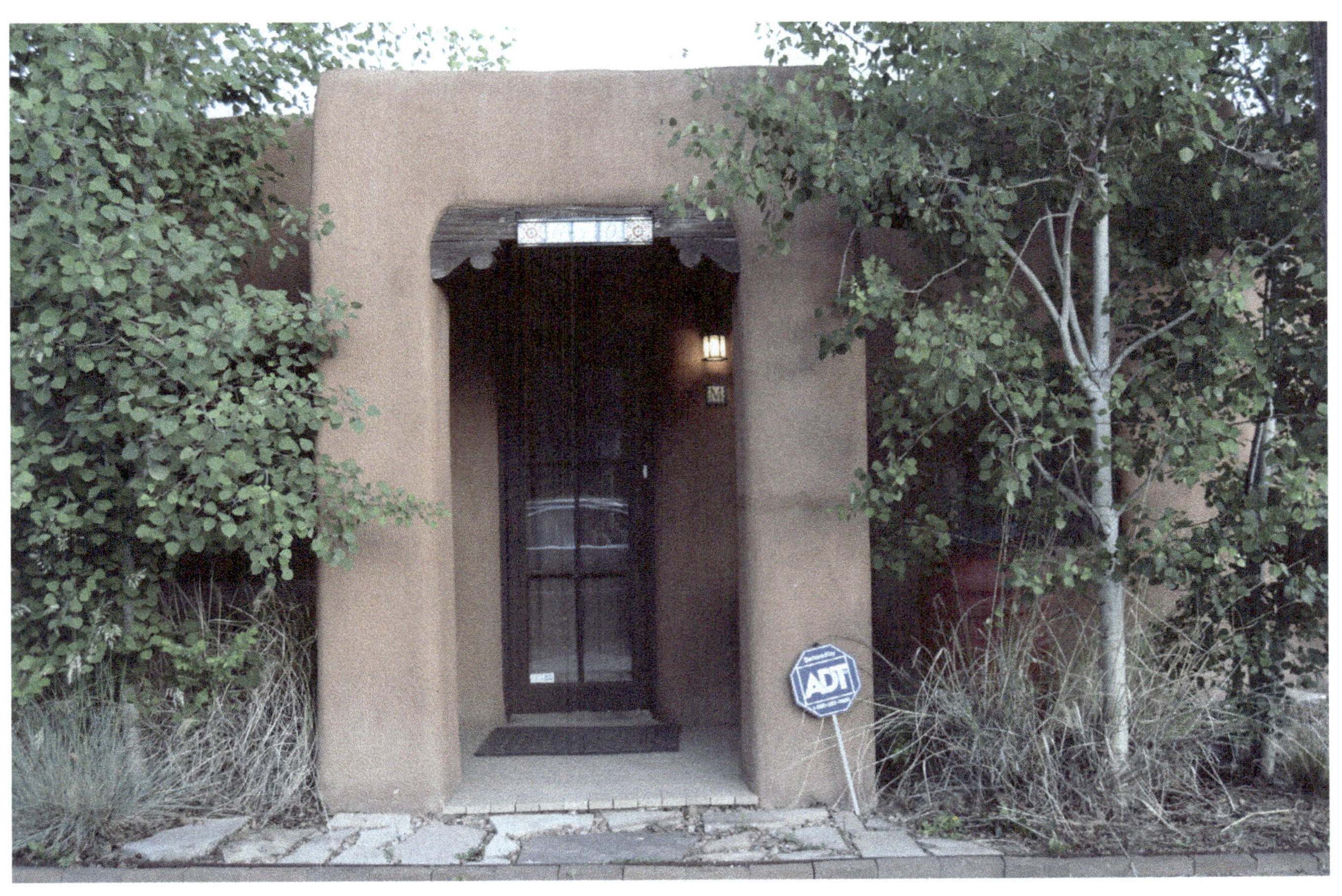

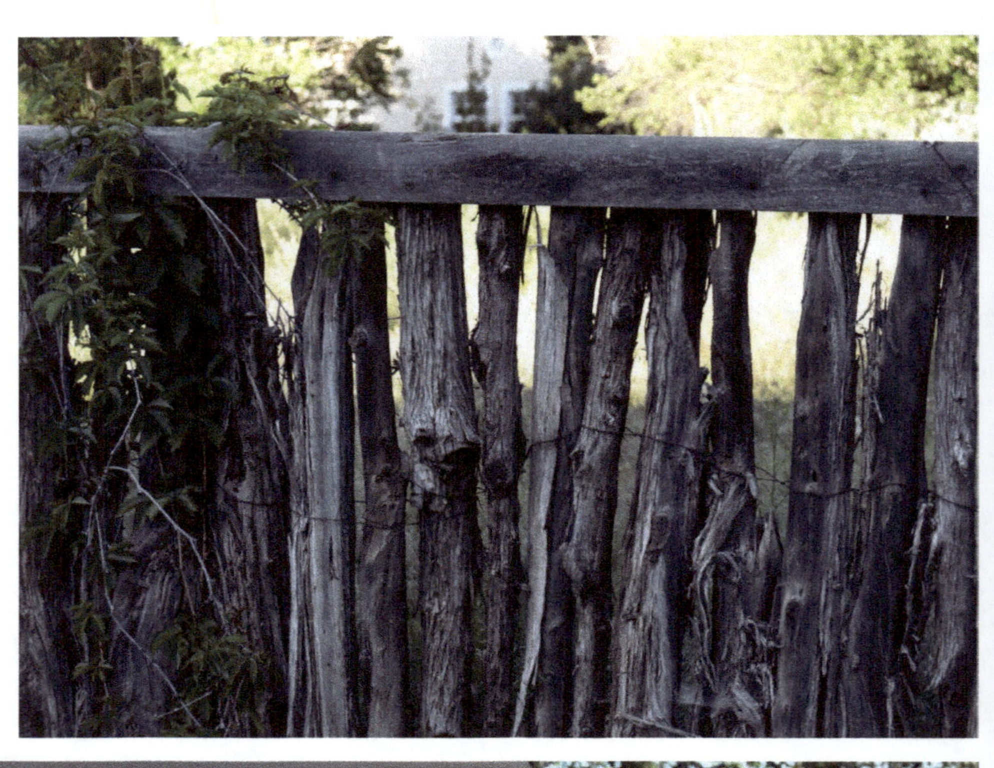

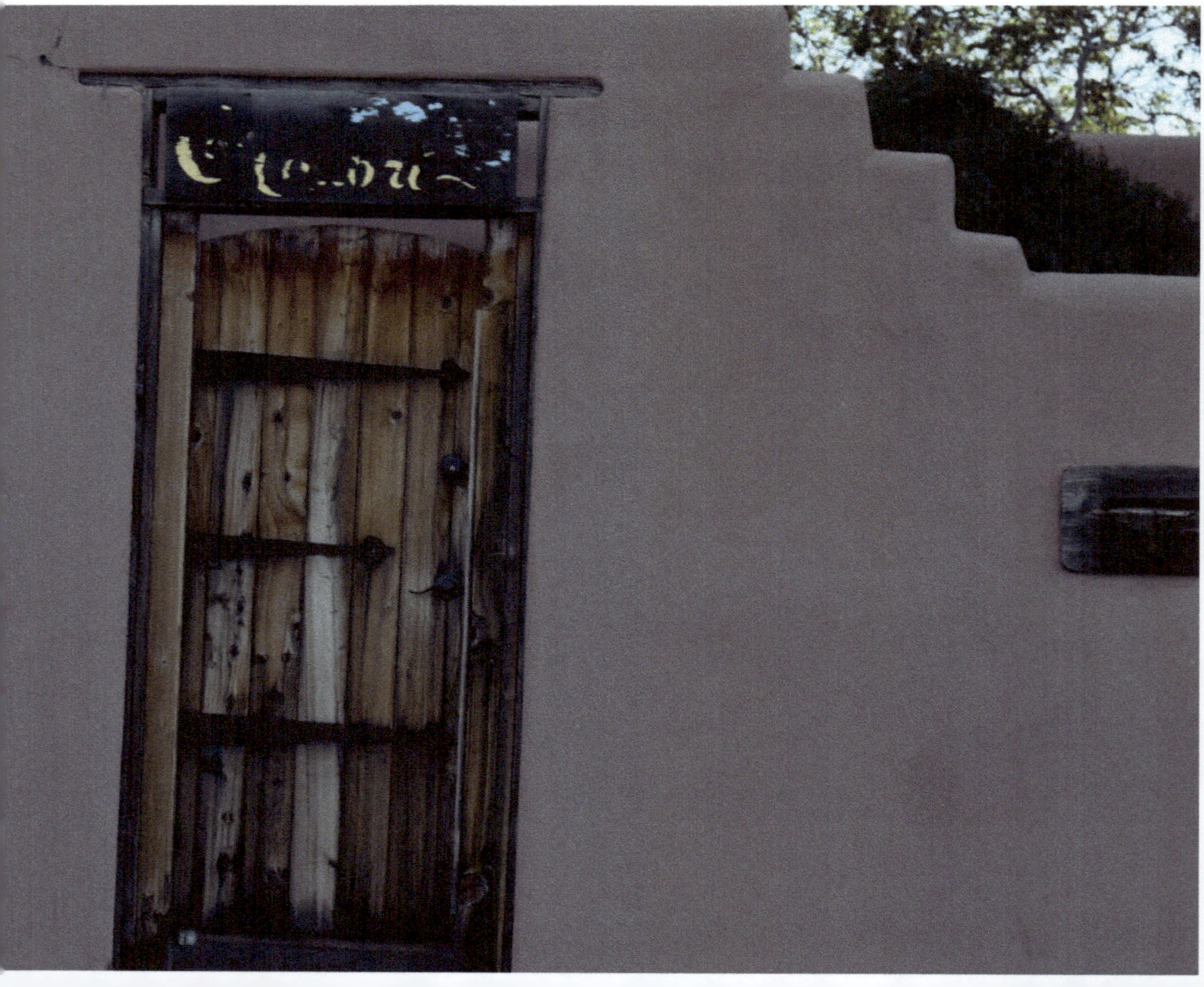

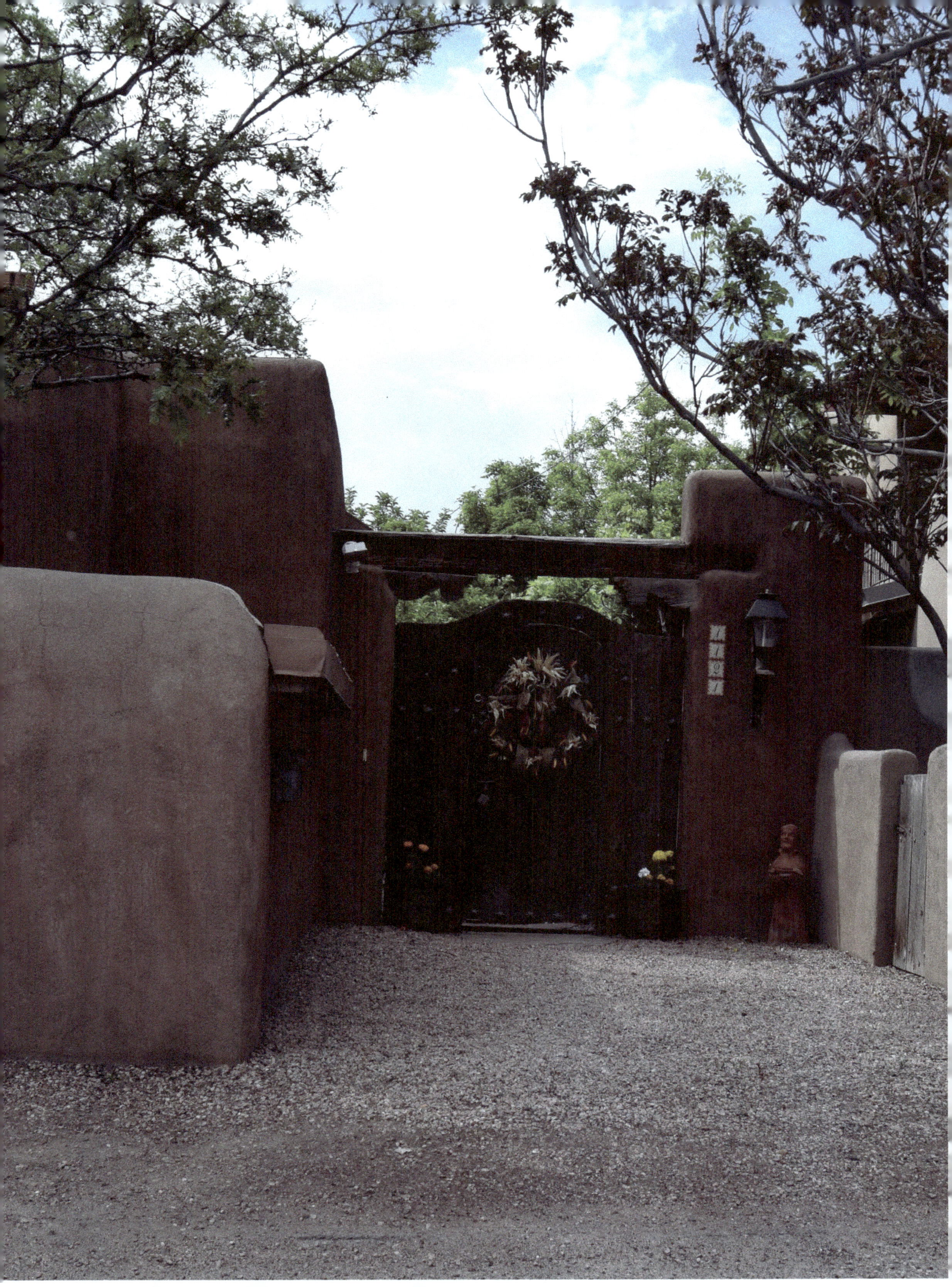

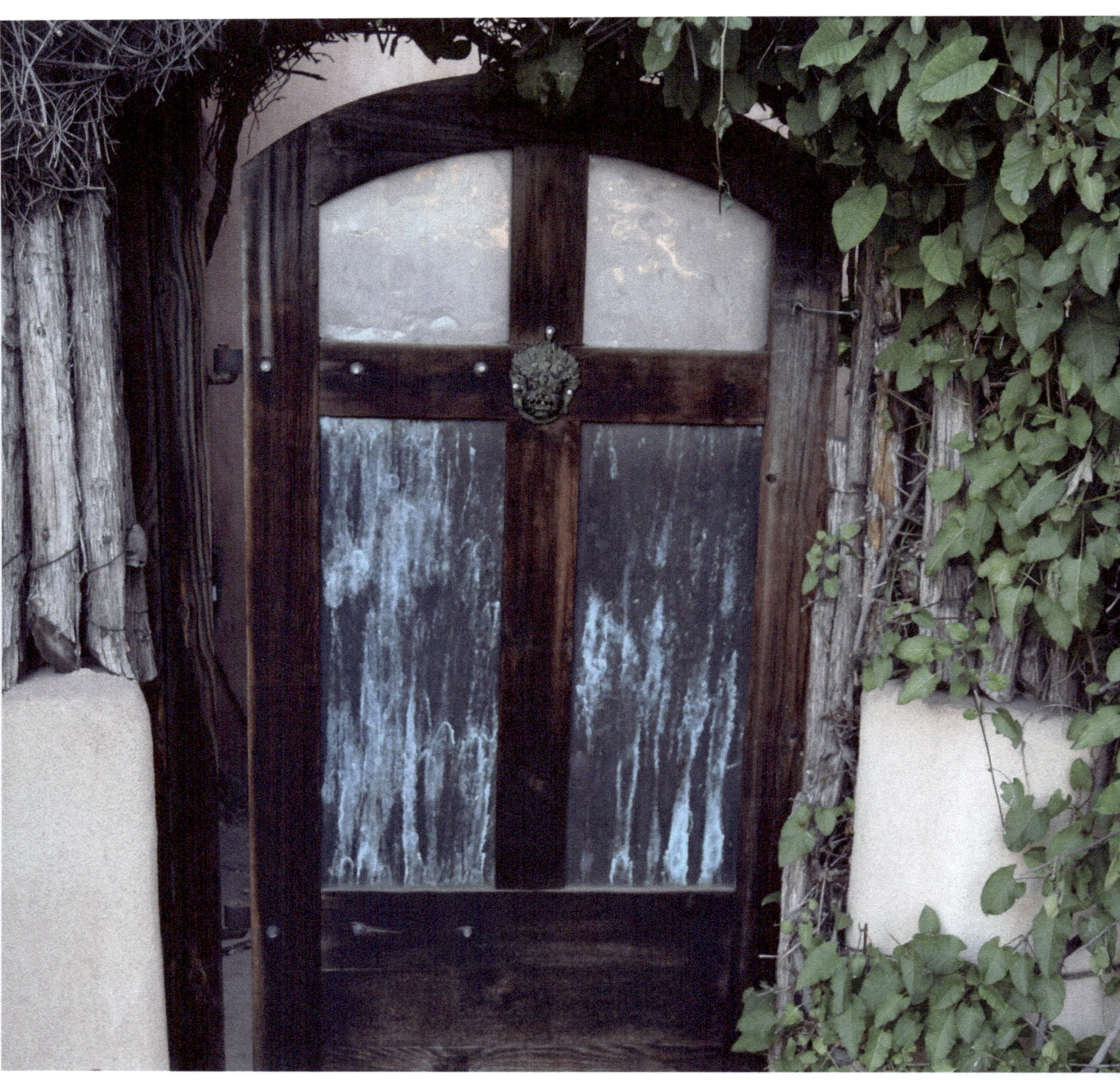

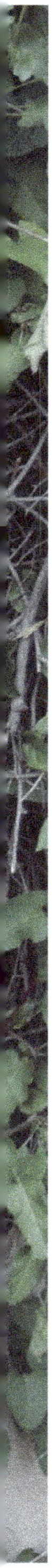

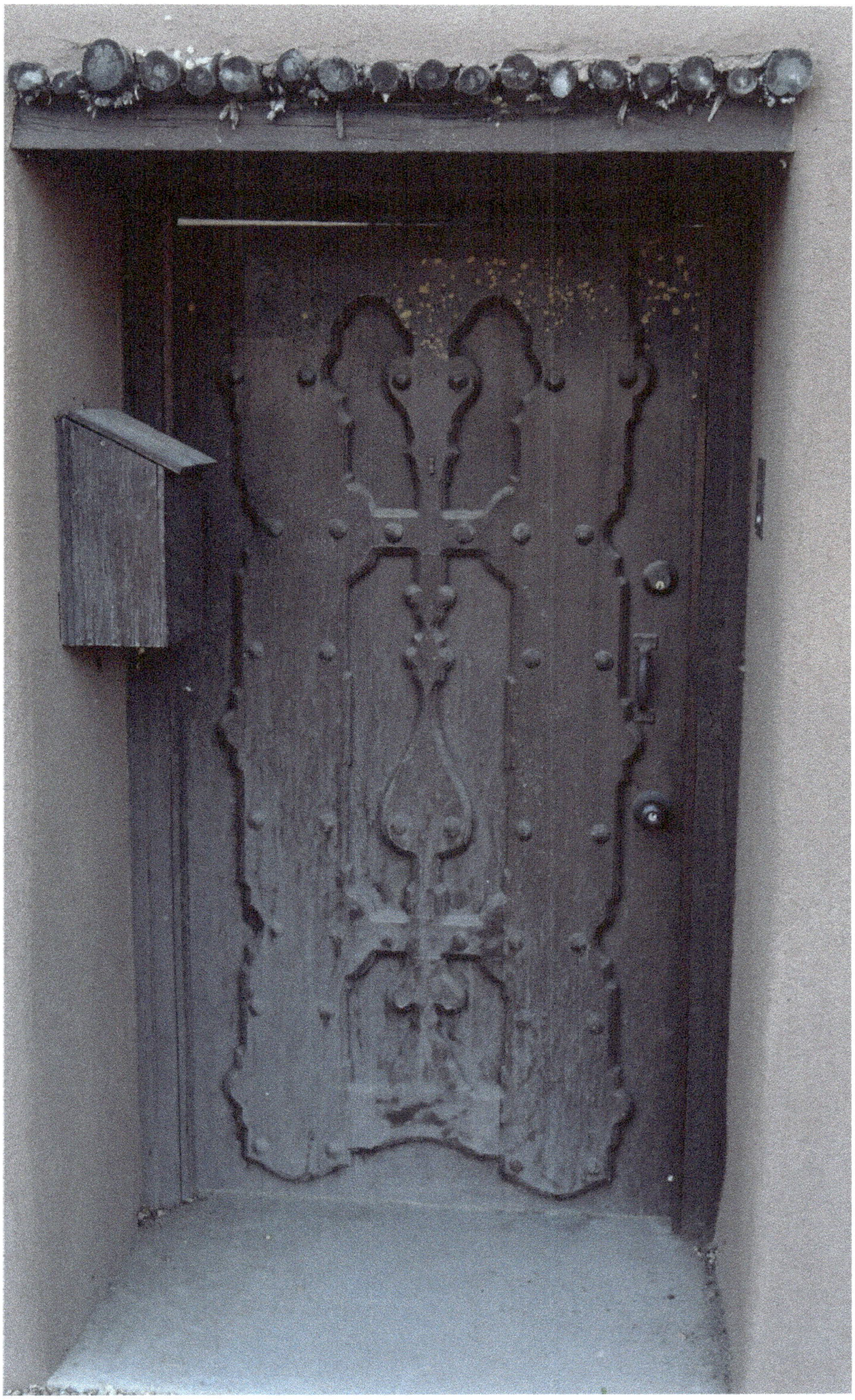

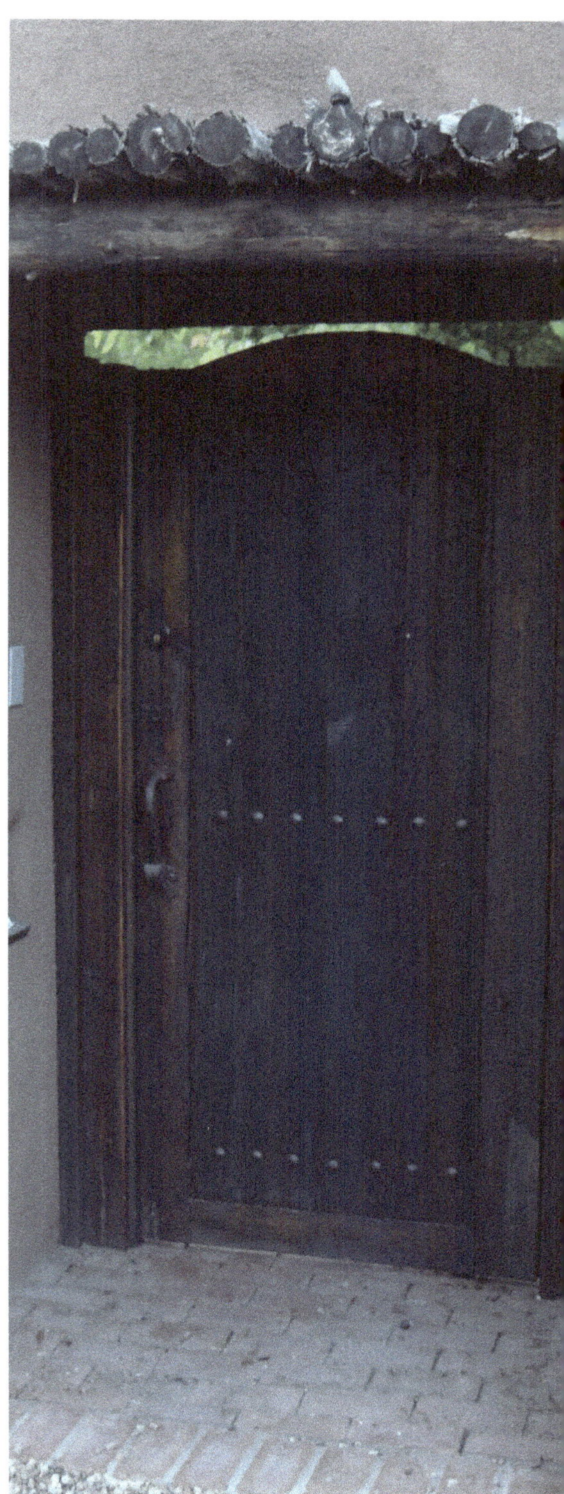

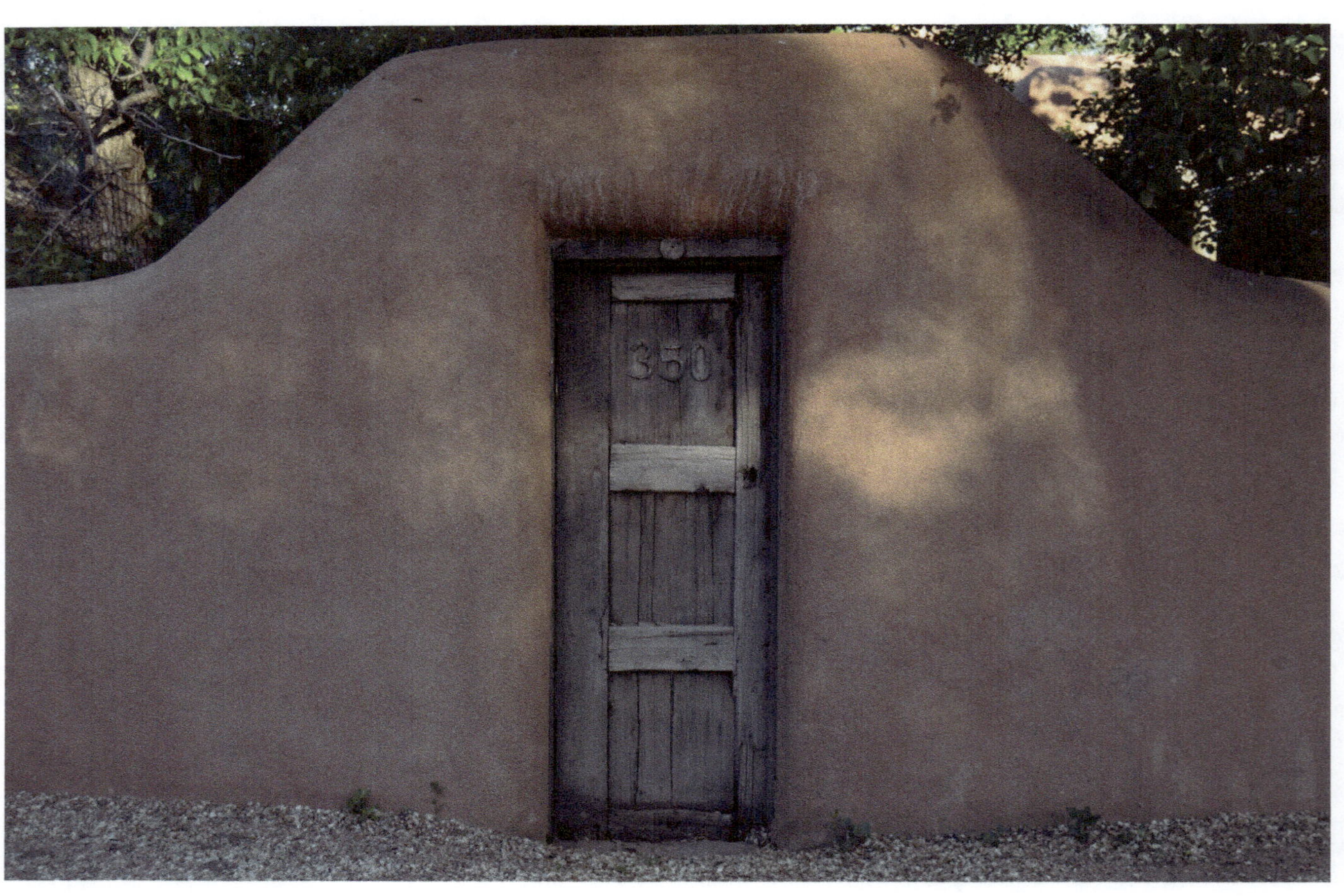

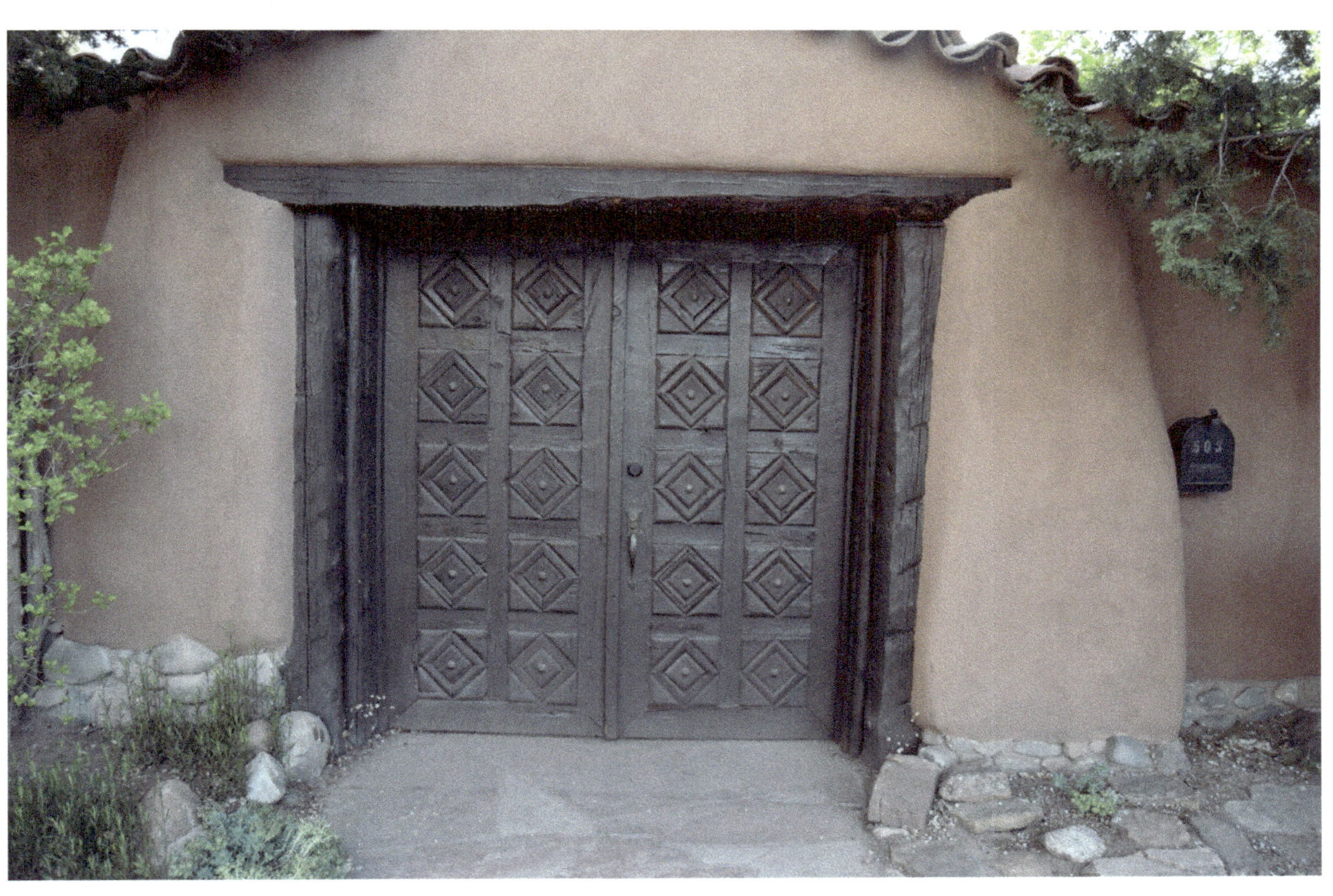

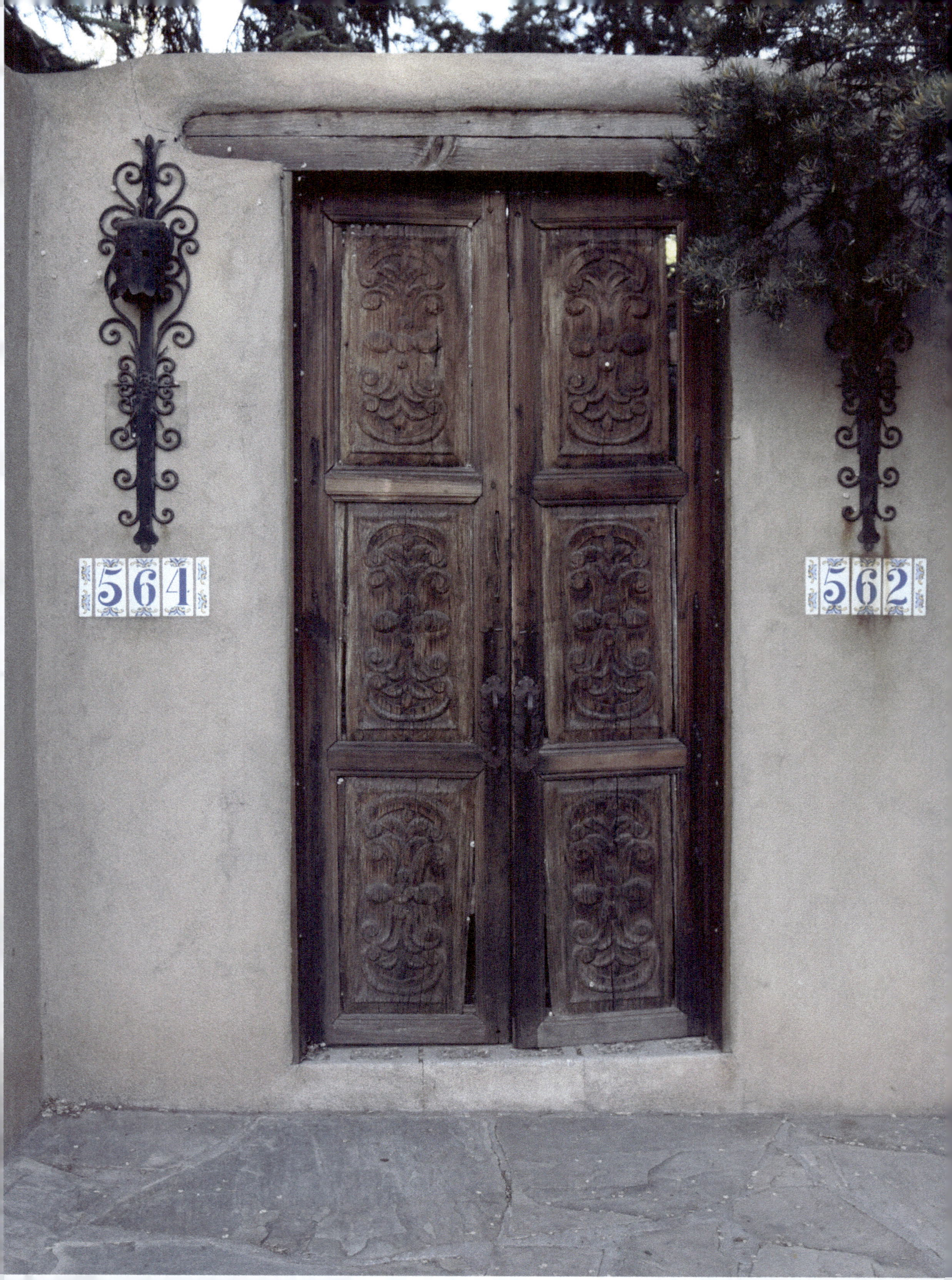
564
562

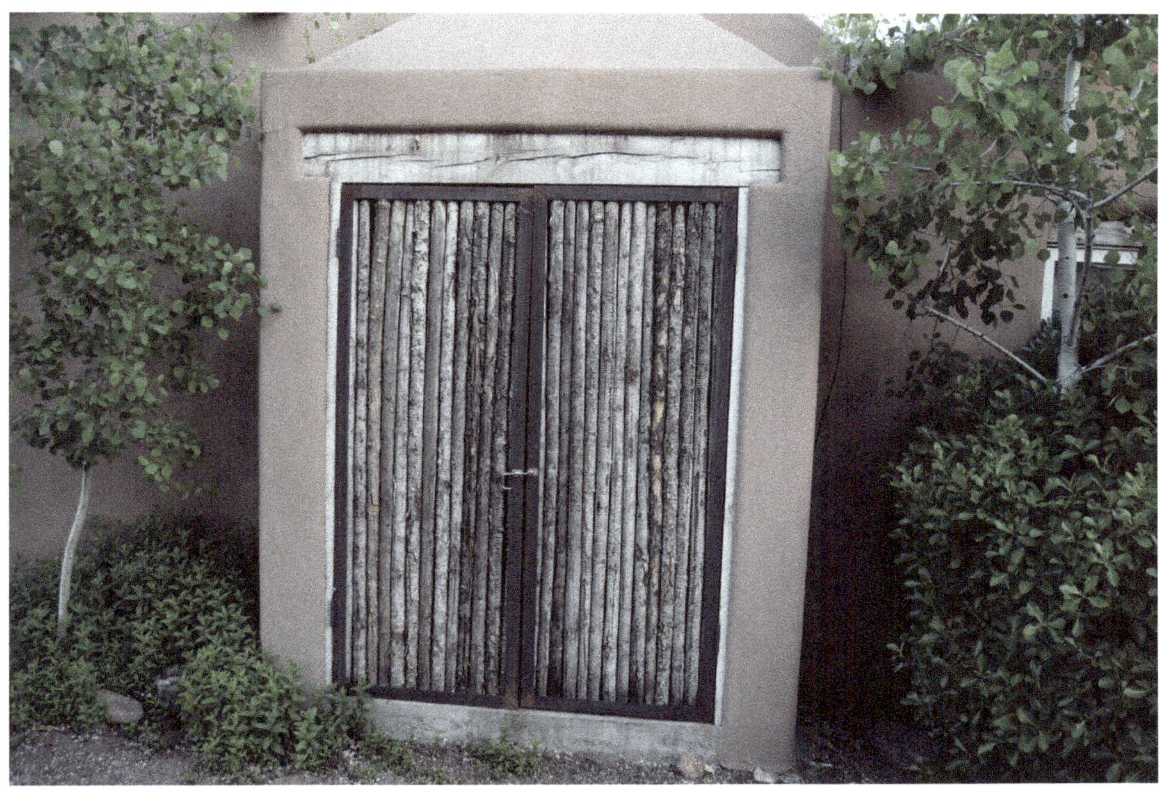

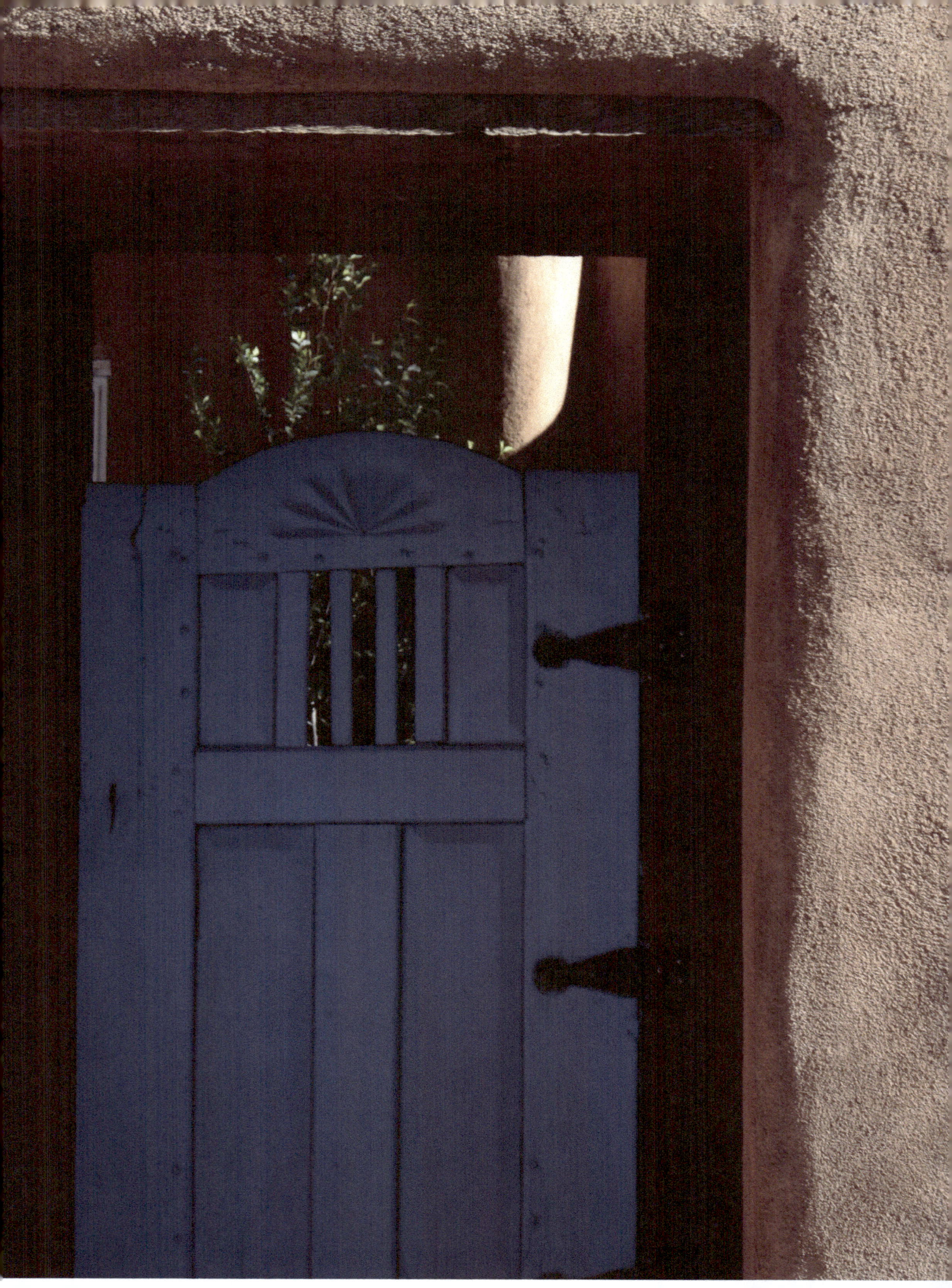

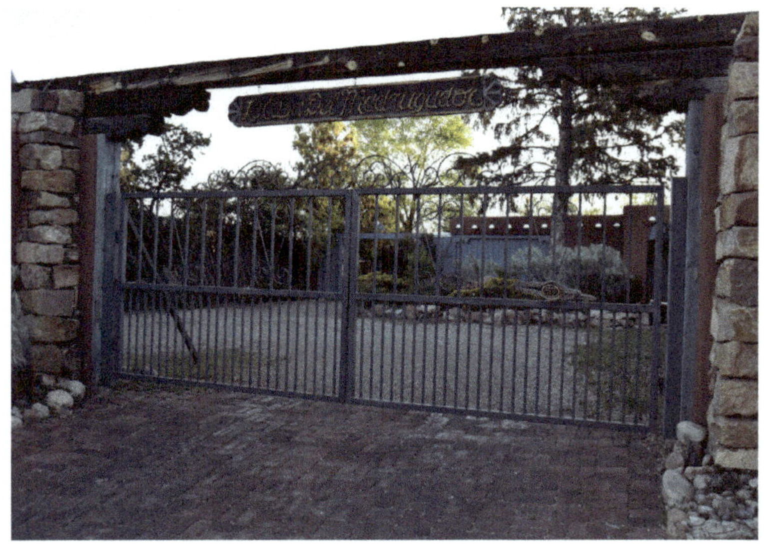

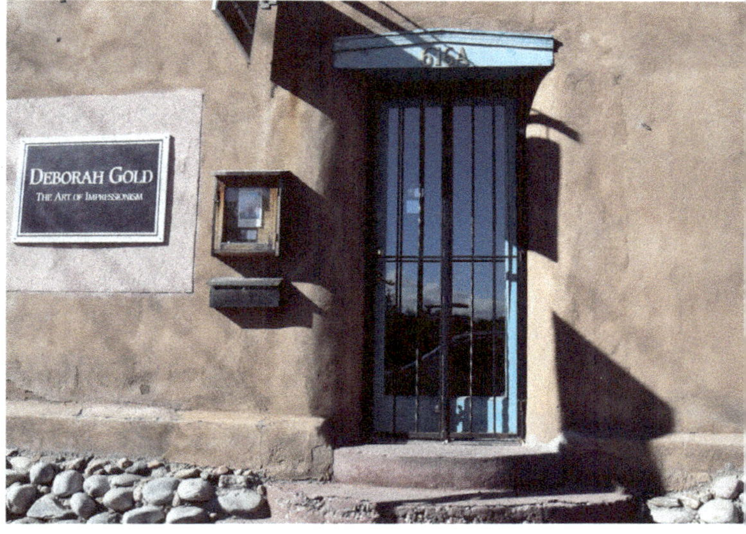

DEBORAH GOLD
THE ART OF IMPRESSIONISM

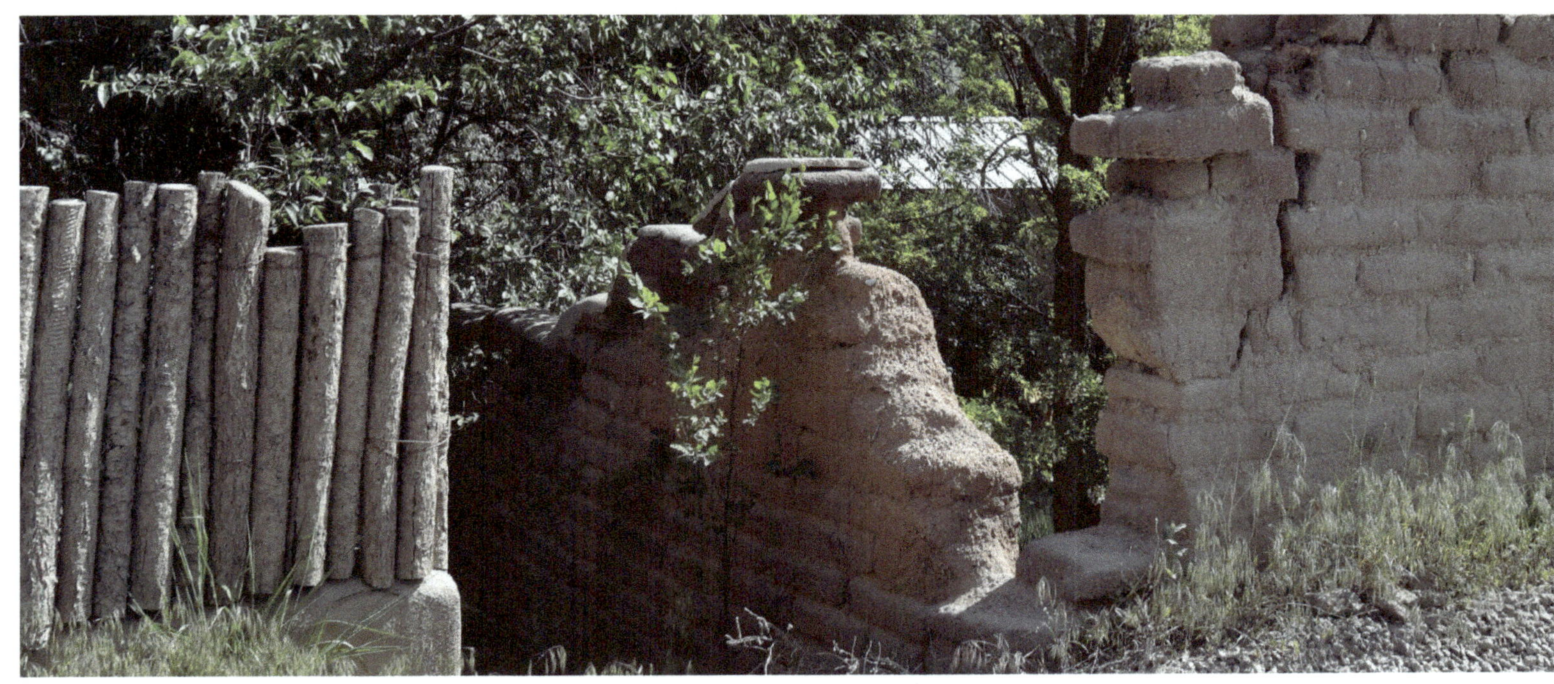

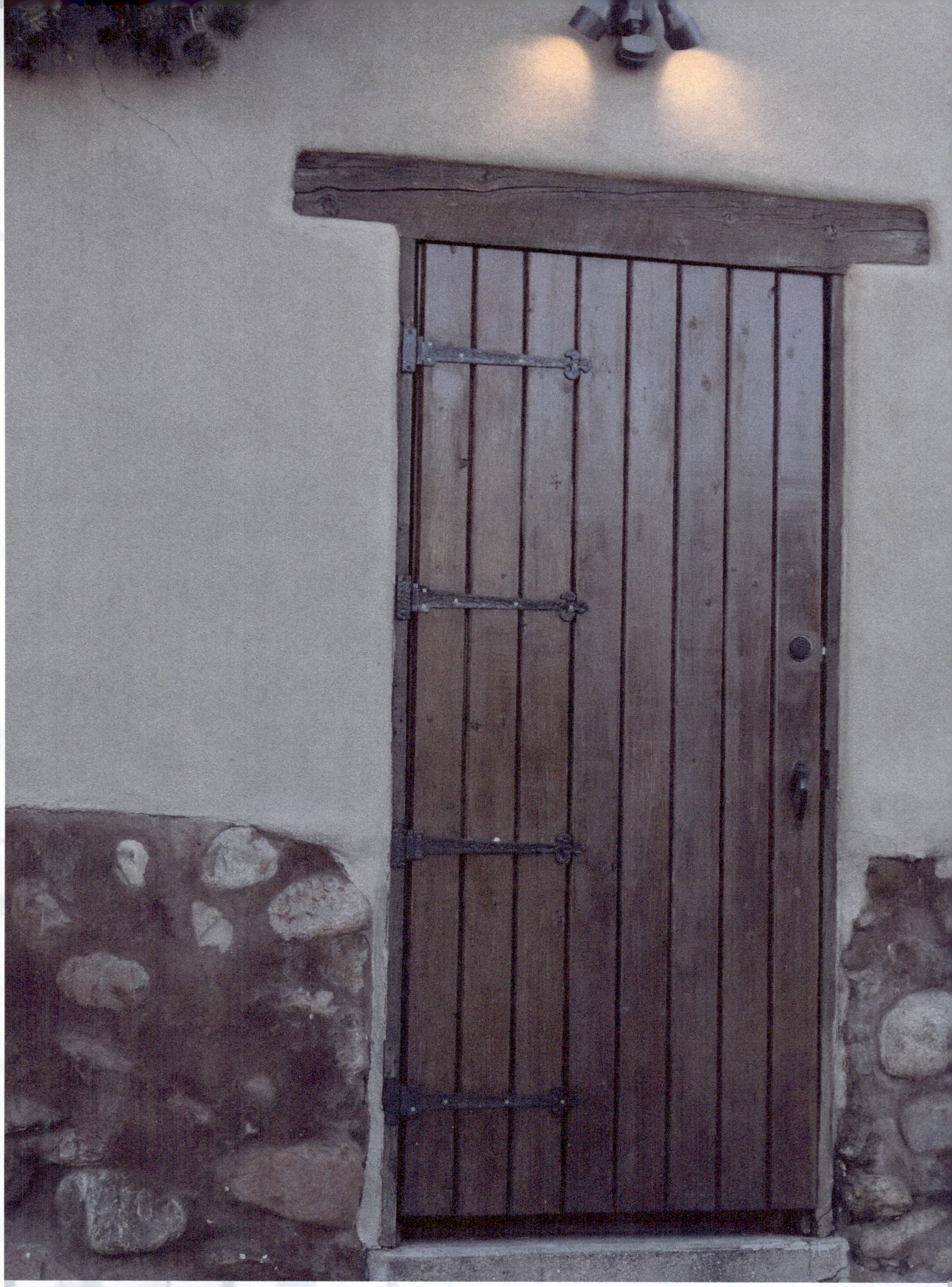

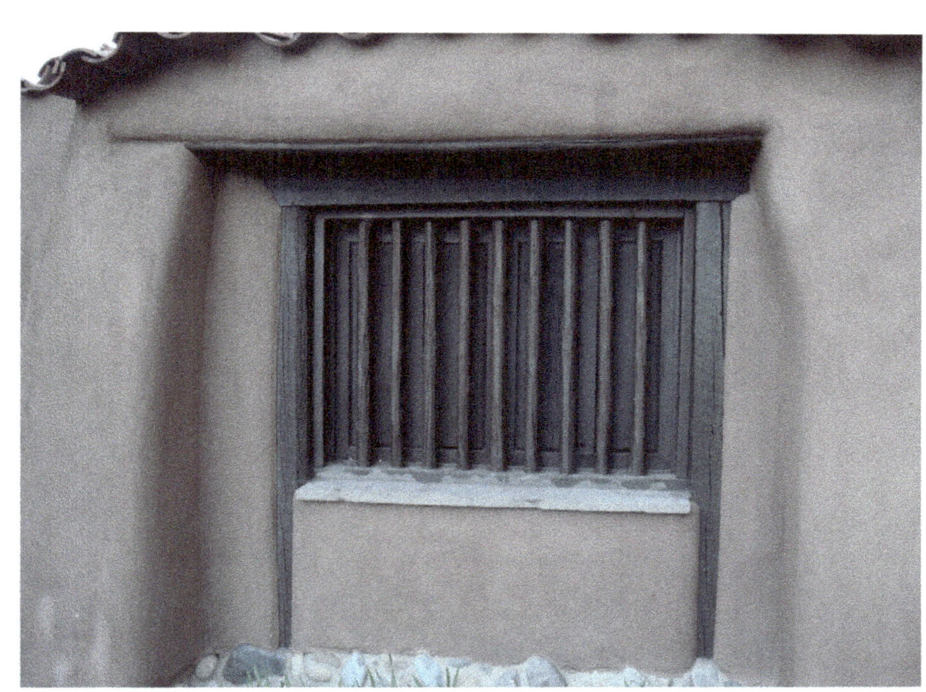
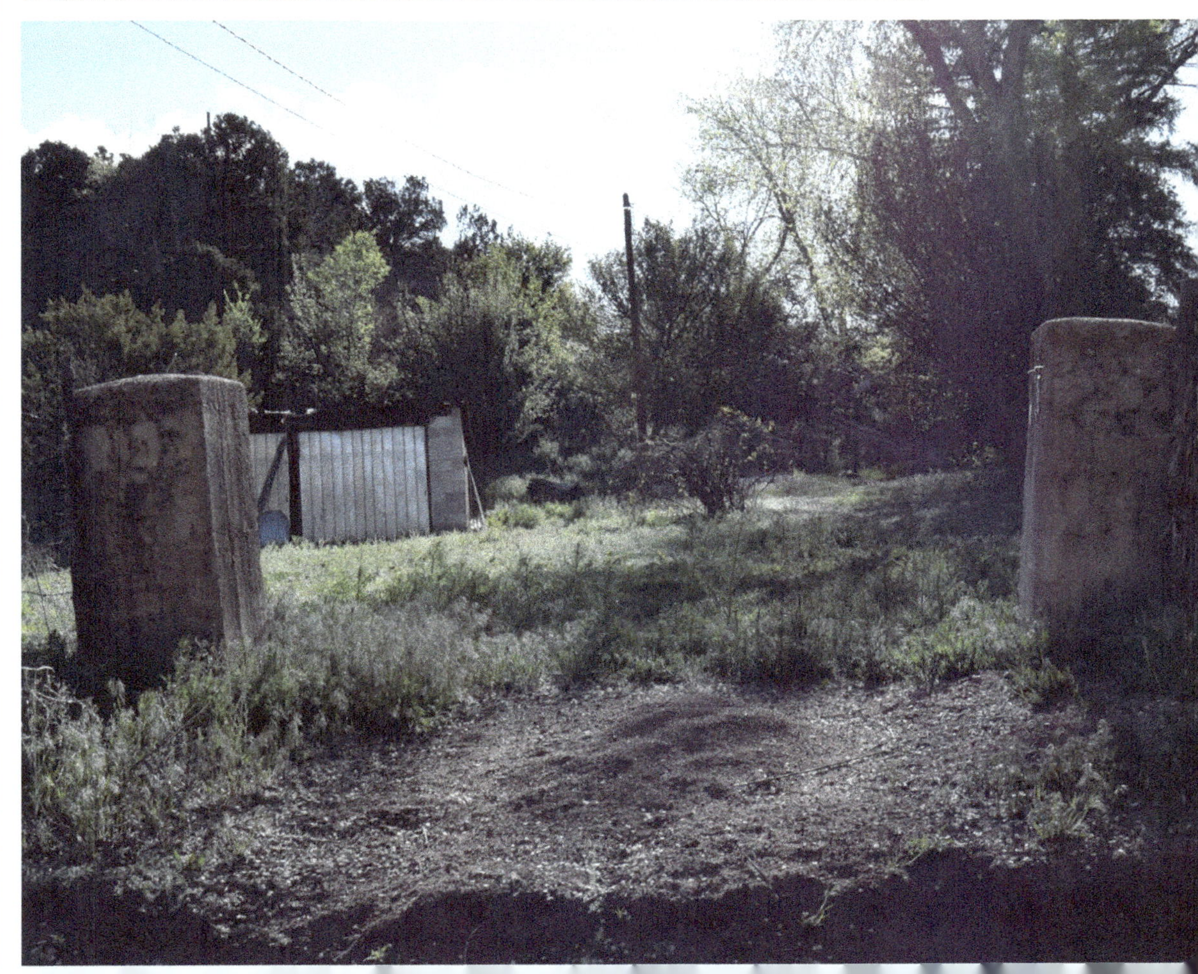

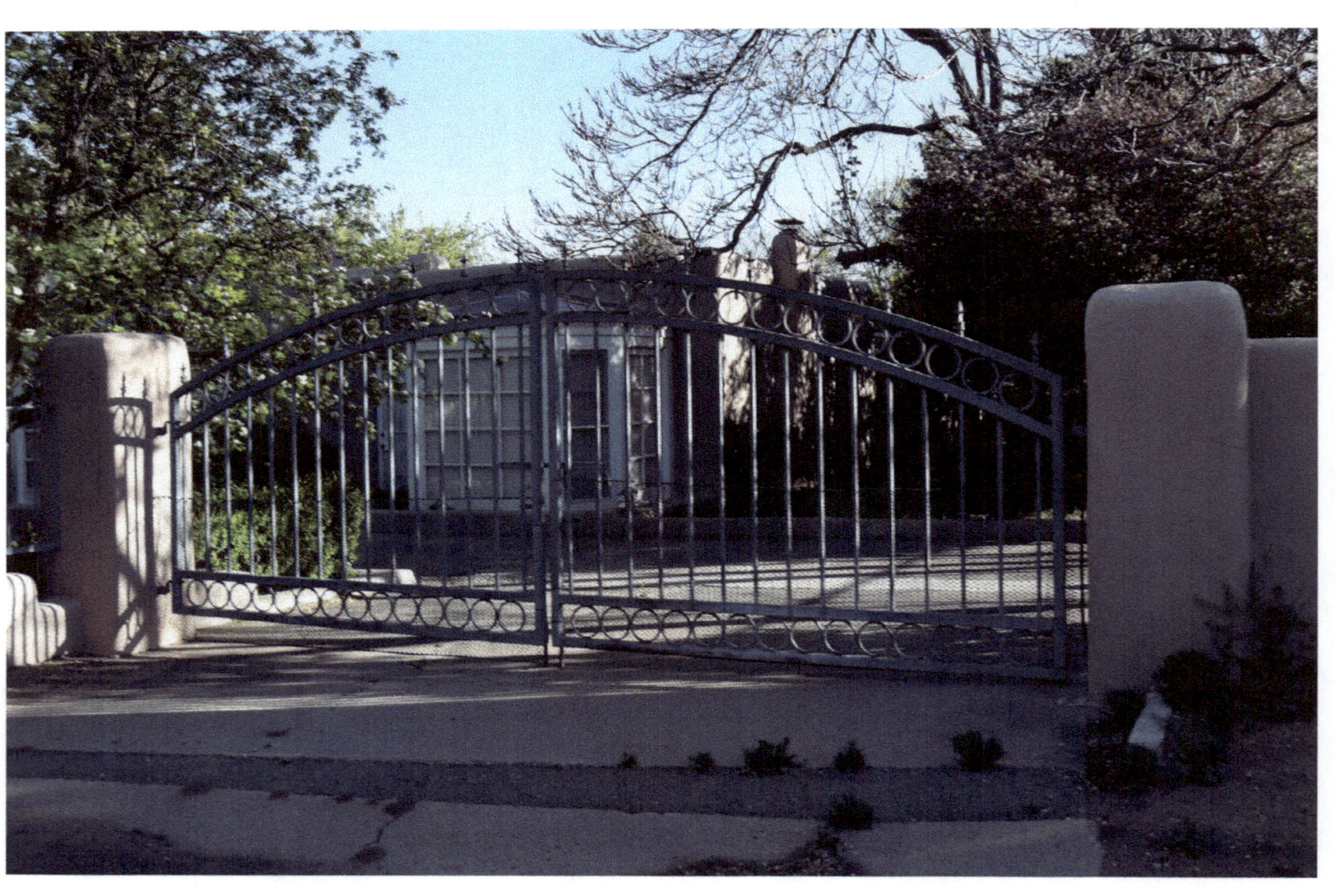

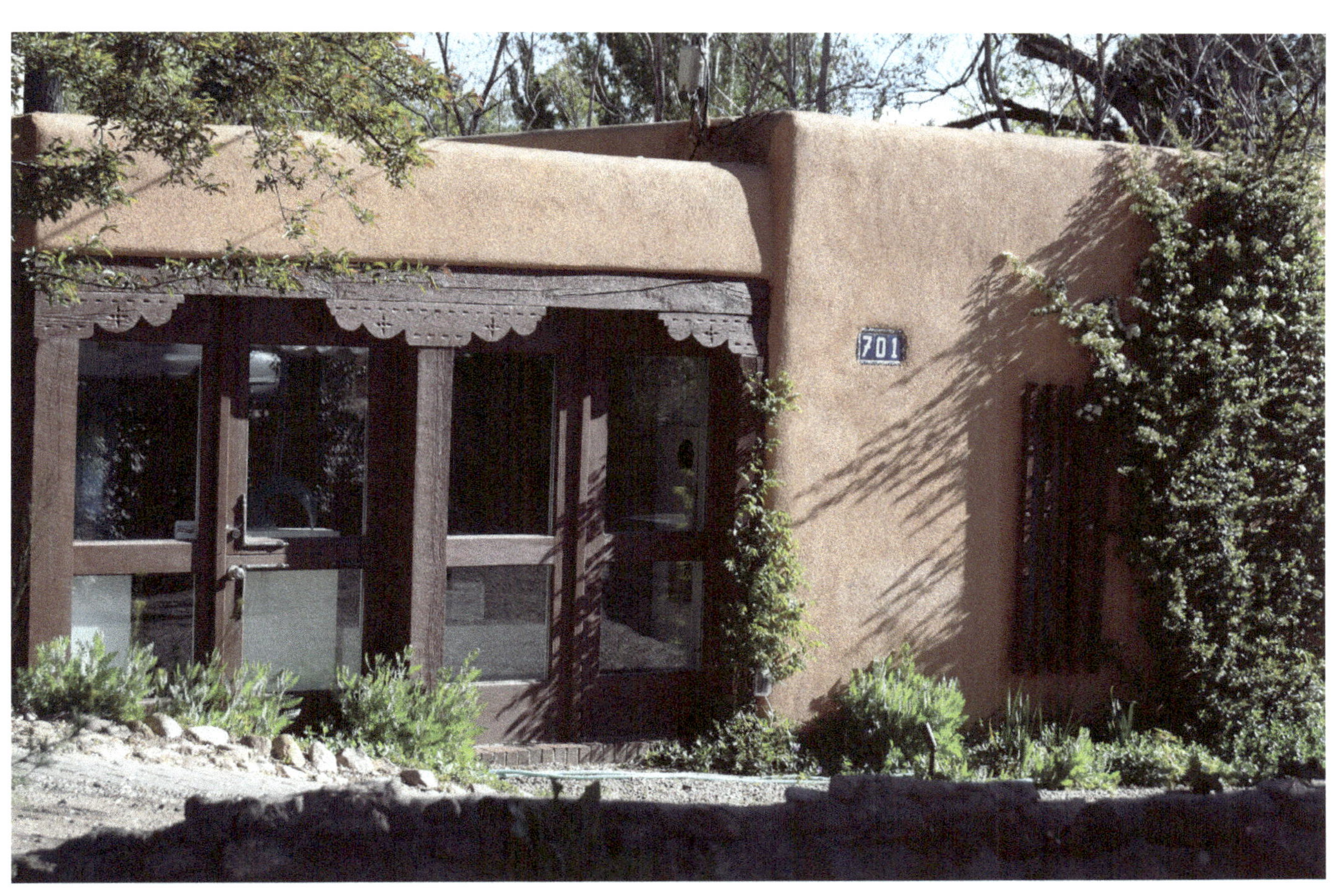

701

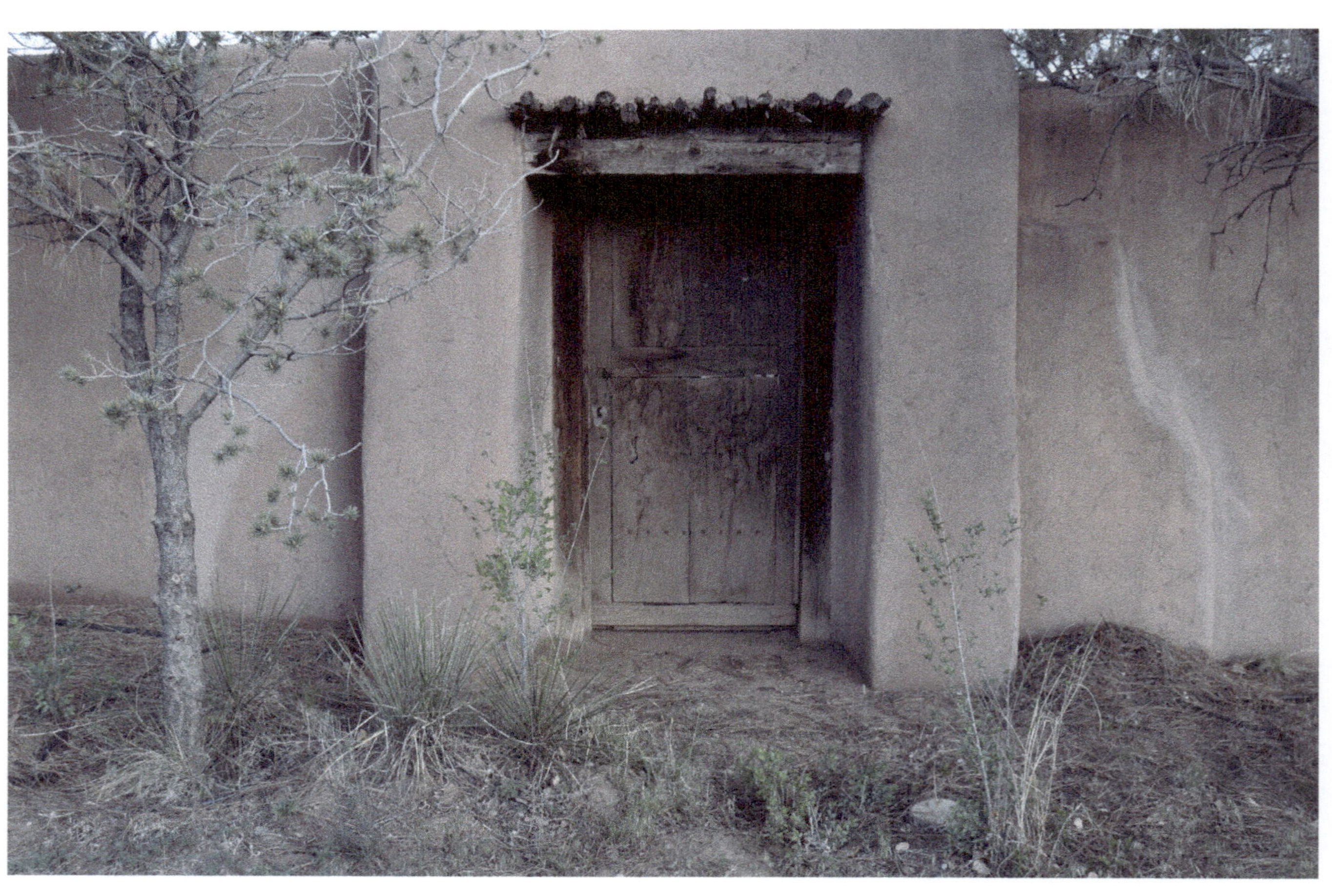

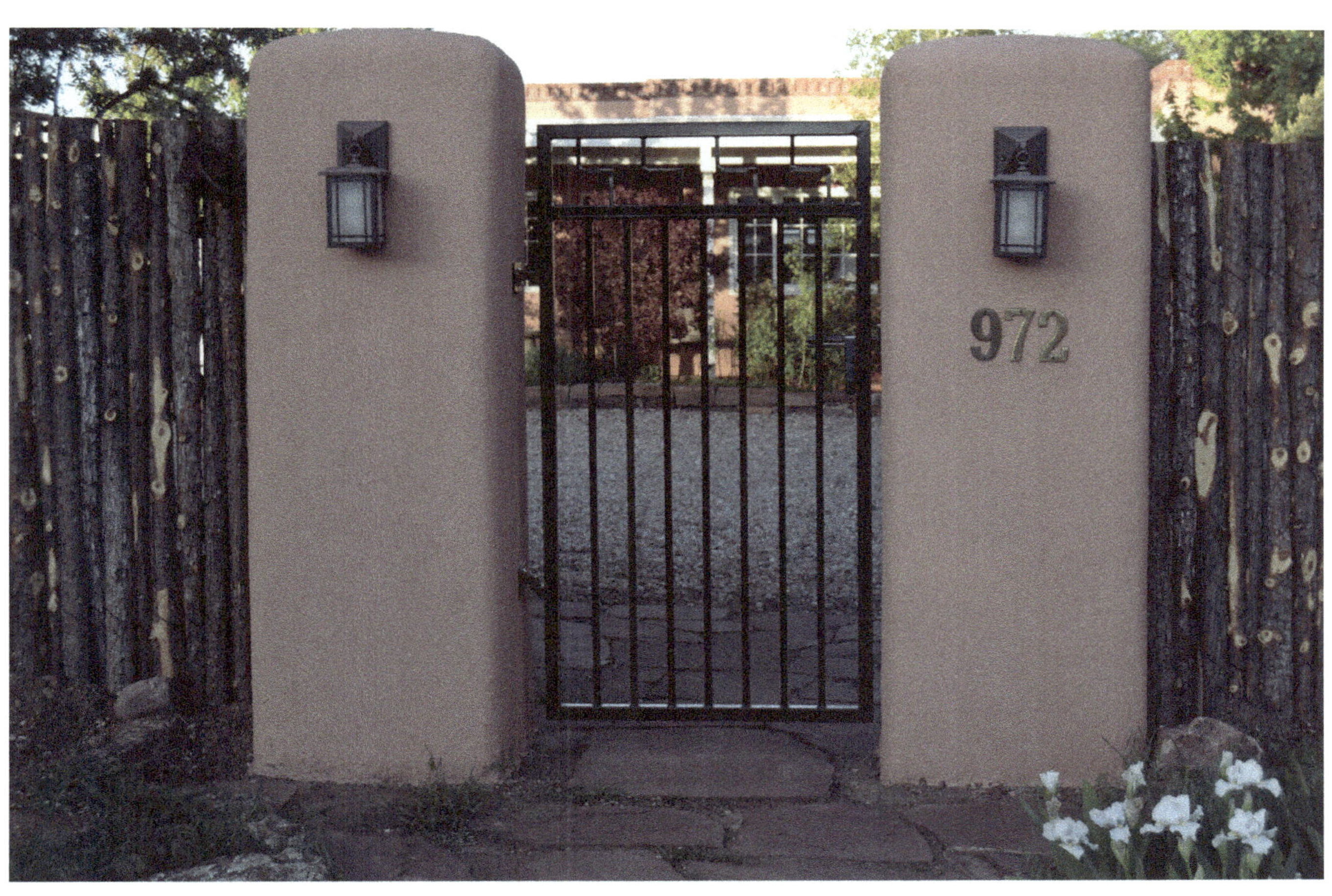

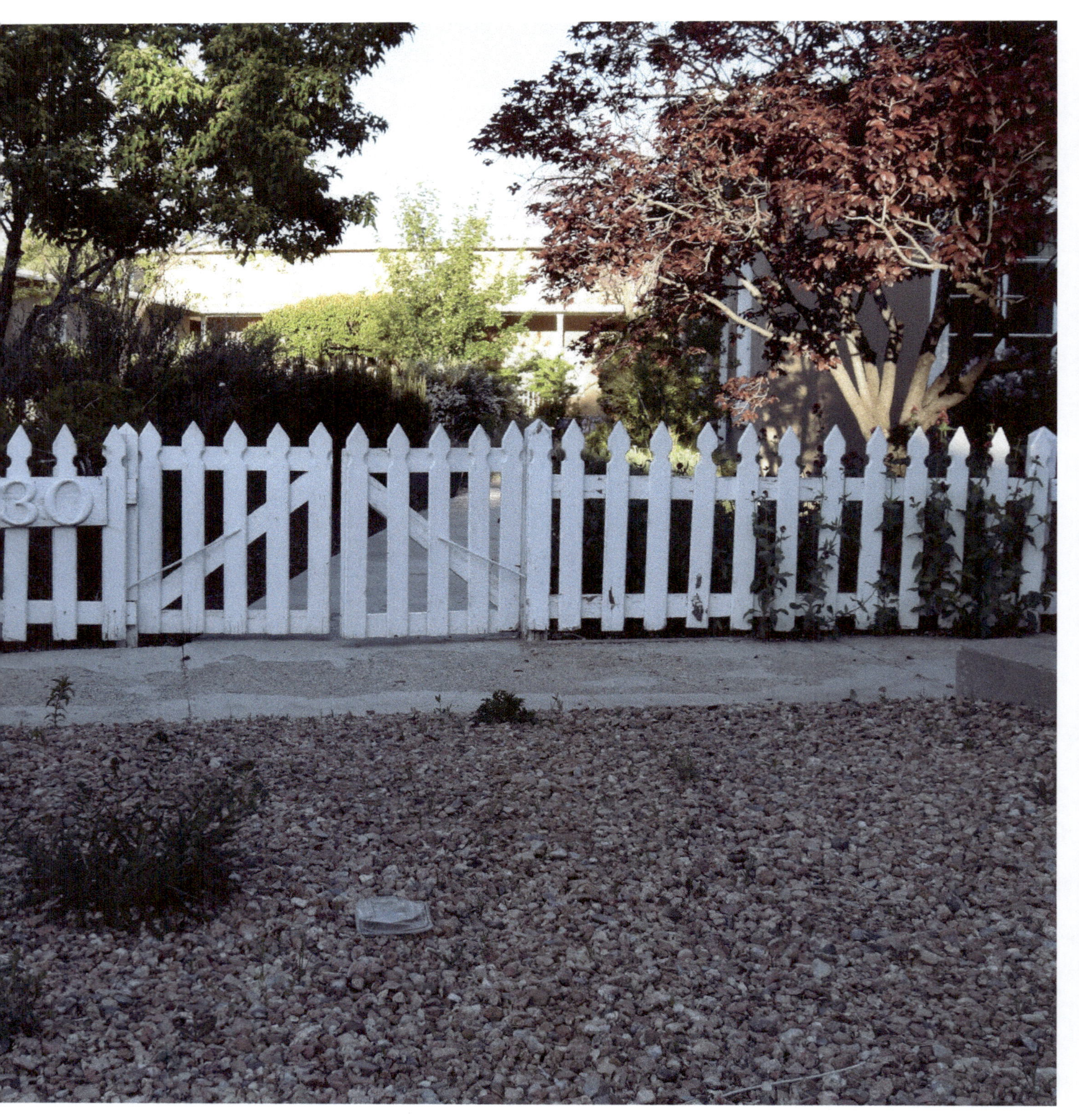

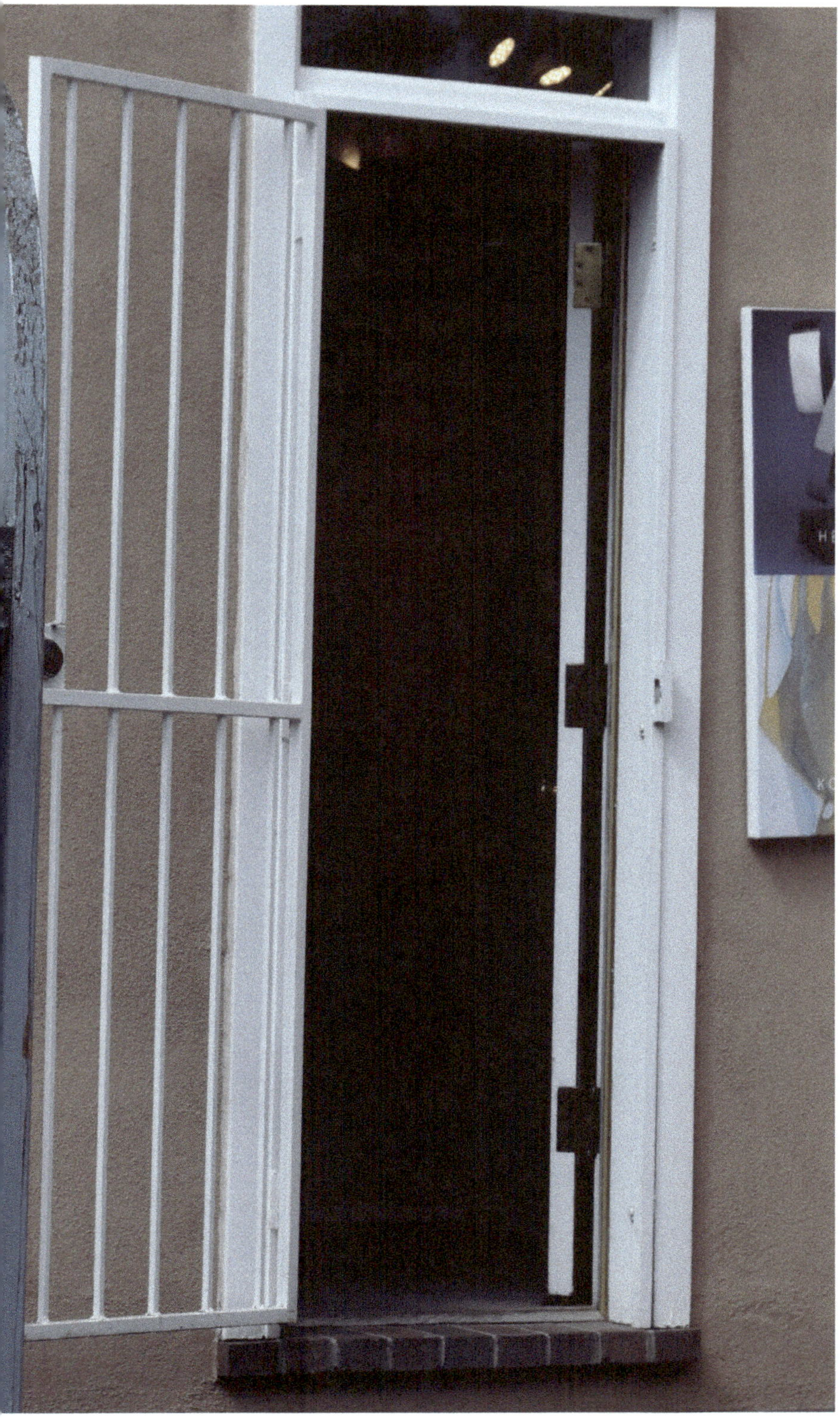

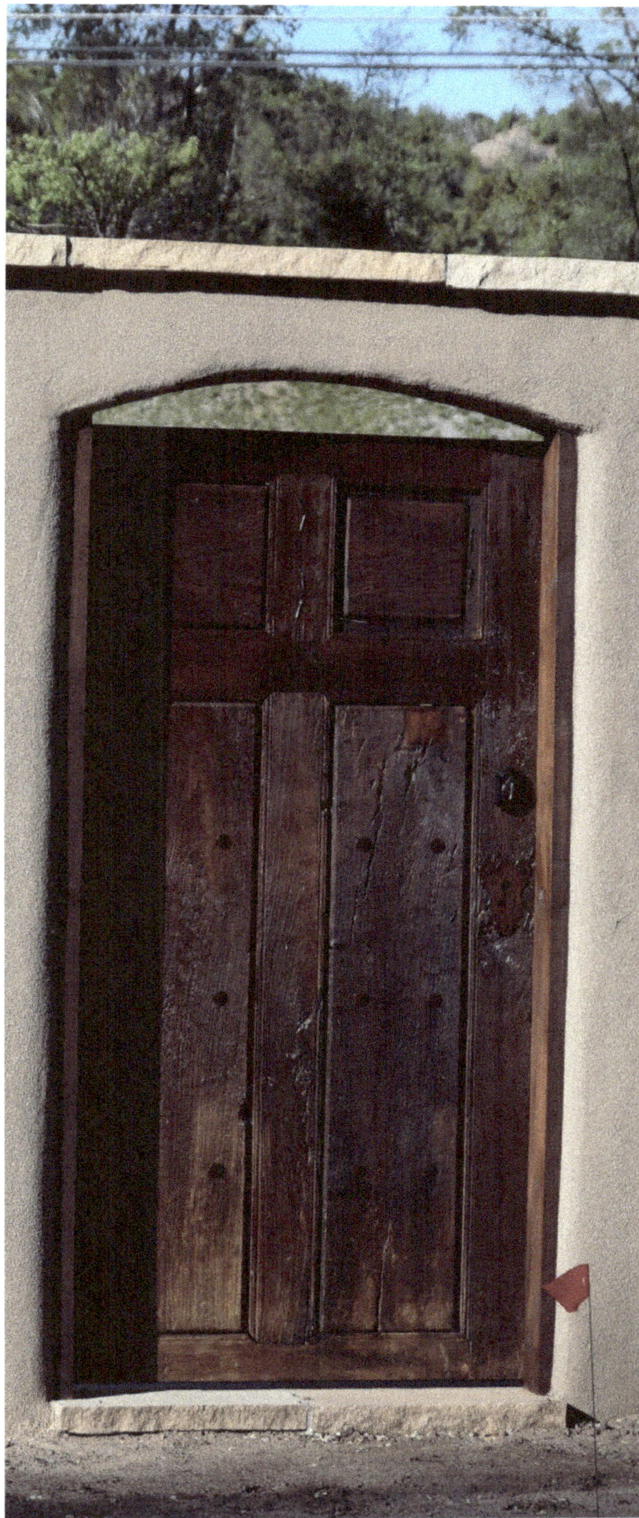

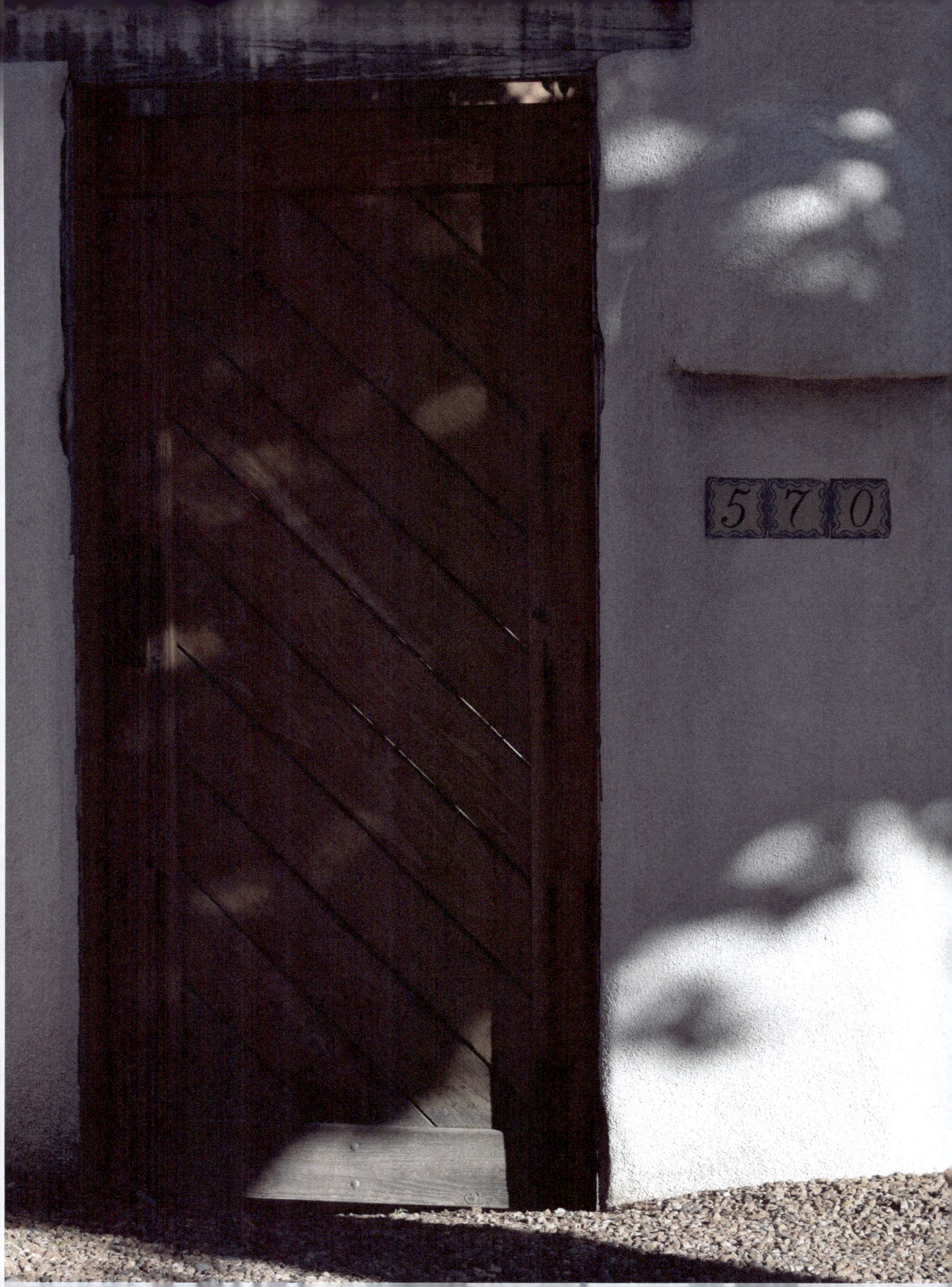

570

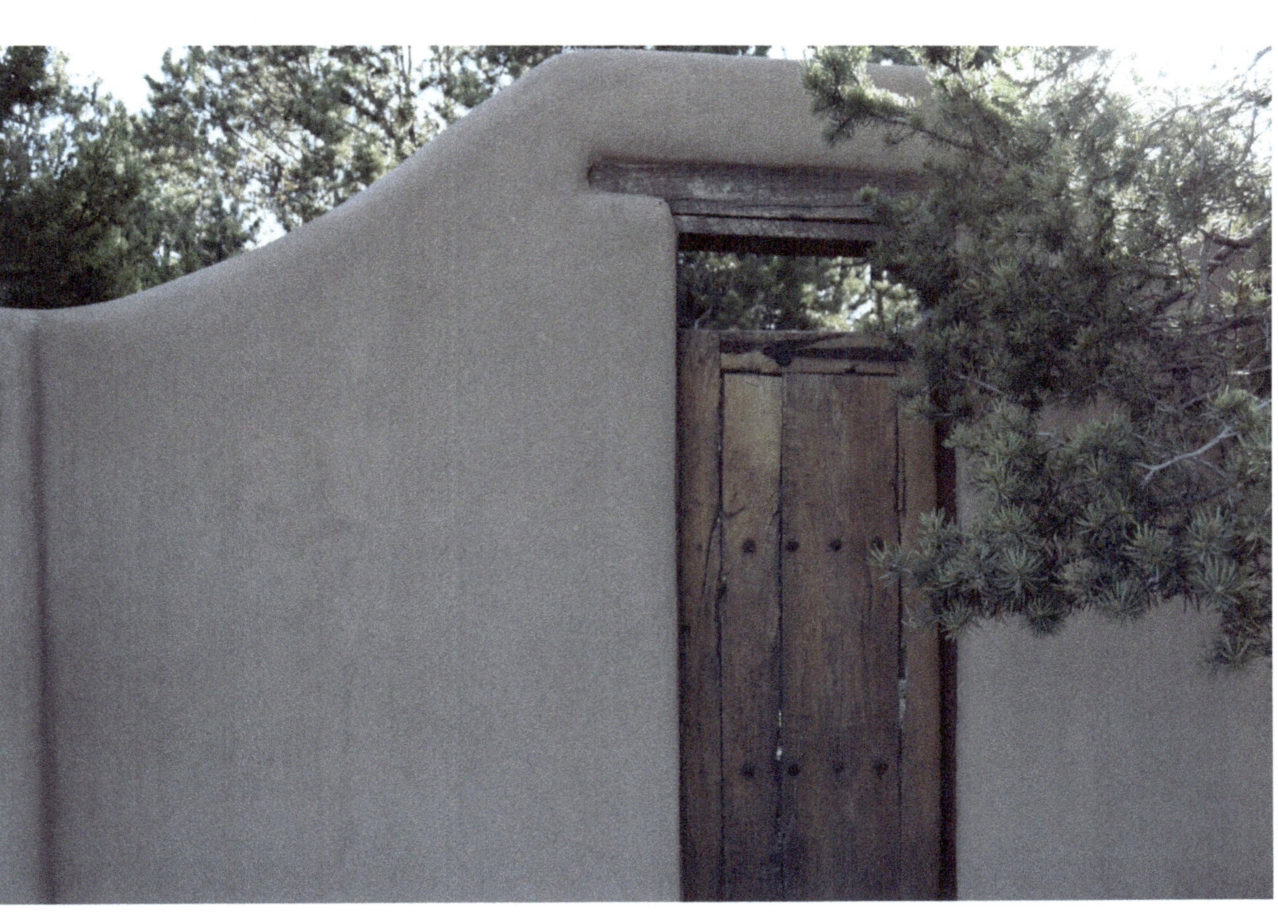

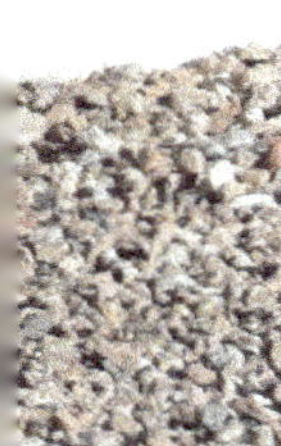

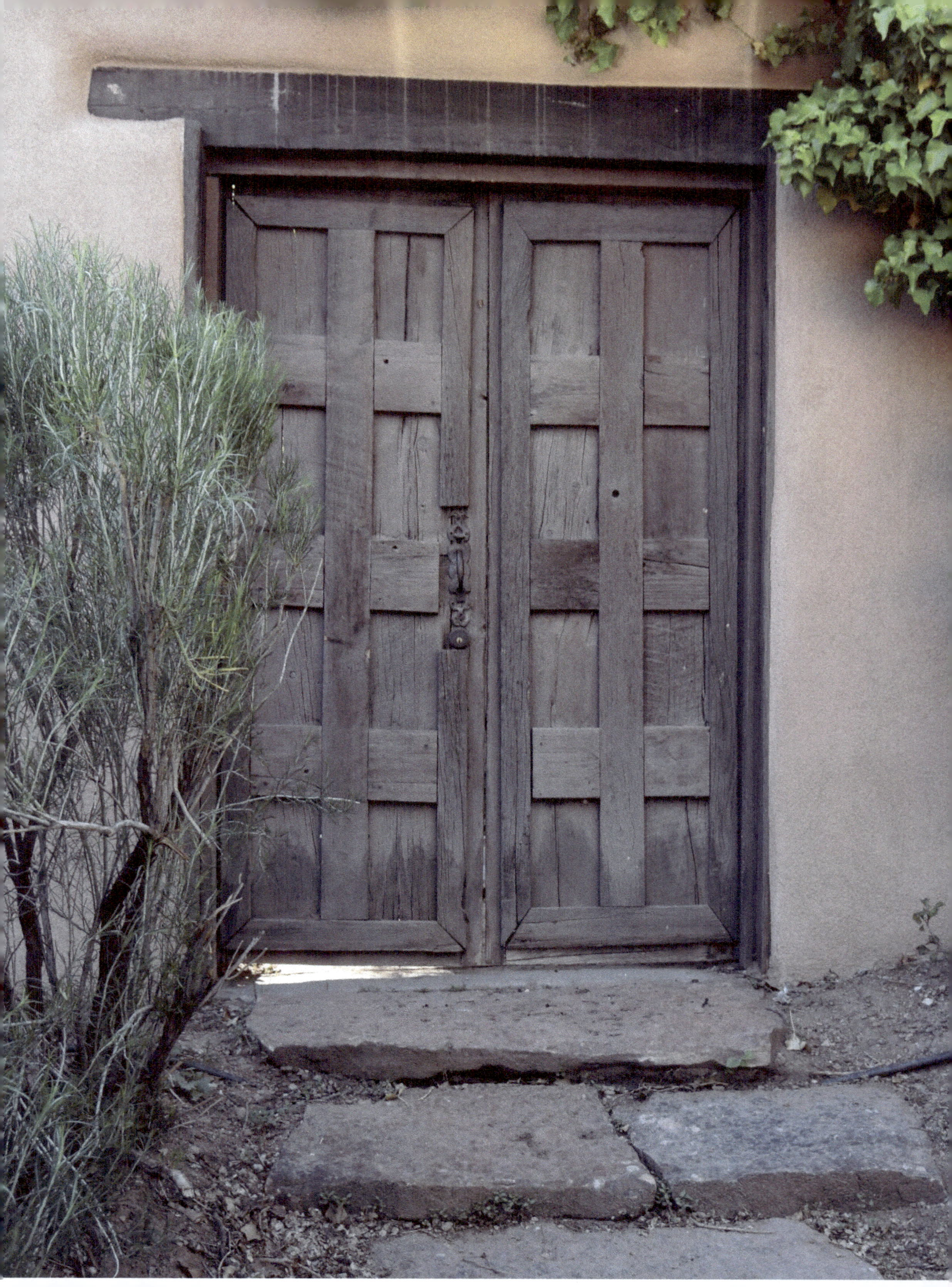

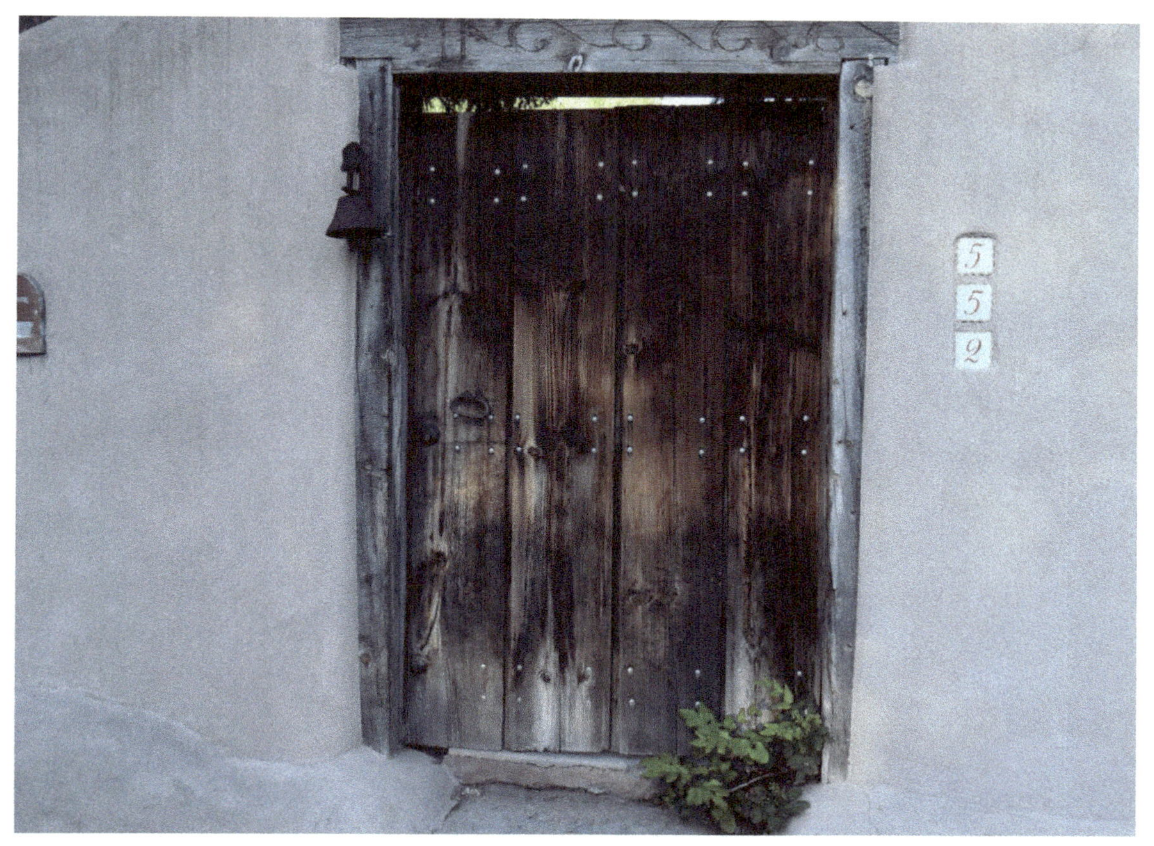

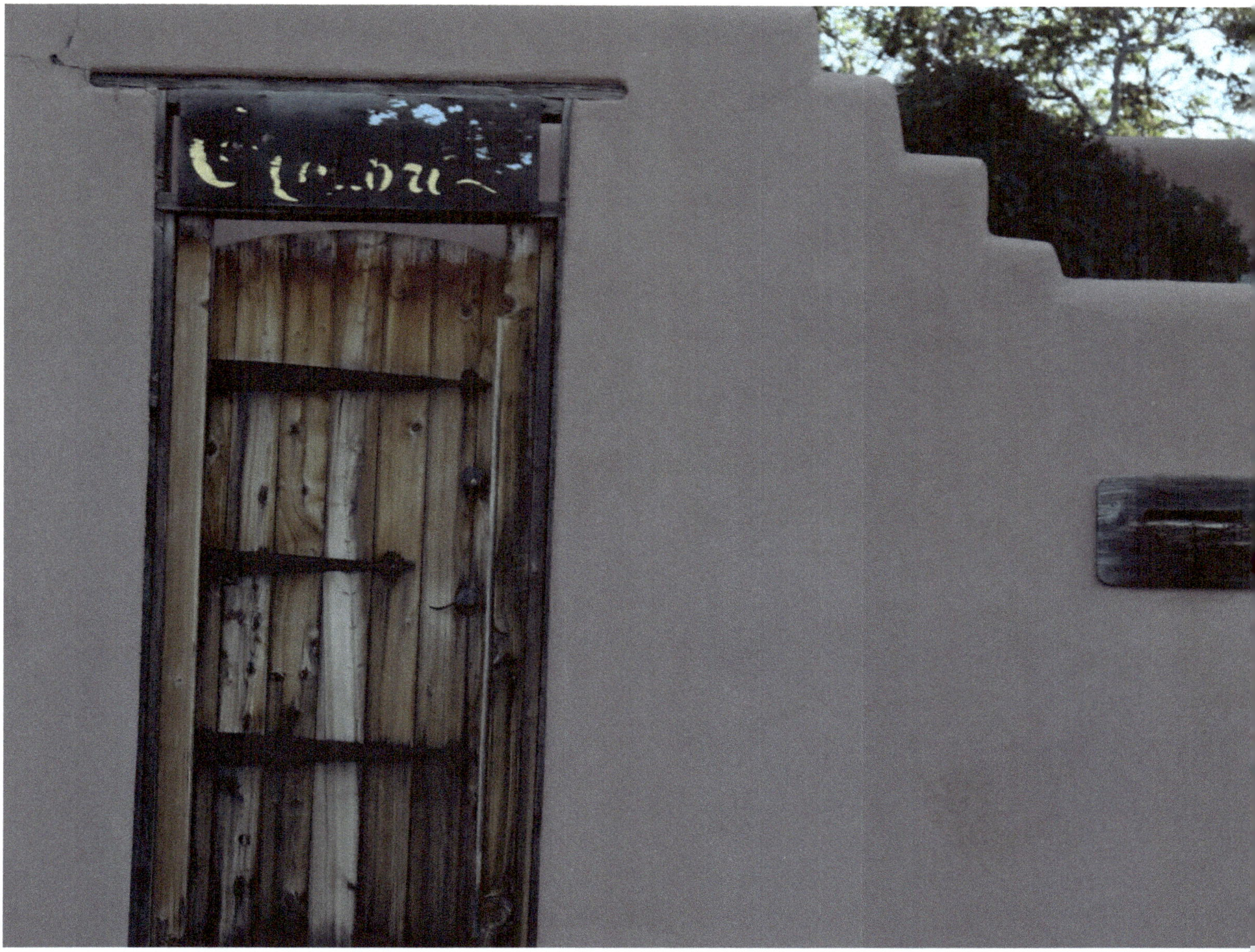